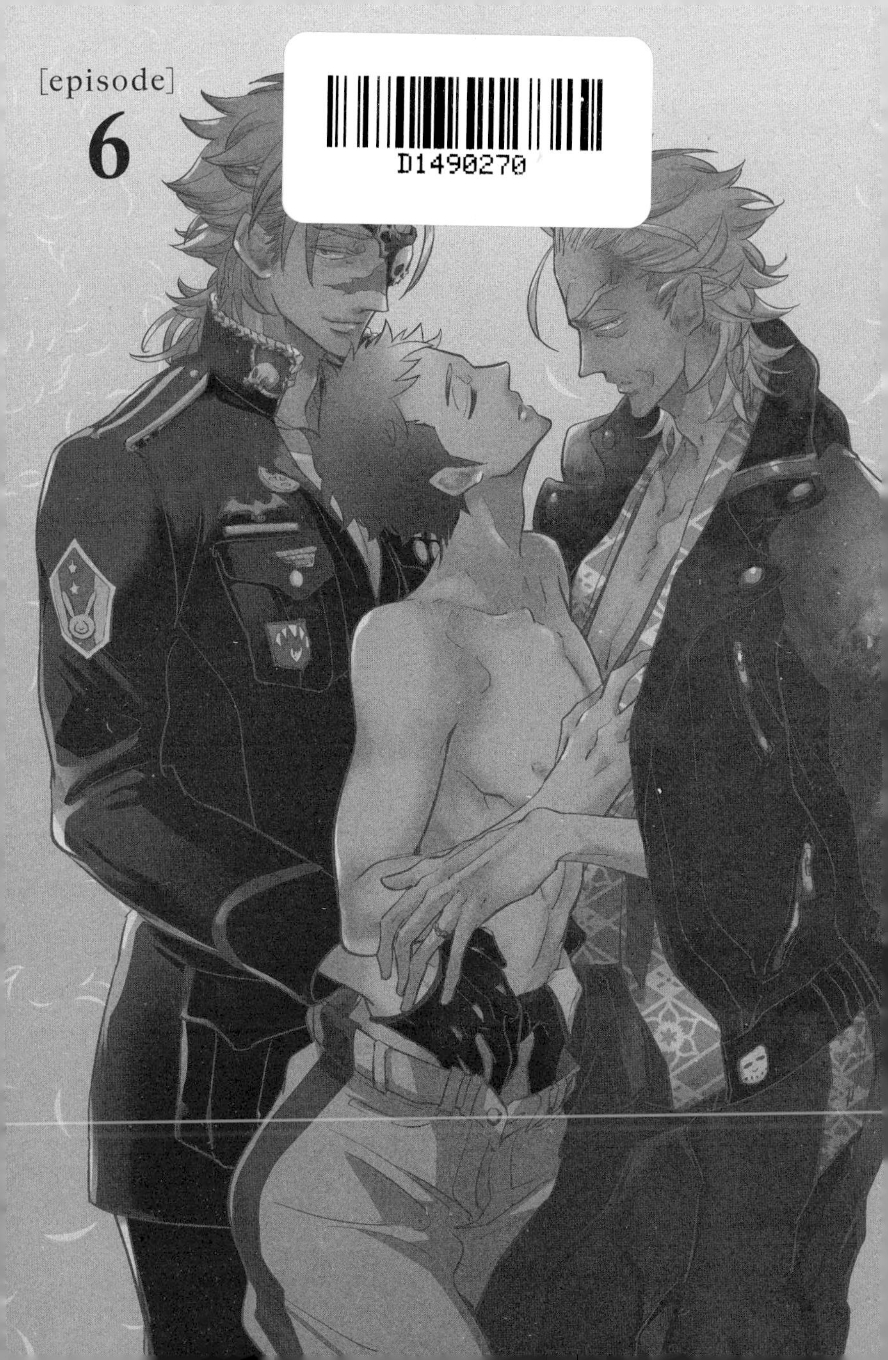
[episode]
6

Love in
Limbo

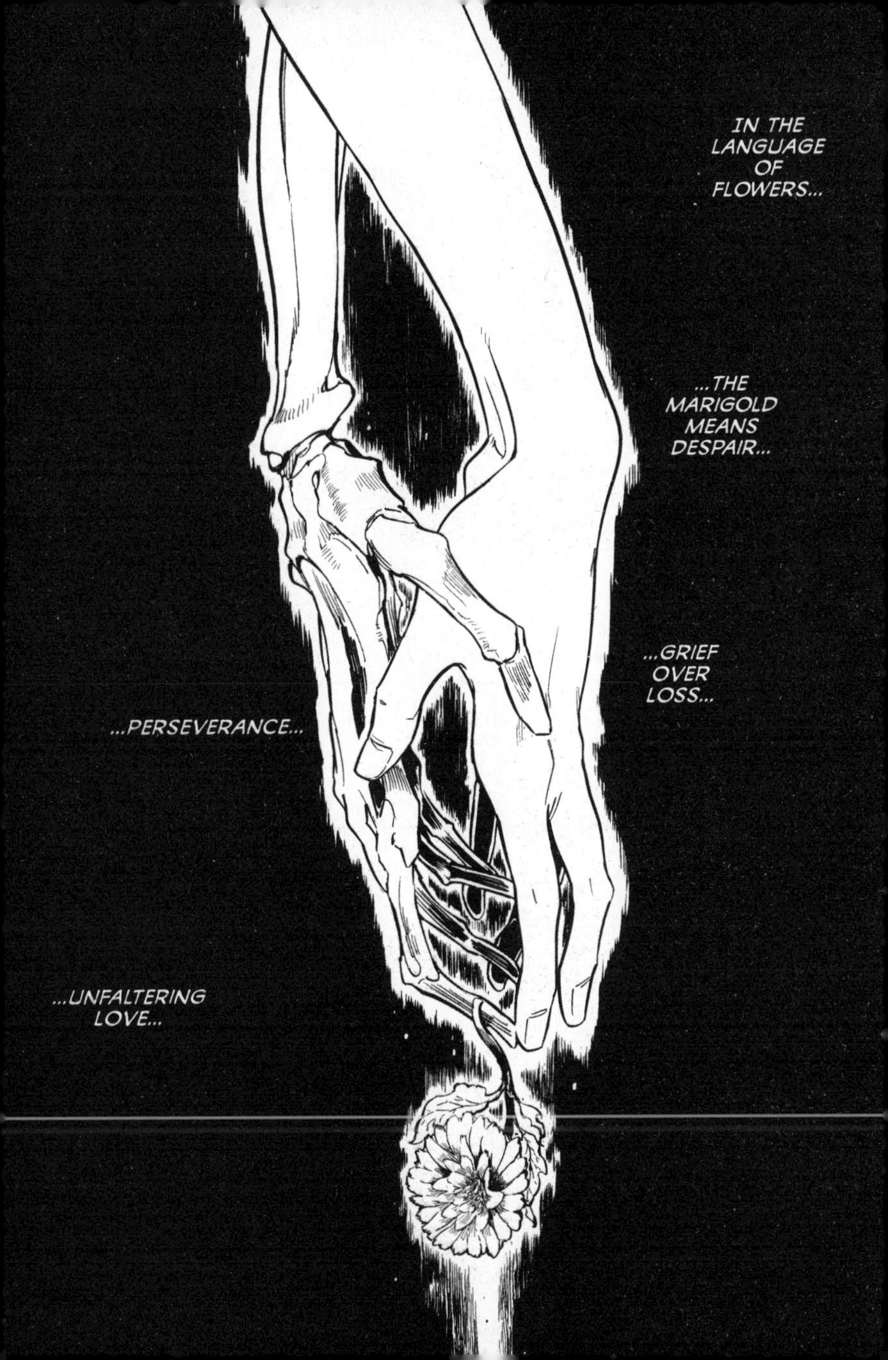
IN THE LANGUAGE OF FLOWERS...
...THE MARIGOLD MEANS DESPAIR...
...GRIEF OVER LOSS...
...PERSEVERANCE...
...UNFALTERING LOVE...

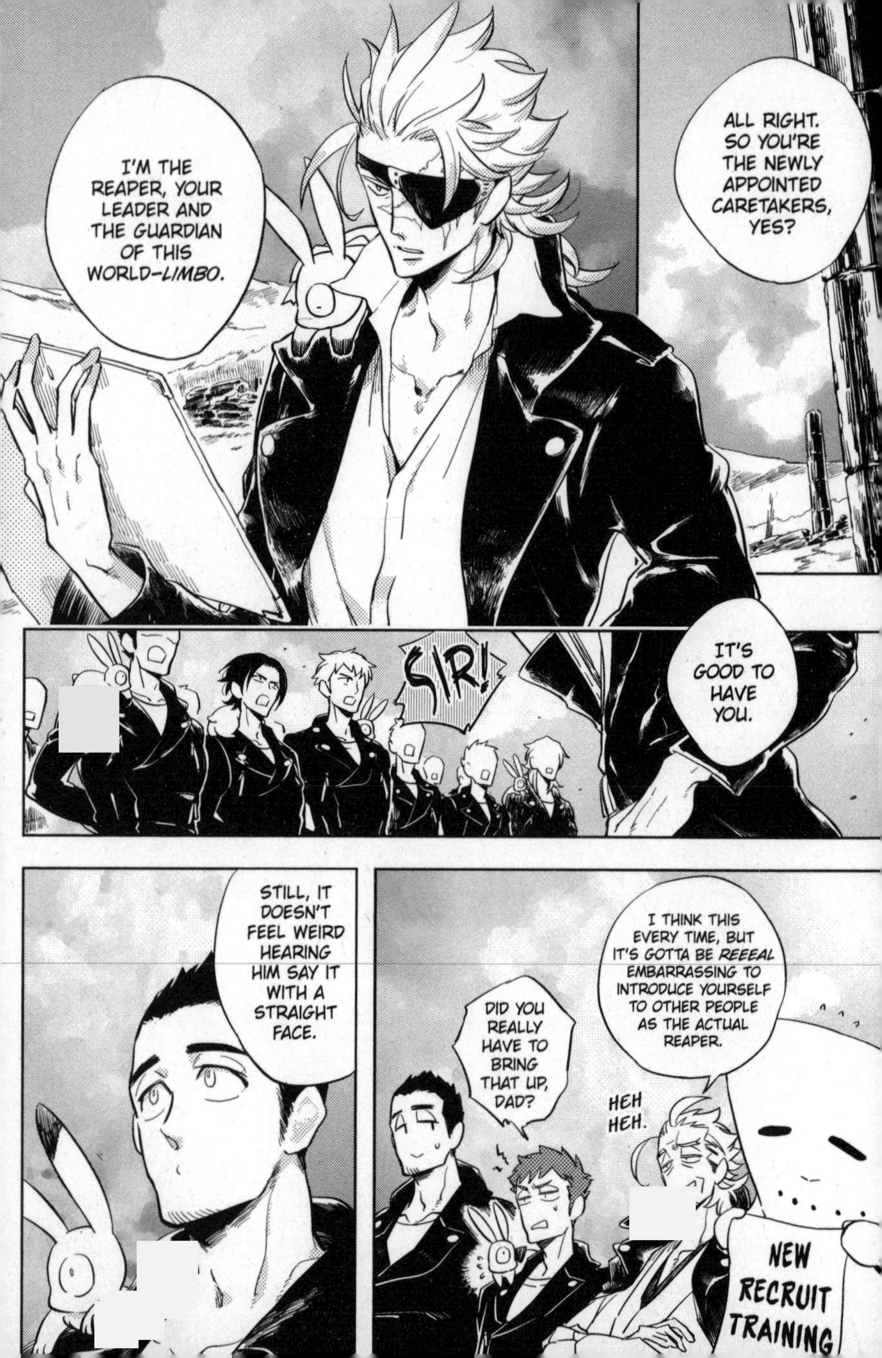
ALL RIGHT. SO YOU'RE THE NEWLY APPOINTED CARETAKERS, YES?
I'M THE REAPER, YOUR LEADER AND THE GUARDIAN OF THIS WORLD—*LIMBO*.
IT'S GOOD TO HAVE YOU.
SIR!
I THINK THIS EVERY TIME, BUT IT'S GOTTA BE *REEEAL* EMBARRASSING TO INTRODUCE YOURSELF TO OTHER PEOPLE AS THE ACTUAL REAPER.
HEH HEH.
DID YOU REALLY HAVE TO BRING THAT UP, DAD?
NEW RECRUIT TRAINING
STILL, IT DOESN'T FEEL WEIRD HEARING HIM SAY IT WITH A STRAIGHT FACE.

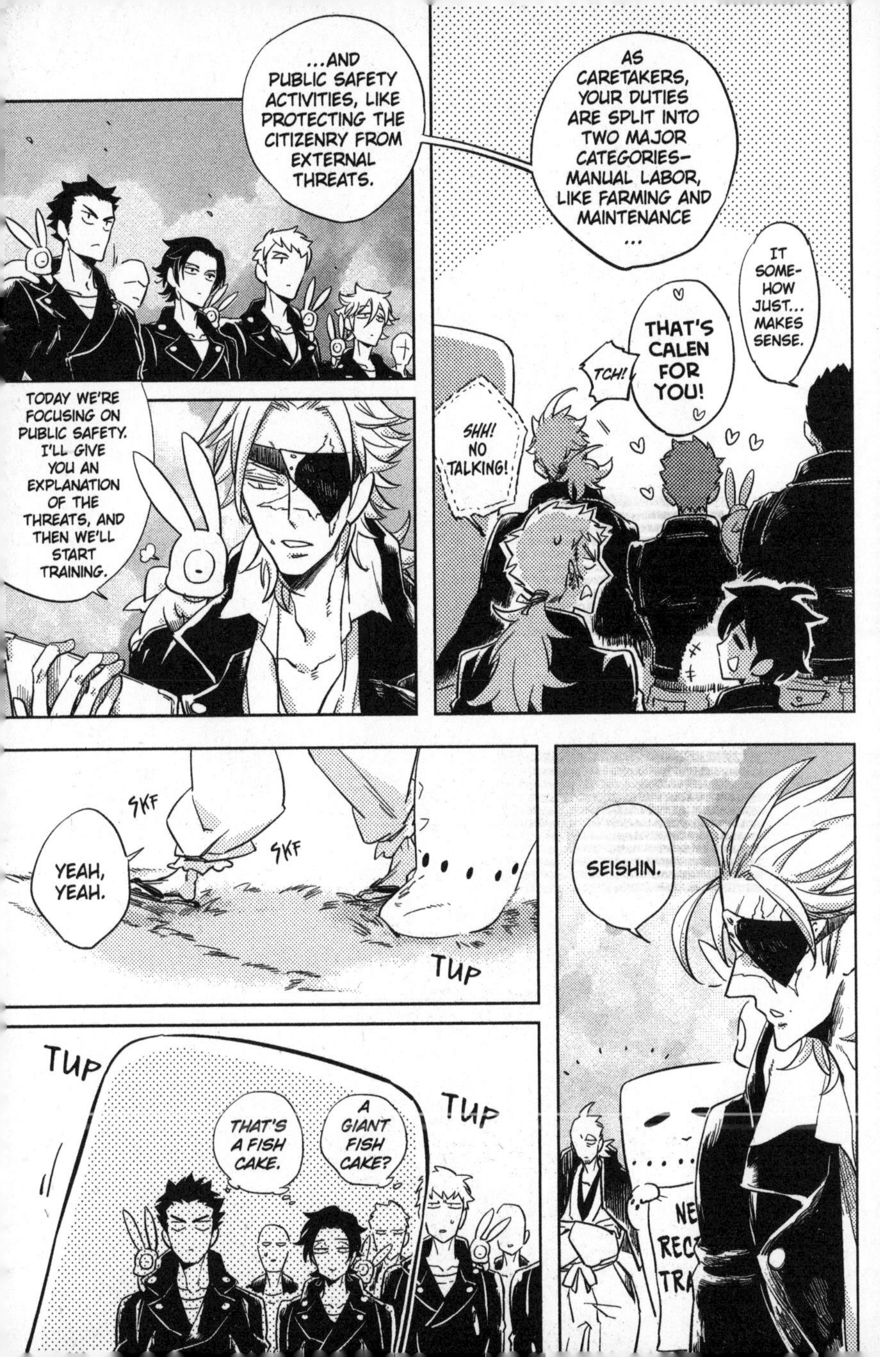
AS CARETAKERS, YOUR DUTIES ARE SPLIT INTO TWO MAJOR CATEGORIES– MANUAL LABOR, LIKE FARMING AND MAINTENANCE ...
IT SOMEHOW JUST... MAKES SENSE.
THAT'S CALEN FOR YOU!
TCH!
SHH! NO TALKING!
...AND PUBLIC SAFETY ACTIVITIES, LIKE PROTECTING THE CITIZENRY FROM EXTERNAL THREATS.
TODAY WE'RE FOCUSING ON PUBLIC SAFETY. I'LL GIVE YOU AN EXPLANATION OF THE THREATS, AND THEN WE'LL START TRAINING.
SEISHIN.
YEAH, YEAH.
SKF
SKF
......
TUP
TUP
TUP
A GIANT FISH CAKE?
THAT'S A FISH CAKE.

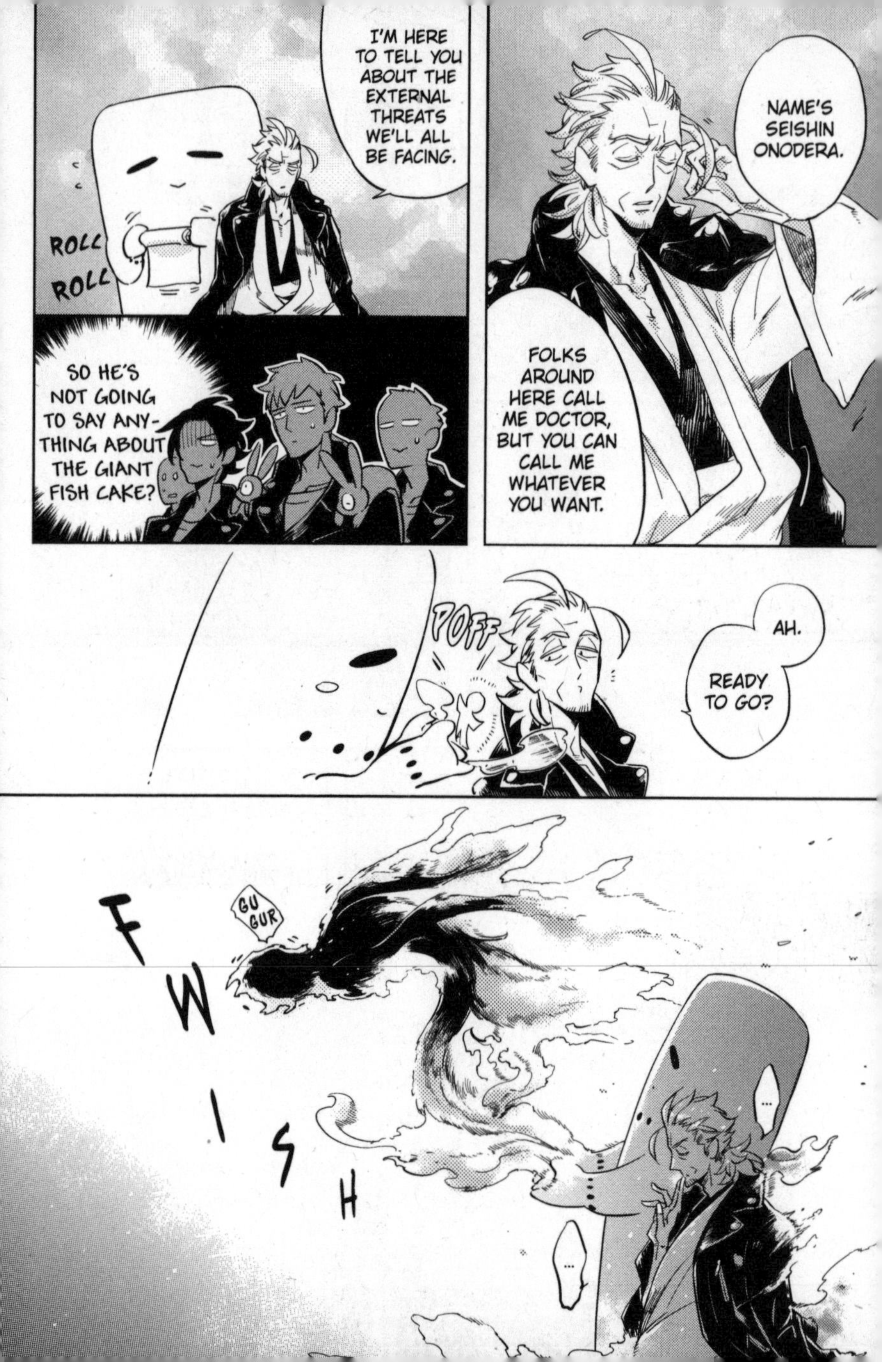
NAME'S SEISHIN ONODERA.
FOLKS AROUND HERE CALL ME DOCTOR, BUT YOU CAN CALL ME WHATEVER YOU WANT.
I'M HERE TO TELL YOU ABOUT THE EXTERNAL THREATS WE'LL ALL BE FACING.
ROLL
ROLL
SO HE'S NOT GOING TO SAY ANY-THING ABOUT THE GIANT FISH CAKE?
AH.
READY TO GO?
POFF
FWISH
GU GUR
...
...

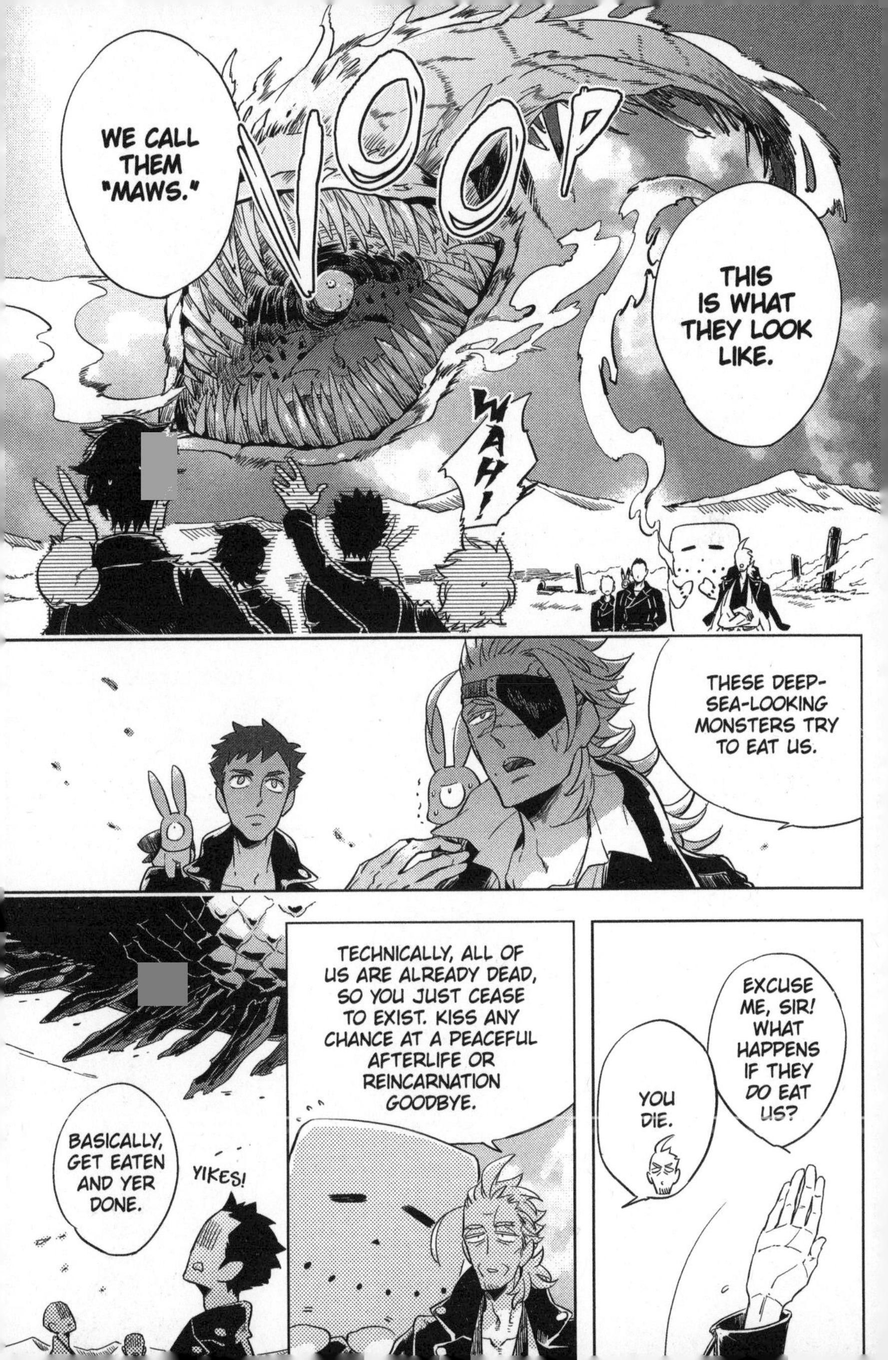

VOOOP
WE CALL THEM "MAWS."
THIS IS WHAT THEY LOOK LIKE.
WAH!
THESE DEEP-SEA-LOOKING MONSTERS TRY TO EAT US.
EXCUSE ME, SIR! WHAT HAPPENS IF THEY DO EAT US?
YOU DIE.
TECHNICALLY, ALL OF US ARE ALREADY DEAD, SO YOU JUST CEASE TO EXIST. KISS ANY CHANCE AT A PEACEFUL AFTERLIFE OR REINCARNATION GOODBYE.
BASICALLY, GET EATEN AND YER DONE.
YIKES!

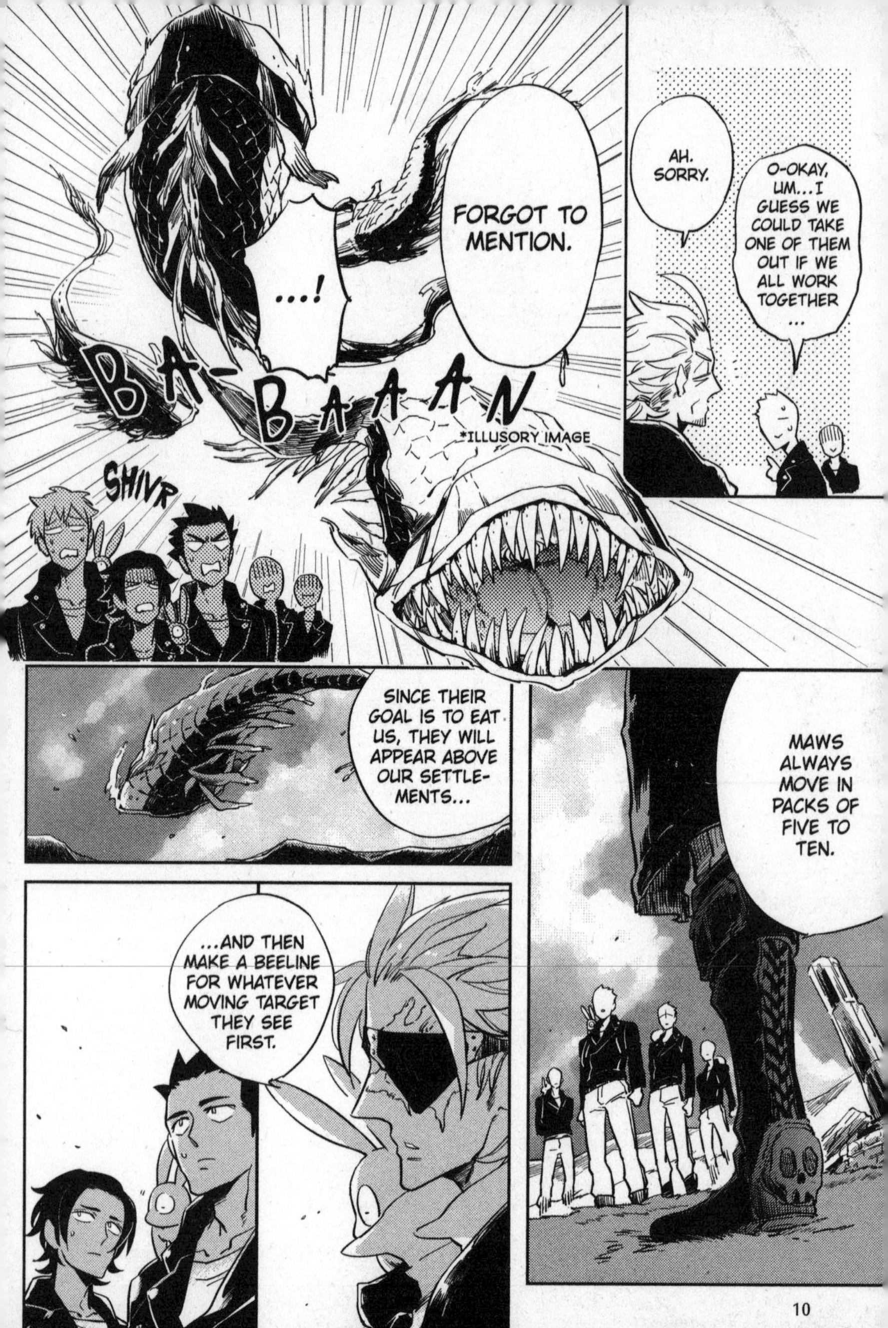
O-OKAY, UM...I GUESS WE COULD TAKE ONE OF THEM OUT IF WE ALL WORK TOGETHER...
AH. SORRY.
FORGOT TO MENTION.
...!
BA-BAAAN
*ILLUSORY IMAGE
SHIVR
MAWS ALWAYS MOVE IN PACKS OF FIVE TO TEN.
SINCE THEIR GOAL IS TO EAT US, THEY WILL APPEAR ABOVE OUR SETTLE-MENTS...
...AND THEN MAKE A BEELINE FOR WHATEVER MOVING TARGET THEY SEE FIRST.

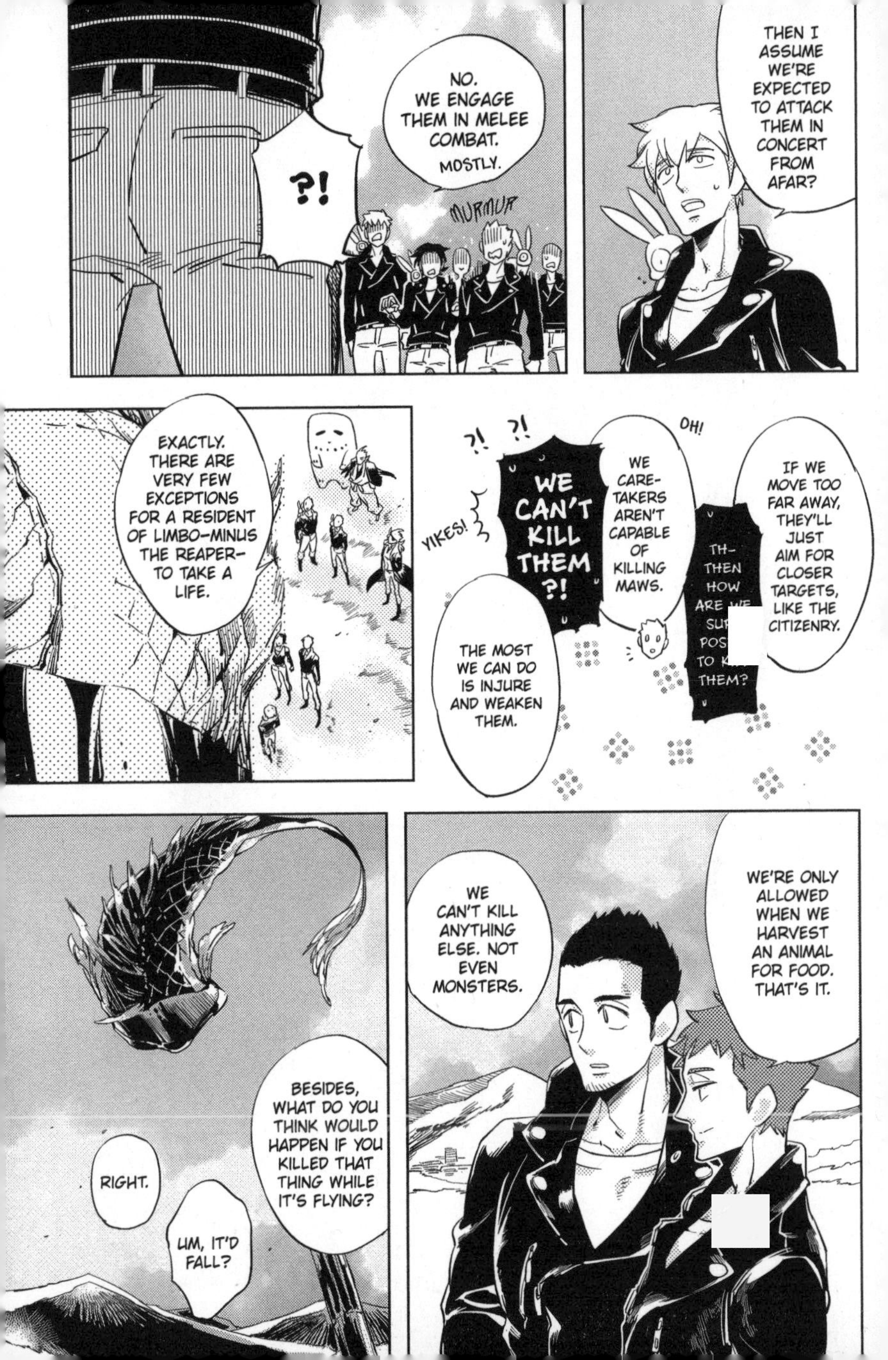
THEN I ASSUME WE'RE EXPECTED TO ATTACK THEM IN CONCERT FROM AFAR?
NO. WE ENGAGE THEM IN MELEE COMBAT.
MOSTLY.
MURMUR
?!
IF WE MOVE TOO FAR AWAY, THEY'LL JUST AIM FOR CLOSER TARGETS, LIKE THE CITIZENRY.
OH!
TH- THEN HOW ARE WE SU POS TO K THEM?
WE CARE-TAKERS AREN'T CAPABLE OF KILLING MAWS.
WE CAN'T KILL THEM?!
?! ?!
YIKES!
THE MOST WE CAN DO IS INJURE AND WEAKEN THEM.
EXACTLY. THERE ARE VERY FEW EXCEPTIONS FOR A RESIDENT OF LIMBO-MINUS THE REAPER-TO TAKE A LIFE.
WE'RE ONLY ALLOWED WHEN WE HARVEST AN ANIMAL FOR FOOD. THAT'S IT.
WE CAN'T KILL ANYTHING ELSE. NOT EVEN MONSTERS.
BESIDES, WHAT DO YOU THINK WOULD HAPPEN IF YOU KILLED THAT THING WHILE IT'S FLYING?
UM, IT'D FALL?
RIGHT.

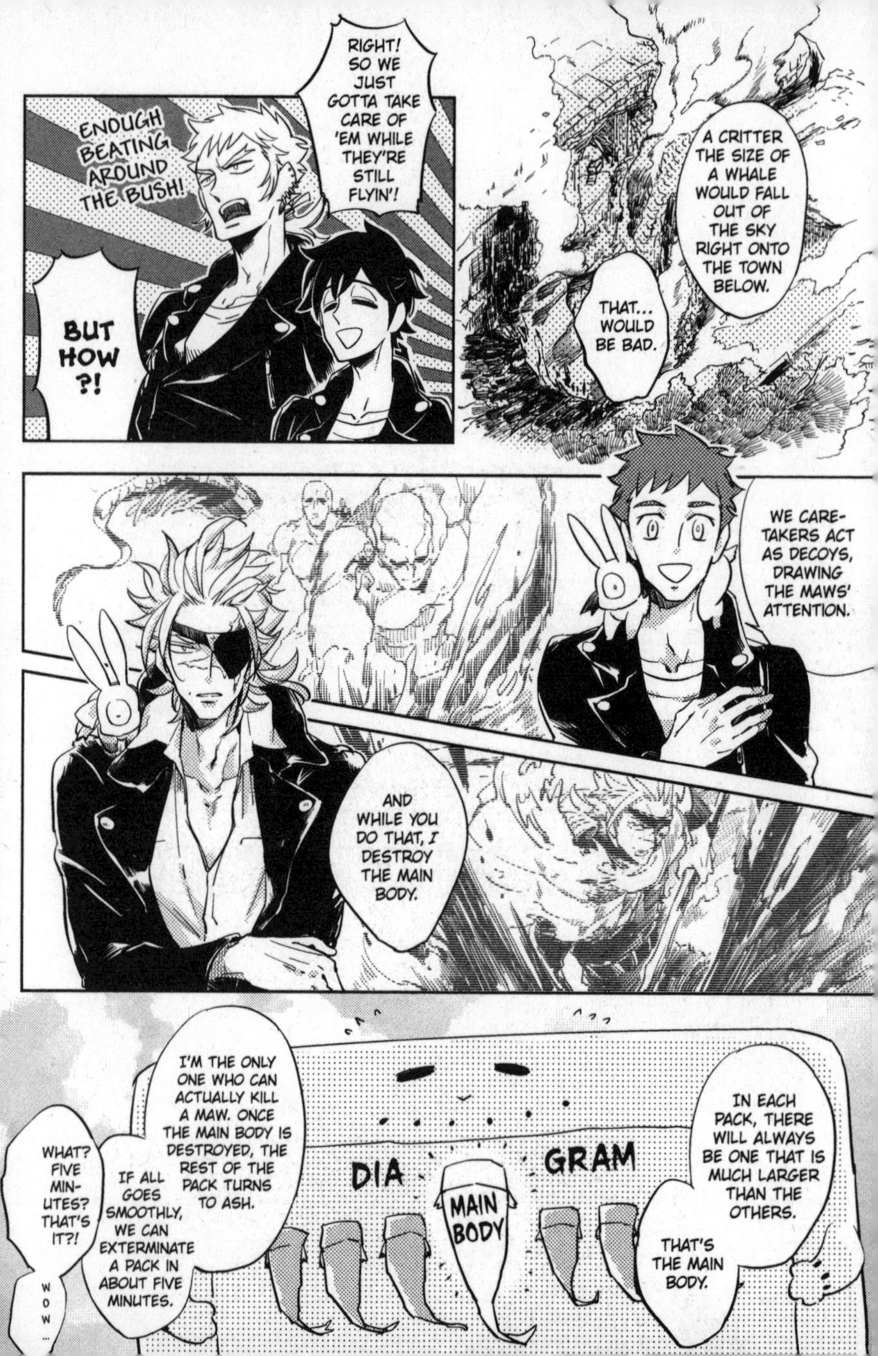
A CRITTER THE SIZE OF A WHALE WOULD FALL OUT OF THE SKY RIGHT ONTO THE TOWN BELOW.
THAT... WOULD BE BAD.
RIGHT! SO WE JUST GOTTA TAKE CARE OF 'EM WHILE THEY'RE STILL FLYIN'!
ENOUGH BEATING AROUND THE BUSH!
BUT HOW?!
WE CARE-TAKERS ACT AS DECOYS, DRAWING THE MAWS' ATTENTION.
AND WHILE YOU DO THAT, *I* DESTROY THE MAIN BODY.
IN EACH PACK, THERE WILL ALWAYS BE ONE THAT IS MUCH LARGER THAN THE OTHERS.
THAT'S THE MAIN BODY.
DIA GRAM
MAIN BODY
I'M THE ONLY ONE WHO CAN ACTUALLY KILL A MAW. ONCE THE MAIN BODY IS DESTROYED, THE REST OF THE PACK TURNS TO ASH.
IF ALL GOES SMOOTHLY, WE CAN EXTERMINATE A PACK IN ABOUT FIVE MINUTES.
WHAT? FIVE MIN-UTES? THAT'S IT?!
WOW...

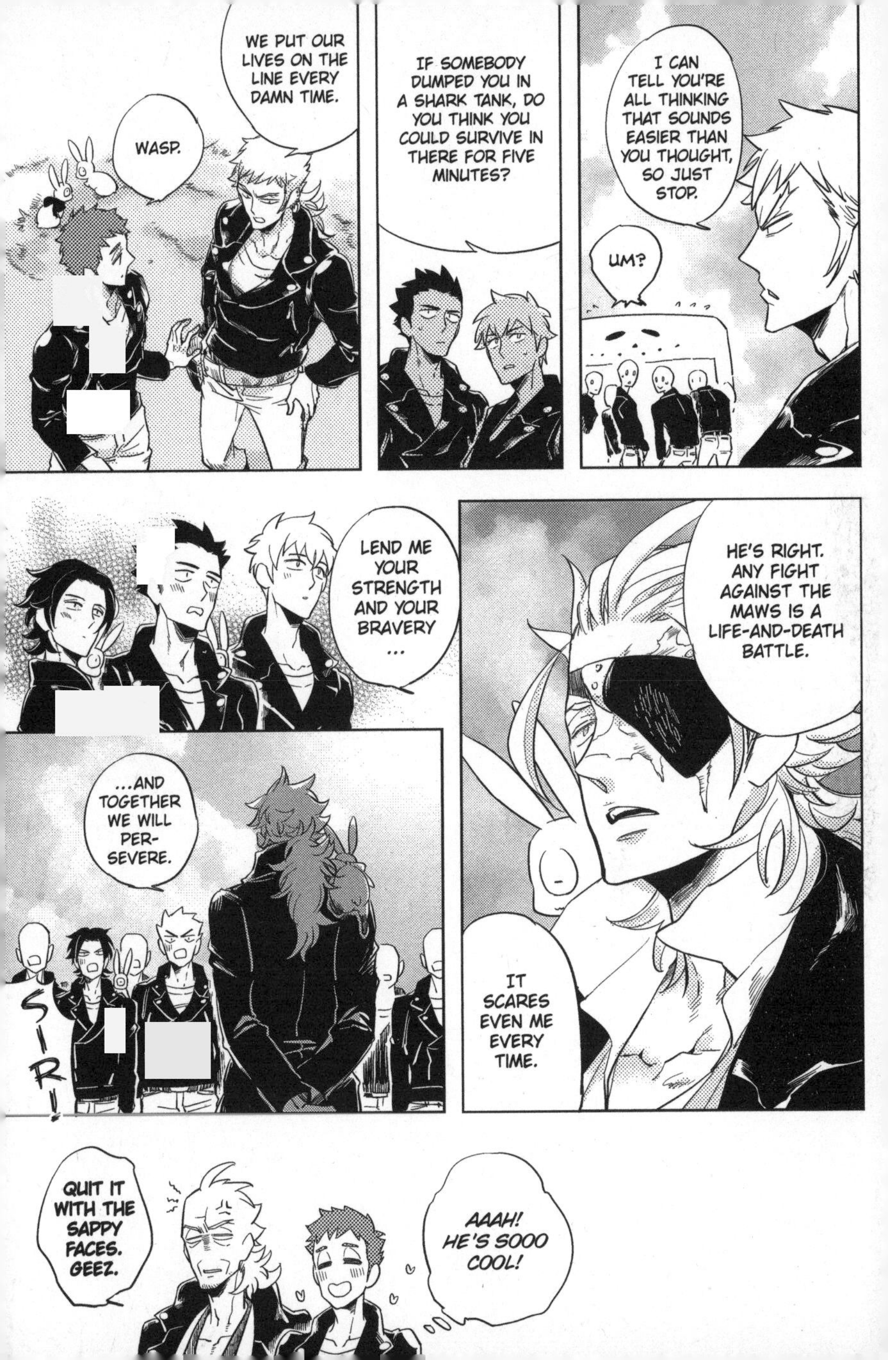
I CAN TELL YOU'RE ALL THINKING THAT SOUNDS EASIER THAN YOU THOUGHT, SO JUST STOP.
UM?
IF SOMEBODY DUMPED YOU IN A SHARK TANK, DO YOU THINK YOU COULD SURVIVE IN THERE FOR FIVE MINUTES?
WE PUT OUR LIVES ON THE LINE EVERY DAMN TIME.
WASP.
HE'S RIGHT. ANY FIGHT AGAINST THE MAWS IS A LIFE-AND-DEATH BATTLE.
IT SCARES EVEN ME EVERY TIME.
LEND ME YOUR STRENGTH AND YOUR BRAVERY ...
...AND TOGETHER WE WILL PER-SEVERE.
SIR!
AAAH! HE'S SOOO COOL!
QUIT IT WITH THE SAPPY FACES. GEEZ.

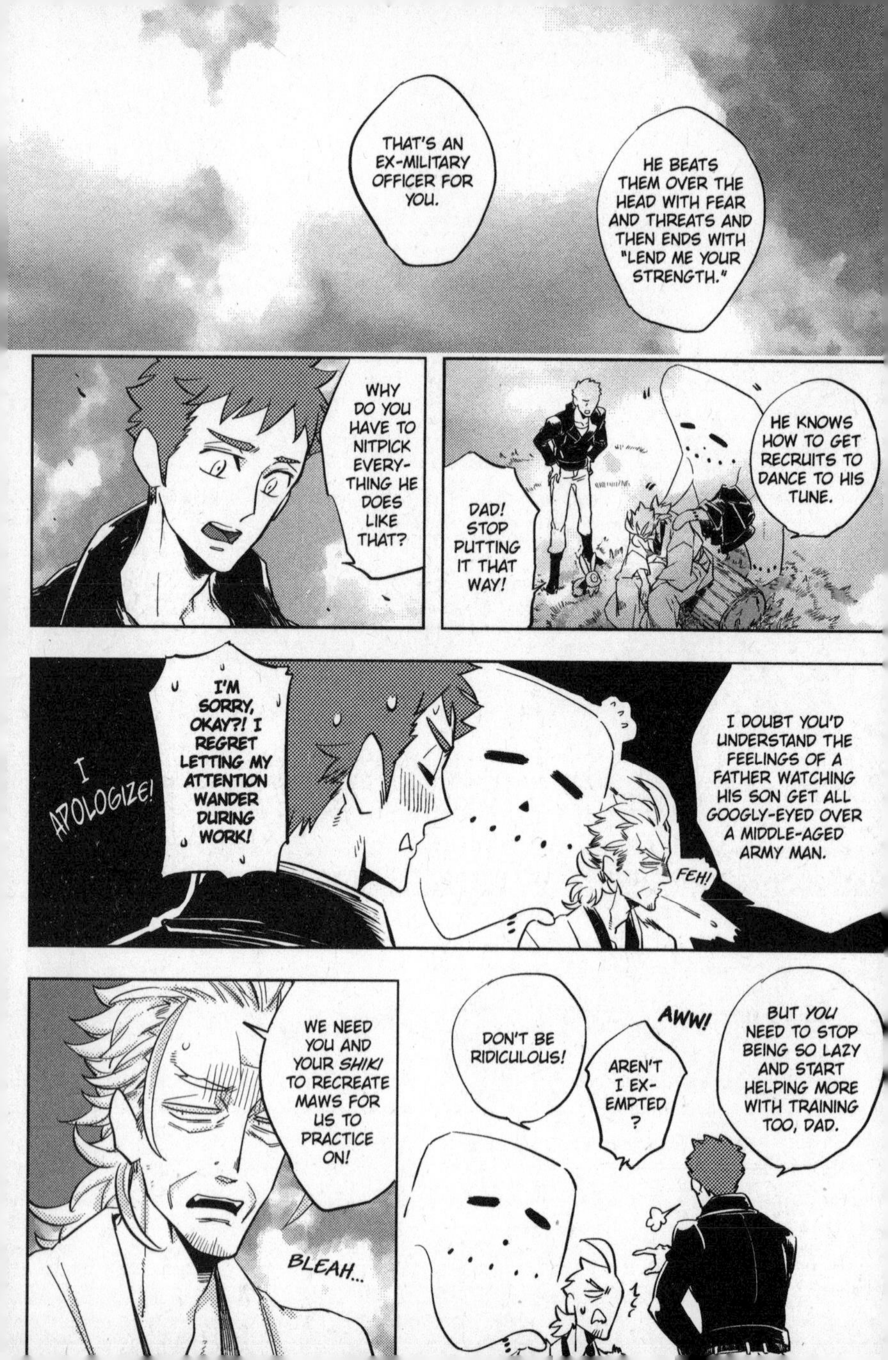
HE BEATS THEM OVER THE HEAD WITH FEAR AND THREATS AND THEN ENDS WITH "LEND ME YOUR STRENGTH."
THAT'S AN EX-MILITARY OFFICER FOR YOU.
HE KNOWS HOW TO GET RECRUITS TO DANCE TO HIS TUNE.
DAD! STOP PUTTING IT THAT WAY!
WHY DO YOU HAVE TO NITPICK EVERY-THING HE DOES LIKE THAT?
I DOUBT YOU'D UNDERSTAND THE FEELINGS OF A FATHER WATCHING HIS SON GET ALL GOOGLY-EYED OVER A MIDDLE-AGED ARMY MAN.
FEH!
I'M SORRY, OKAY?! I REGRET LETTING MY ATTENTION WANDER DURING WORK!
I APOLOGIZE!
BUT YOU NEED TO STOP BEING SO LAZY AND START HELPING MORE WITH TRAINING TOO, DAD.
AWW!
AREN'T I EX-EMPTED?
DON'T BE RIDICULOUS!
WE NEED YOU AND YOUR SHIKI TO RECREATE MAWS FOR US TO PRACTICE ON!
BLEAH...

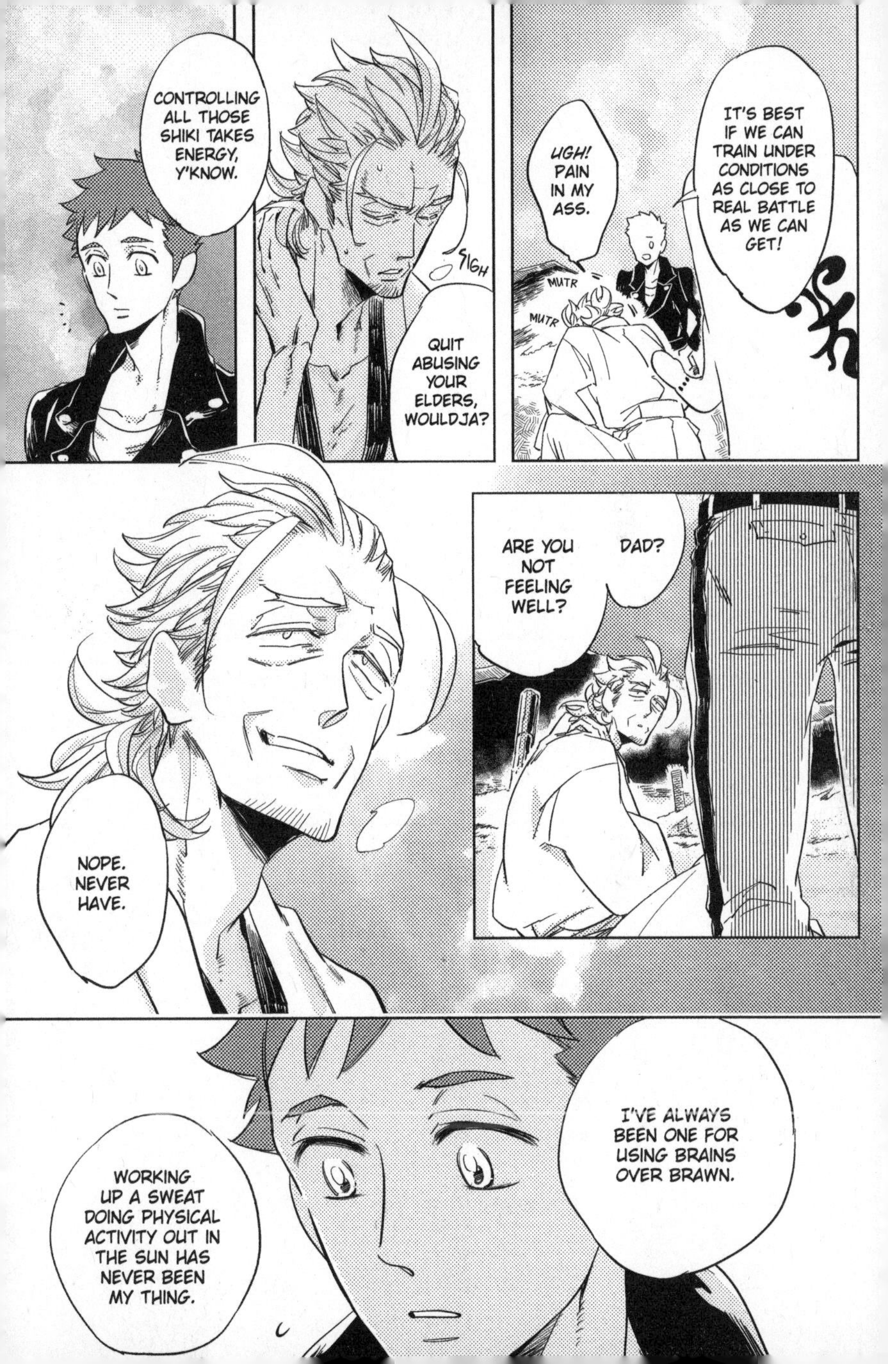
IT'S BEST IF WE CAN TRAIN UNDER CONDITIONS AS CLOSE TO REAL BATTLE AS WE CAN GET!
UGH! PAIN IN MY ASS.
MUTR
MUTR
SIGH
QUIT ABUSING YOUR ELDERS, WOULDJA?
CONTROLLING ALL THOSE SHIKI TAKES ENERGY, Y'KNOW.
ARE YOU NOT FEELING WELL? DAD?
NOPE. NEVER HAVE.
I'VE ALWAYS BEEN ONE FOR USING BRAINS OVER BRAWN.
WORKING UP A SWEAT DOING PHYSICAL ACTIVITY OUT IN THE SUN HAS NEVER BEEN MY THING.

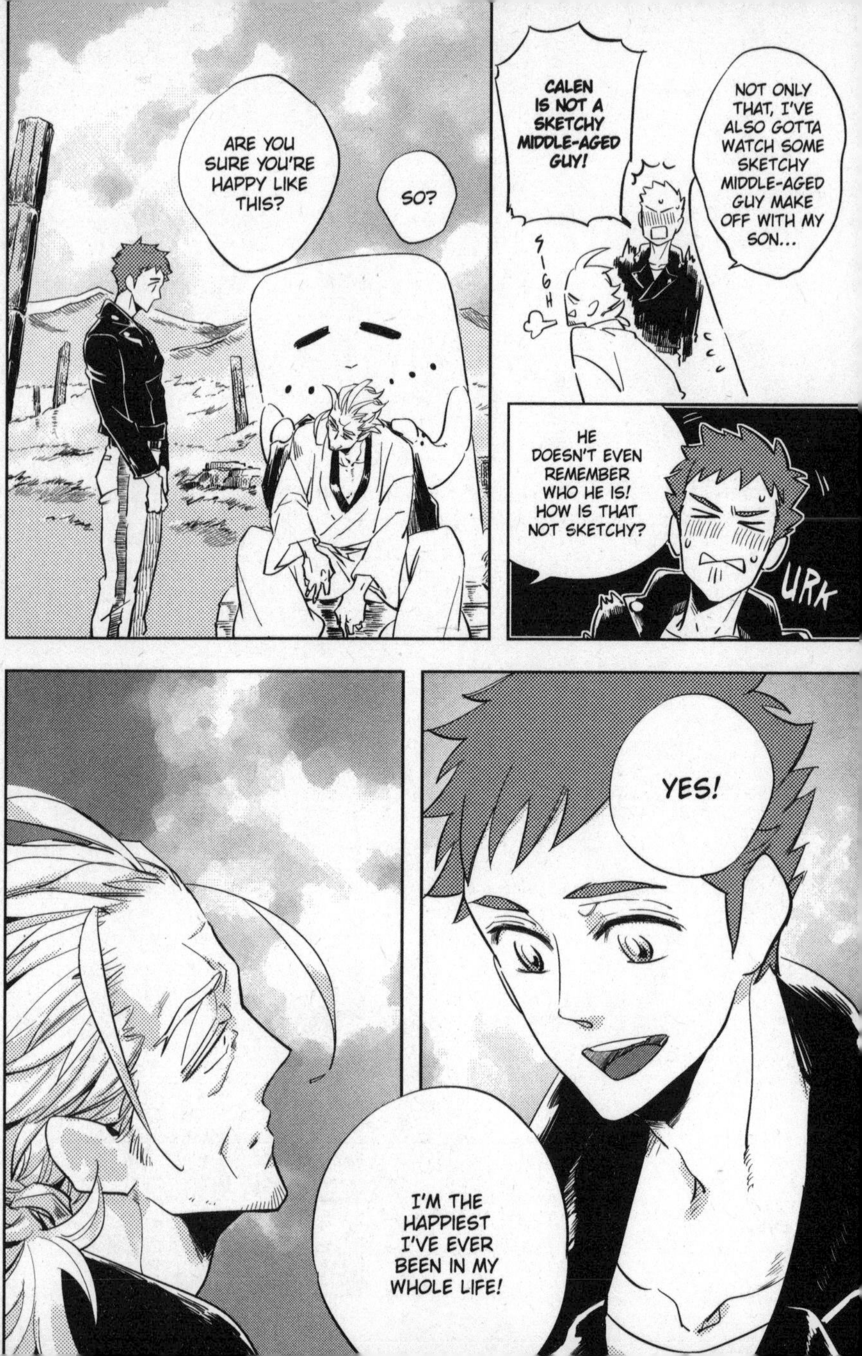
NOT ONLY THAT, I'VE ALSO GOTTA WATCH SOME SKETCHY MIDDLE-AGED GUY MAKE OFF WITH MY SON...
CALEN IS NOT A SKETCHY MIDDLE-AGED GUY!
SIGH
HE DOESN'T EVEN REMEMBER WHO HE IS! HOW IS THAT NOT SKETCHY?
URK
SO?
ARE YOU SURE YOU'RE HAPPY LIKE THIS?
YES!
I'M THE HAPPIEST I'VE EVER BEEN IN MY WHOLE LIFE!

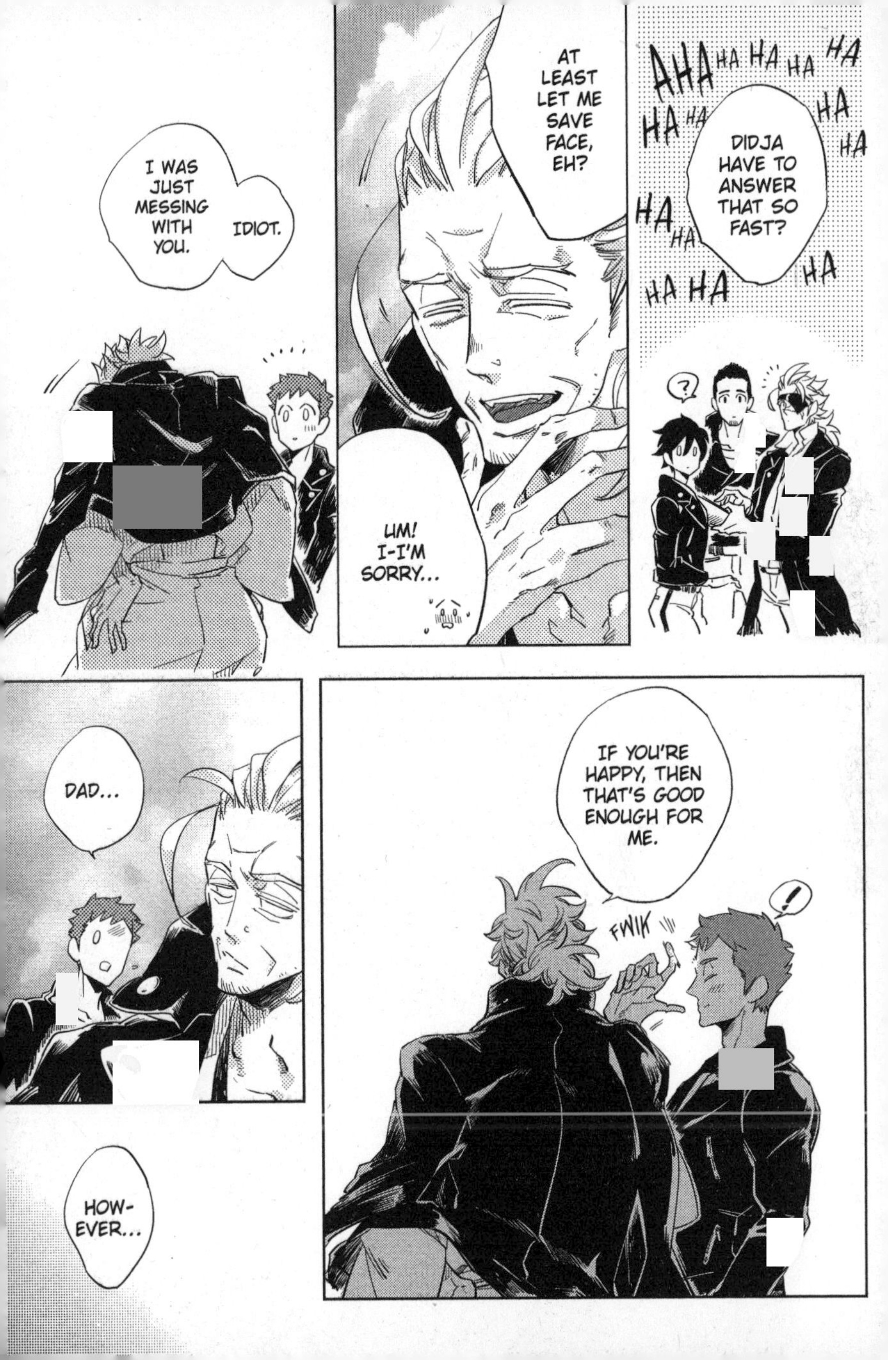
AHAHA HA HA HA HA HA HA HA HA HA HA HA HA HA HA
DIDJA HAVE TO ANSWER THAT SO FAST?
AT LEAST LET ME SAVE FACE, EH?
UM! I-I'M SORRY...
I WAS JUST MESSING WITH YOU.
IDIOT.
IF YOU'RE HAPPY, THEN THAT'S GOOD ENOUGH FOR ME.
FWIK
!
DAD...
HOW-EVER...

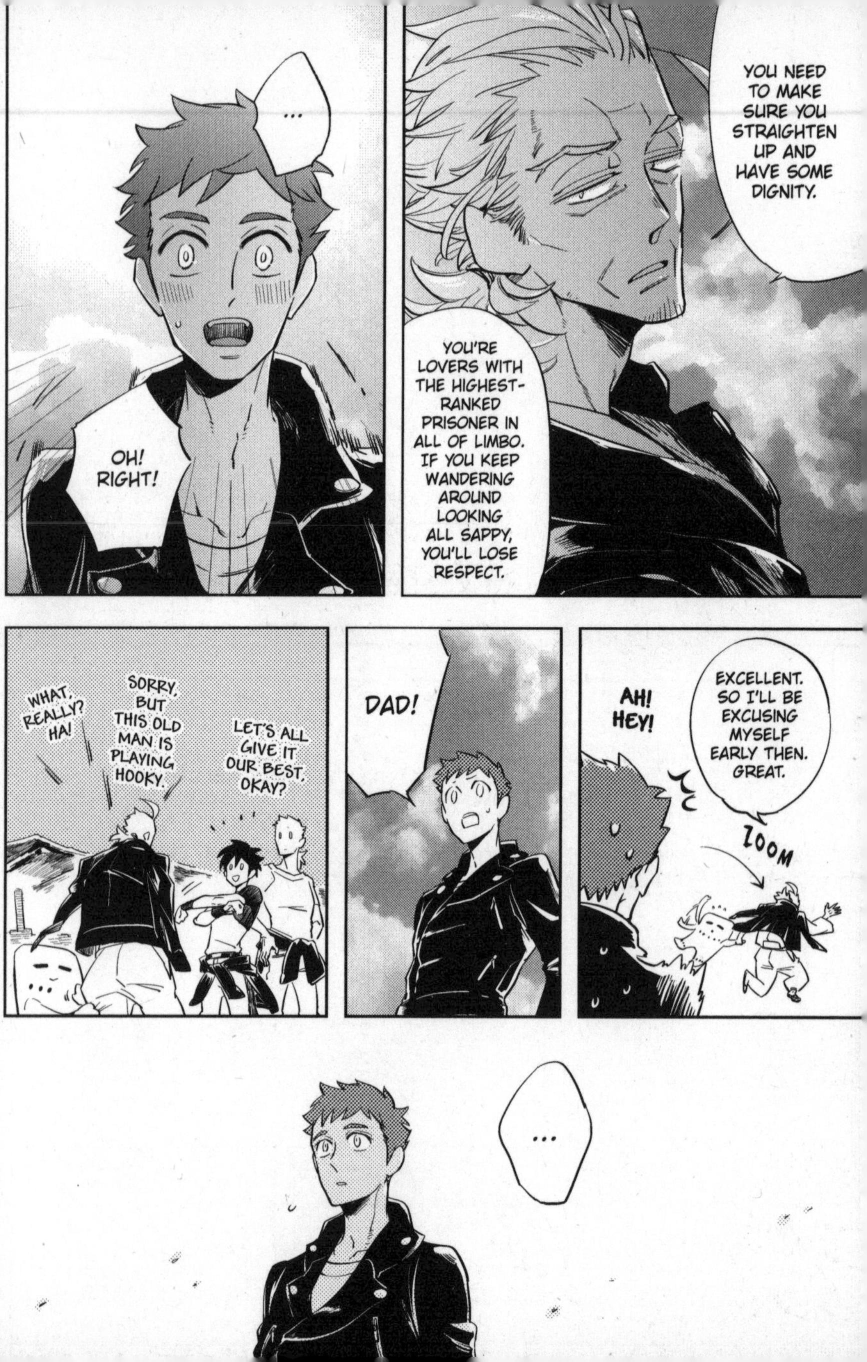

YOU NEED TO MAKE SURE YOU STRAIGHTEN UP AND HAVE SOME DIGNITY.
YOU'RE LOVERS WITH THE HIGHEST-RANKED PRISONER IN ALL OF LIMBO. IF YOU KEEP WANDERING AROUND LOOKING ALL SAPPY, YOU'LL LOSE RESPECT.
...
OH! RIGHT!
EXCELLENT. SO I'LL BE EXCUSING MYSELF EARLY THEN. GREAT.
AH! HEY!
ZOOM
DAD!
LET'S ALL GIVE IT OUR BEST, OKAY?
SORRY, BUT THIS OLD MAN IS PLAYING HOOKY.
WHAT, REALLY? HA!
...

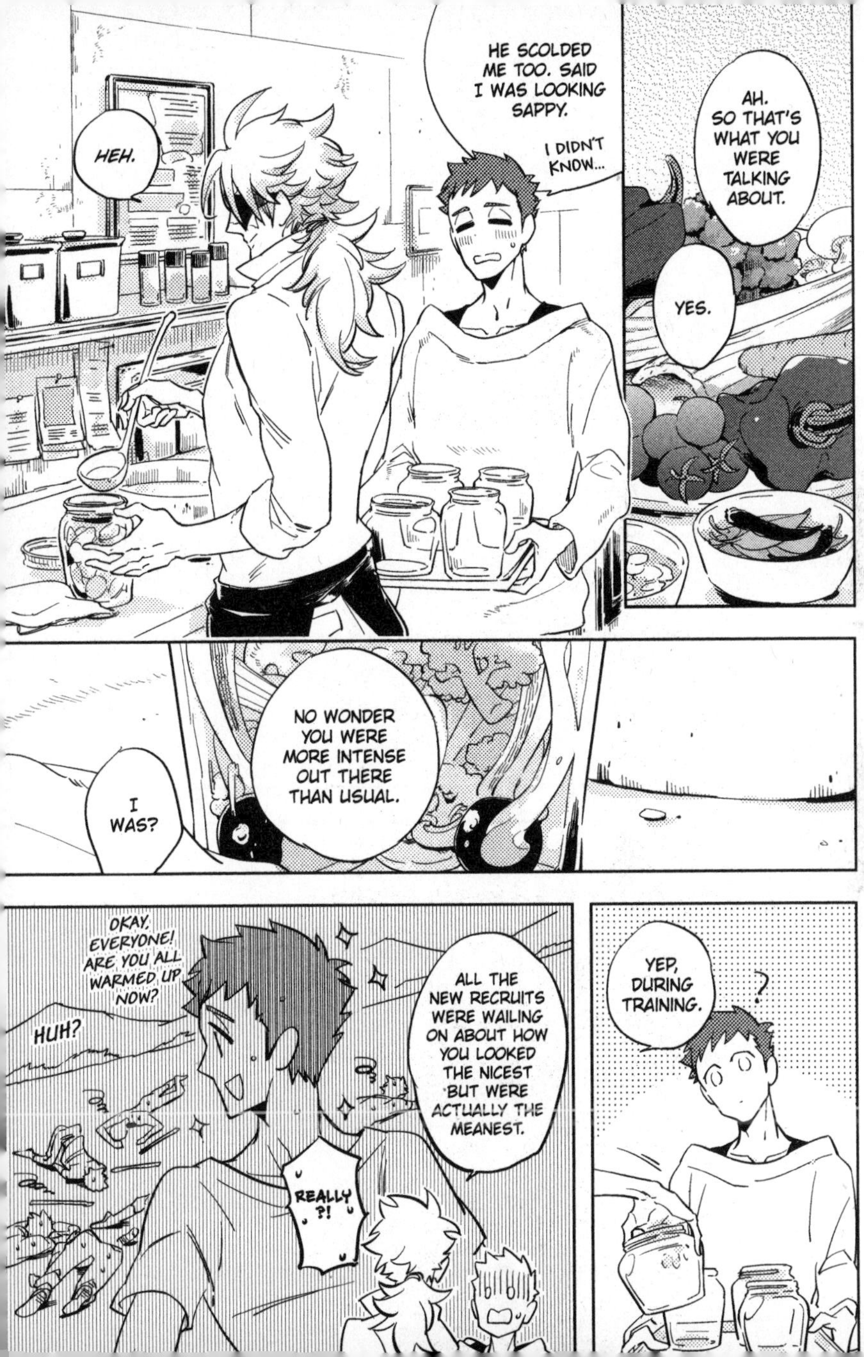
AH. SO THAT'S WHAT YOU WERE TALKING ABOUT.
YES.
HE SCOLDED ME TOO. SAID I WAS LOOKING SAPPY.
I DIDN'T KNOW...
HEH.
NO WONDER YOU WERE MORE INTENSE OUT THERE THAN USUAL.
I WAS?
YEP, DURING TRAINING.
?
ALL THE NEW RECRUITS WERE WAILING ON ABOUT HOW YOU LOOKED THE NICEST BUT WERE ACTUALLY THE MEANEST.
REALLY?!
OKAY, EVERYONE! ARE YOU ALL WARMED UP NOW?
HUH?

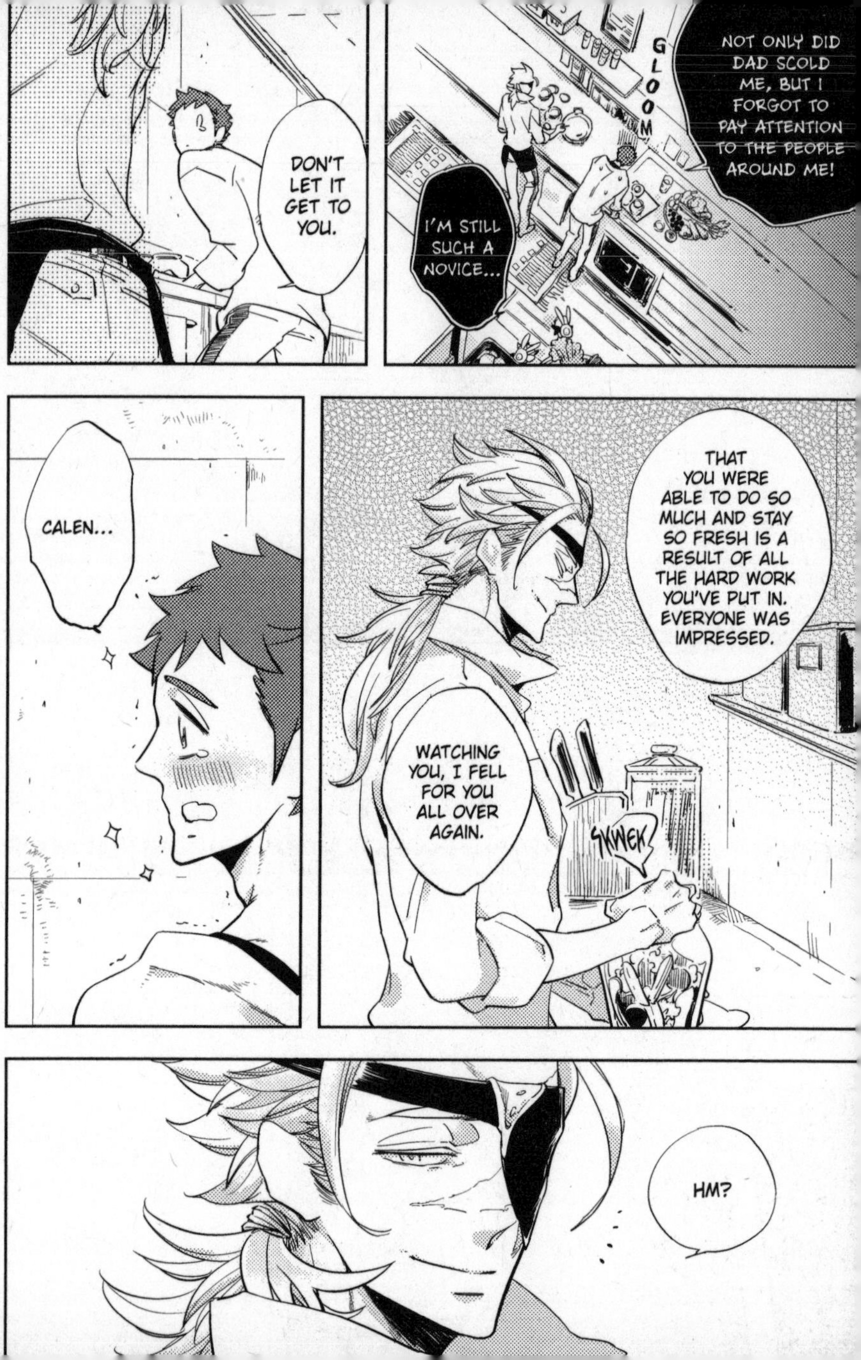
NOT ONLY DID DAD SCOLD ME, BUT I FORGOT TO PAY ATTENTION TO THE PEOPLE AROUND ME!
GLOOM
I'M STILL SUCH A NOVICE...
DON'T LET IT GET TO YOU.
THAT YOU WERE ABLE TO DO SO MUCH AND STAY SO FRESH IS A RESULT OF ALL THE HARD WORK YOU'VE PUT IN. EVERYONE WAS IMPRESSED.
WATCHING YOU, I FELL FOR YOU ALL OVER AGAIN.
SKWEK
CALEN...
HM?

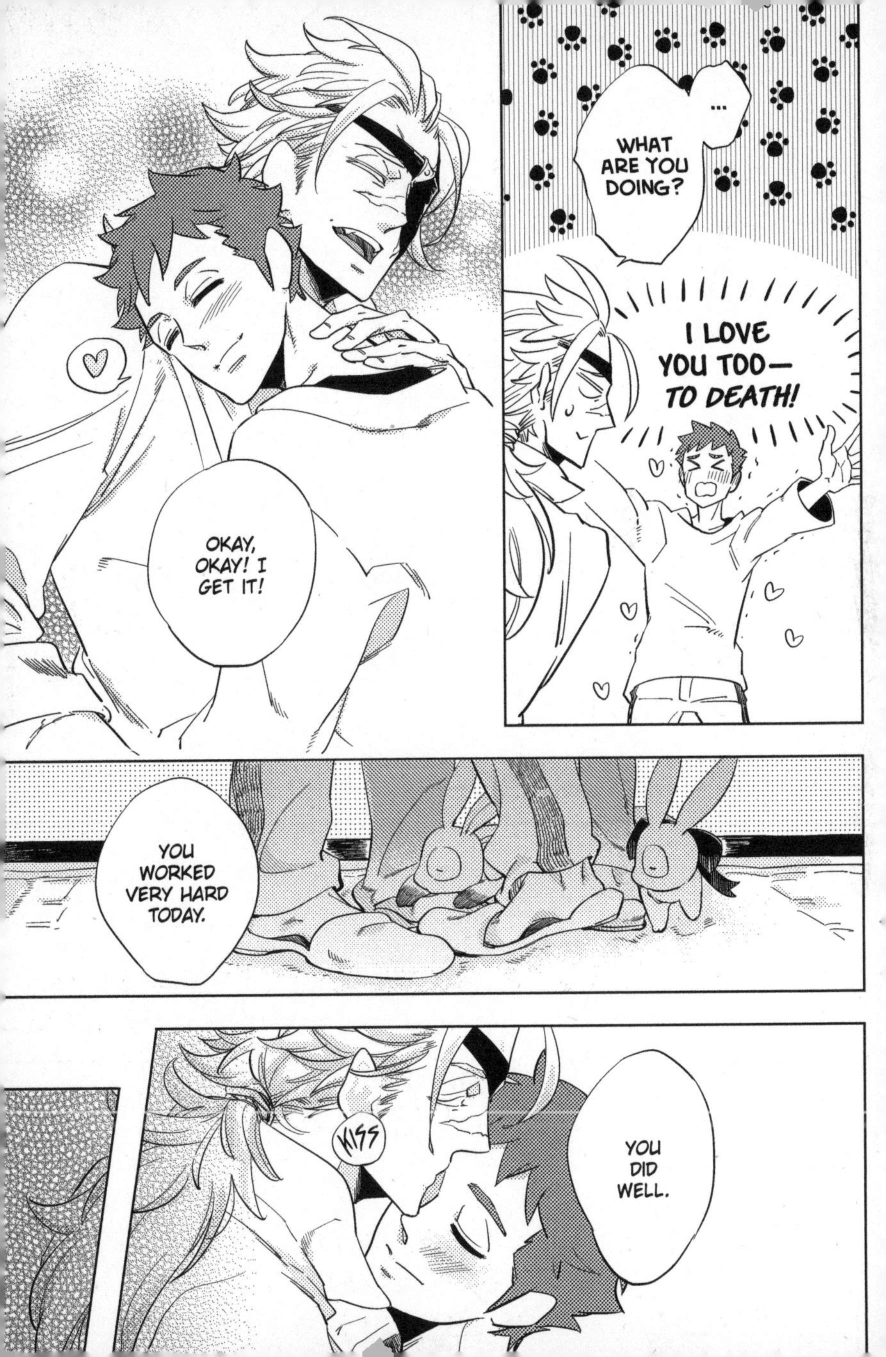
...
WHAT ARE YOU DOING?
I LOVE YOU TOO— TO DEATH!
OKAY, OKAY! I GET IT!
YOU WORKED VERY HARD TODAY.
YOU DID WELL.
KISS

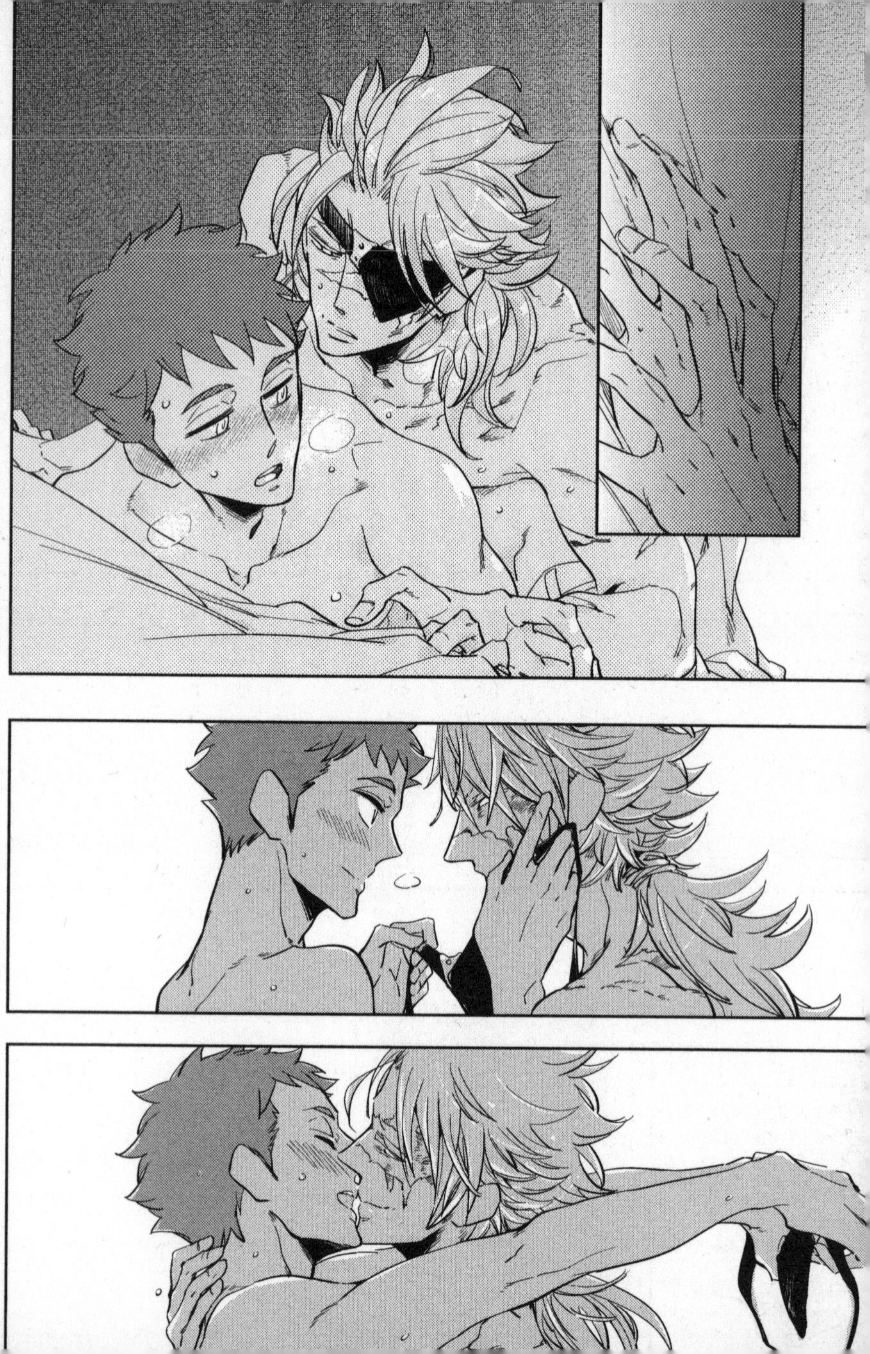

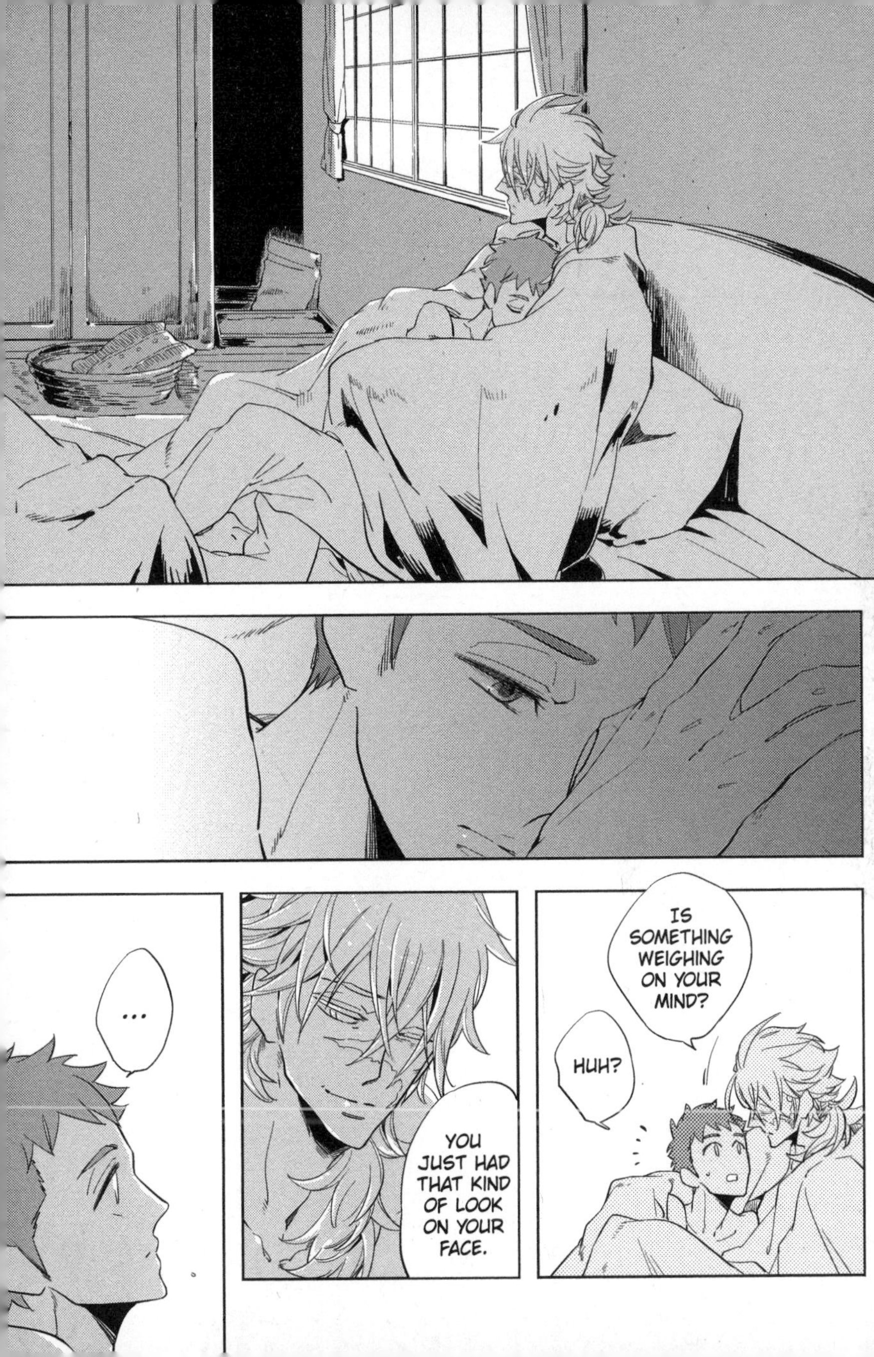
IS SOMETHING WEIGHING ON YOUR MIND?
HUH?
YOU JUST HAD THAT KIND OF LOOK ON YOUR FACE.
...

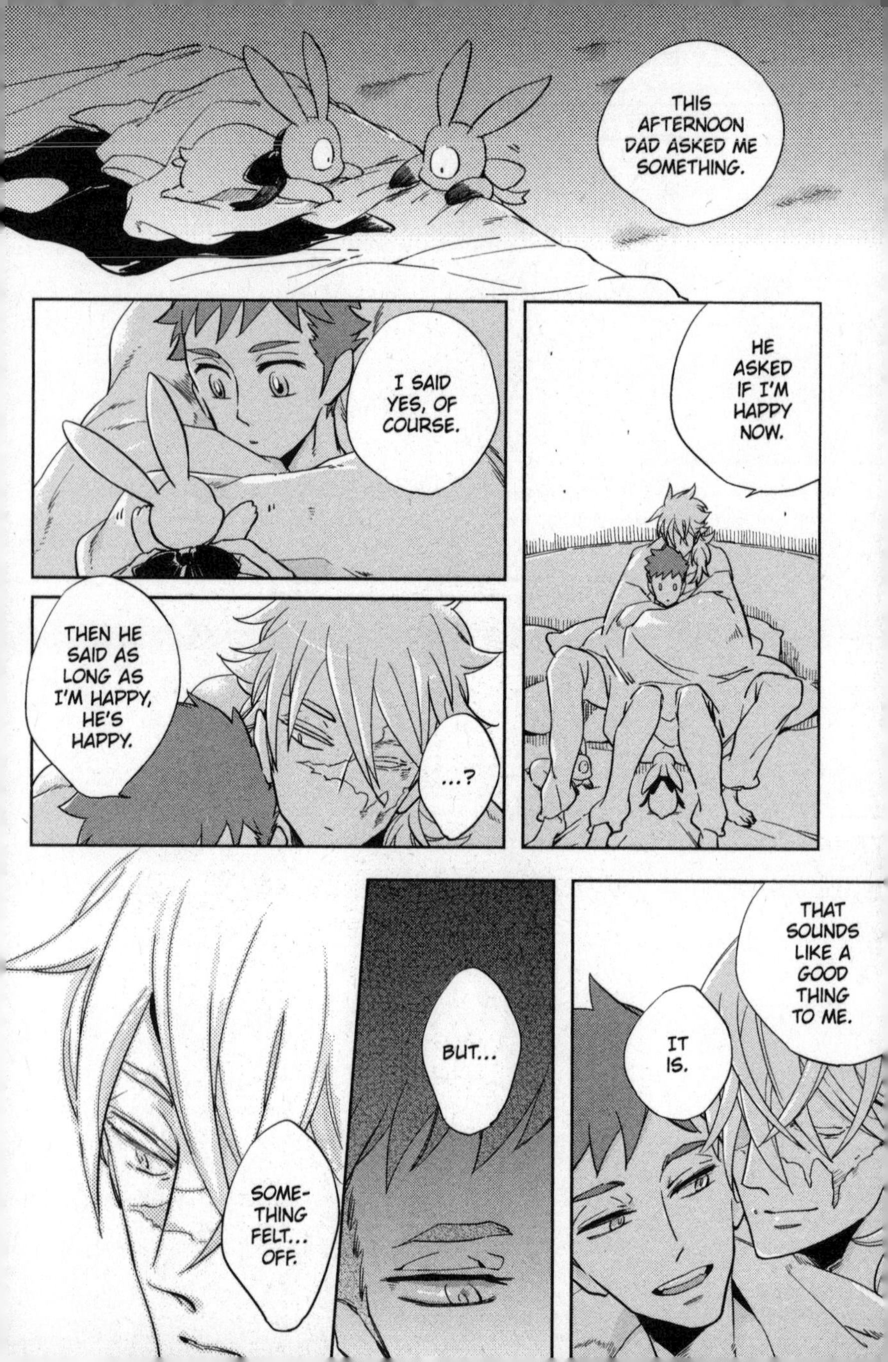
THIS AFTERNOON DAD ASKED ME SOMETHING.
HE ASKED IF I'M HAPPY NOW.
I SAID YES, OF COURSE.
THEN HE SAID AS LONG AS I'M HAPPY, HE'S HAPPY.
...?
THAT SOUNDS LIKE A GOOD THING TO ME.
IT IS.
BUT...
SOME-THING FELT... OFF.

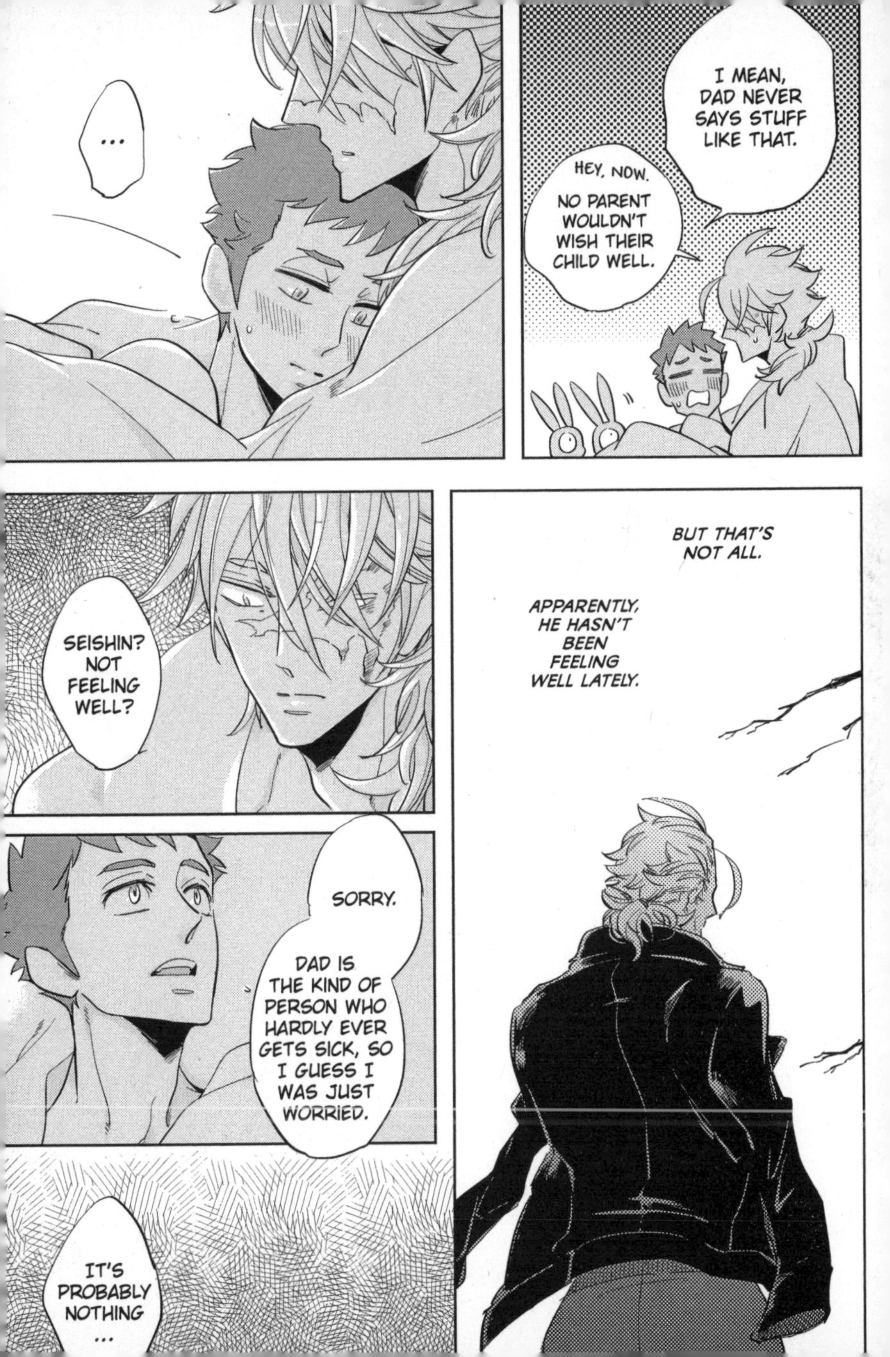
I MEAN, DAD NEVER SAYS STUFF LIKE THAT.
HEY, NOW.
NO PARENT WOULDN'T WISH THEIR CHILD WELL.
...
BUT THAT'S NOT ALL.
APPARENTLY, HE HASN'T BEEN FEELING WELL LATELY.
SEISHIN? NOT FEELING WELL?
SORRY.
DAD IS THE KIND OF PERSON WHO HARDLY EVER GETS SICK, SO I GUESS I WAS JUST WORRIED.
IT'S PROBABLY NOTHING ...

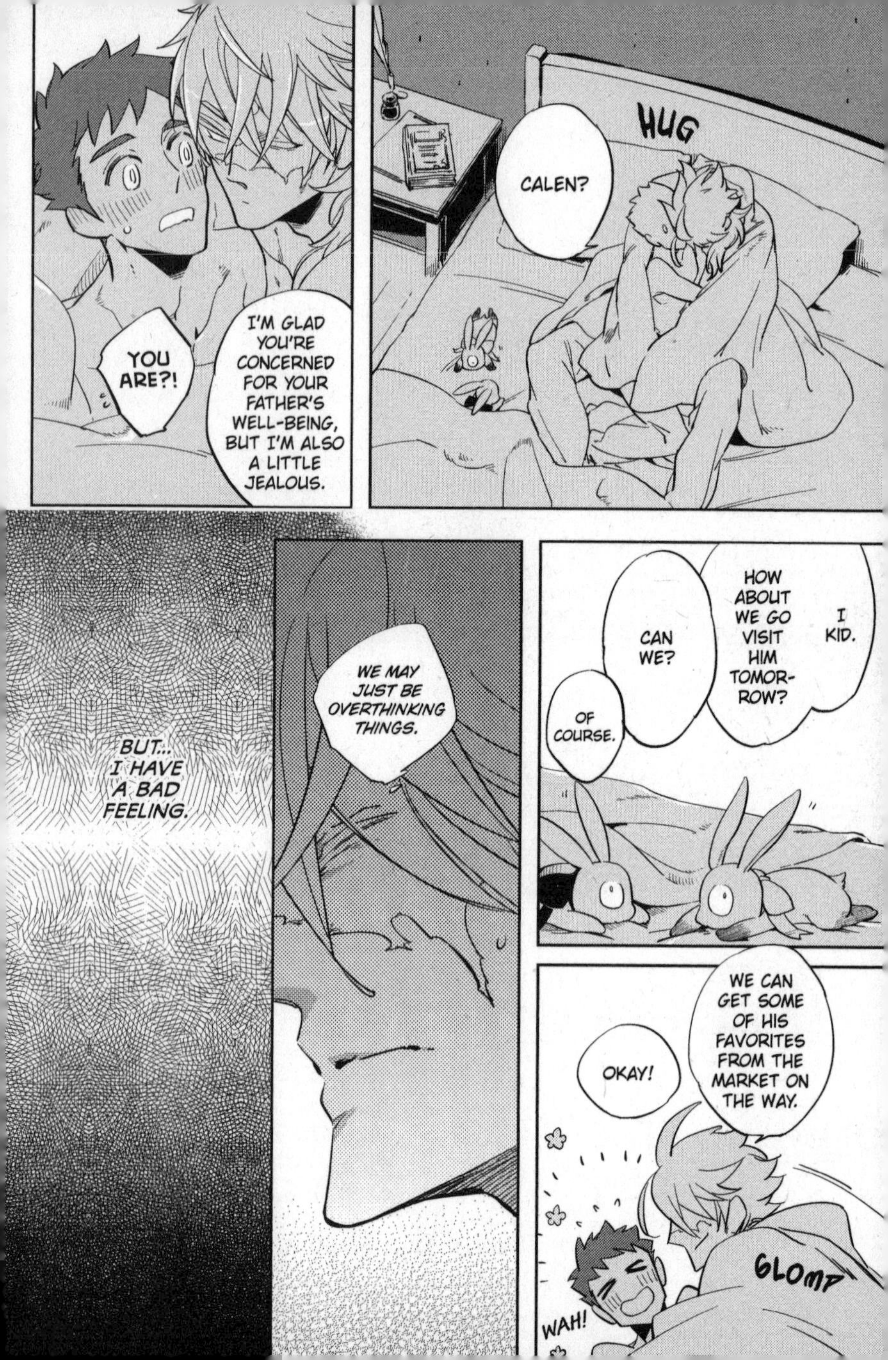
CALEN?
HUG
I'M GLAD YOU'RE CONCERNED FOR YOUR FATHER'S WELL-BEING, BUT I'M ALSO A LITTLE JEALOUS.
YOU ARE?!
I KID.
HOW ABOUT WE GO VISIT HIM TOMOR-ROW?
CAN WE?
OF COURSE.
WE CAN GET SOME OF HIS FAVORITES FROM THE MARKET ON THE WAY.
OKAY!
GLOMP
WAH!
WE MAY JUST BE OVERTHINKING THINGS.
BUT... I HAVE A BAD FEELING.

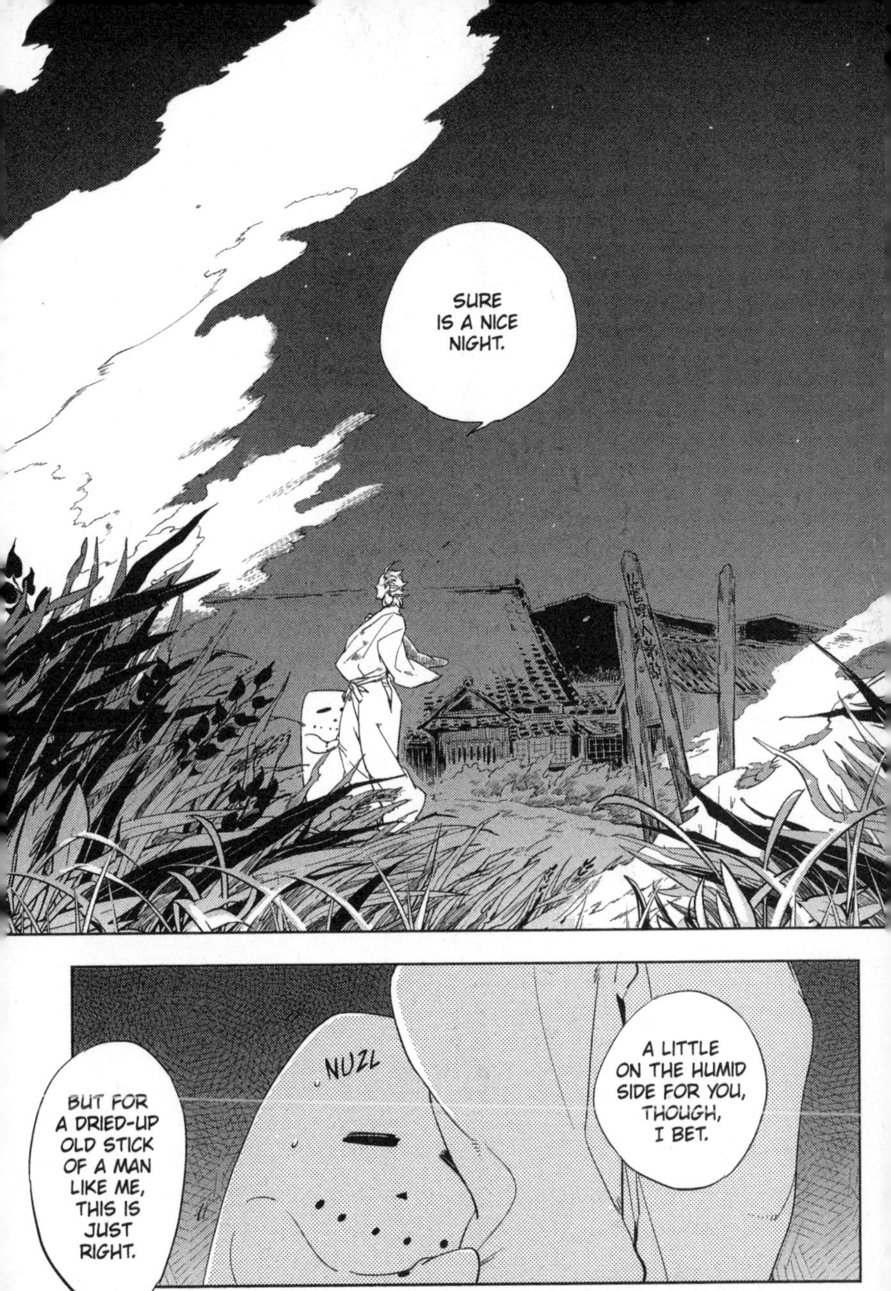
SURE IS A NICE NIGHT.
A LITTLE ON THE HUMID SIDE FOR YOU, THOUGH, I BET.
NUZL
BUT FOR A DRIED-UP OLD STICK OF A MAN LIKE ME, THIS IS JUST RIGHT.

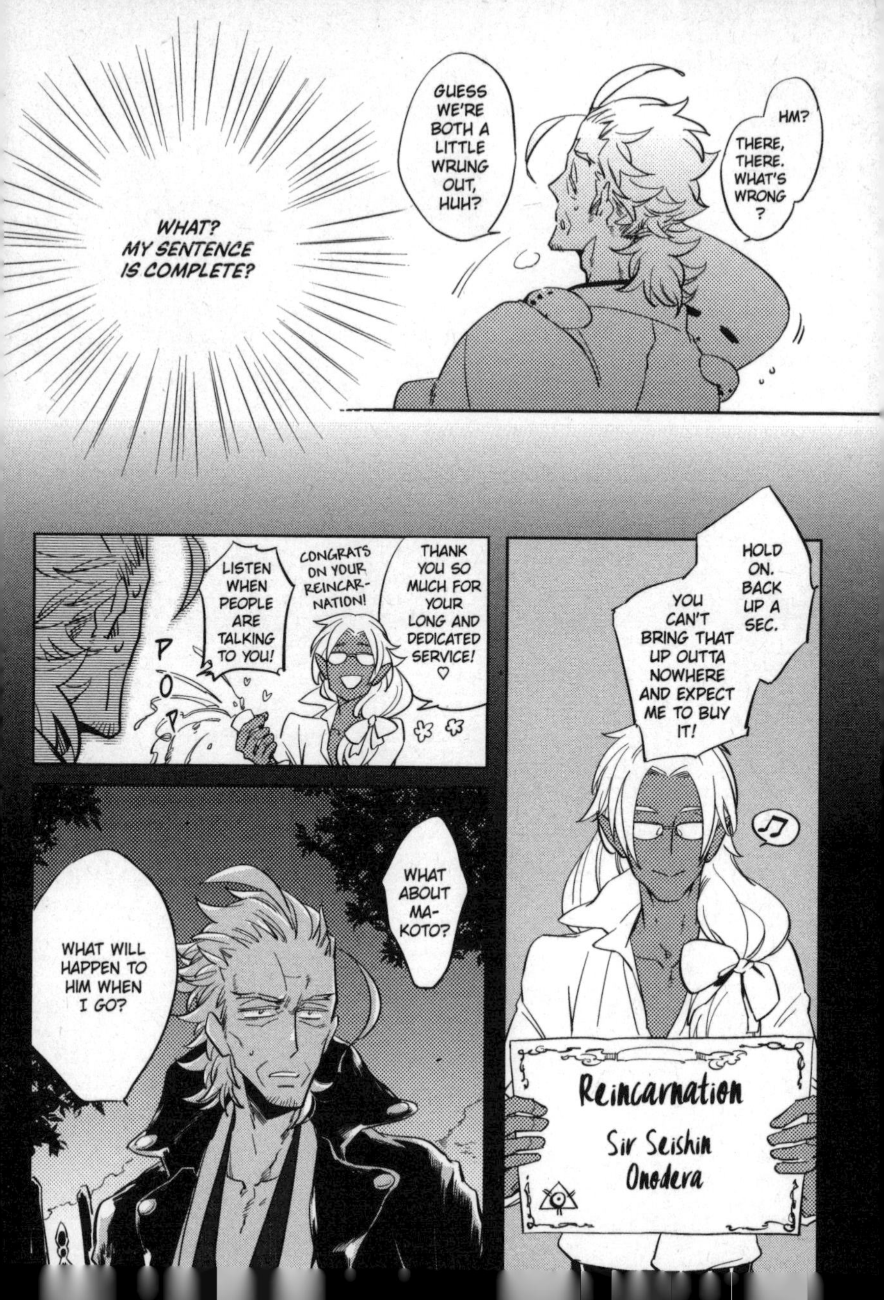
HM?
THERE, THERE. WHAT'S WRONG?
GUESS WE'RE BOTH A LITTLE WRUNG OUT, HUH?
WHAT? MY SENTENCE IS COMPLETE?
HOLD ON. BACK UP A SEC.
YOU CAN'T BRING THAT UP OUTTA NOWHERE AND EXPECT ME TO BUY IT!
Reincarnation
Sir Seishin Onodera
THANK YOU SO MUCH FOR YOUR LONG AND DEDICATED SERVICE! ♡
CONGRATS ON YOUR REINCAR-NATION!
LISTEN WHEN PEOPLE ARE TALKING TO YOU!
POP
WHAT ABOUT MA-KOTO?
WHAT WILL HAPPEN TO HIM WHEN I GO?

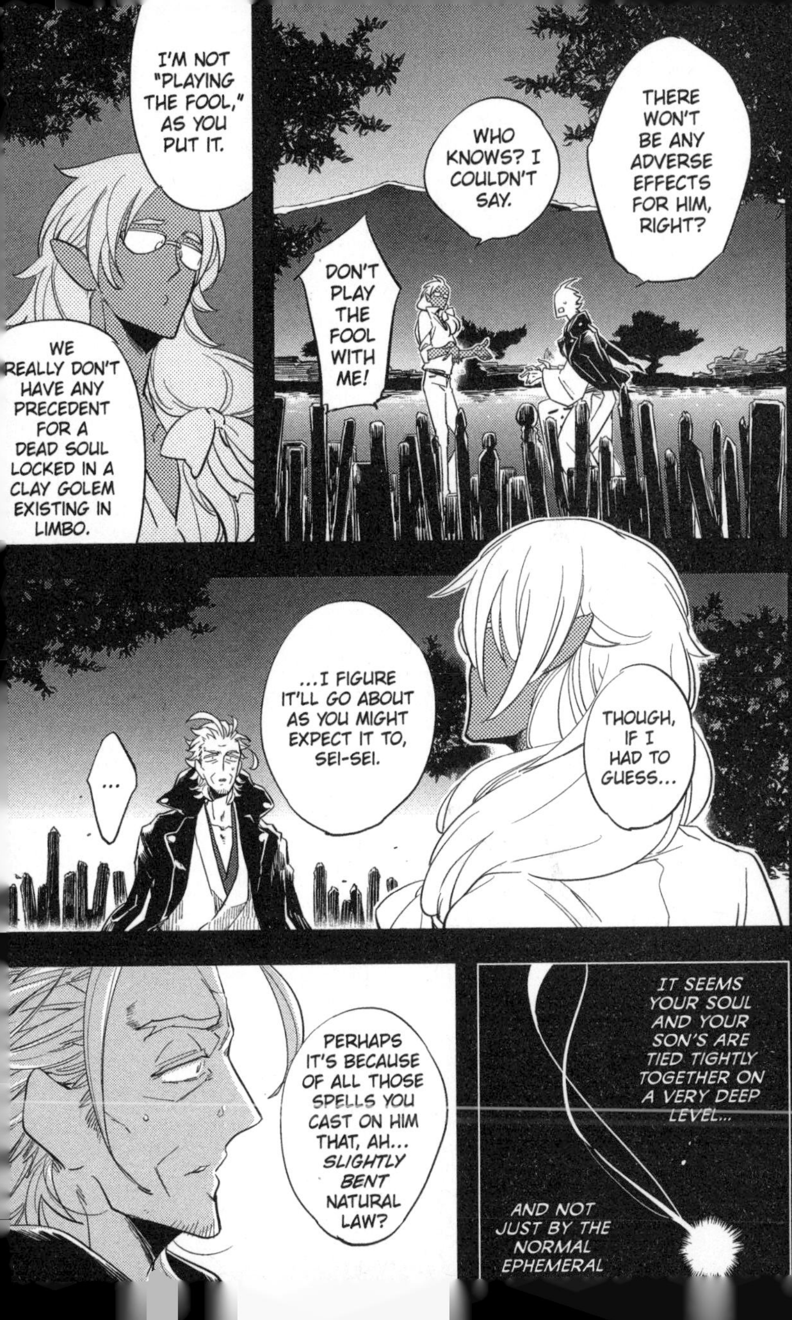
THERE WON'T BE ANY ADVERSE EFFECTS FOR HIM, RIGHT?
WHO KNOWS? I COULDN'T SAY.
DON'T PLAY THE FOOL WITH ME!
I'M NOT "PLAYING THE FOOL," AS YOU PUT IT.
WE REALLY DON'T HAVE ANY PRECEDENT FOR A DEAD SOUL LOCKED IN A CLAY GOLEM EXISTING IN LIMBO.
THOUGH, IF I HAD TO GUESS...
...I FIGURE IT'LL GO ABOUT AS YOU MIGHT EXPECT IT TO, SEI-SEI.
...
IT SEEMS YOUR SOUL AND YOUR SON'S ARE TIED TIGHTLY TOGETHER ON A VERY DEEP LEVEL...
AND NOT JUST BY THE NORMAL EPHEMERAL
PERHAPS IT'S BECAUSE OF ALL THOSE SPELLS YOU CAST ON HIM THAT, AH... *SLIGHTLY BENT* NATURAL LAW?

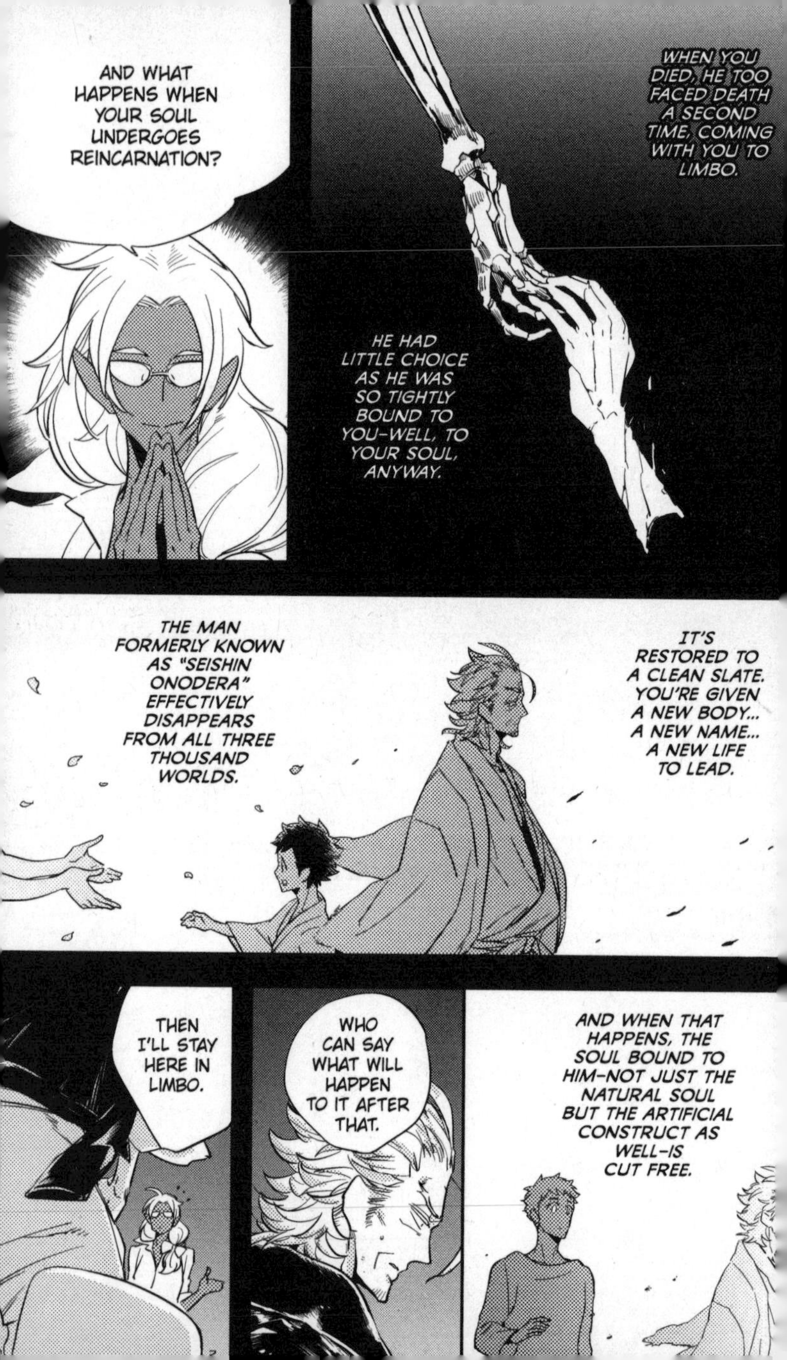
WHEN YOU DIED, HE TOO FACED DEATH A SECOND TIME, COMING WITH YOU TO LIMBO.
HE HAD LITTLE CHOICE AS HE WAS SO TIGHTLY BOUND TO YOU—WELL, TO YOUR SOUL, ANYWAY.
AND WHAT HAPPENS WHEN YOUR SOUL UNDERGOES REINCARNATION?
IT'S RESTORED TO A CLEAN SLATE. YOU'RE GIVEN A NEW BODY... A NEW NAME... A NEW LIFE TO LEAD.
THE MAN FORMERLY KNOWN AS "SEISHIN ONODERA" EFFECTIVELY DISAPPEARS FROM ALL THREE THOUSAND WORLDS.
AND WHEN THAT HAPPENS, THE SOUL BOUND TO HIM—NOT JUST THE NATURAL SOUL BUT THE ARTIFICIAL CONSTRUCT AS WELL—IS CUT FREE.
WHO CAN SAY WHAT WILL HAPPEN TO IT AFTER THAT.
THEN I'LL STAY HERE IN LIMBO.

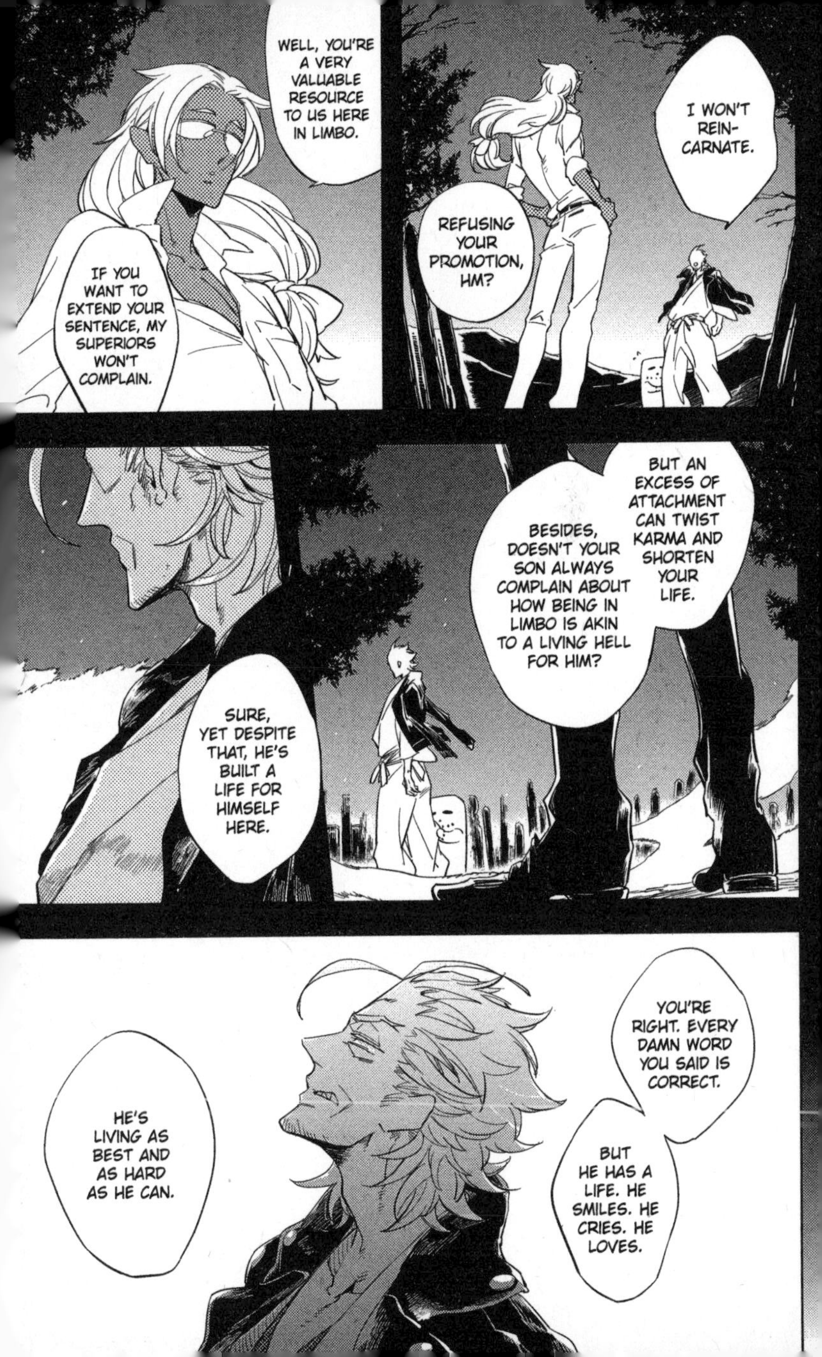
I WON'T REIN-CARNATE.
REFUSING YOUR PROMOTION, HM?
WELL, YOU'RE A VERY VALUABLE RESOURCE TO US HERE IN LIMBO.
IF YOU WANT TO EXTEND YOUR SENTENCE, MY SUPERIORS WON'T COMPLAIN.
BUT AN EXCESS OF ATTACHMENT CAN TWIST KARMA AND SHORTEN YOUR LIFE.
BESIDES, DOESN'T YOUR SON ALWAYS COMPLAIN ABOUT HOW BEING IN LIMBO IS AKIN TO A LIVING HELL FOR HIM?
SURE, YET DESPITE THAT, HE'S BUILT A LIFE FOR HIMSELF HERE.
YOU'RE RIGHT. EVERY DAMN WORD YOU SAID IS CORRECT.
BUT HE HAS A LIFE. HE SMILES. HE CRIES. HE LOVES.
HE'S LIVING AS BEST AND AS HARD AS HE CAN.

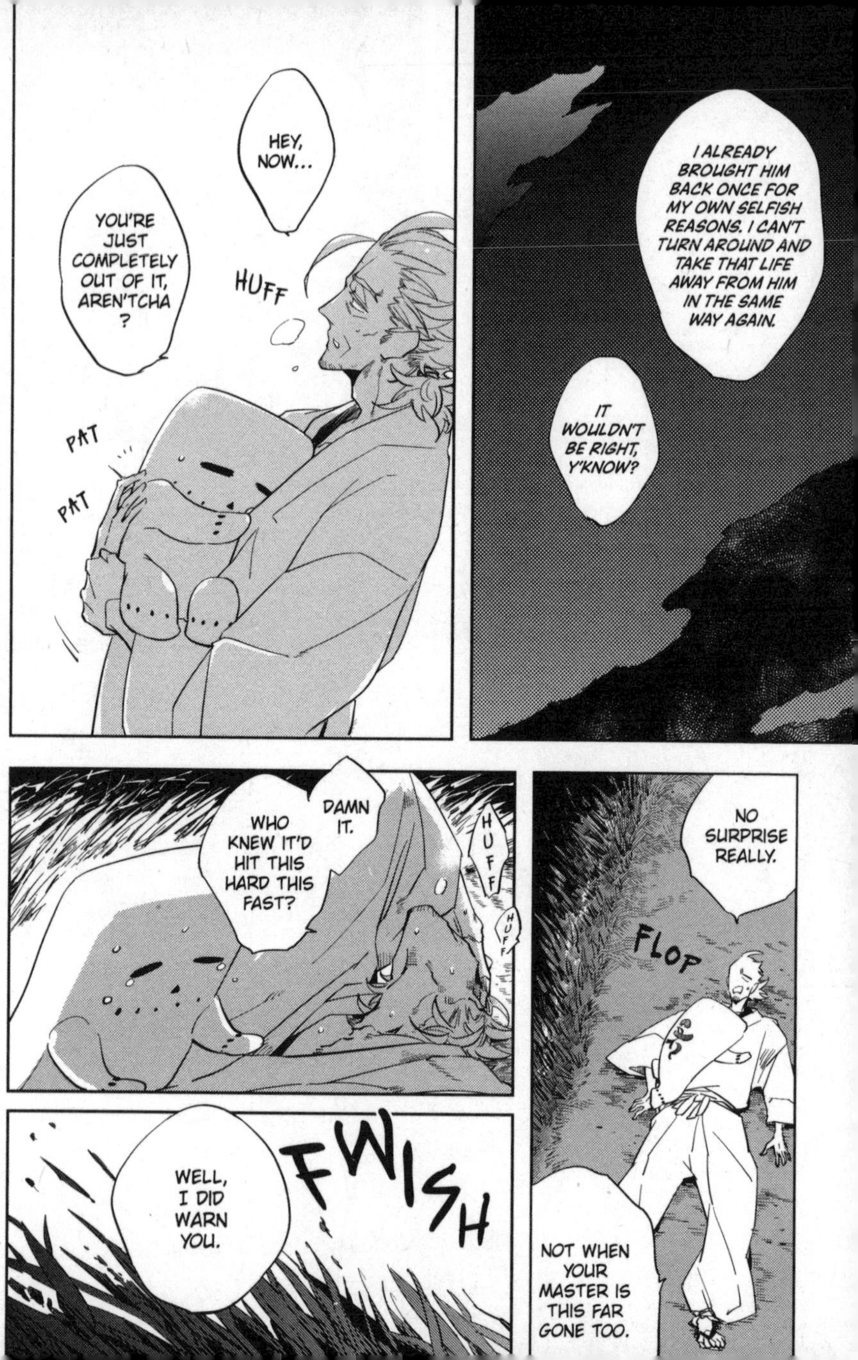
I ALREADY BROUGHT HIM BACK ONCE FOR MY OWN SELFISH REASONS. I CAN'T TURN AROUND AND TAKE THAT LIFE AWAY FROM HIM IN THE SAME WAY AGAIN.
IT WOULDN'T BE RIGHT, Y'KNOW?
HEY, NOW...
YOU'RE JUST COMPLETELY OUT OF IT, AREN'TCHA?
HUFF
PAT
PAT
NO SURPRISE REALLY.
FLOP
NOT WHEN YOUR MASTER IS THIS FAR GONE TOO.
DAMN IT.
WHO KNEW IT'D HIT THIS HARD THIS FAST?
HUFF
HUFF
FWISH
WELL, I DID WARN YOU.

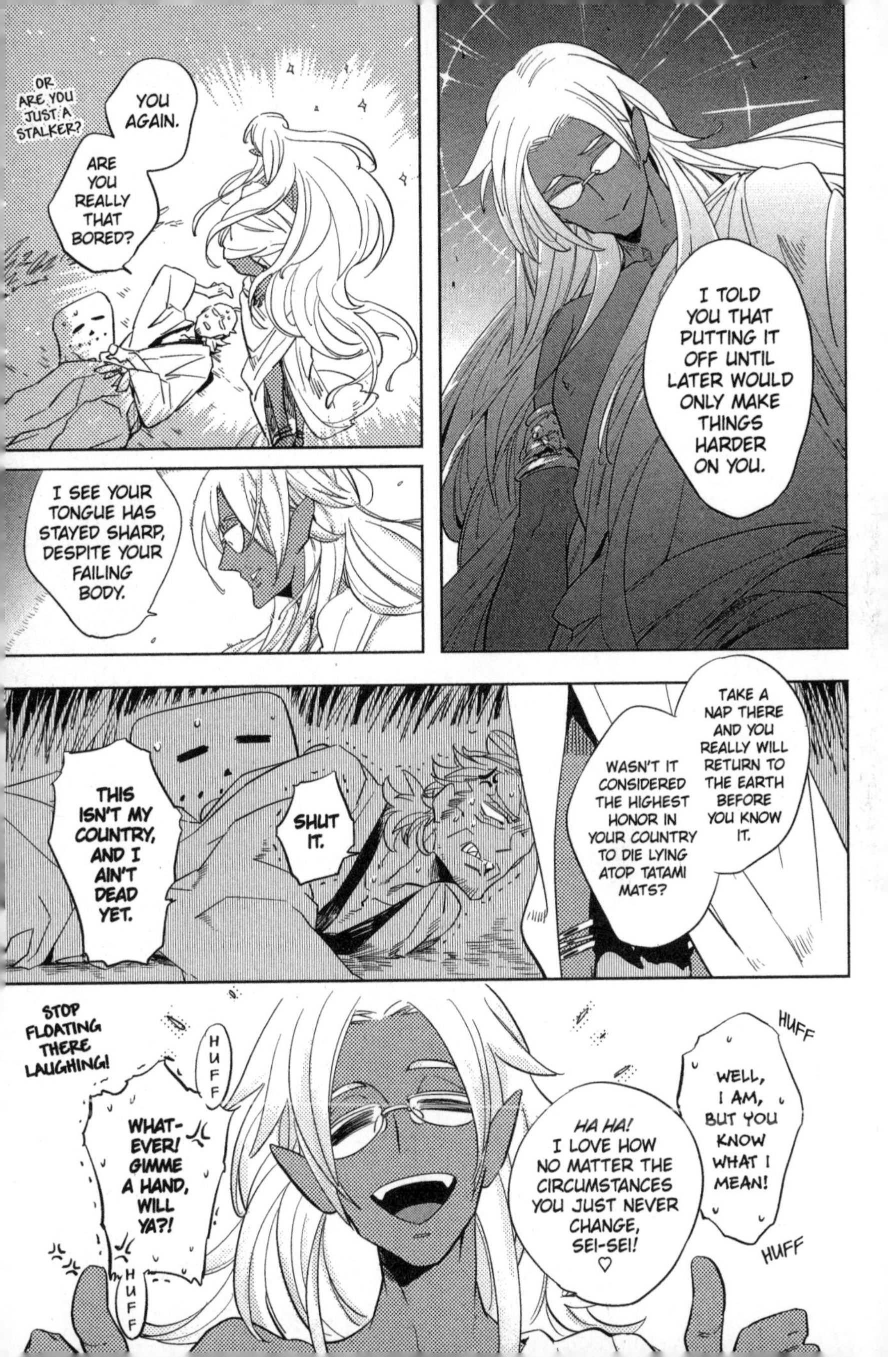
I TOLD YOU THAT PUTTING IT OFF UNTIL LATER WOULD ONLY MAKE THINGS HARDER ON YOU.
YOU AGAIN.
ARE YOU REALLY THAT BORED?
OR ARE YOU JUST A STALKER?
I SEE YOUR TONGUE HAS STAYED SHARP, DESPITE YOUR FAILING BODY.
TAKE A NAP THERE AND YOU REALLY WILL RETURN TO THE EARTH BEFORE YOU KNOW IT.
WASN'T IT CONSIDERED THE HIGHEST HONOR IN YOUR COUNTRY TO DIE LYING ATOP TATAMI MATS?
SHUT IT.
THIS ISN'T MY COUNTRY, AND I AIN'T DEAD YET.
HUFF
WELL, I AM, BUT YOU KNOW WHAT I MEAN!
HUFF
HA HA! I LOVE HOW NO MATTER THE CIRCUMSTANCES YOU JUST NEVER CHANGE, SEI-SEI! ♡
HUFF
WHAT-EVER! GIMME A HAND, WILL YA?!
HUFF
STOP FLOATING THERE LAUGHING!

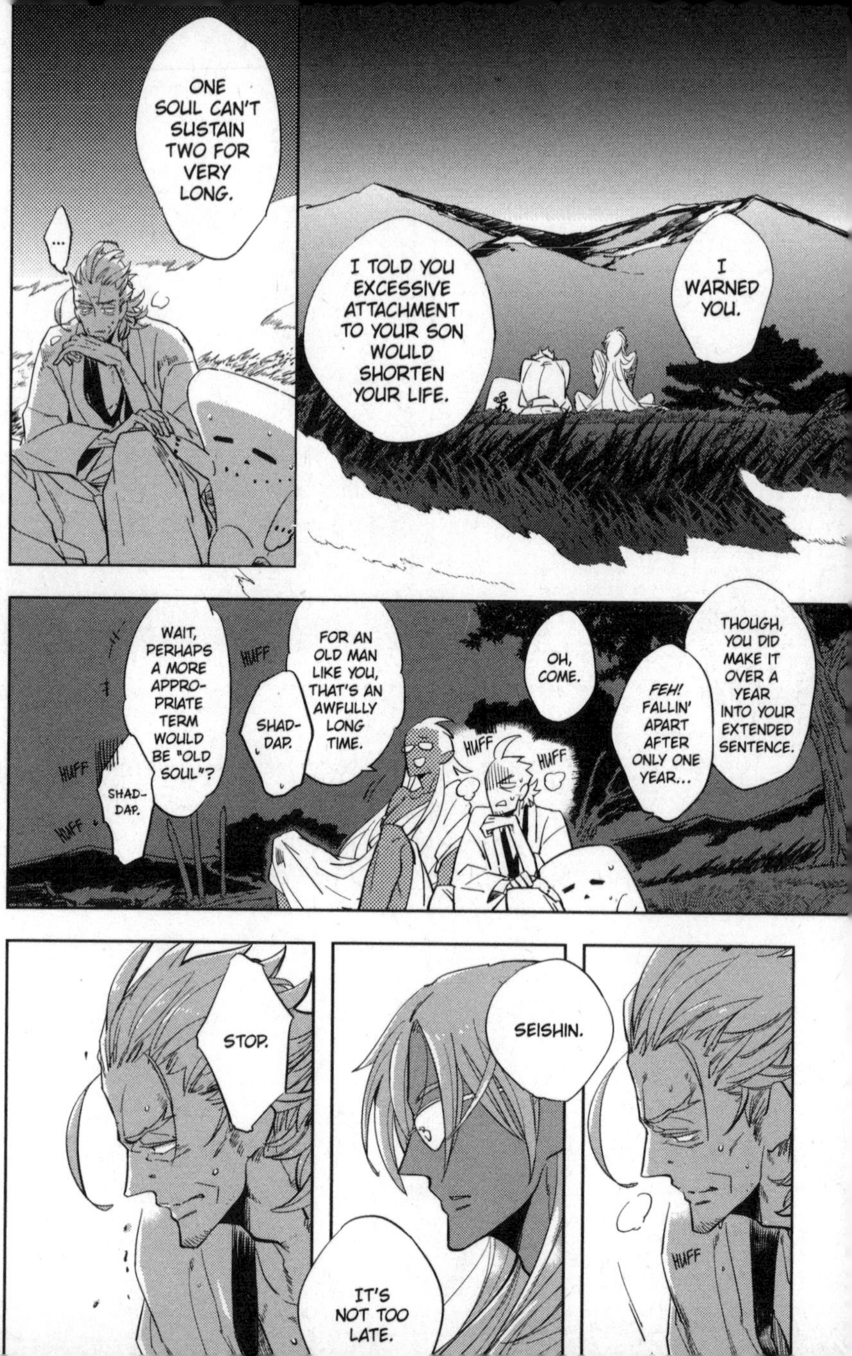
I WARNED YOU.
I TOLD YOU EXCESSIVE ATTACHMENT TO YOUR SON WOULD SHORTEN YOUR LIFE.
ONE SOUL CAN'T SUSTAIN TWO FOR VERY LONG.
...
THOUGH, YOU DID MAKE IT OVER A YEAR INTO YOUR EXTENDED SENTENCE.
FEH! FALLIN' APART AFTER ONLY ONE YEAR...
OH, COME.
HUFF
HUFF
FOR AN OLD MAN LIKE YOU, THAT'S AN AWFULLY LONG TIME.
SHAD-DAP.
HUFF
WAIT, PERHAPS A MORE APPROPRIATE TERM WOULD BE "OLD SOUL"?
HUFF
SHAD-DAP.
HUFF
HUFF
SEISHIN.
IT'S NOT TOO LATE.
STOP.

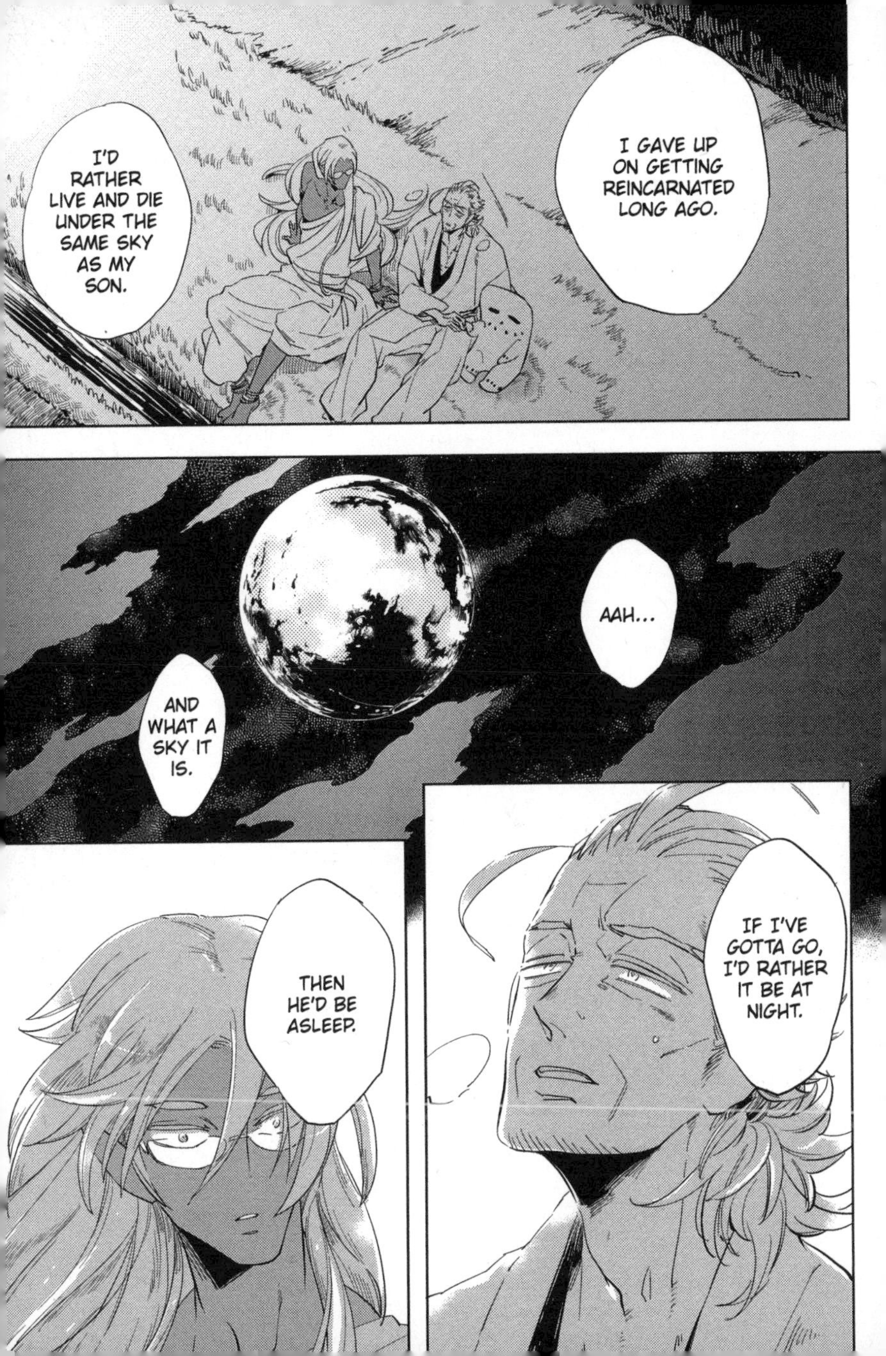
I GAVE UP ON GETTING REINCARNATED LONG AGO.
I'D RATHER LIVE AND DIE UNDER THE SAME SKY AS MY SON.
AAH...
AND WHAT A SKY IT IS.
IF I'VE GOTTA GO, I'D RATHER IT BE AT NIGHT.
THEN HE'D BE ASLEEP.

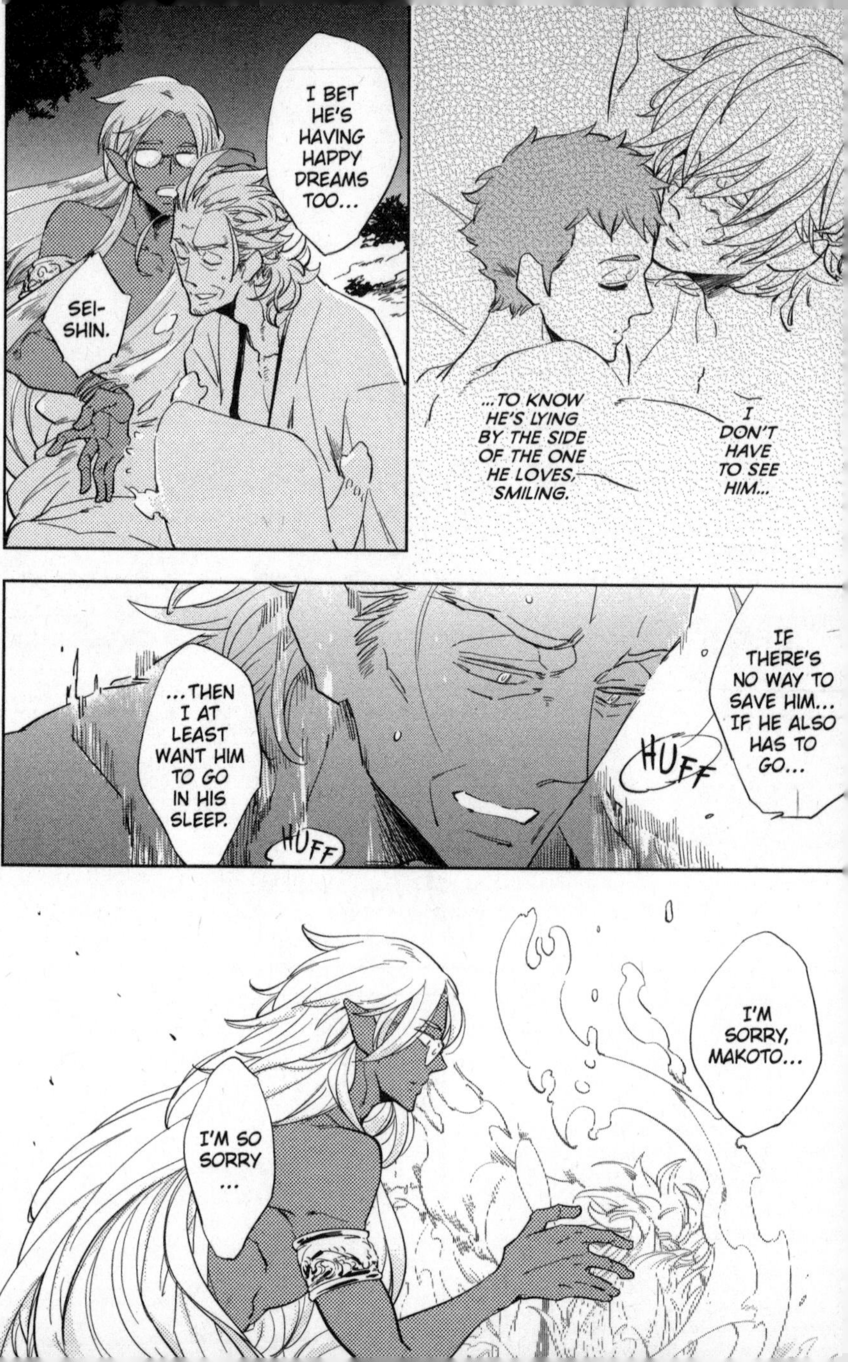
I DON'T HAVE TO SEE HIM...
...TO KNOW HE'S LYING BY THE SIDE OF THE ONE HE LOVES, SMILING.
I BET HE'S HAVING HAPPY DREAMS TOO...
SEI-SHIN.
IF THERE'S NO WAY TO SAVE HIM... IF HE ALSO HAS TO GO...
HUFF
...THEN I AT LEAST WANT HIM TO GO IN HIS SLEEP.
HUFF
I'M SORRY, MAKOTO...
I'M SO SORRY ...

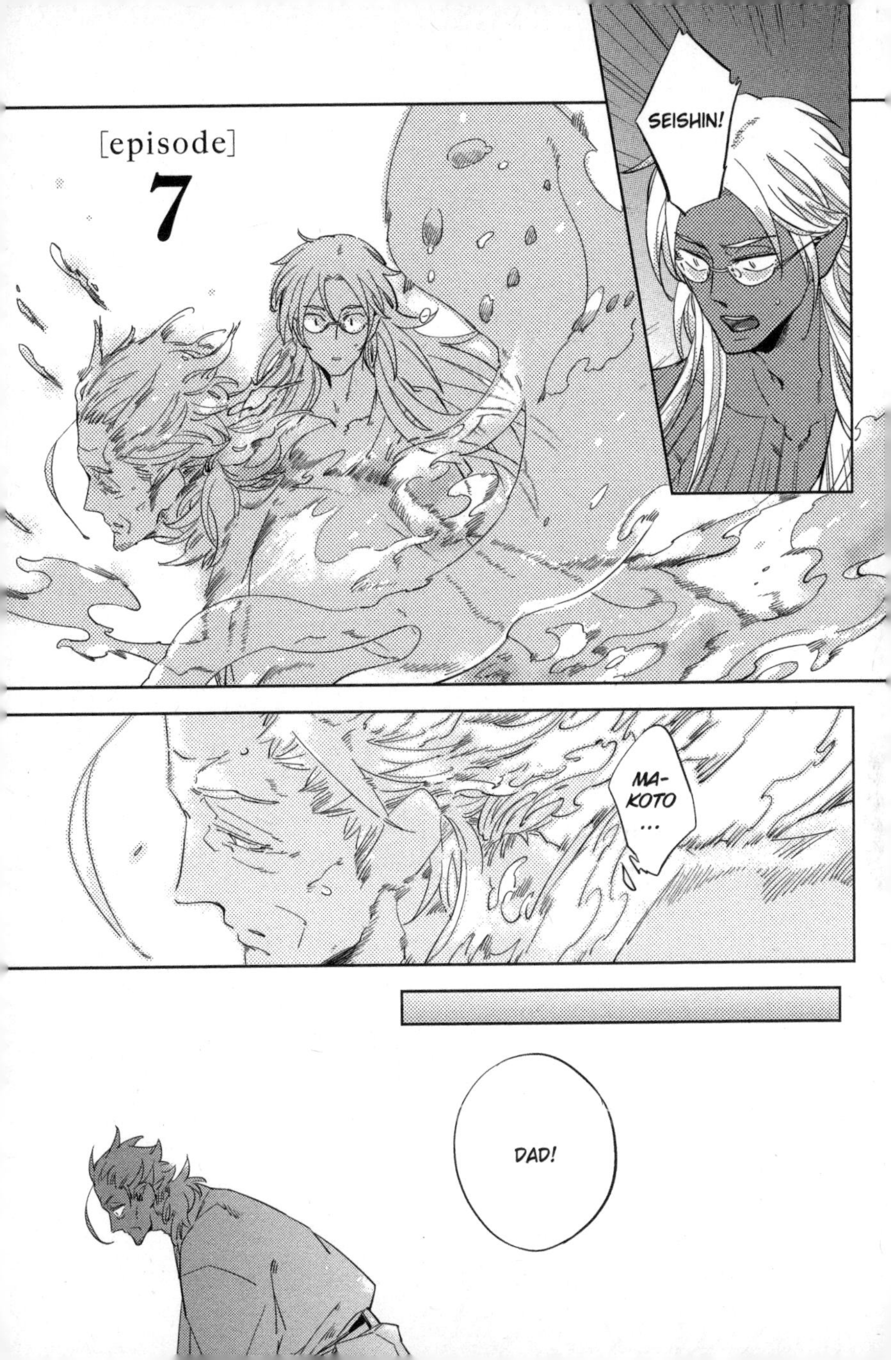
SEISHIN!
[episode] 7
MA-KOTO ...
DAD!

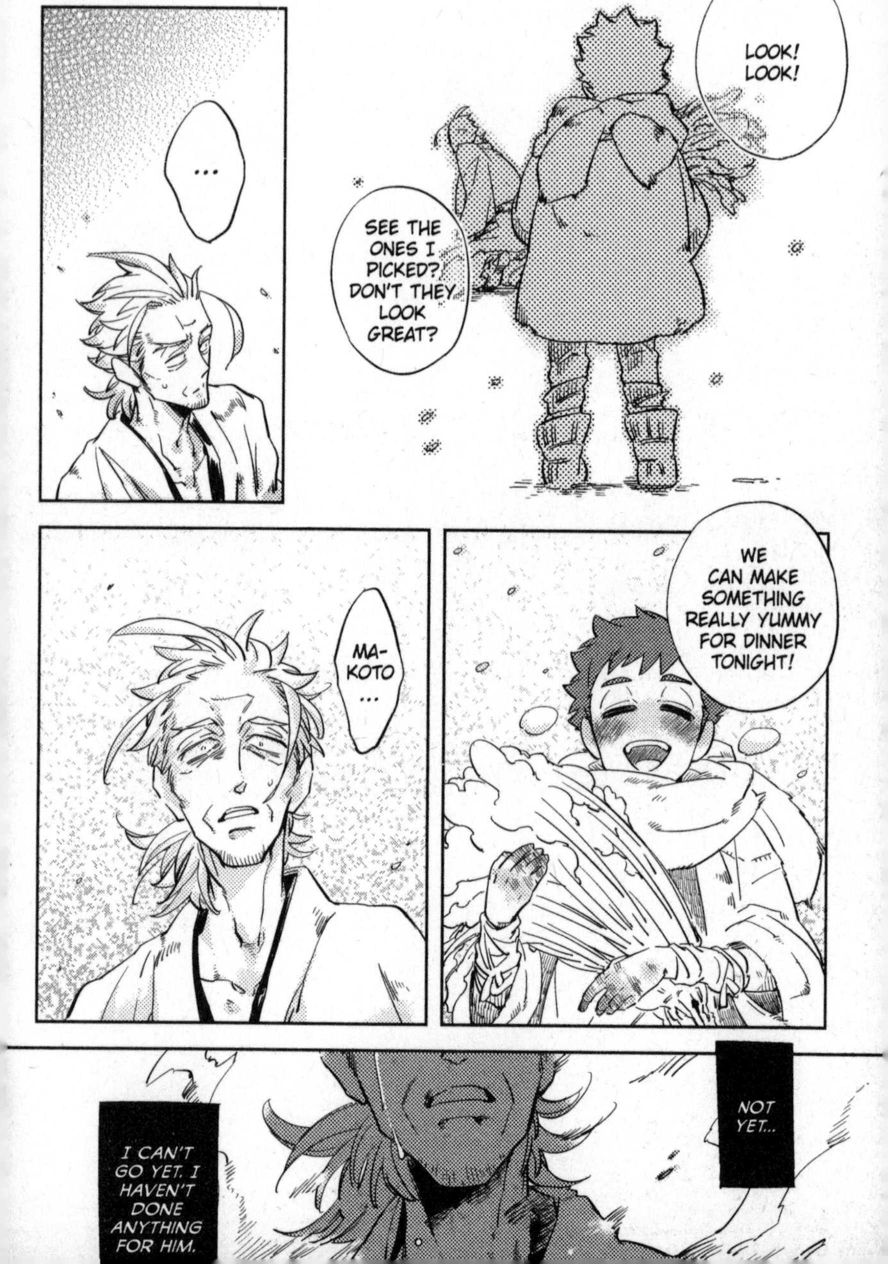
LOOK! LOOK!
SEE THE ONES I PICKED? DON'T THEY LOOK GREAT?
...
WE CAN MAKE SOMETHING REALLY YUMMY FOR DINNER TONIGHT!
MA-KOTO ...
NOT YET...
I CAN'T GO YET. I HAVEN'T DONE ANYTHING FOR HIM.

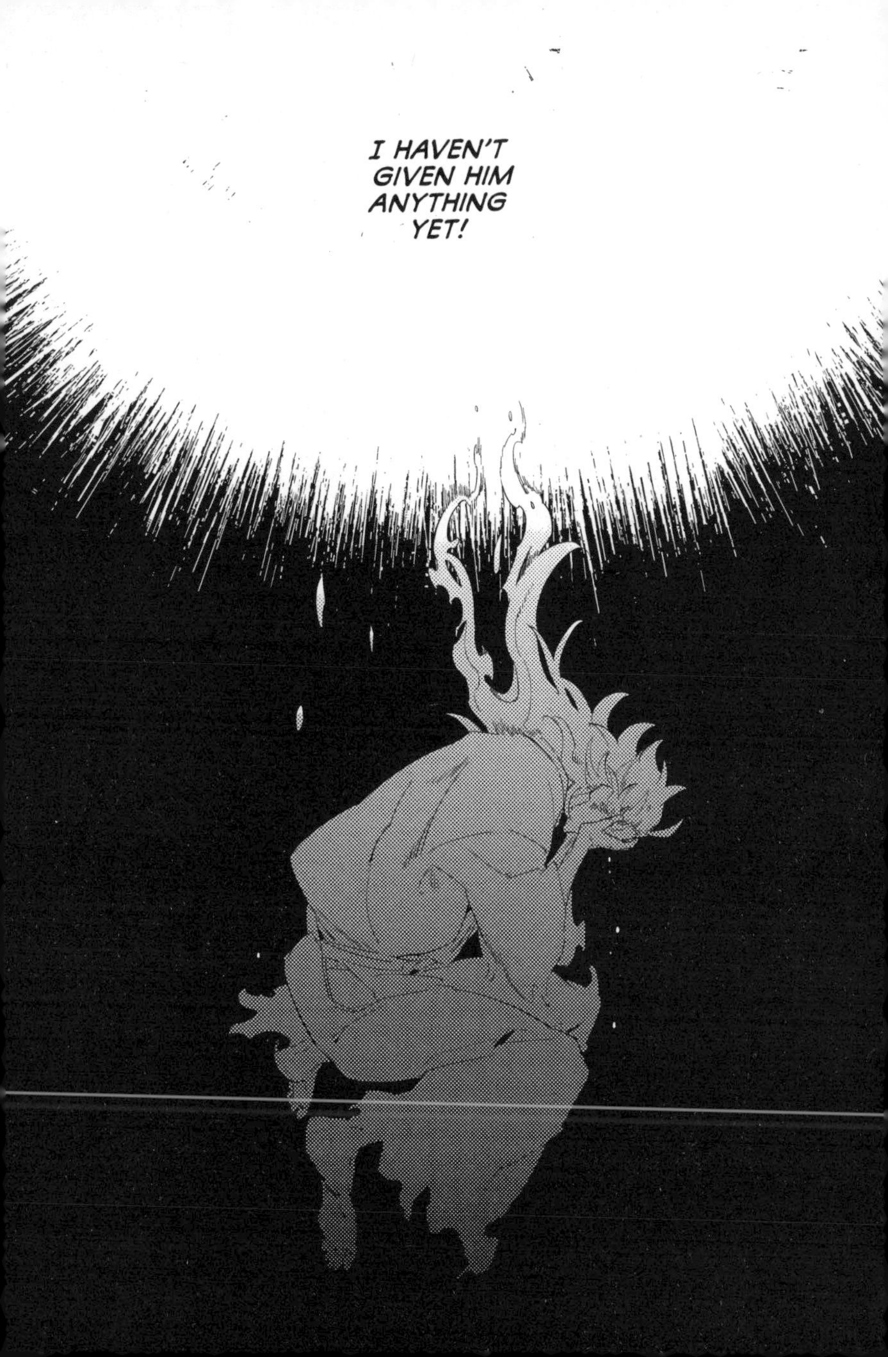
I HAVEN'T GIVEN HIM ANYTHING YET!

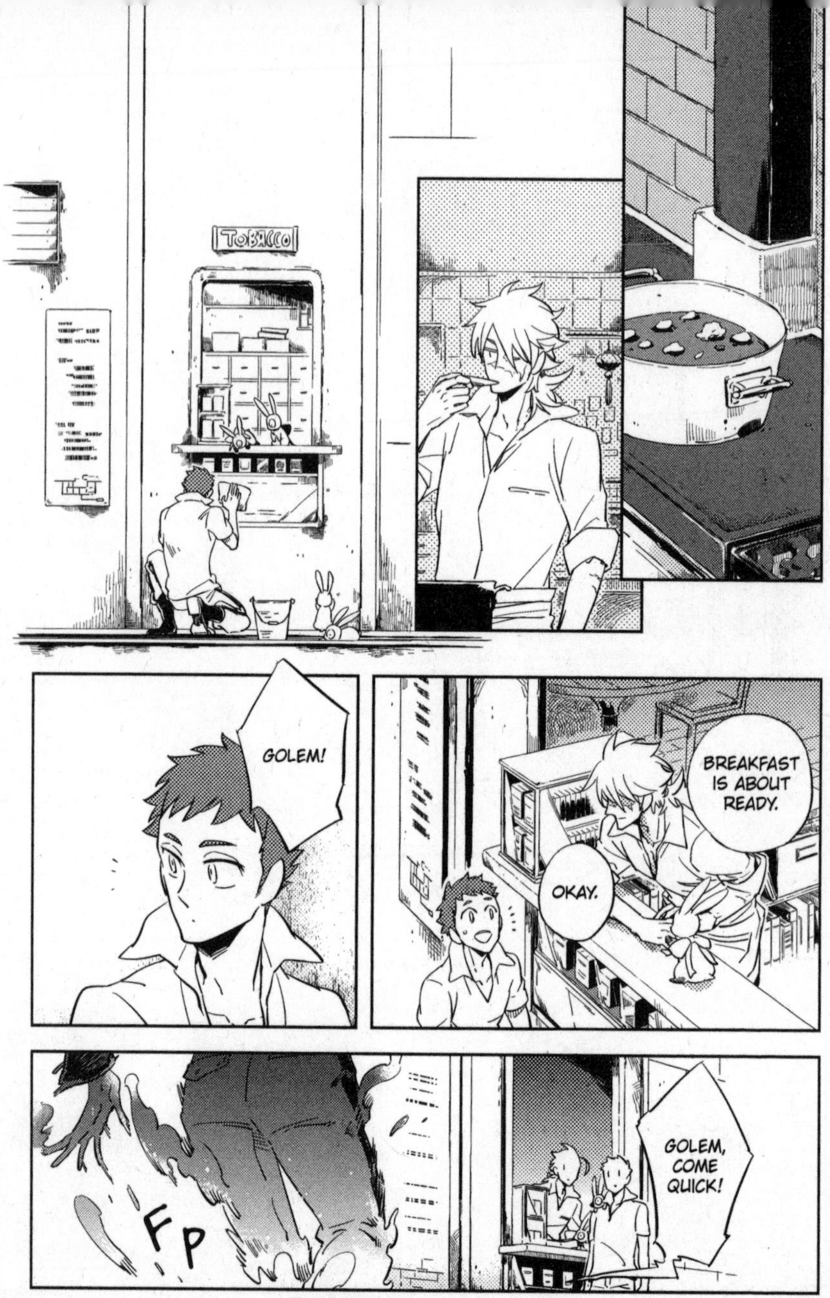
TOBACCO
BREAKFAST IS ABOUT READY.
OKAY.
GOLEM!
GOLEM, COME QUICK!
FP

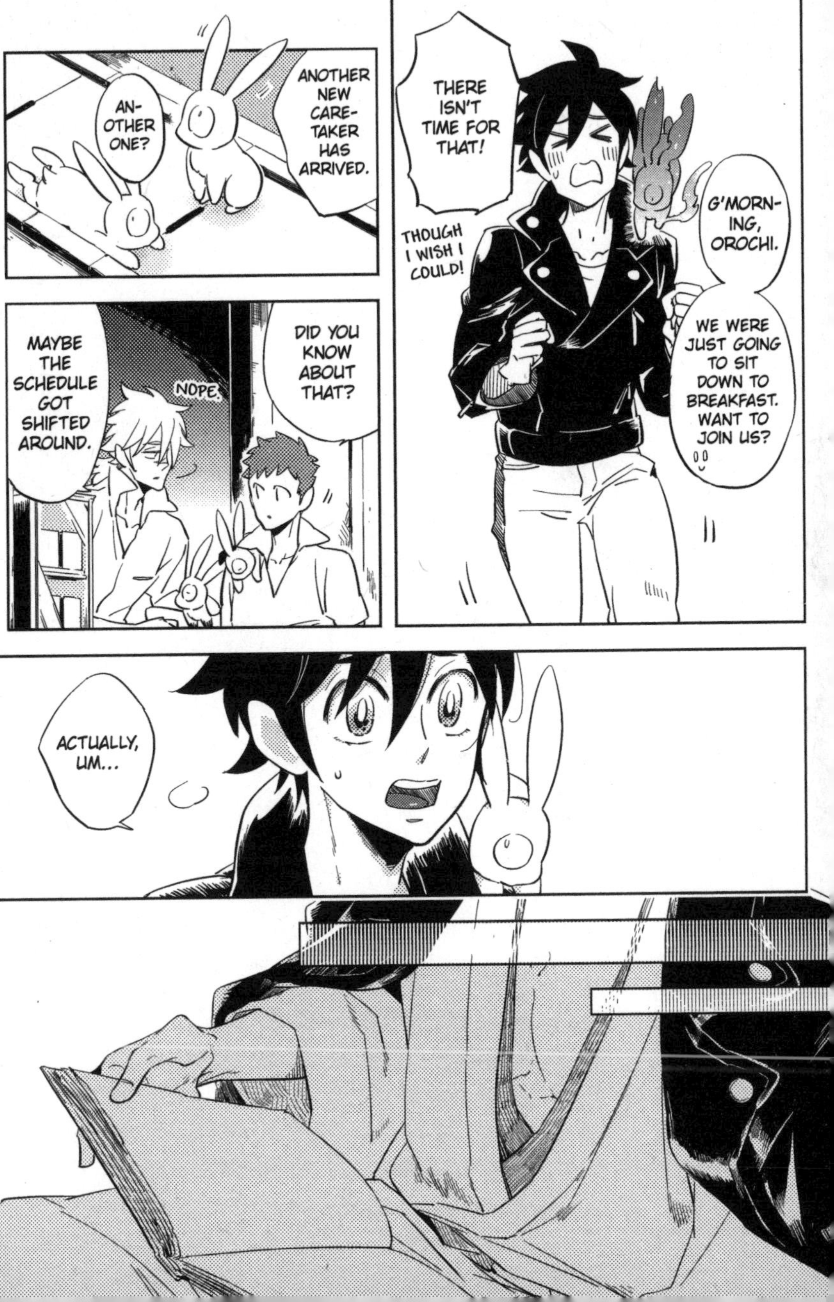
G'MORN-ING, OROCHI.
WE WERE JUST GOING TO SIT DOWN TO BREAKFAST. WANT TO JOIN US?
THERE ISN'T TIME FOR THAT!
THOUGH I WISH I COULD!
ANOTHER NEW CARE-TAKER HAS ARRIVED.
AN-OTHER ONE?
DID YOU KNOW ABOUT THAT?
NOPE.
MAYBE THE SCHEDULE GOT SHIFTED AROUND.
ACTUALLY, UM...

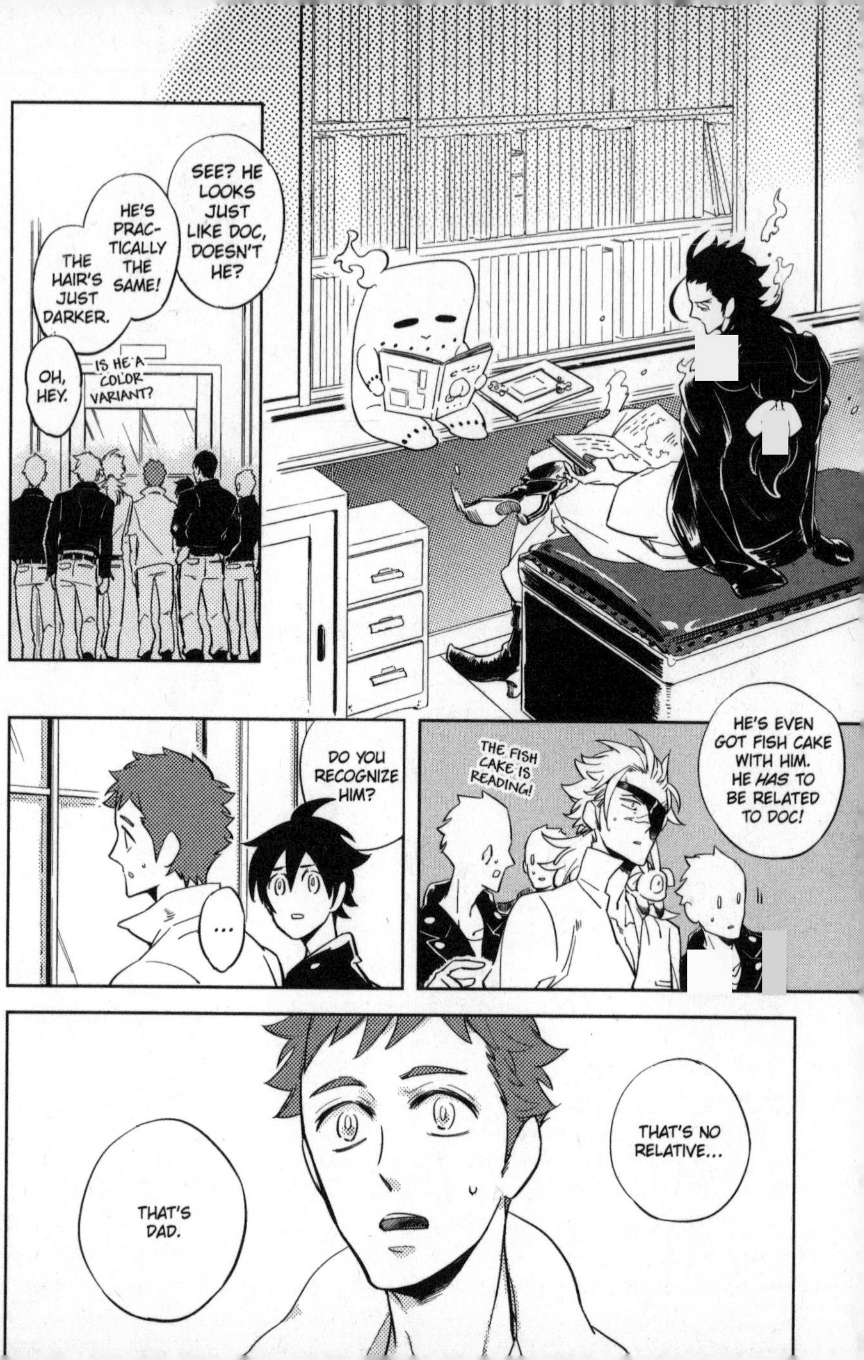
SEE? HE LOOKS JUST LIKE DOC, DOESN'T HE?
HE'S PRAC-TICALLY THE SAME!
THE HAIR'S JUST DARKER.
IS HE A COLOR VARIANT?
OH, HEY.
HE'S EVEN GOT FISH CAKE WITH HIM. HE *HAS* TO BE RELATED TO DOC!
THE FISH CAKE IS READING!
DO YOU RECOGNIZE HIM?
...
THAT'S NO RELATIVE...
THAT'S DAD.

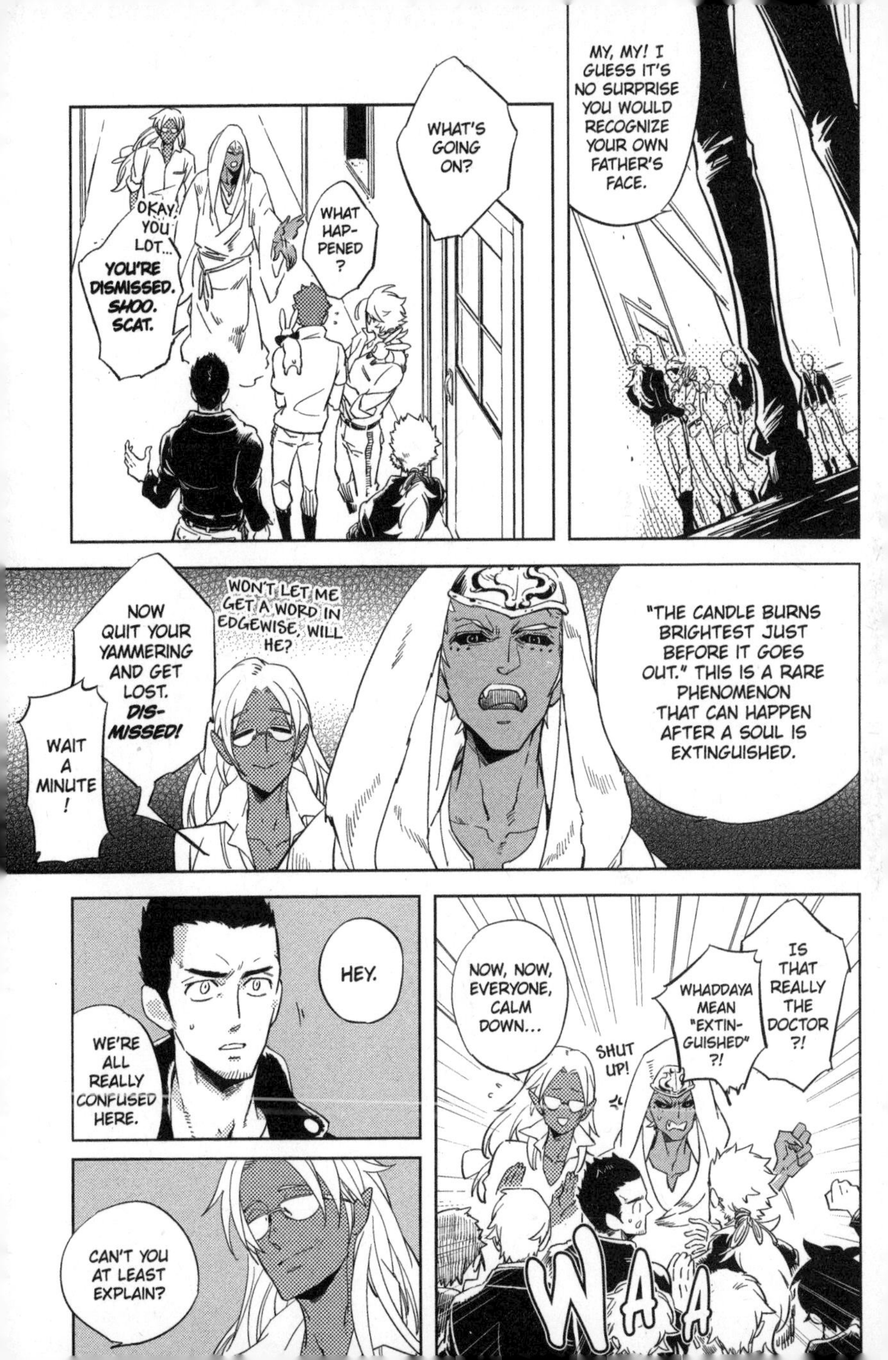
MY, MY! I GUESS IT'S NO SURPRISE YOU WOULD RECOGNIZE YOUR OWN FATHER'S FACE.
WHAT'S GOING ON?
WHAT HAPPENED?
OKAY, YOU LOT... YOU'RE DISMISSED. SHOO. SCAT.
"THE CANDLE BURNS BRIGHTEST JUST BEFORE IT GOES OUT." THIS IS A RARE PHENOMENON THAT CAN HAPPEN AFTER A SOUL IS EXTINGUISHED.
WON'T LET ME GET A WORD IN EDGEWISE, WILL HE?
NOW QUIT YOUR YAMMERING AND GET LOST. DISMISSED!
WAIT A MINUTE!
IS THAT REALLY THE DOCTOR?!
WHADDAYA MEAN "EXTINGUISHED"?!
SHUT UP!
NOW, NOW, EVERYONE, CALM DOWN...
WAAA
HEY.
WE'RE ALL REALLY CONFUSED HERE.
CAN'T YOU AT LEAST EXPLAIN?

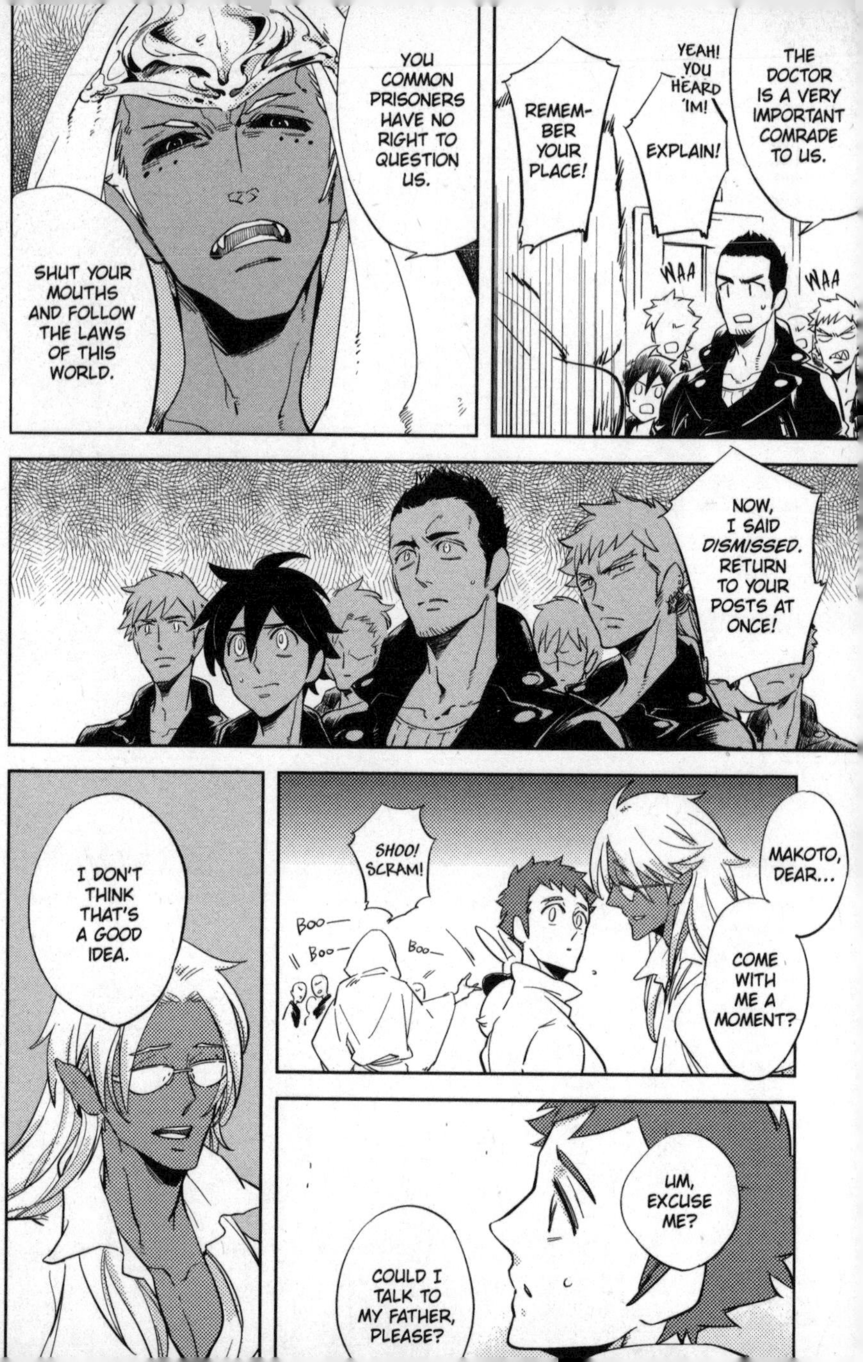
THE DOCTOR IS A VERY IMPORTANT COMRADE TO US.
YEAH! YOU HEARD 'IM!
EXPLAIN!
REMEMBER YOUR PLACE!
WAA
WAA
YOU COMMON PRISONERS HAVE NO RIGHT TO QUESTION US.
SHUT YOUR MOUTHS AND FOLLOW THE LAWS OF THIS WORLD.
NOW, I SAID *DISMISSED.* RETURN TO YOUR POSTS AT ONCE!
MAKOTO, DEAR...
COME WITH ME A MOMENT?
SHOO! SCRAM!
BOO—
BOO—
BOO—
UM, EXCUSE ME?
COULD I TALK TO MY FATHER, PLEASE?
I DON'T THINK THAT'S A GOOD IDEA.

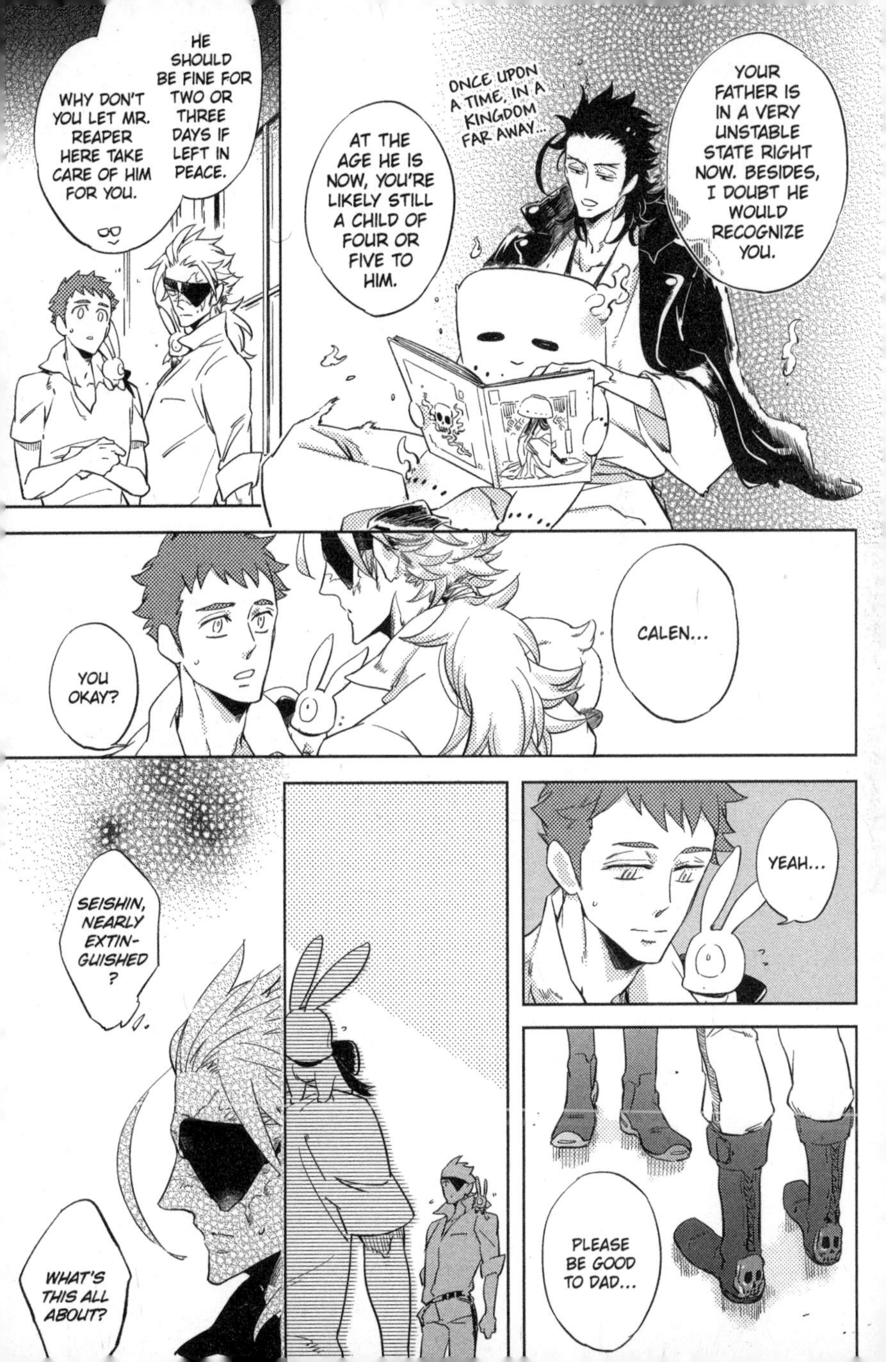
YOUR FATHER IS IN A VERY UNSTABLE STATE RIGHT NOW. BESIDES, I DOUBT HE WOULD RECOGNIZE YOU.
ONCE UPON A TIME, IN A KINGDOM FAR AWAY...
AT THE AGE HE IS NOW, YOU'RE LIKELY STILL A CHILD OF FOUR OR FIVE TO HIM.
HE SHOULD BE FINE FOR TWO OR THREE DAYS IF LEFT IN PEACE.
WHY DON'T YOU LET MR. REAPER HERE TAKE CARE OF HIM FOR YOU.
CALEN...
YOU OKAY?
YEAH...
PLEASE BE GOOD TO DAD...
SEISHIN, NEARLY EXTIN-GUISHED?
WHAT'S THIS ALL ABOUT?

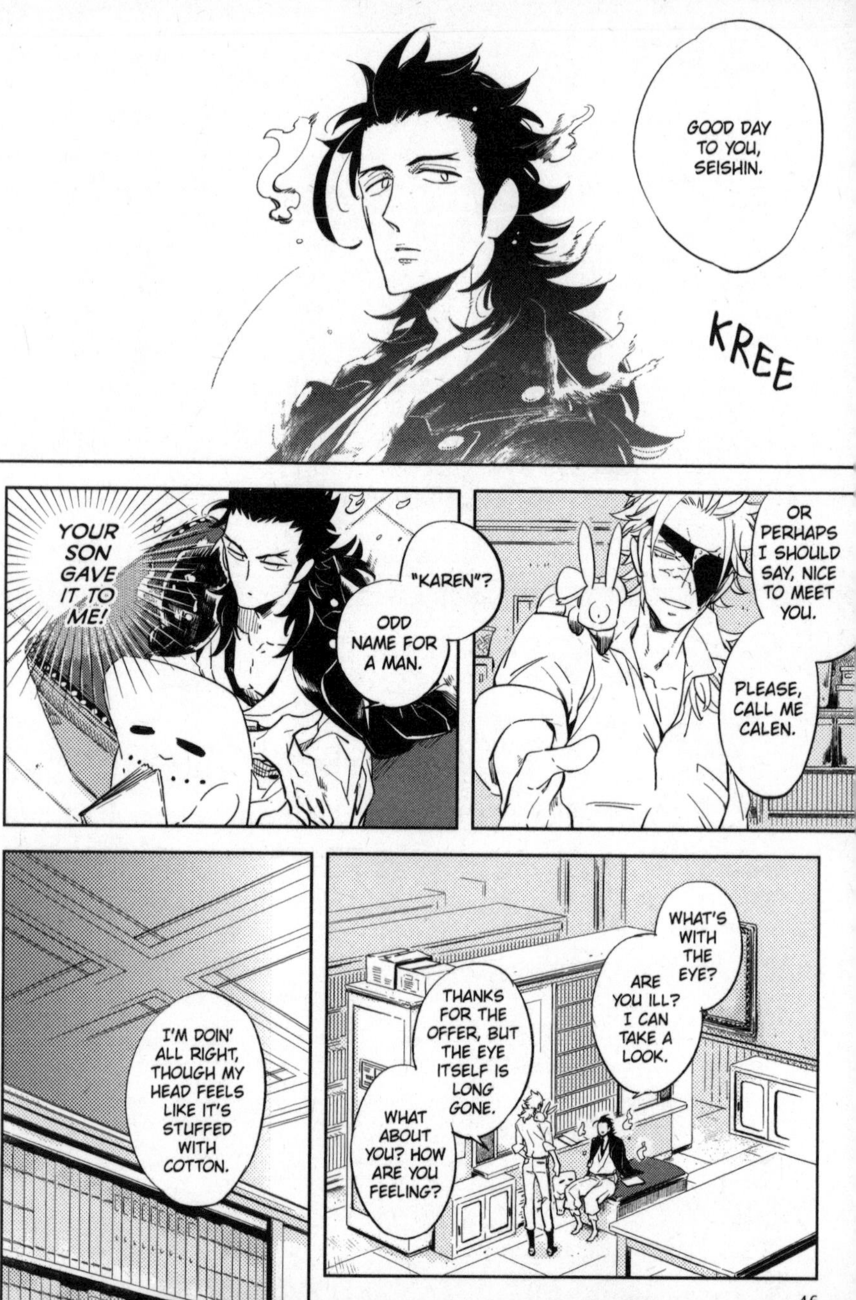
GOOD DAY TO YOU, SEISHIN.
KREE
OR PERHAPS I SHOULD SAY, NICE TO MEET YOU.
PLEASE, CALL ME CALEN.
"KAREN"?
ODD NAME FOR A MAN.
YOUR SON GAVE IT TO ME!
WHAT'S WITH THE EYE?
ARE YOU ILL? I CAN TAKE A LOOK.
THANKS FOR THE OFFER, BUT THE EYE ITSELF IS LONG GONE.
WHAT ABOUT YOU? HOW ARE YOU FEELING?
I'M DOIN' ALL RIGHT, THOUGH MY HEAD FEELS LIKE IT'S STUFFED WITH COTTON.

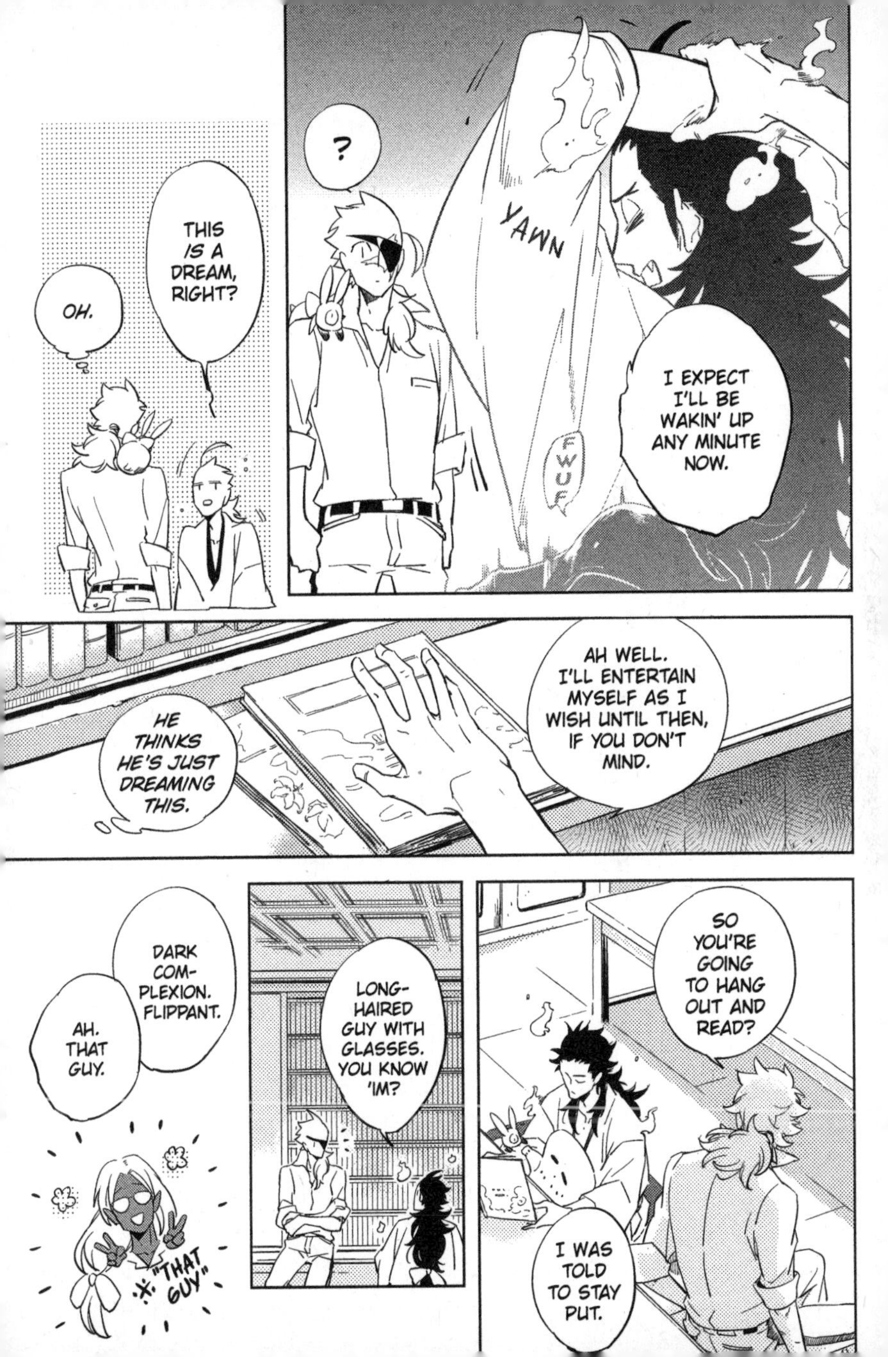
?
YAWN
FWUF
I EXPECT I'LL BE WAKIN' UP ANY MINUTE NOW.
THIS IS A DREAM, RIGHT?
OH.
AH WELL. I'LL ENTERTAIN MYSELF AS I WISH UNTIL THEN, IF YOU DON'T MIND.
HE THINKS HE'S JUST DREAMING THIS.
SO YOU'RE GOING TO HANG OUT AND READ?
I WAS TOLD TO STAY PUT.
LONG-HAIRED GUY WITH GLASSES. YOU KNOW 'IM?
DARK COMPLEXION. FLIPPANT.
AH. THAT GUY.
※"THAT GUY"

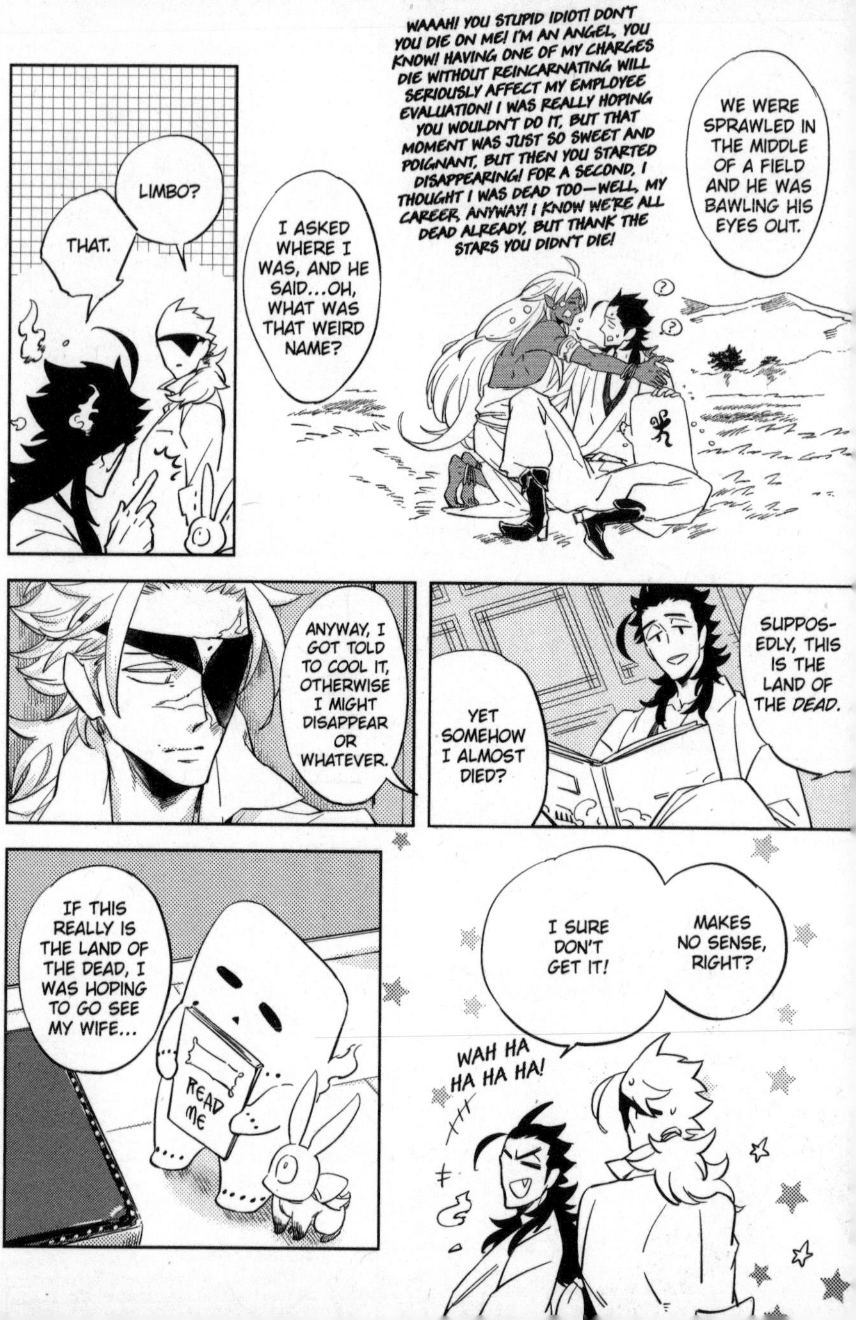
WE WERE SPRAWLED IN THE MIDDLE OF A FIELD AND HE WAS BAWLING HIS EYES OUT.
WAAAH! YOU STUPID IDIOT! DON'T YOU DIE ON ME! I'M AN ANGEL, YOU KNOW! HAVING ONE OF MY CHARGES DIE WITHOUT REINCARNATING WILL SERIOUSLY AFFECT MY EMPLOYEE EVALUATION! I WAS REALLY HOPING YOU WOULDN'T DO IT, BUT THAT MOMENT WAS JUST SO SWEET AND POIGNANT, BUT THEN YOU STARTED DISAPPEARING! FOR A SECOND, I THOUGHT I WAS DEAD TOO—WELL, MY CAREER, ANYWAY! I KNOW WE'RE ALL DEAD ALREADY, BUT THANK THE STARS YOU DIDN'T DIE!
I ASKED WHERE I WAS, AND HE SAID...OH, WHAT WAS THAT WEIRD NAME?
LIMBO?
THAT.
SUPPOS-EDLY, THIS IS THE LAND OF THE *DEAD*.
YET SOMEHOW I ALMOST DIED?
ANYWAY, I GOT TOLD TO COOL IT, OTHERWISE I MIGHT DISAPPEAR OR WHATEVER.
MAKES NO SENSE, RIGHT?
I SURE DON'T GET IT!
WAH HA HA HA HA!
IF THIS REALLY IS THE LAND OF THE DEAD, I WAS HOPING TO GO SEE MY WIFE...
READ ME

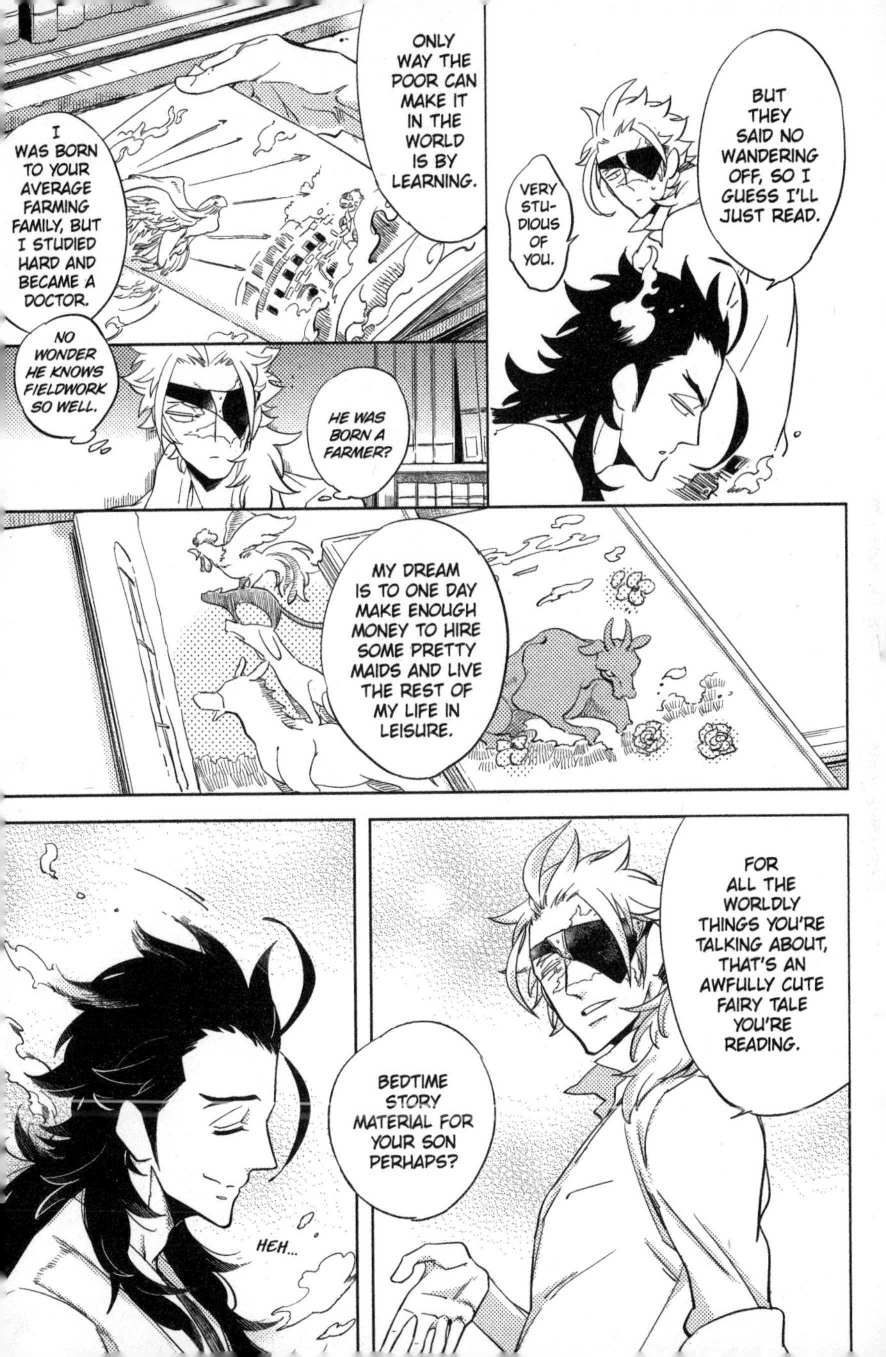

BUT THEY SAID NO WANDERING OFF, SO I GUESS I'LL JUST READ.
VERY STUDIOUS OF YOU.
ONLY WAY THE POOR CAN MAKE IT IN THE WORLD IS BY LEARNING.
I WAS BORN TO YOUR AVERAGE FARMING FAMILY, BUT I STUDIED HARD AND BECAME A DOCTOR.
HE WAS BORN A FARMER?
NO WONDER HE KNOWS FIELDWORK SO WELL.
MY DREAM IS TO ONE DAY MAKE ENOUGH MONEY TO HIRE SOME PRETTY MAIDS AND LIVE THE REST OF MY LIFE IN LEISURE.
FOR ALL THE WORLDLY THINGS YOU'RE TALKING ABOUT, THAT'S AN AWFULLY CUTE FAIRY TALE YOU'RE READING.
BEDTIME STORY MATERIAL FOR YOUR SON PERHAPS?
HEH...

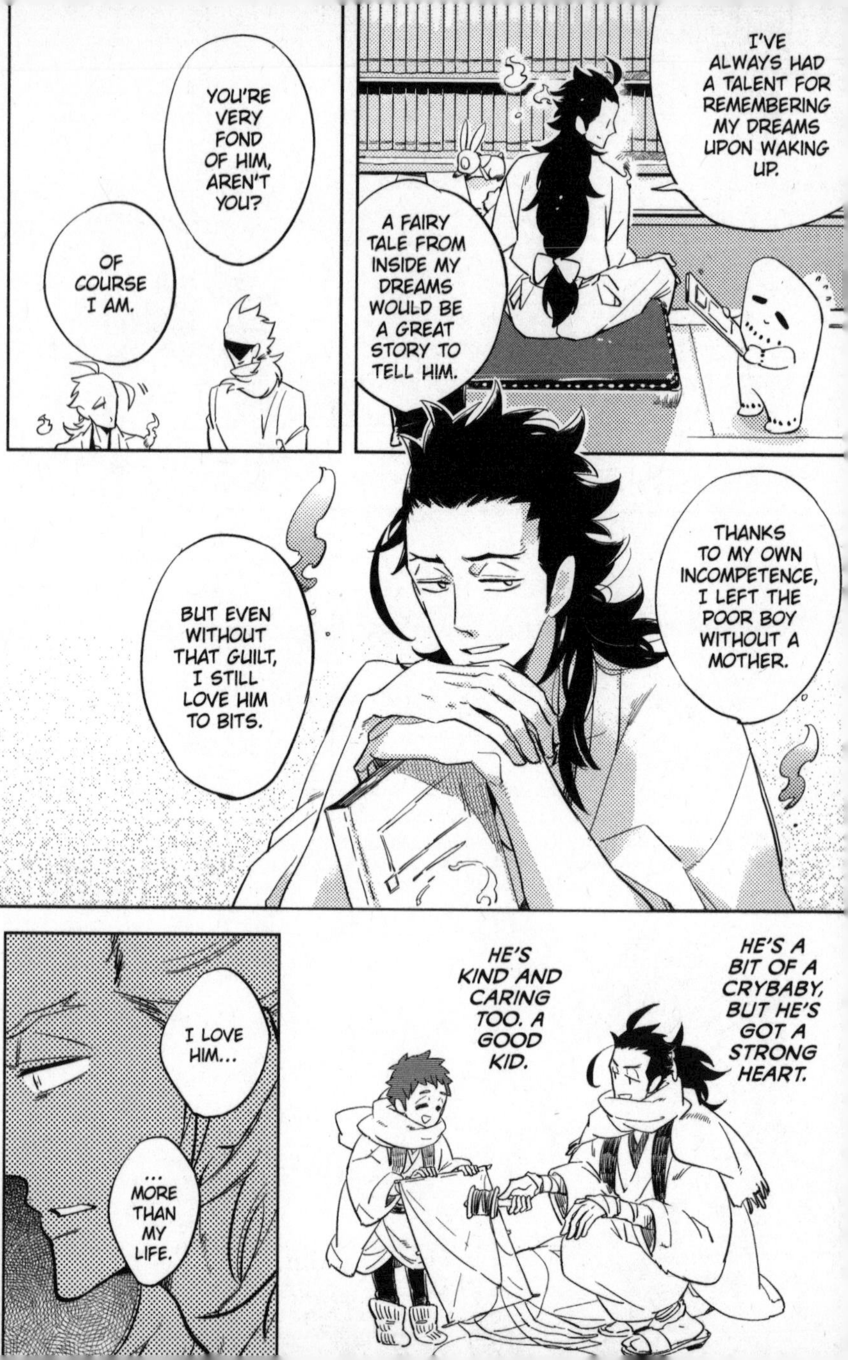
I'VE ALWAYS HAD A TALENT FOR REMEMBERING MY DREAMS UPON WAKING UP.
A FAIRY TALE FROM INSIDE MY DREAMS WOULD BE A GREAT STORY TO TELL HIM.
YOU'RE VERY FOND OF HIM, AREN'T YOU?
OF COURSE I AM.
THANKS TO MY OWN INCOMPETENCE, I LEFT THE POOR BOY WITHOUT A MOTHER.
BUT EVEN WITHOUT THAT GUILT, I STILL LOVE HIM TO BITS.
HE'S A BIT OF A CRYBABY, BUT HE'S GOT A STRONG HEART.
HE'S KIND AND CARING TOO. A GOOD KID.
I LOVE HIM...
...MORE THAN MY LIFE.

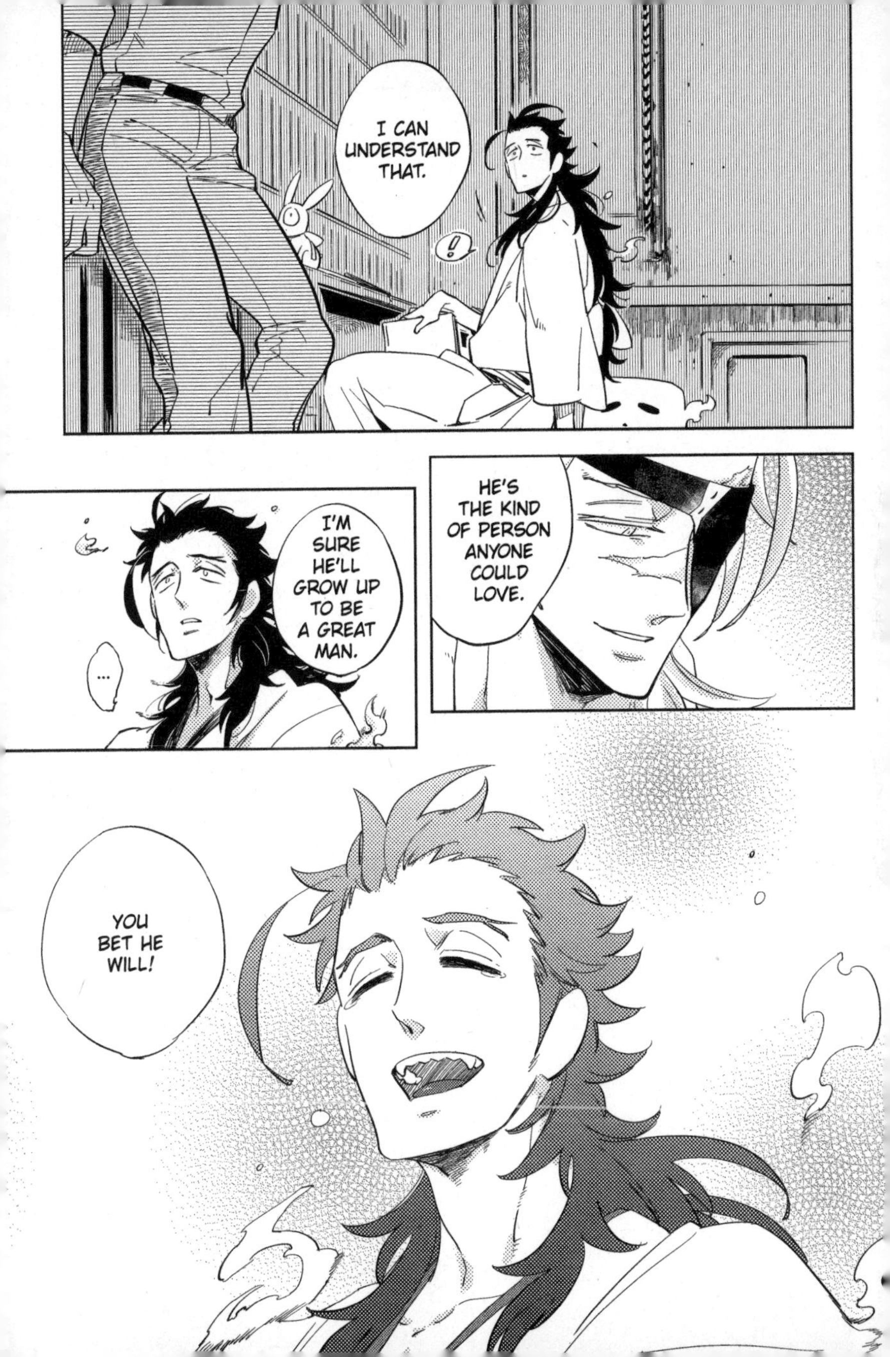
I CAN UNDERSTAND THAT.
!
HE'S THE KIND OF PERSON ANYONE COULD LOVE.
I'M SURE HE'LL GROW UP TO BE A GREAT MAN.
...
YOU BET HE WILL!

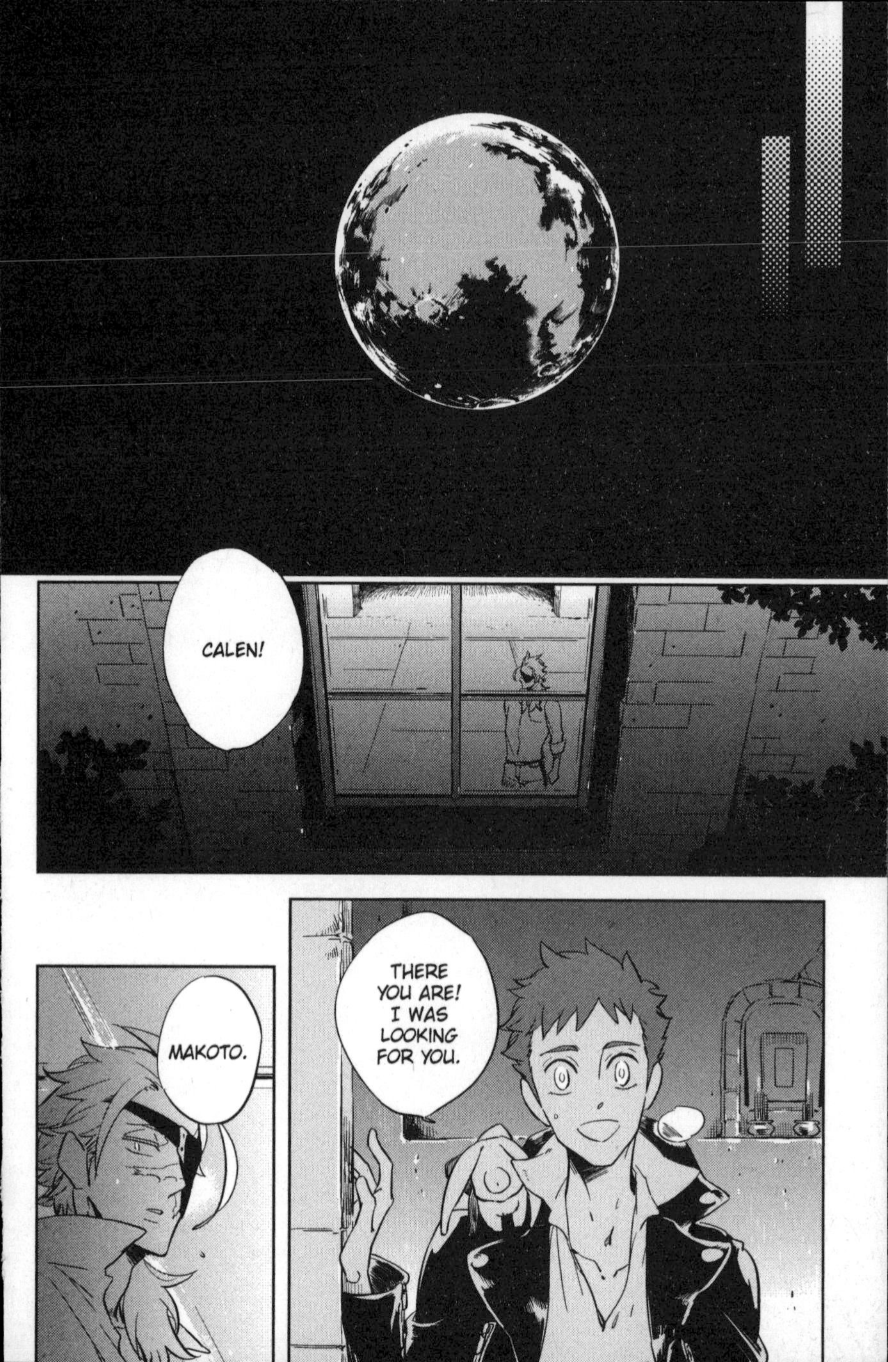
CALEN!
THERE YOU ARE! I WAS LOOKING FOR YOU.
MAKOTO.

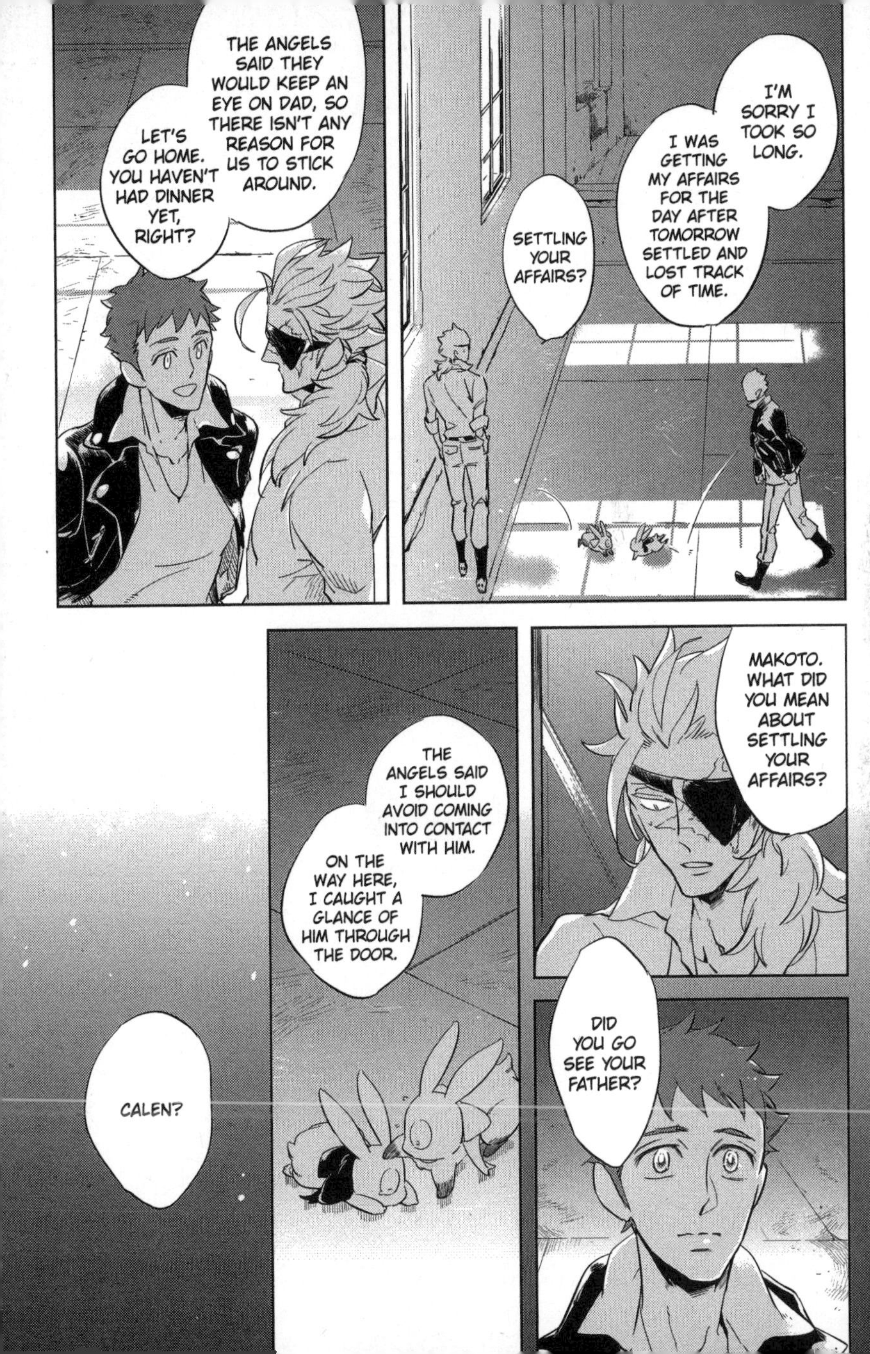
I'M SORRY I TOOK SO LONG.
I WAS GETTING MY AFFAIRS FOR THE DAY AFTER TOMORROW SETTLED AND LOST TRACK OF TIME.
SETTLING YOUR AFFAIRS?
THE ANGELS SAID THEY WOULD KEEP AN EYE ON DAD, SO THERE ISN'T ANY REASON FOR US TO STICK AROUND.
LET'S GO HOME. YOU HAVEN'T HAD DINNER YET, RIGHT?
MAKOTO. WHAT DID YOU MEAN ABOUT SETTLING YOUR AFFAIRS?
DID YOU GO SEE YOUR FATHER?
THE ANGELS SAID I SHOULD AVOID COMING INTO CONTACT WITH HIM.
ON THE WAY HERE, I CAUGHT A GLANCE OF HIM THROUGH THE DOOR.
CALEN?

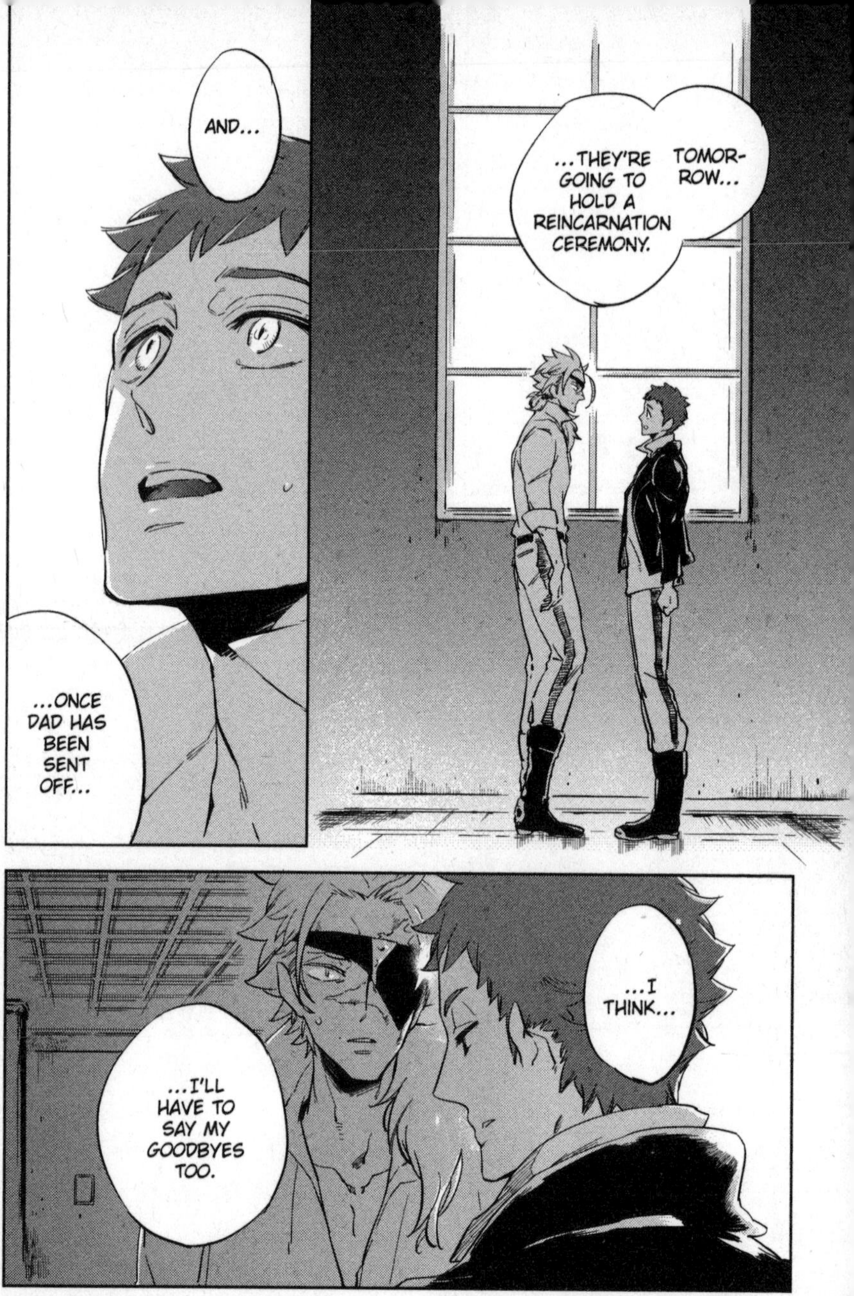
TOMOR-ROW... ...THEY'RE GOING TO HOLD A REINCARNATION CEREMONY.
AND...
...ONCE DAD HAS BEEN SENT OFF...
...I THINK...
...I'LL HAVE TO SAY MY GOODBYES TOO.

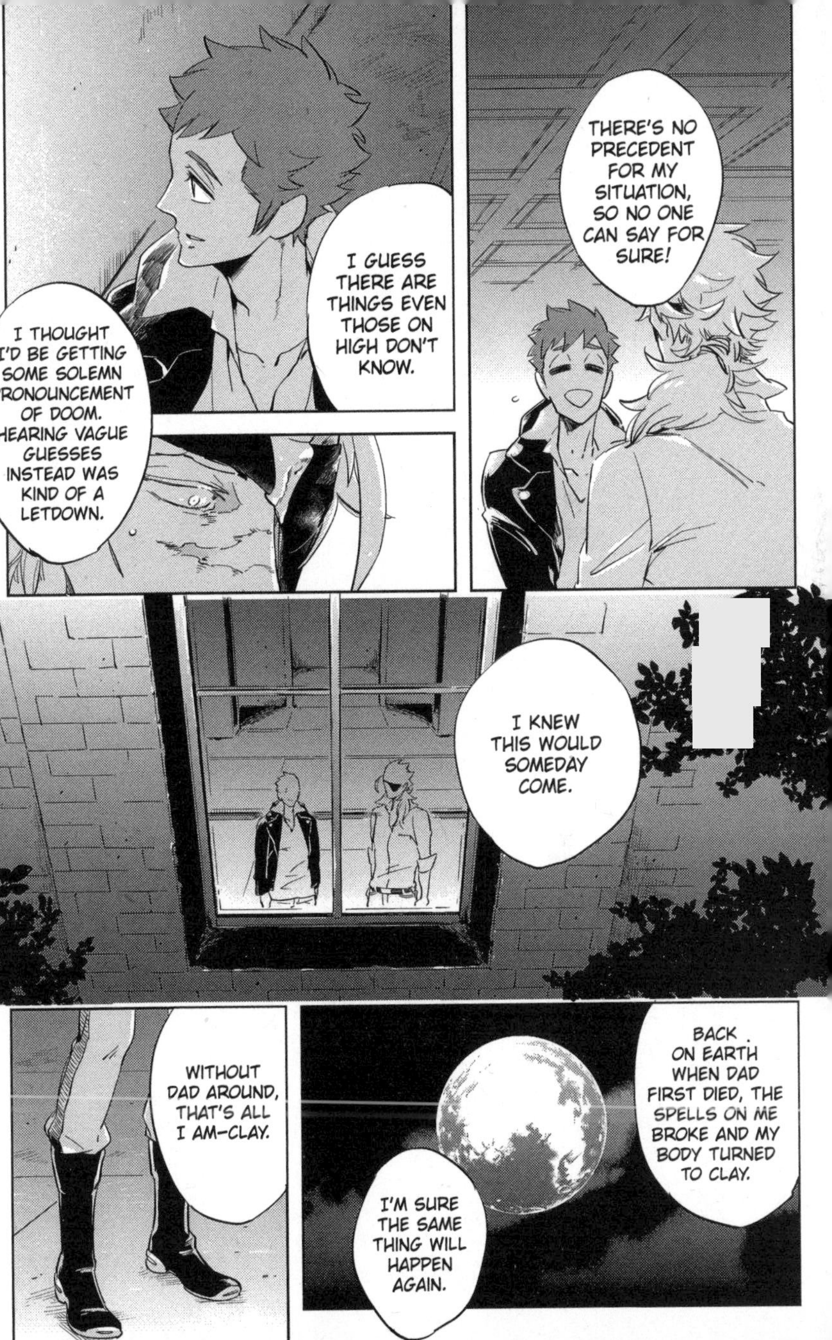
THERE'S NO PRECEDENT FOR MY SITUATION, SO NO ONE CAN SAY FOR SURE!
I GUESS THERE ARE THINGS EVEN THOSE ON HIGH DON'T KNOW.
I THOUGHT I'D BE GETTING SOME SOLEMN PRONOUNCEMENT OF DOOM. HEARING VAGUE GUESSES INSTEAD WAS KIND OF A LETDOWN.
I KNEW THIS WOULD SOMEDAY COME.
BACK ON EARTH WHEN DAD FIRST DIED, THE SPELLS ON ME BROKE AND MY BODY TURNED TO CLAY.
I'M SURE THE SAME THING WILL HAPPEN AGAIN.
WITHOUT DAD AROUND, THAT'S ALL I AM—CLAY.

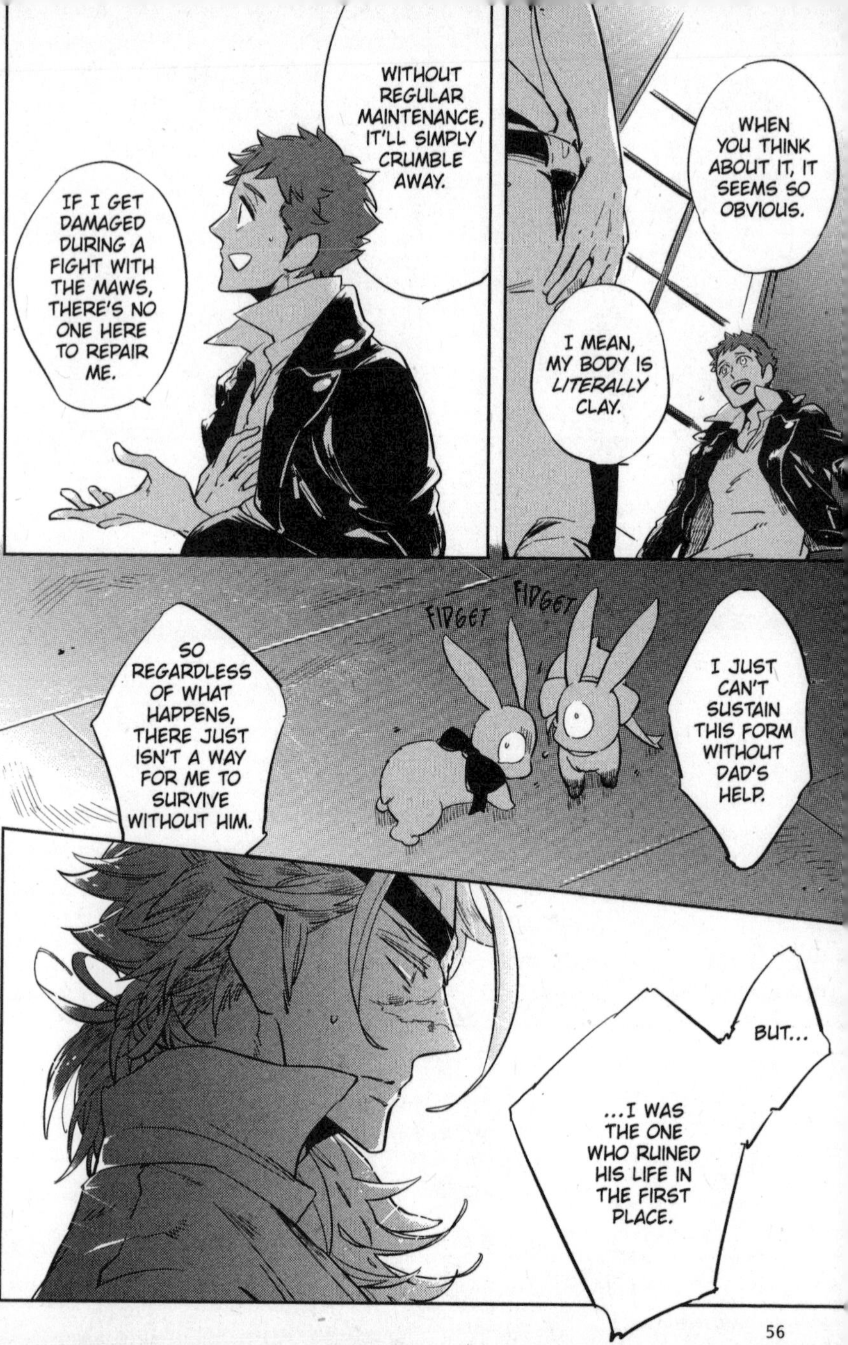
WHEN YOU THINK ABOUT IT, IT SEEMS SO OBVIOUS.
I MEAN, MY BODY IS *LITERALLY* CLAY.
WITHOUT REGULAR MAINTENANCE, IT'LL SIMPLY CRUMBLE AWAY.
IF I GET DAMAGED DURING A FIGHT WITH THE MAWS, THERE'S NO ONE HERE TO REPAIR ME.
I JUST CAN'T SUSTAIN THIS FORM WITHOUT DAD'S HELP.
FIDGET
FIDGET
SO REGARDLESS OF WHAT HAPPENS, THERE JUST ISN'T A WAY FOR ME TO SURVIVE WITHOUT HIM.
BUT...
...I WAS THE ONE WHO RUINED HIS LIFE IN THE FIRST PLACE.

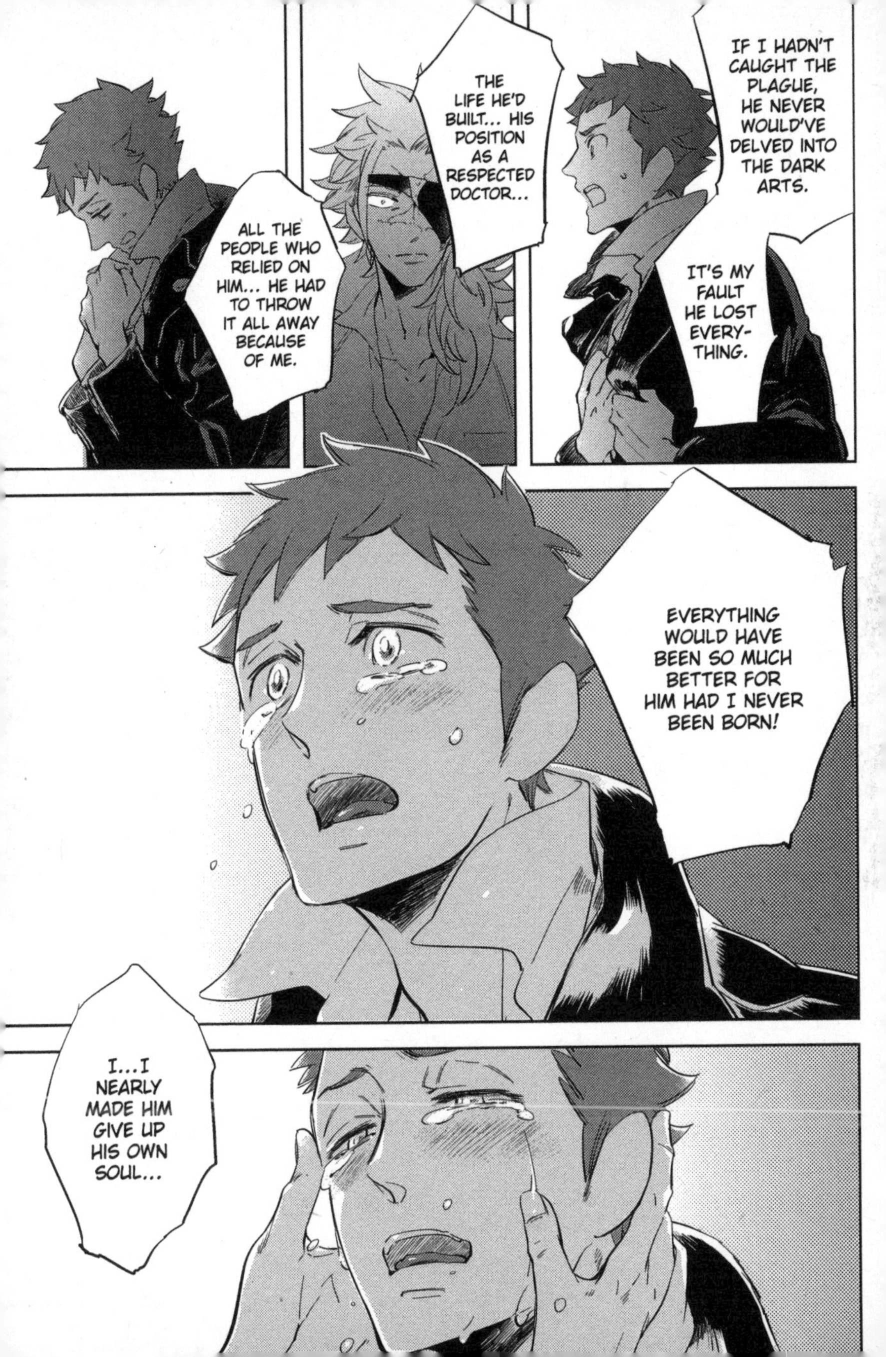
IF I HADN'T CAUGHT THE PLAGUE, HE NEVER WOULD'VE DELVED INTO THE DARK ARTS.
IT'S MY FAULT HE LOST EVERY-THING.
THE LIFE HE'D BUILT... HIS POSITION AS A RESPECTED DOCTOR...
ALL THE PEOPLE WHO RELIED ON HIM... HE HAD TO THROW IT ALL AWAY BECAUSE OF ME.
EVERYTHING WOULD HAVE BEEN SO MUCH BETTER FOR HIM HAD I NEVER BEEN BORN!
I...I NEARLY MADE HIM GIVE UP HIS OWN SOUL...

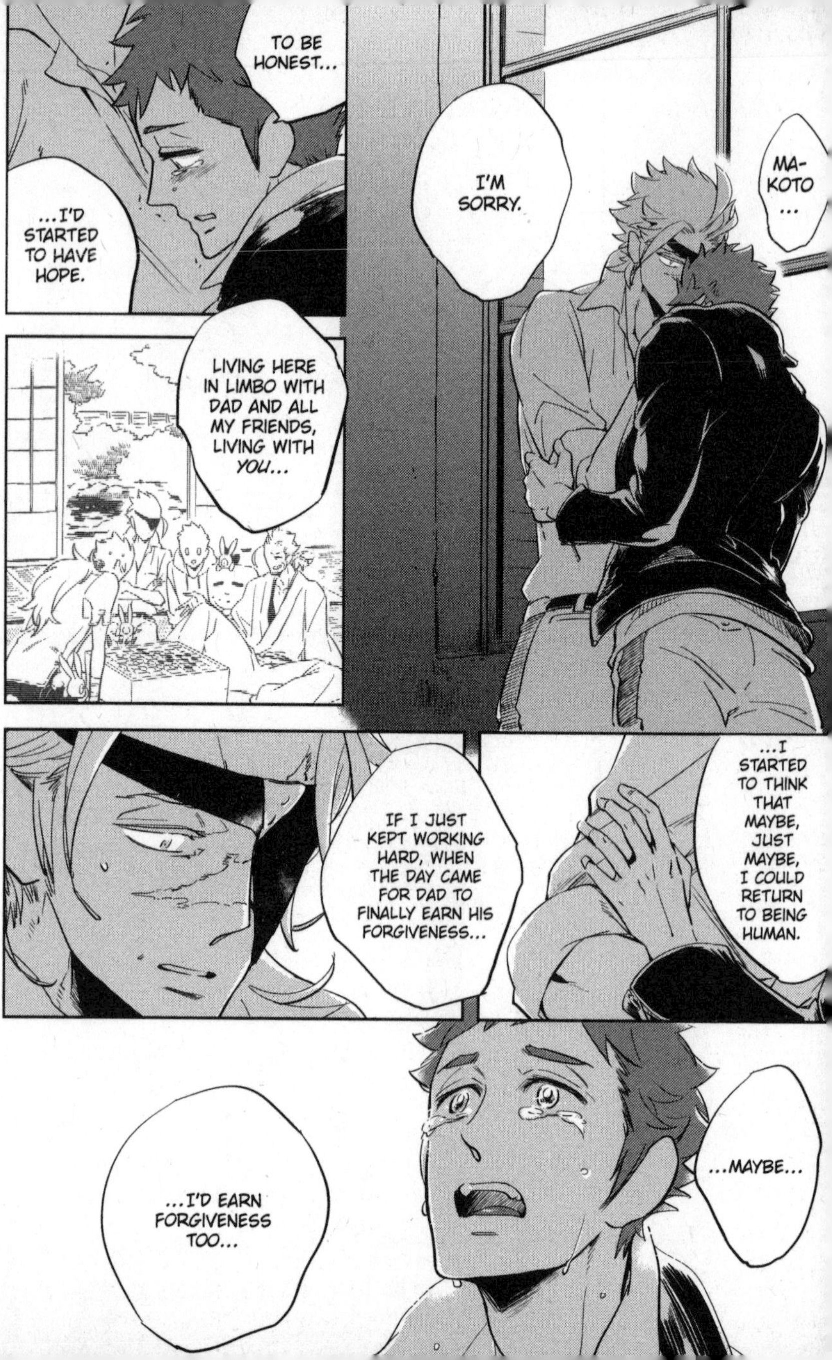
MA-KOTO...
I'M SORRY.
TO BE HONEST...
...I'D STARTED TO HAVE HOPE.
LIVING HERE IN LIMBO WITH DAD AND ALL MY FRIENDS, LIVING WITH *YOU*...
...I STARTED TO THINK THAT MAYBE, JUST MAYBE, I COULD RETURN TO BEING HUMAN.
IF I JUST KEPT WORKING HARD, WHEN THE DAY CAME FOR DAD TO FINALLY EARN HIS FORGIVENESS...
...MAYBE...
...I'D EARN FORGIVENESS TOO...

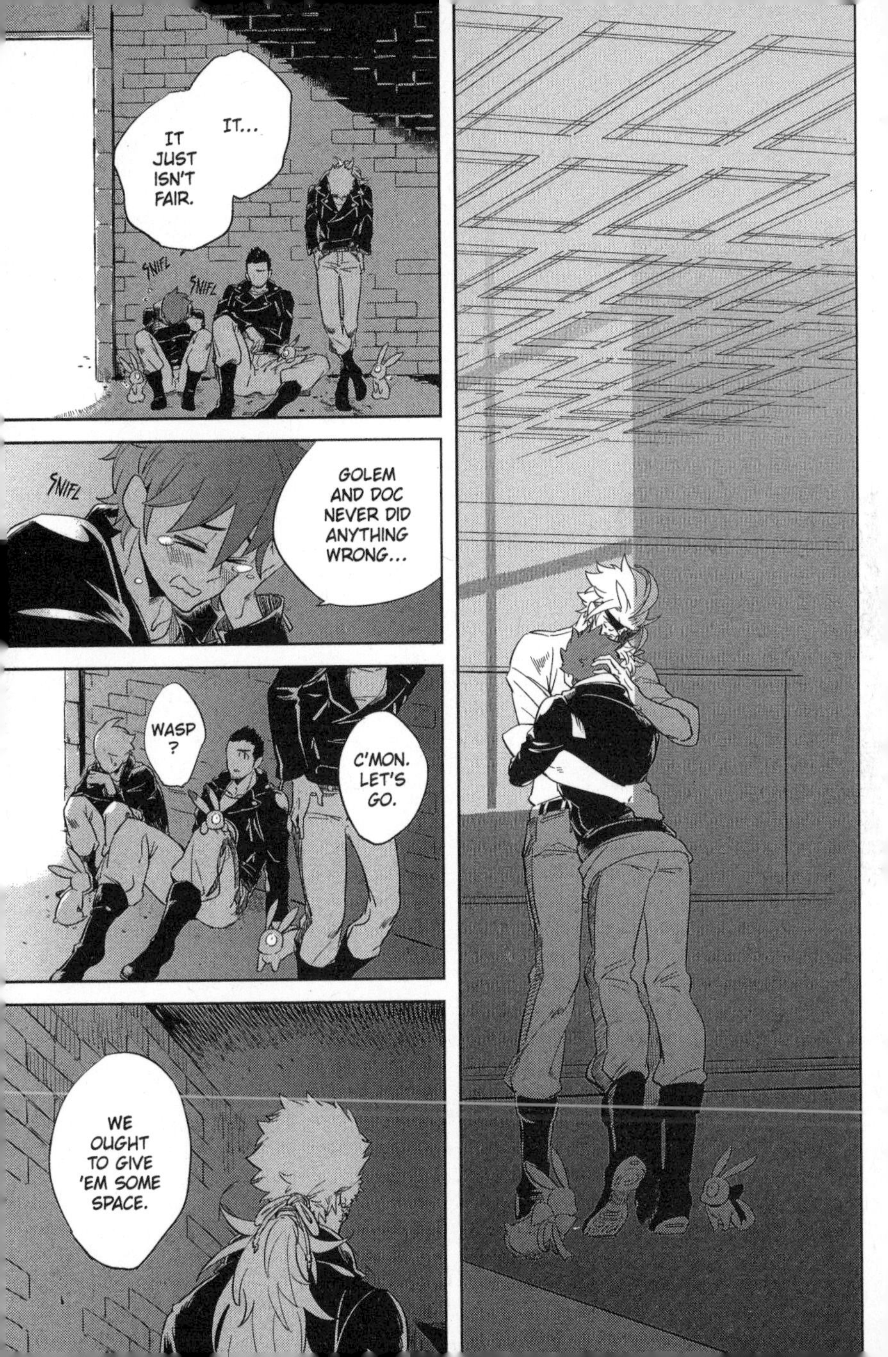
IT...
IT JUST ISN'T FAIR.
SNIFL
SNIFL
GOLEM AND DOC NEVER DID ANYTHING WRONG...
SNIFL
WASP?
C'MON. LET'S GO.
WE OUGHT TO GIVE 'EM SOME SPACE.

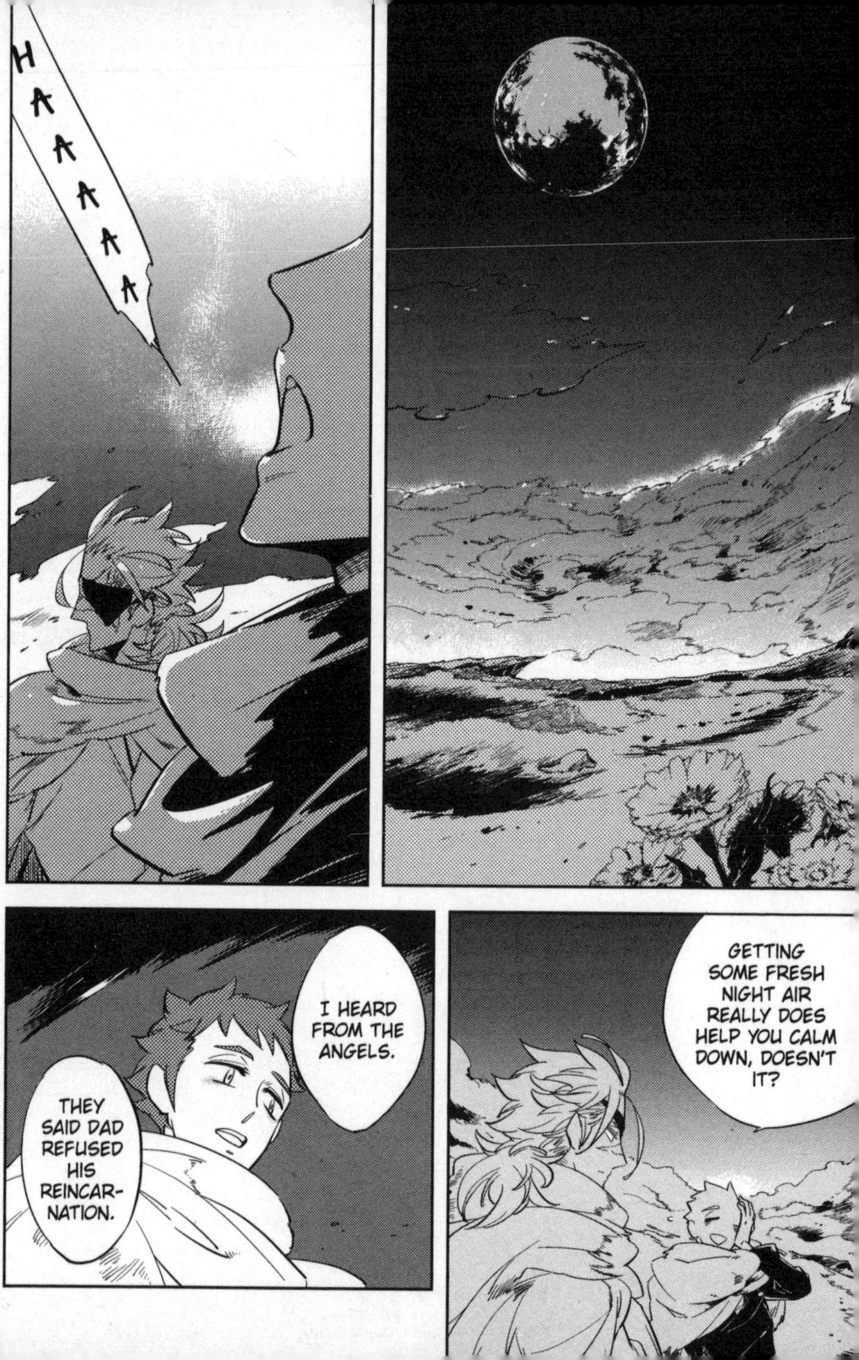
HAAAAAA
GETTING SOME FRESH NIGHT AIR REALLY DOES HELP YOU CALM DOWN, DOESN'T IT?
I HEARD FROM THE ANGELS.
THEY SAID DAD REFUSED HIS REINCAR-NATION.

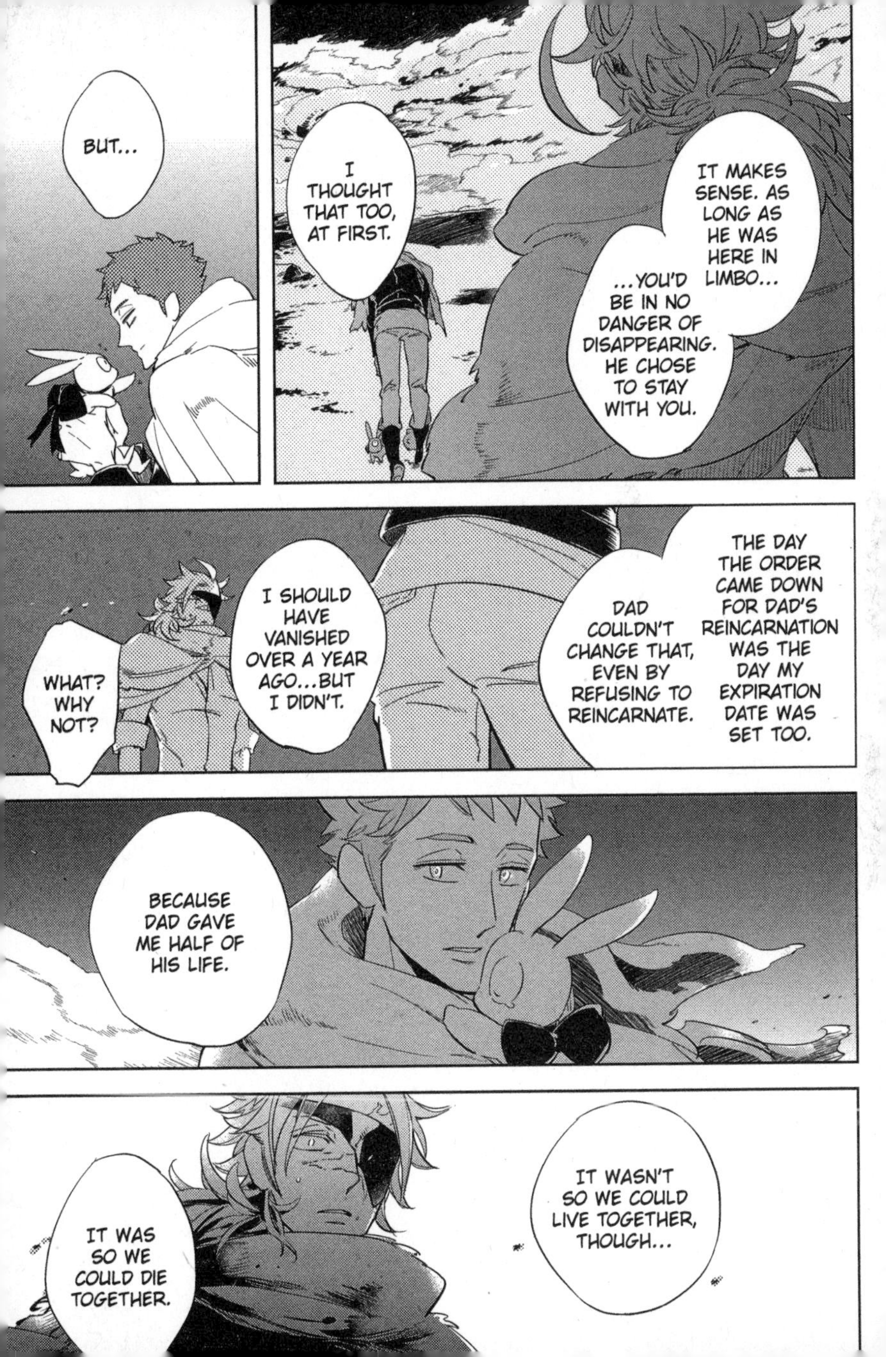
IT MAKES SENSE. AS LONG AS HE WAS HERE IN LIMBO...
...YOU'D BE IN NO DANGER OF DISAPPEARING. HE CHOSE TO STAY WITH YOU.
I THOUGHT THAT TOO, AT FIRST.
BUT...
THE DAY THE ORDER CAME DOWN FOR DAD'S REINCARNATION WAS THE DAY MY EXPIRATION DATE WAS SET TOO.
DAD COULDN'T CHANGE THAT, EVEN BY REFUSING TO REINCARNATE.
I SHOULD HAVE VANISHED OVER A YEAR AGO...BUT I DIDN'T.
WHAT? WHY NOT?
BECAUSE DAD GAVE ME HALF OF HIS LIFE.
IT WASN'T SO WE COULD LIVE TOGETHER, THOUGH...
IT WAS SO WE COULD DIE TOGETHER.

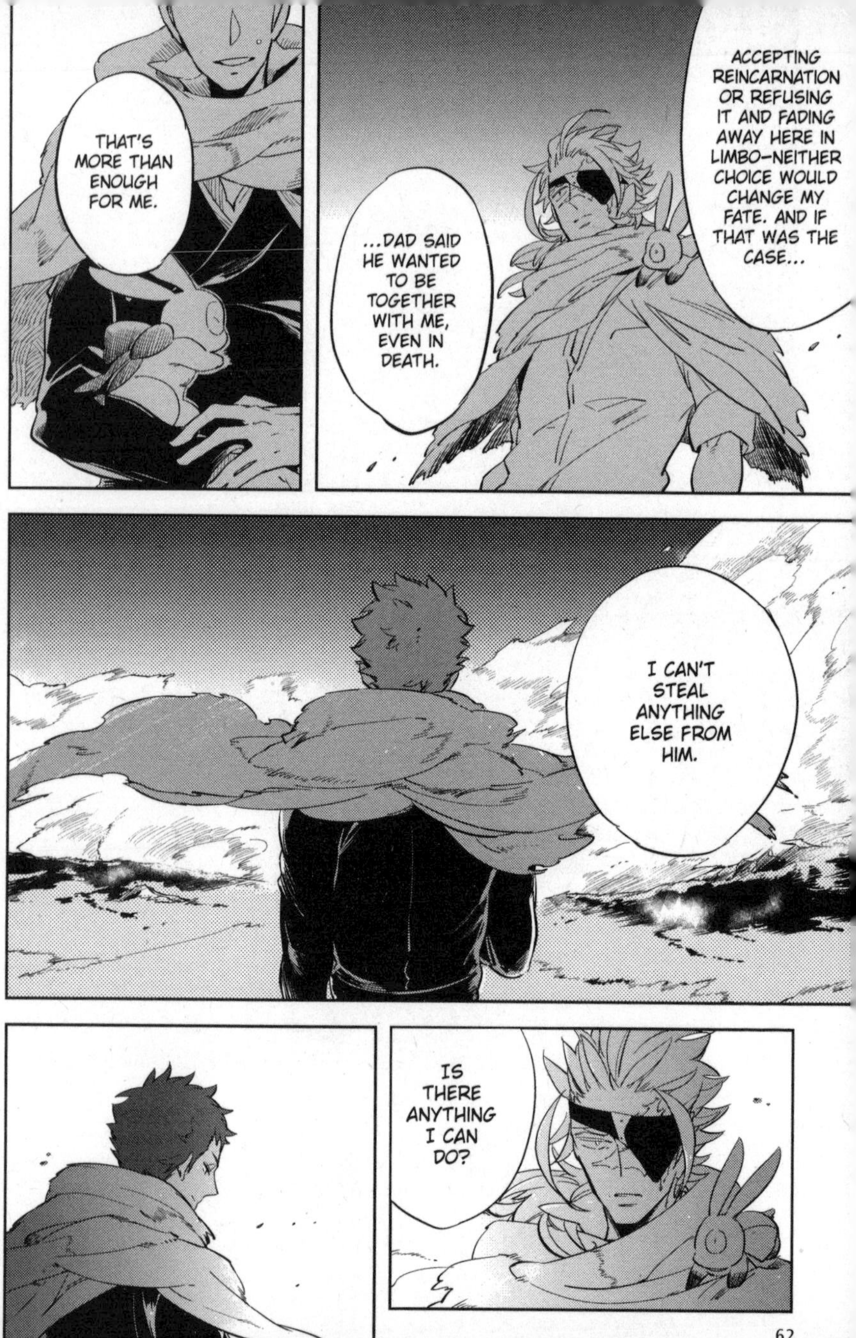
ACCEPTING REINCARNATION OR REFUSING IT AND FADING AWAY HERE IN LIMBO—NEITHER CHOICE WOULD CHANGE MY FATE. AND IF THAT WAS THE CASE...
...DAD SAID HE WANTED TO BE TOGETHER WITH ME, EVEN IN DEATH.
THAT'S MORE THAN ENOUGH FOR ME.
I CAN'T STEAL ANYTHING ELSE FROM HIM.
IS THERE ANYTHING I CAN DO?

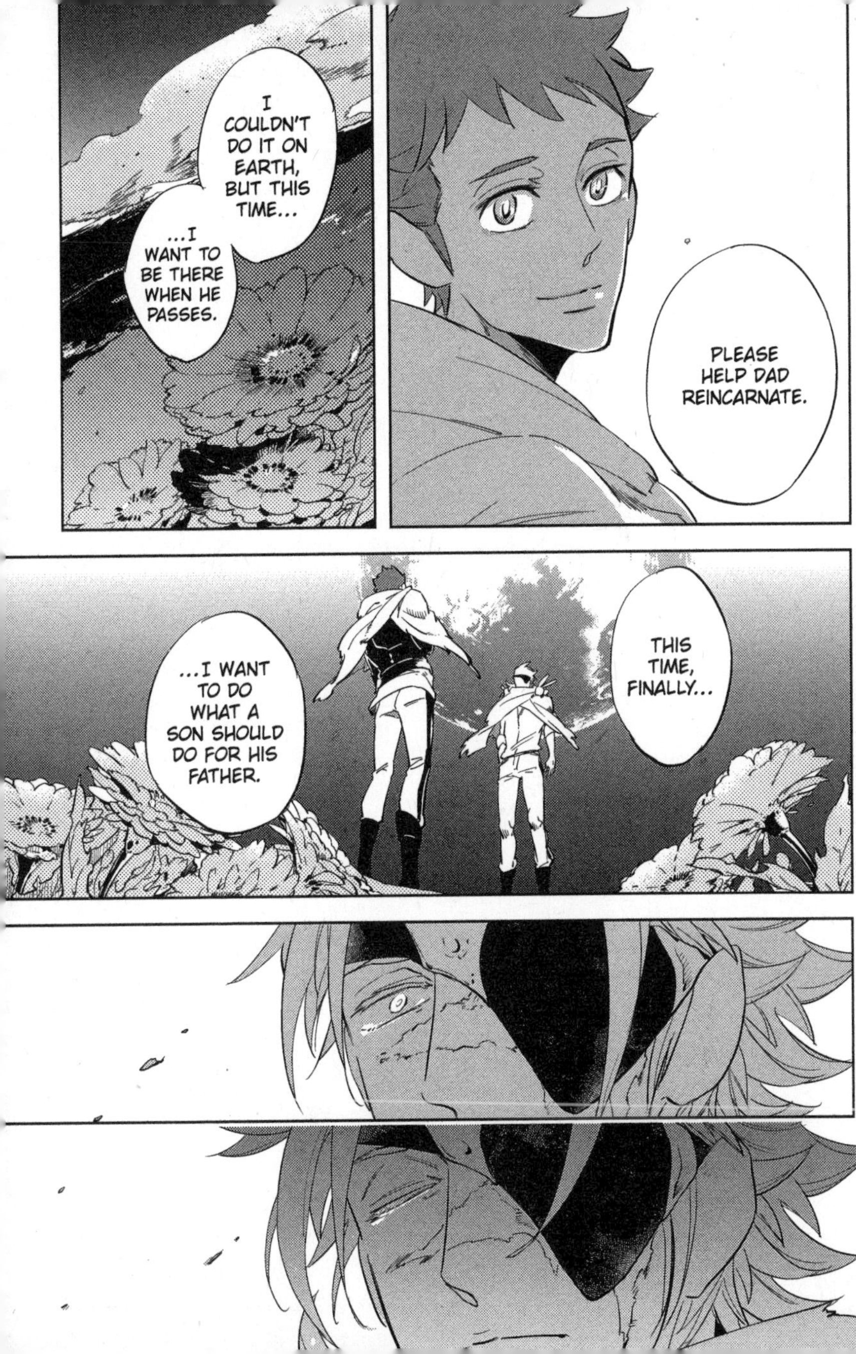
PLEASE HELP DAD REINCARNATE.
I COULDN'T DO IT ON EARTH, BUT THIS TIME...
...I WANT TO BE THERE WHEN HE PASSES.
THIS TIME, FINALLY...
...I WANT TO DO WHAT A SON SHOULD DO FOR HIS FATHER.

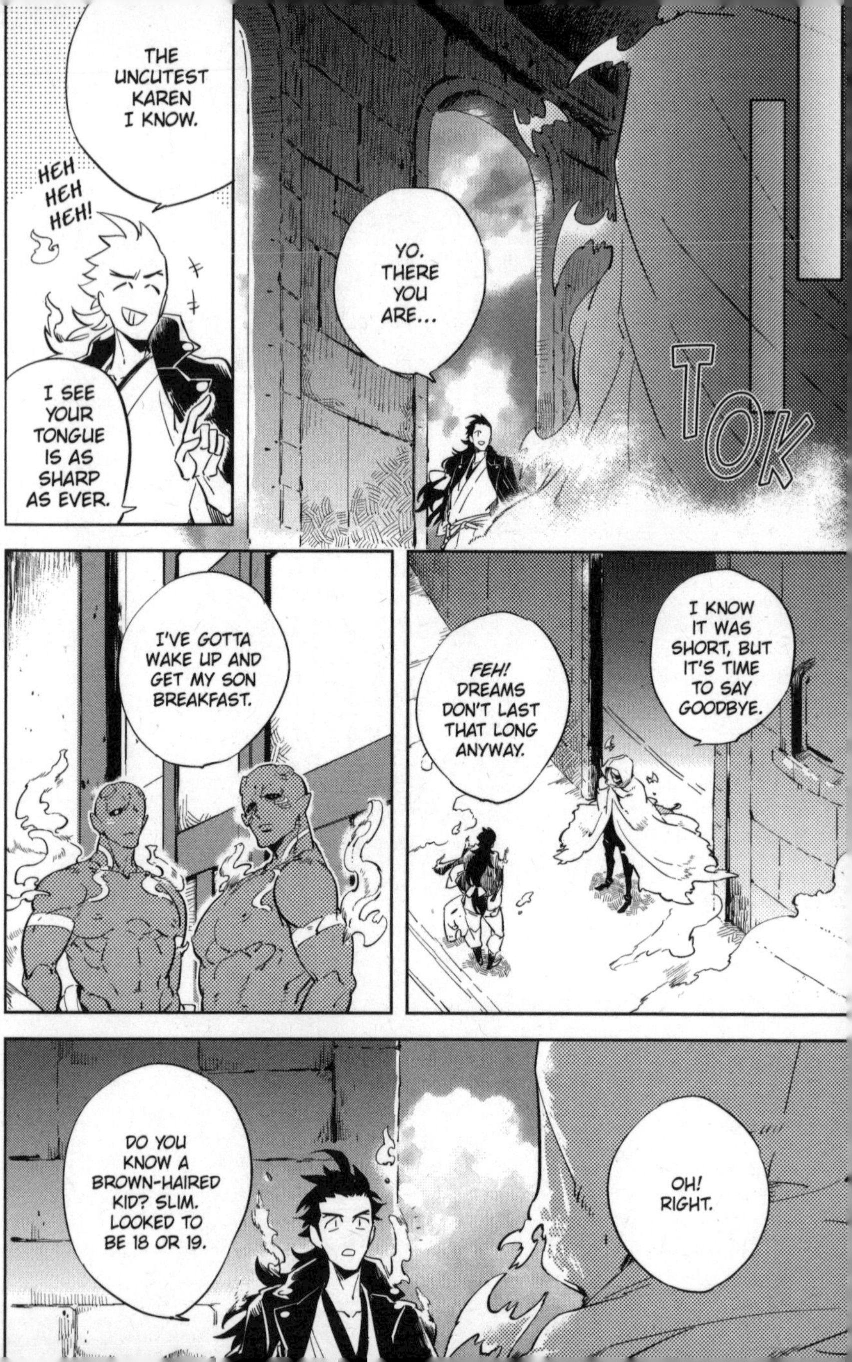
YO. THERE YOU ARE...
TOK
THE UNCUTEST KAREN I KNOW.
HEH HEH HEH!
I SEE YOUR TONGUE IS AS SHARP AS EVER.
I KNOW IT WAS SHORT, BUT IT'S TIME TO SAY GOODBYE.
FEH! DREAMS DON'T LAST THAT LONG ANYWAY.
I'VE GOTTA WAKE UP AND GET MY SON BREAKFAST.
OH! RIGHT.
DO YOU KNOW A BROWN-HAIRED KID? SLIM. LOOKED TO BE 18 OR 19.

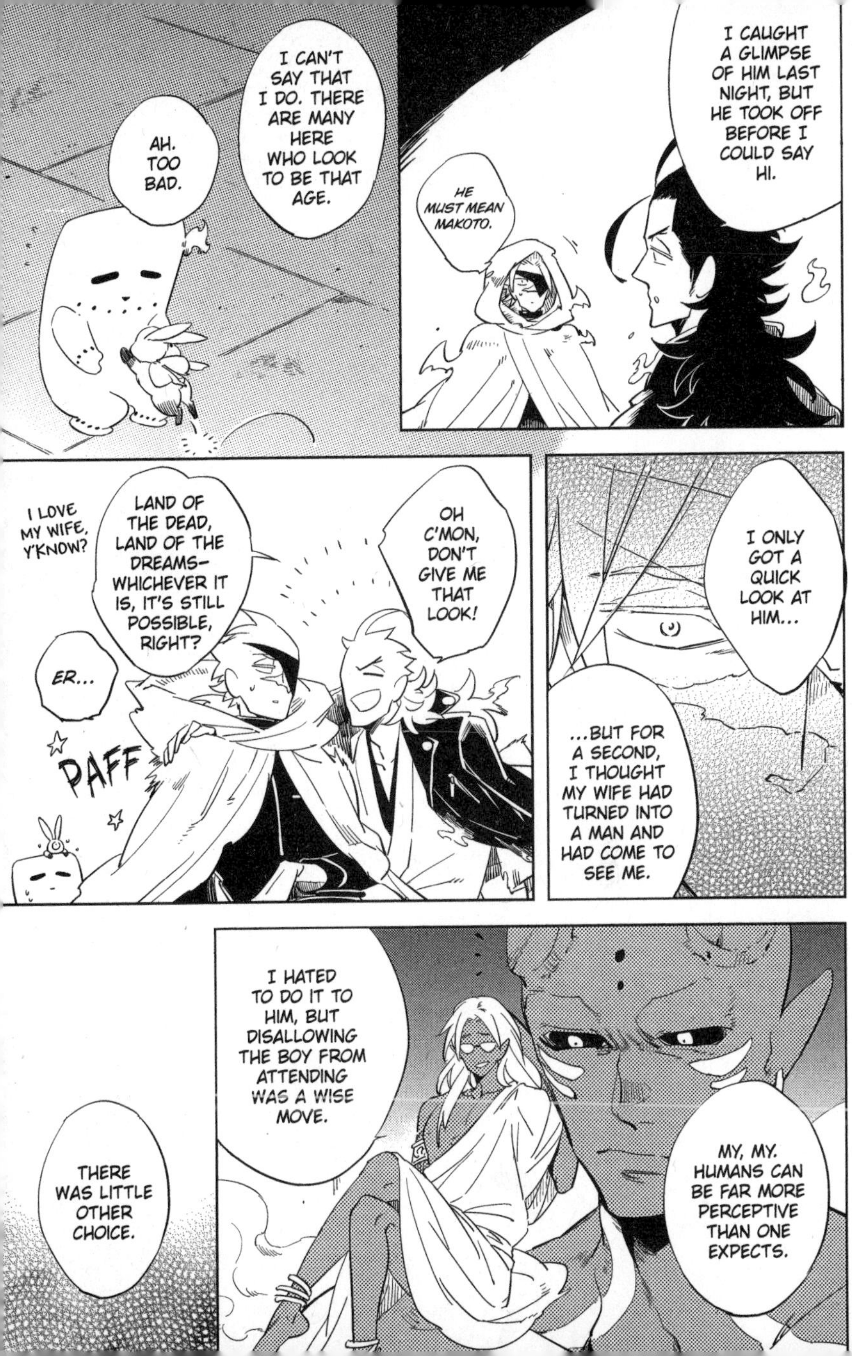
I CAUGHT A GLIMPSE OF HIM LAST NIGHT, BUT HE TOOK OFF BEFORE I COULD SAY HI.
HE MUST MEAN MAKOTO.
I CAN'T SAY THAT I DO. THERE ARE MANY HERE WHO LOOK TO BE THAT AGE.
AH. TOO BAD.
I ONLY GOT A QUICK LOOK AT HIM...
...BUT FOR A SECOND, I THOUGHT MY WIFE HAD TURNED INTO A MAN AND HAD COME TO SEE ME.
OH C'MON, DON'T GIVE ME THAT LOOK!
LAND OF THE DEAD, LAND OF THE DREAMS–WHICHEVER IT IS, IT'S STILL POSSIBLE, RIGHT?
I LOVE MY WIFE, Y'KNOW?
ER...
PAFF
MY, MY. HUMANS CAN BE FAR MORE PERCEPTIVE THAN ONE EXPECTS.
I HATED TO DO IT TO HIM, BUT DISALLOWING THE BOY FROM ATTENDING WAS A WISE MOVE.
THERE WAS LITTLE OTHER CHOICE.

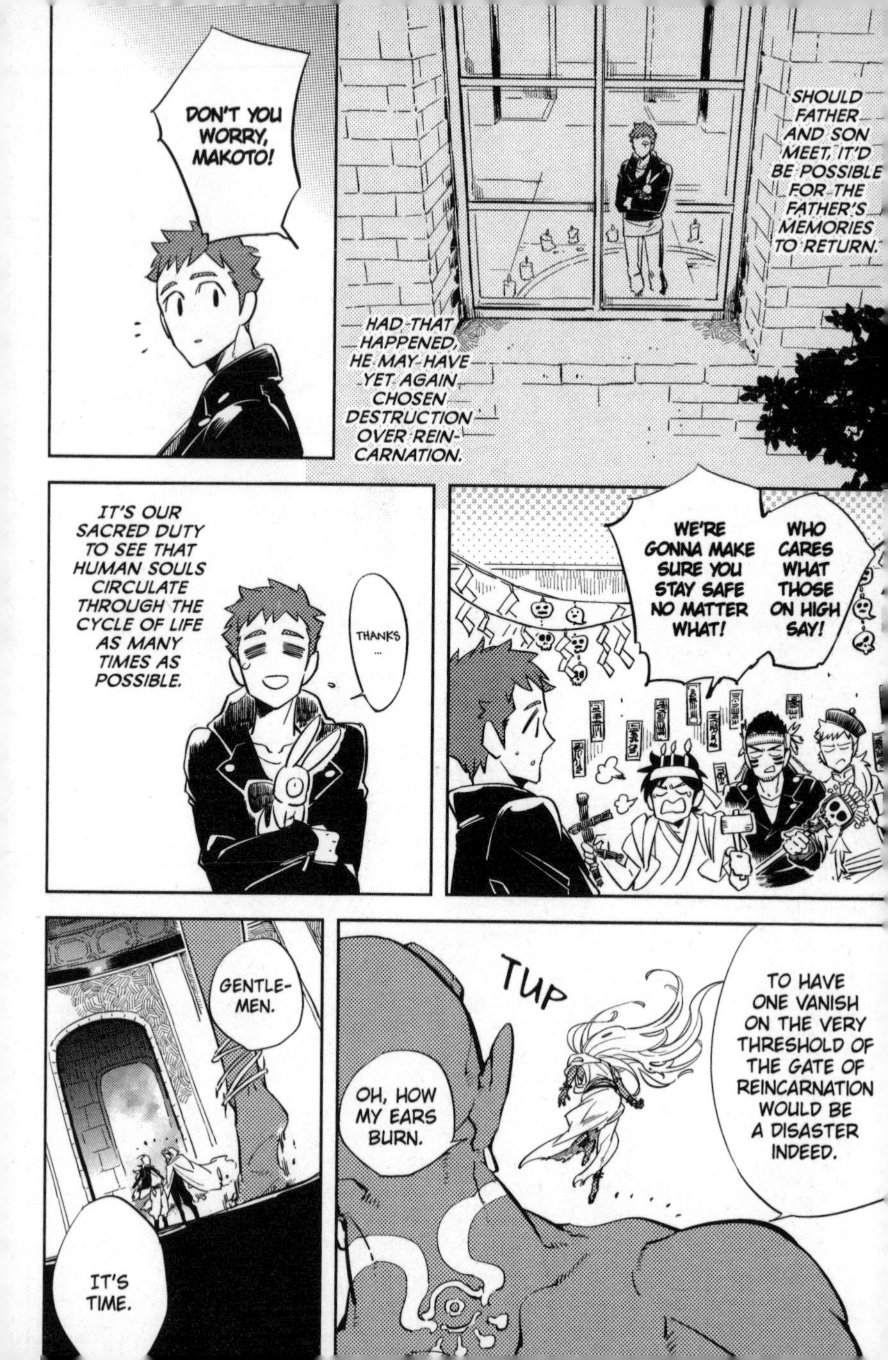
SHOULD FATHER AND SON MEET, IT'D BE POSSIBLE FOR THE FATHER'S MEMORIES TO RETURN.
HAD THAT HAPPENED, HE MAY HAVE YET AGAIN CHOSEN DESTRUCTION OVER REIN-CARNATION.
DON'T YOU WORRY, MAKOTO!
WHO CARES WHAT THOSE ON HIGH SAY!
WE'RE GONNA MAKE SURE YOU STAY SAFE NO MATTER WHAT!
IT'S OUR SACRED DUTY TO SEE THAT HUMAN SOULS CIRCULATE THROUGH THE CYCLE OF LIFE AS MANY TIMES AS POSSIBLE.
THANKS...
TO HAVE ONE VANISH ON THE VERY THRESHOLD OF THE GATE OF REINCARNATION WOULD BE A DISASTER INDEED.
TUP
OH, HOW MY EARS BURN.
GENTLE-MEN.
IT'S TIME.

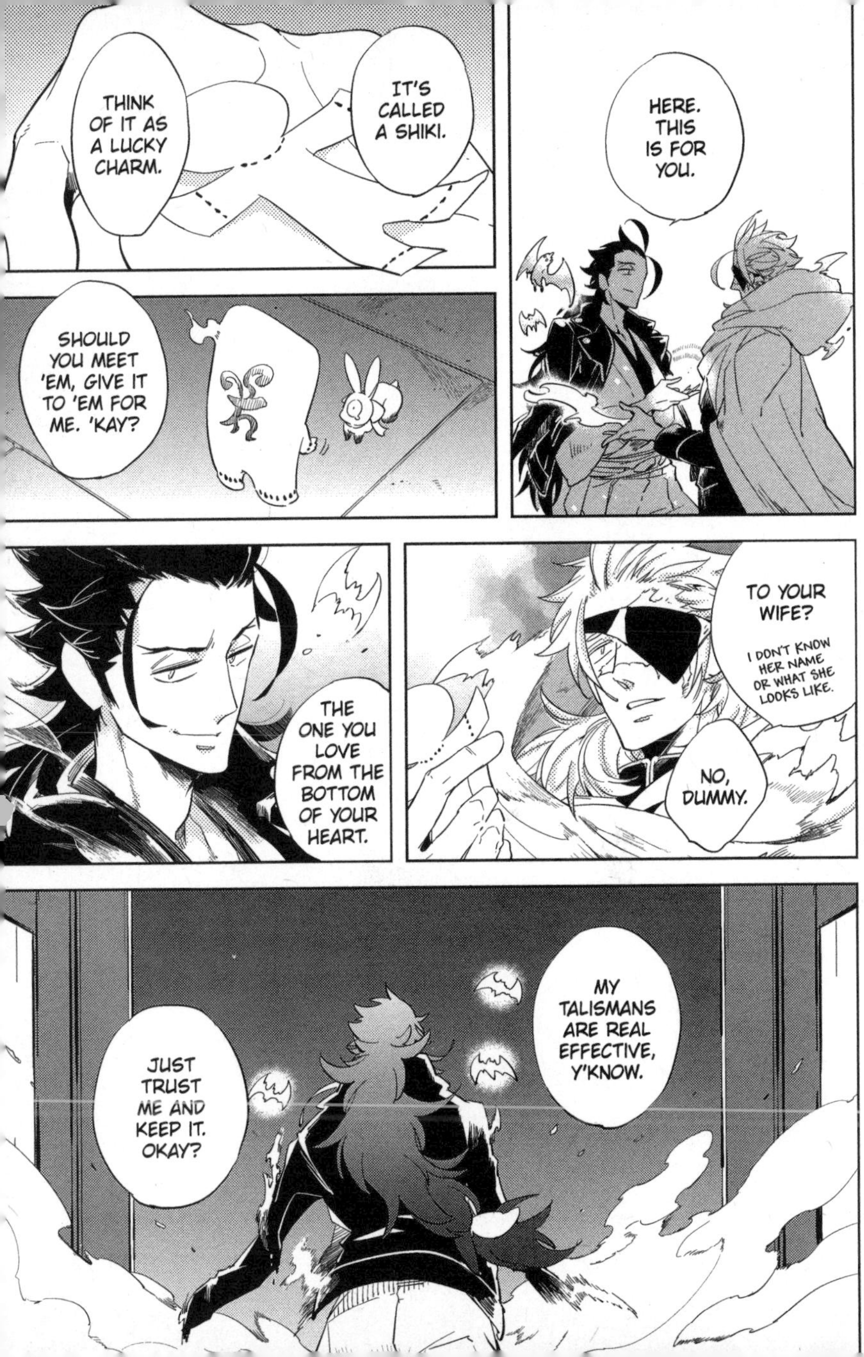
HERE. THIS IS FOR YOU.
IT'S CALLED A SHIKI.
THINK OF IT AS A LUCKY CHARM.
SHOULD YOU MEET 'EM, GIVE IT TO 'EM FOR ME. 'KAY?
TO YOUR WIFE?
I DON'T KNOW HER NAME OR WHAT SHE LOOKS LIKE.
NO, DUMMY.
THE ONE YOU LOVE FROM THE BOTTOM OF YOUR HEART.
MY TALISMANS ARE REAL EFFECTIVE, Y'KNOW.
JUST TRUST ME AND KEEP IT. OKAY?

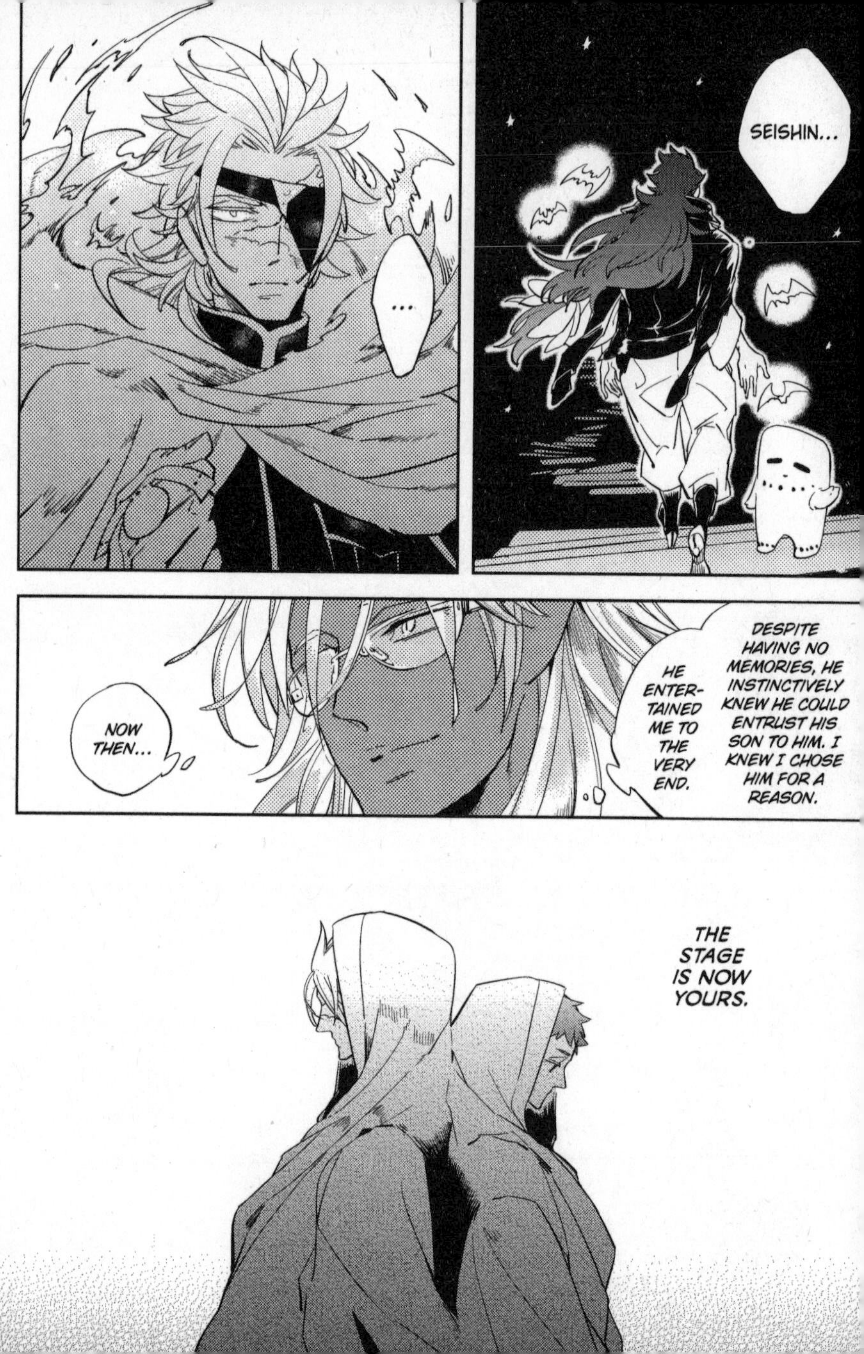
SEISHIN...
...
DESPITE HAVING NO MEMORIES, HE INSTINCTIVELY KNEW HE COULD ENTRUST HIS SON TO HIM. I KNEW I CHOSE HIM FOR A REASON.
HE ENTER-TAINED ME TO THE VERY END.
NOW THEN...
THE STAGE IS NOW YOURS.

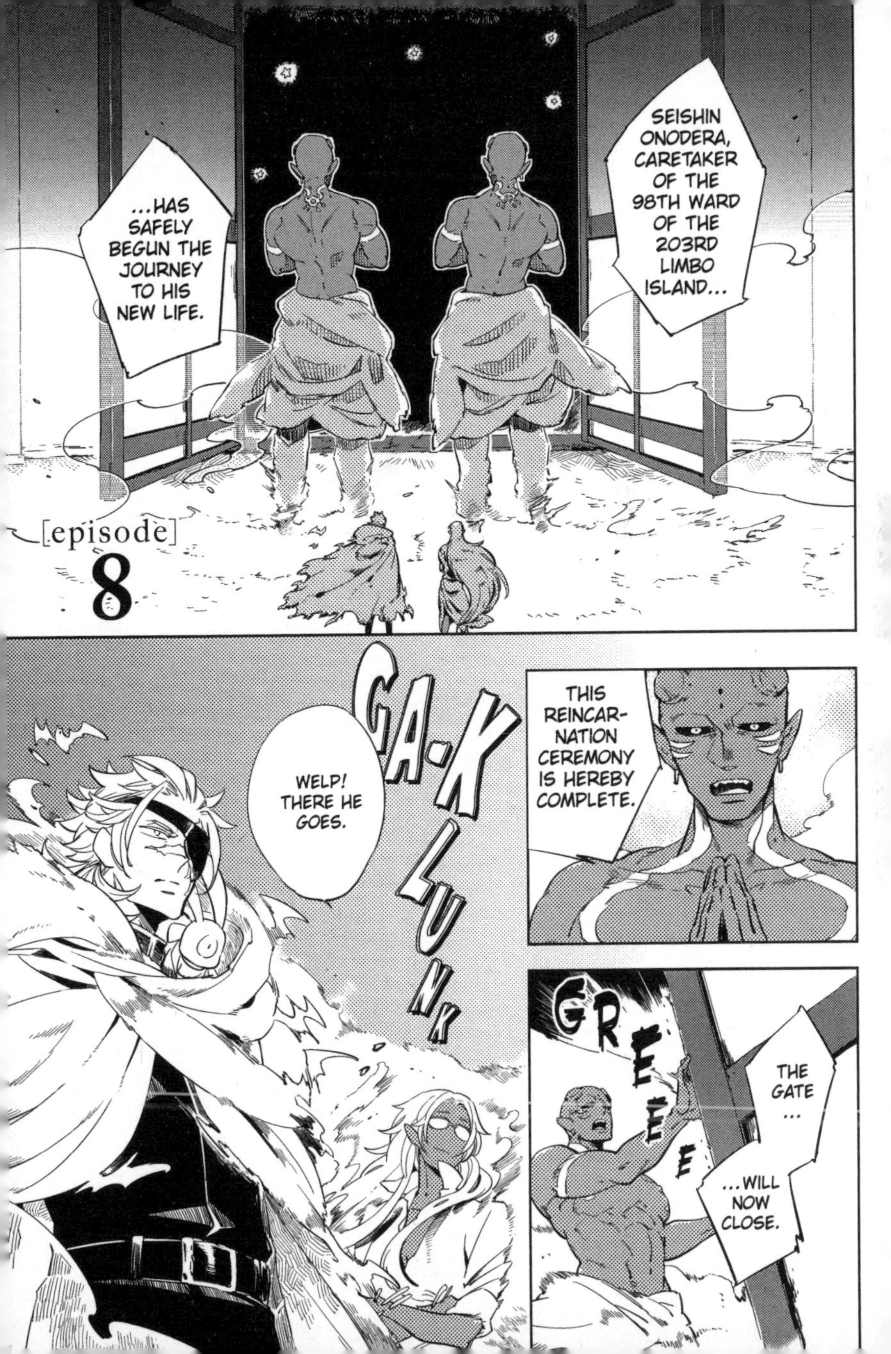
SEISHIN ONODERA, CARETAKER OF THE 98TH WARD OF THE 203RD LIMBO ISLAND...
...HAS SAFELY BEGUN THE JOURNEY TO HIS NEW LIFE.
[episode] 8
THIS REINCAR-NATION CEREMONY IS HEREBY COMPLETE.
GREEEE
THE GATE ...
...WILL NOW CLOSE.
GA-KLUNK
WELP! THERE HE GOES.

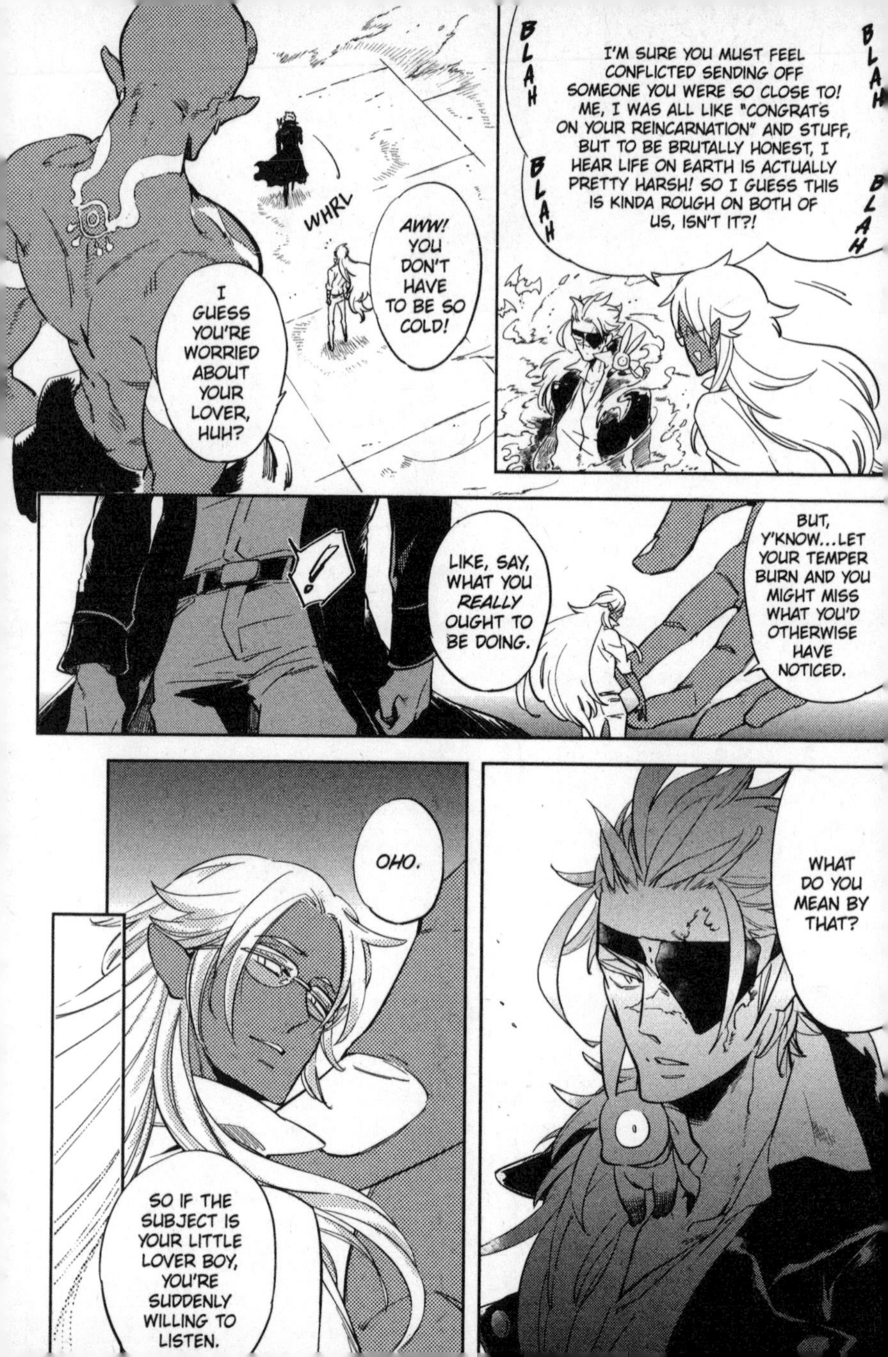
BLAH BLAH
I'M SURE YOU MUST FEEL CONFLICTED SENDING OFF SOMEONE YOU WERE SO CLOSE TO! ME, I WAS ALL LIKE "CONGRATS ON YOUR REINCARNATION" AND STUFF, BUT TO BE BRUTALLY HONEST, I HEAR LIFE ON EARTH IS ACTUALLY PRETTY HARSH! SO I GUESS THIS IS KINDA ROUGH ON BOTH OF US, ISN'T IT?!
BLAH BLAH
AWW! YOU DON'T HAVE TO BE SO COLD!
WHRL
I GUESS YOU'RE WORRIED ABOUT YOUR LOVER, HUH?
BUT, Y'KNOW...LET YOUR TEMPER BURN AND YOU MIGHT MISS WHAT YOU'D OTHERWISE HAVE NOTICED.
LIKE, SAY, WHAT YOU *REALLY* OUGHT TO BE DOING.
!
WHAT DO YOU MEAN BY THAT?
OHO.
SO IF THE SUBJECT IS YOUR LITTLE LOVER BOY, YOU'RE SUDDENLY WILLING TO LISTEN.

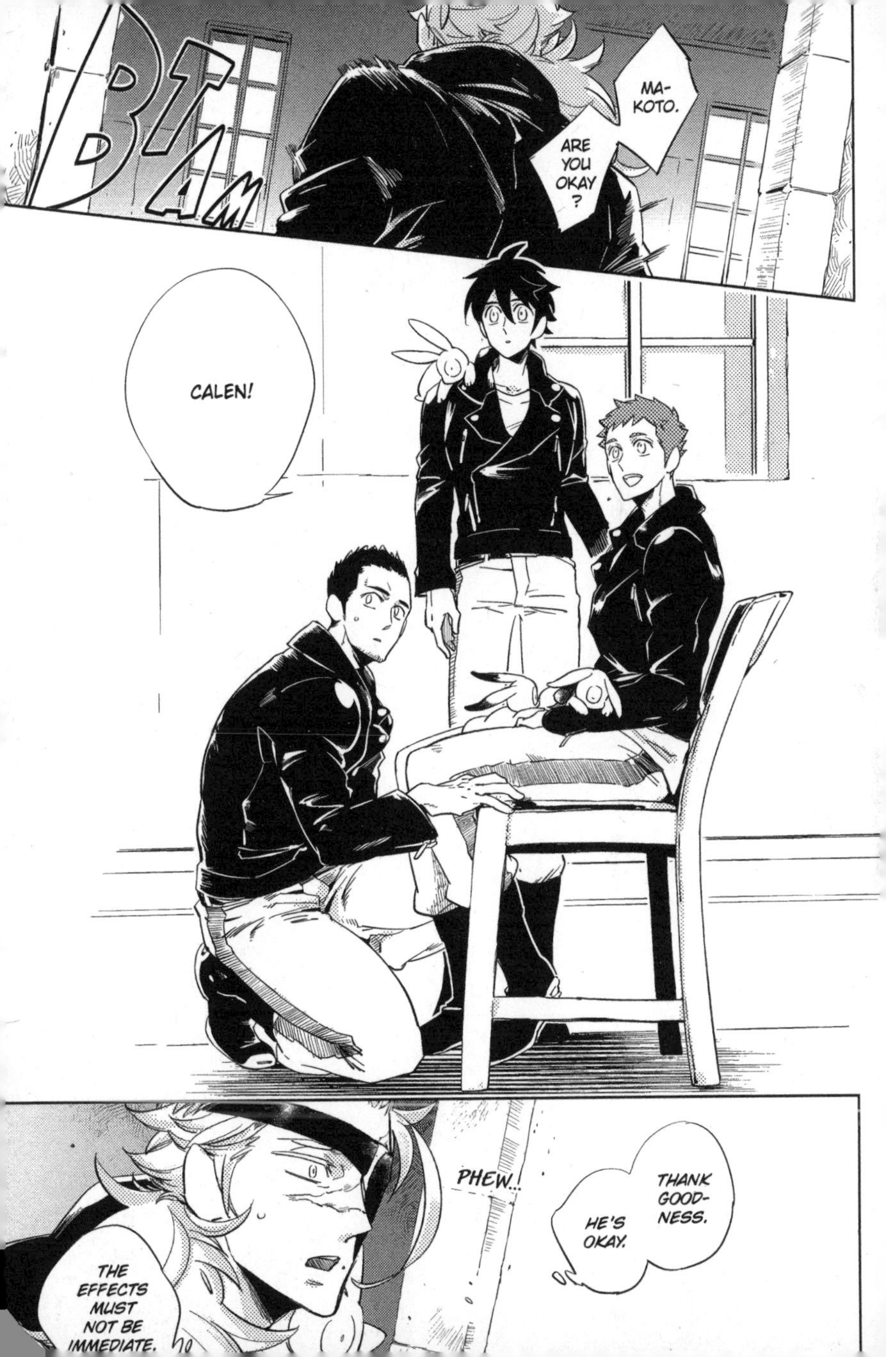
MA-KOTO.
ARE YOU OKAY?
CALEN!
THANK GOODNESS.
HE'S OKAY.
PHEW...
THE EFFECTS MUST NOT BE IMMEDIATE.

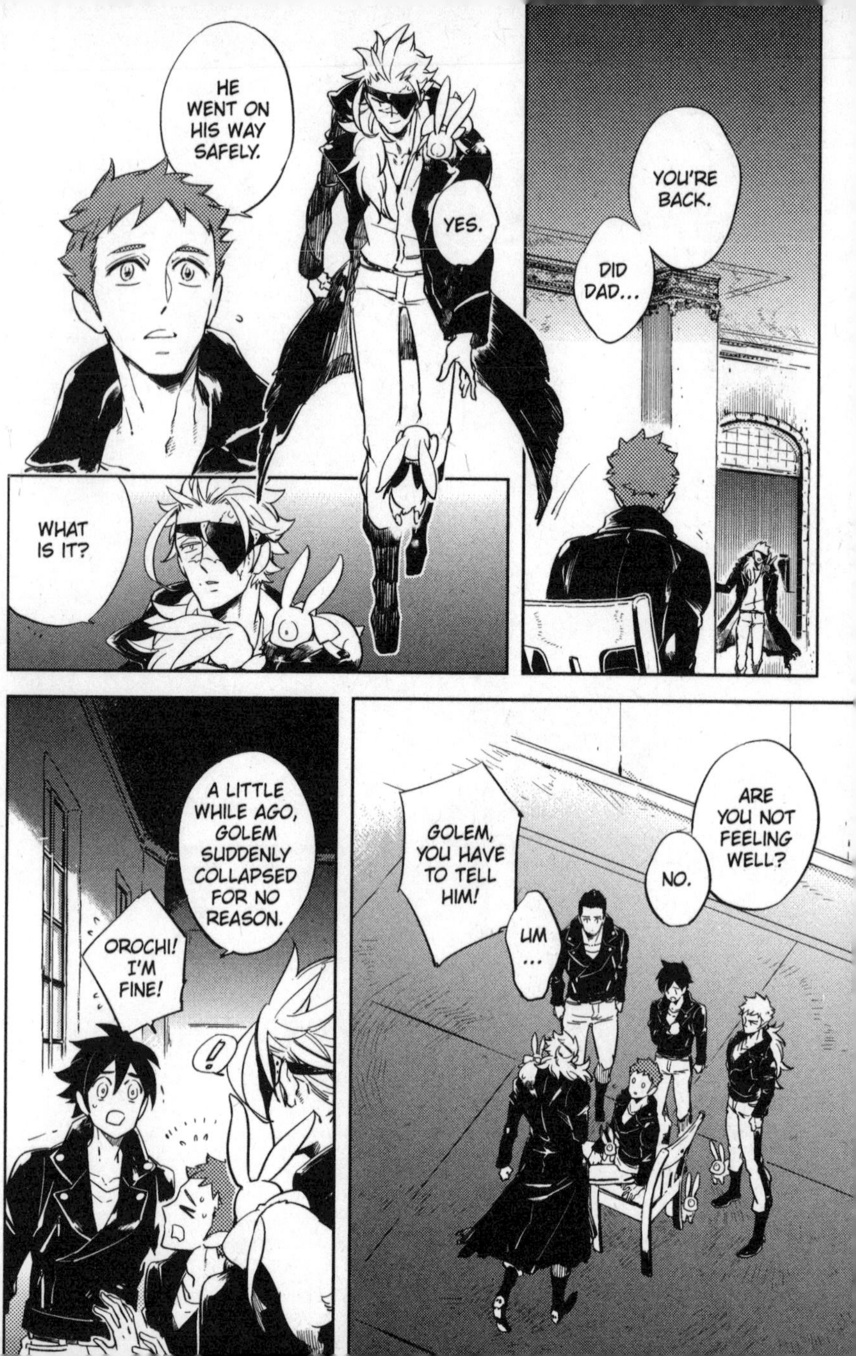
YOU'RE BACK.
DID DAD...
YES.
HE WENT ON HIS WAY SAFELY.
WHAT IS IT?
ARE YOU NOT FEELING WELL?
NO.
GOLEM, YOU HAVE TO TELL HIM!
UM ...
A LITTLE WHILE AGO, GOLEM SUDDENLY COLLAPSED FOR NO REASON.
OROCHI! I'M FINE!
!

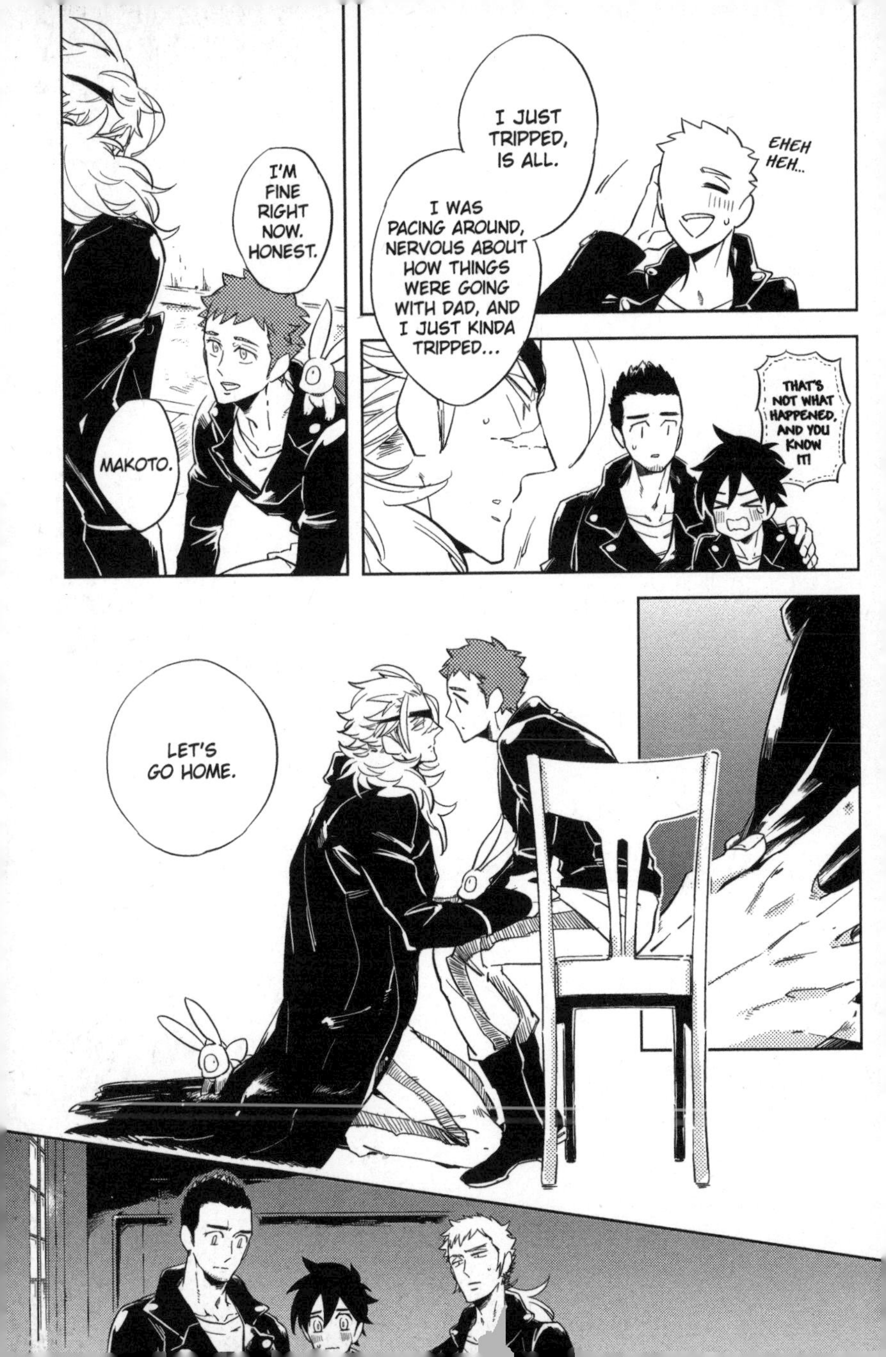
EHEH HEH...
I JUST TRIPPED, IS ALL.
I WAS PACING AROUND, NERVOUS ABOUT HOW THINGS WERE GOING WITH DAD, AND I JUST KINDA TRIPPED...
THAT'S NOT WHAT HAPPENED, AND YOU KNOW IT!
I'M FINE RIGHT NOW. HONEST.
MAKOTO.
LET'S GO HOME.

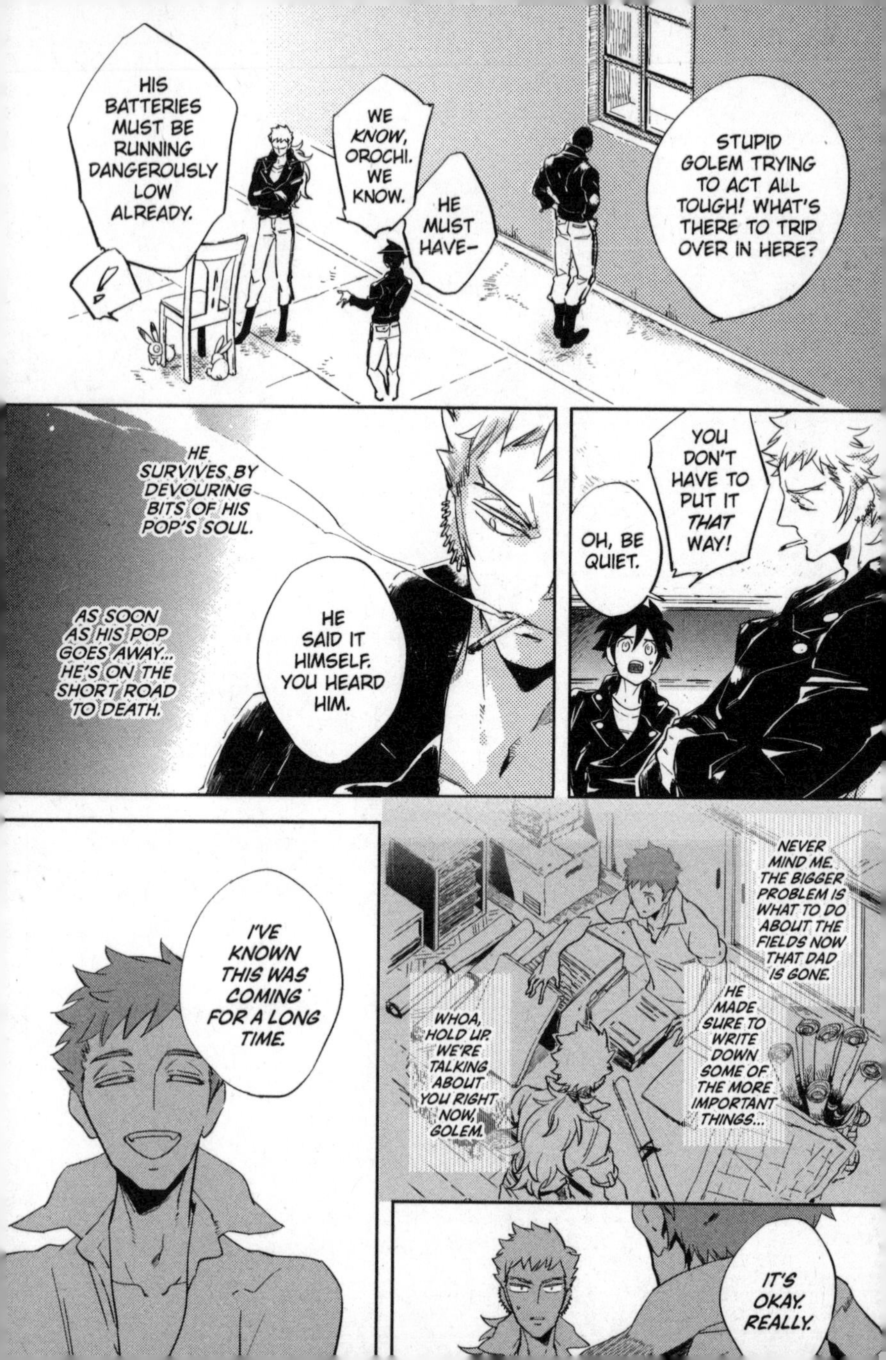
STUPID GOLEM TRYING TO ACT ALL TOUGH! WHAT'S THERE TO TRIP OVER IN HERE?
HE MUST HAVE–
WE KNOW, OROCHI. WE KNOW.
HIS BATTERIES MUST BE RUNNING DANGEROUSLY LOW ALREADY.
!
YOU DON'T HAVE TO PUT IT THAT WAY!
OH, BE QUIET.
HE SURVIVES BY DEVOURING BITS OF HIS POP'S SOUL.
HE SAID IT HIMSELF. YOU HEARD HIM.
AS SOON AS HIS POP GOES AWAY... HE'S ON THE SHORT ROAD TO DEATH.
NEVER MIND ME. THE BIGGER PROBLEM IS WHAT TO DO ABOUT THE FIELDS NOW THAT DAD IS GONE.
HE MADE SURE TO WRITE DOWN SOME OF THE MORE IMPORTANT THINGS...
WHOA, HOLD UP. WE'RE TALKING ABOUT YOU RIGHT NOW, GOLEM.
IT'S OKAY. REALLY.
I'VE KNOWN THIS WAS COMING FOR A LONG TIME.

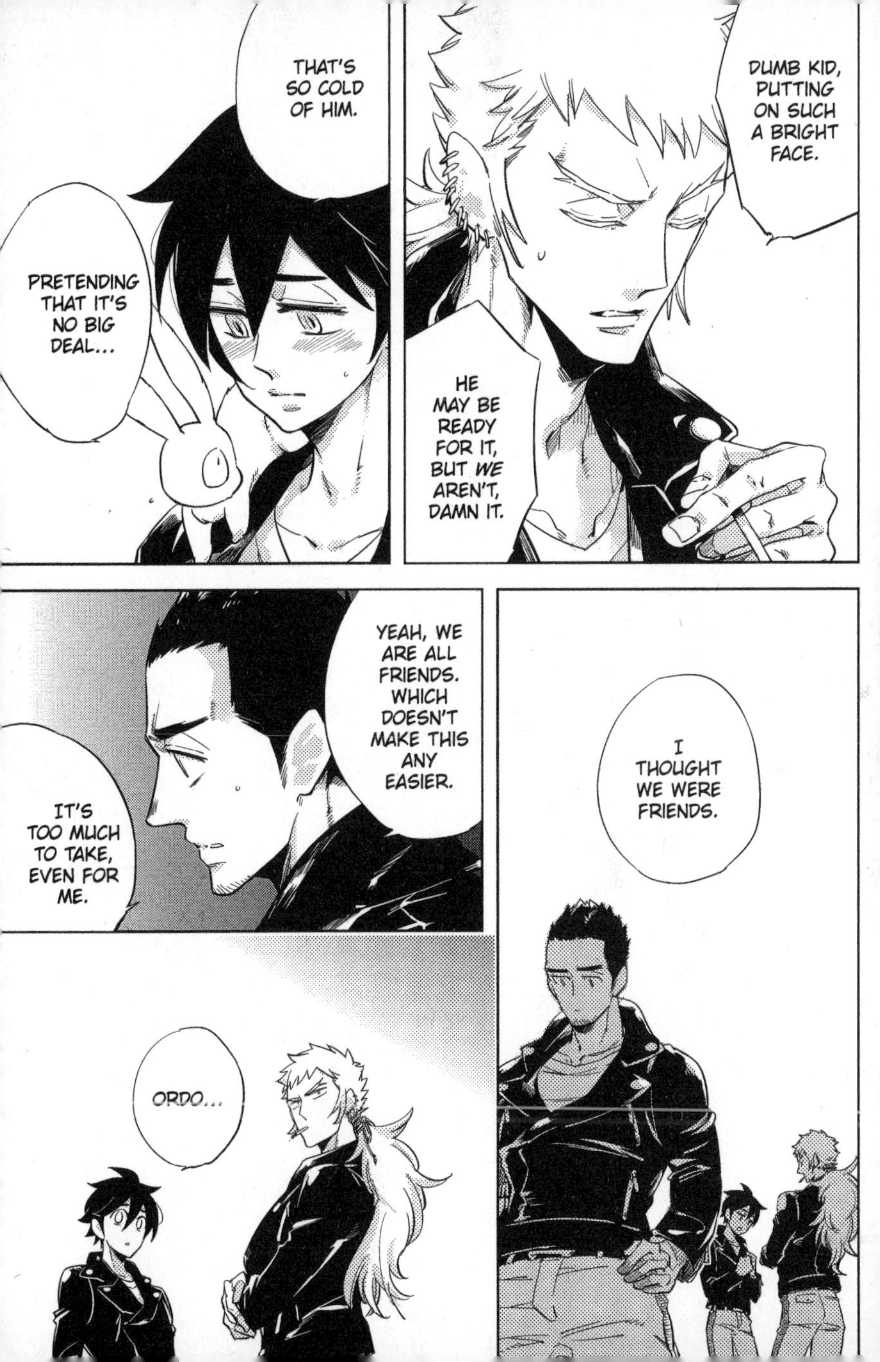
DUMB KID, PUTTING ON SUCH A BRIGHT FACE.
HE MAY BE READY FOR IT, BUT *WE* AREN'T, DAMN IT.
THAT'S SO COLD OF HIM.
PRETENDING THAT IT'S NO BIG DEAL...
I THOUGHT WE WERE FRIENDS.
YEAH, WE ARE ALL FRIENDS. WHICH DOESN'T MAKE THIS ANY EASIER.
IT'S TOO MUCH TO TAKE, EVEN FOR ME.
ORDO...

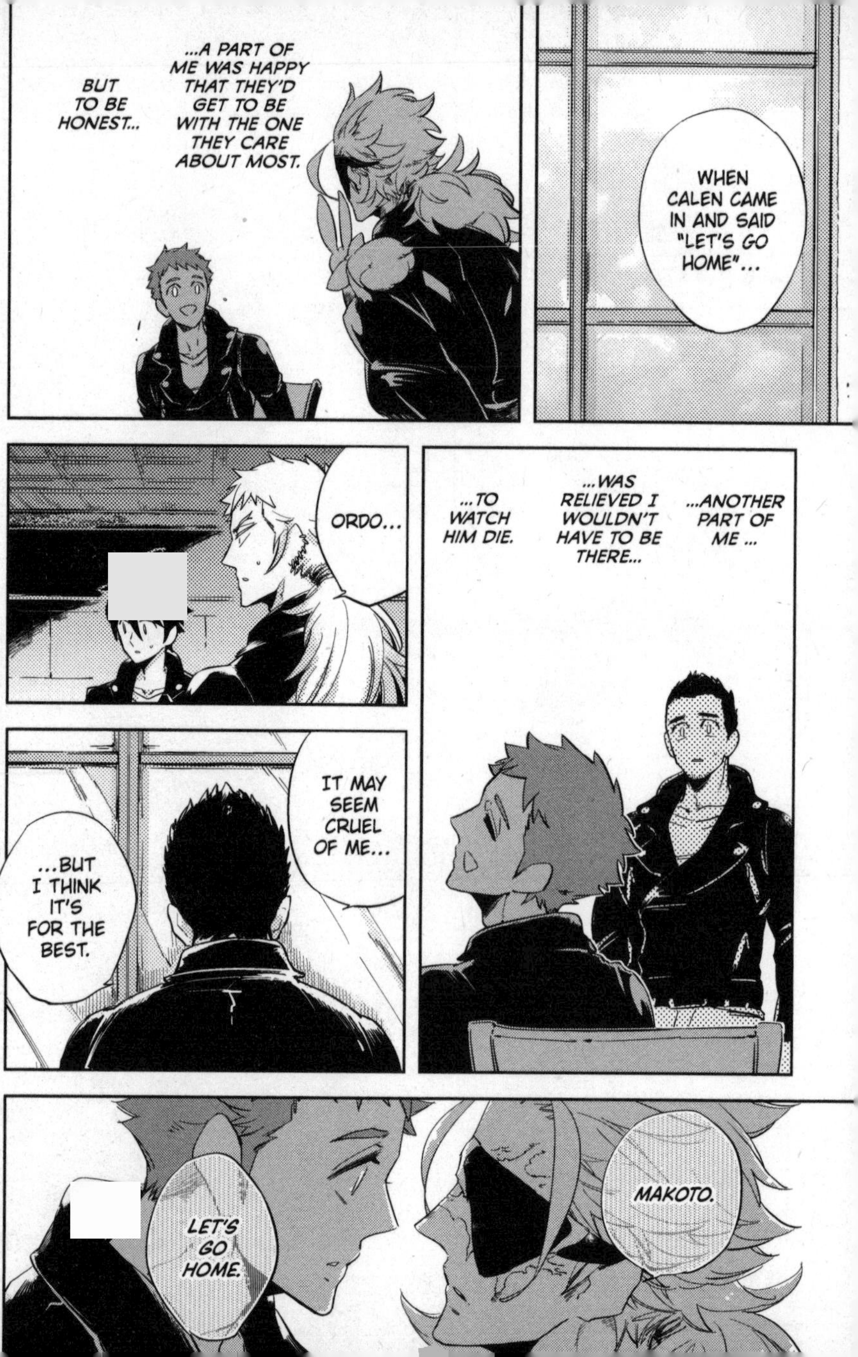
WHEN CALEN CAME IN AND SAID "LET'S GO HOME"...
BUT TO BE HONEST...
...A PART OF ME WAS HAPPY THAT THEY'D GET TO BE WITH THE ONE THEY CARE ABOUT MOST.
...ANOTHER PART OF ME ...
...WAS RELIEVED I WOULDN'T HAVE TO BE THERE...
...TO WATCH HIM DIE.
ORDO...
IT MAY SEEM CRUEL OF ME...
...BUT I THINK IT'S FOR THE BEST.
MAKOTO.
LET'S GO HOME.

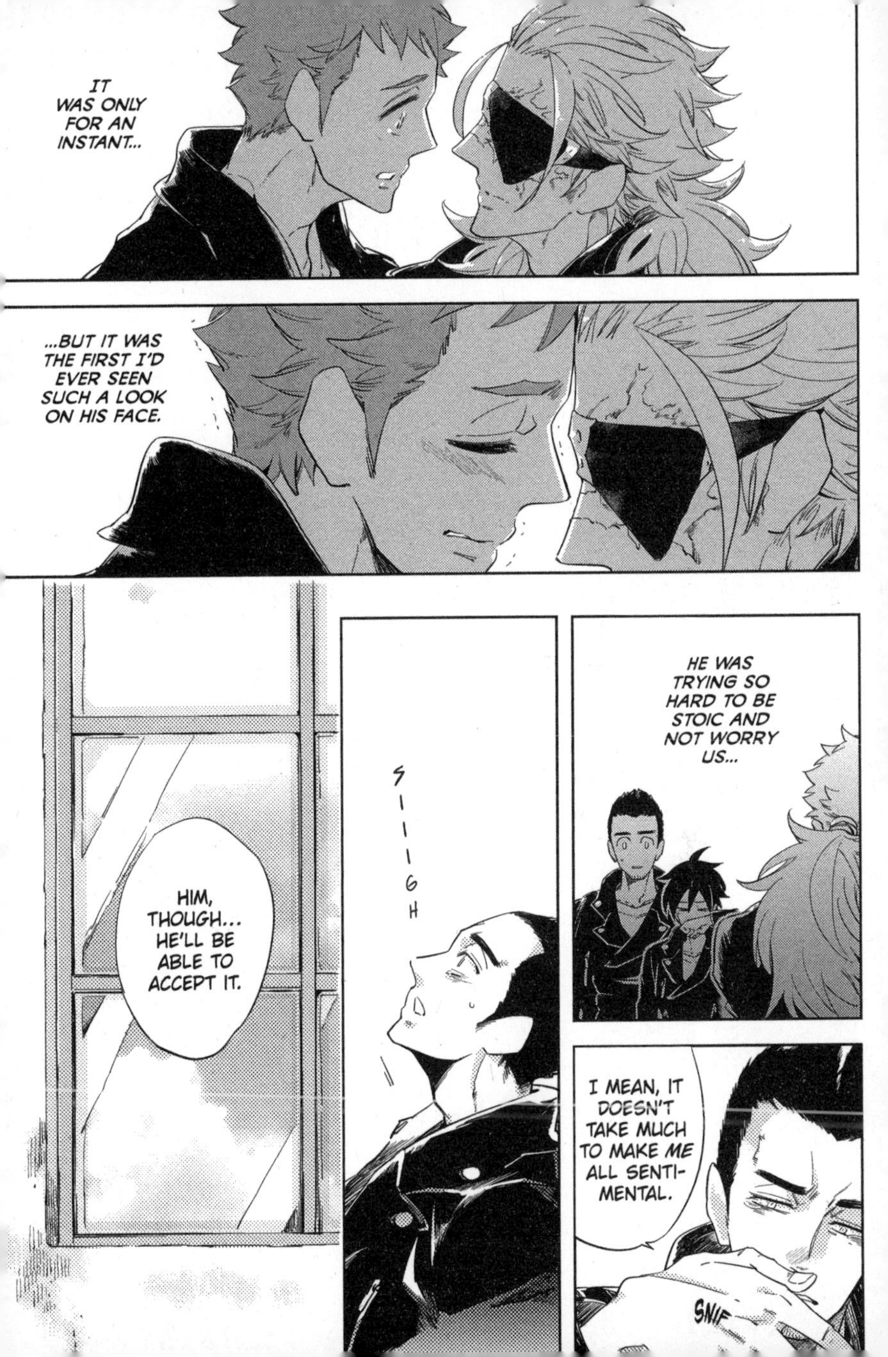
IT WAS ONLY FOR AN INSTANT...
...BUT IT WAS THE FIRST I'D EVER SEEN SUCH A LOOK ON HIS FACE.
HE WAS TRYING SO HARD TO BE STOIC AND NOT WORRY US...
I MEAN, IT DOESN'T TAKE MUCH TO MAKE ME ALL SENTI-MENTAL.
SNIF
SIIIGH
HIM, THOUGH... HE'LL BE ABLE TO ACCEPT IT.

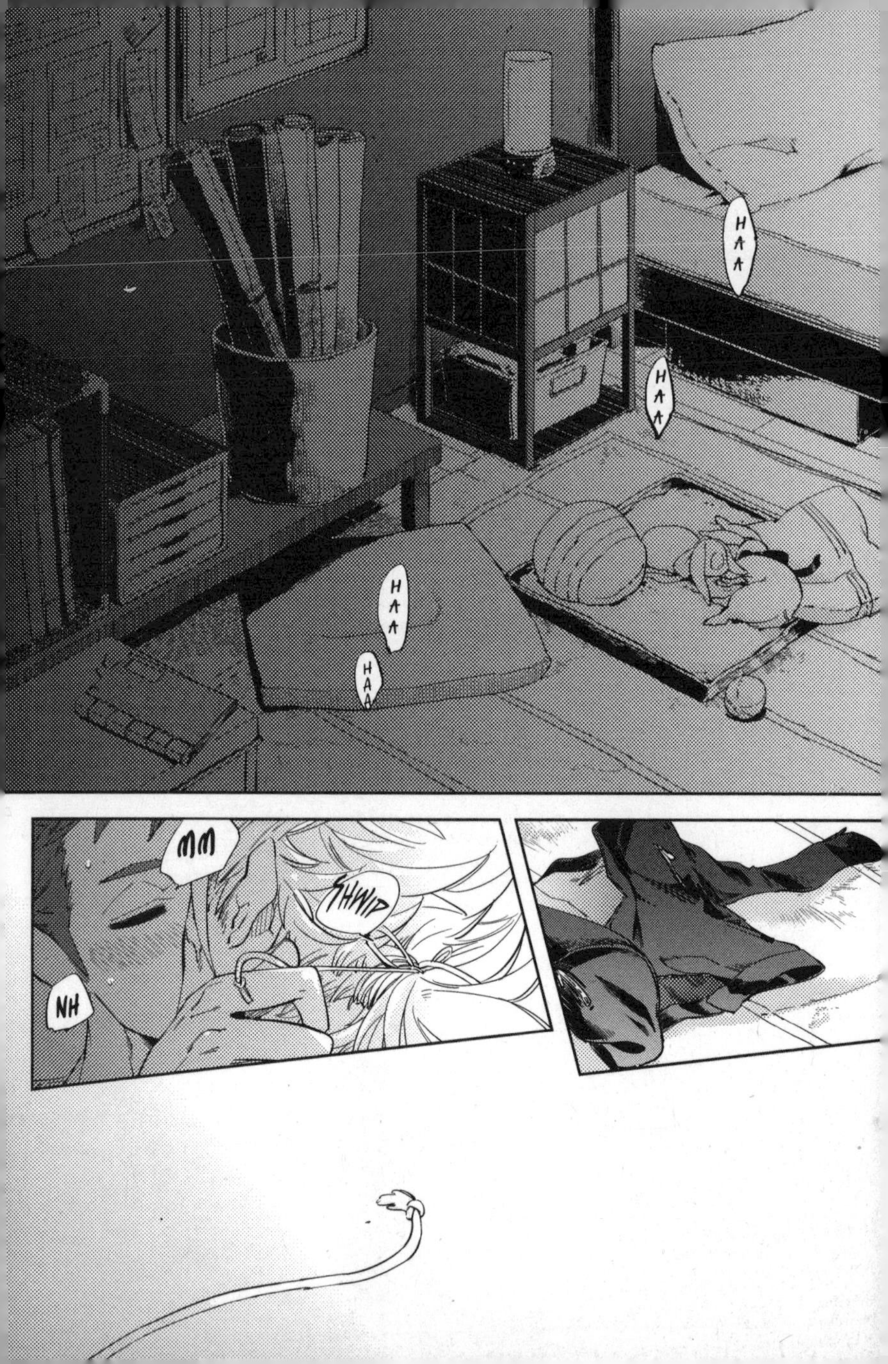
HAA
HAA
HAA
HAA
MM
SHWIP
NH

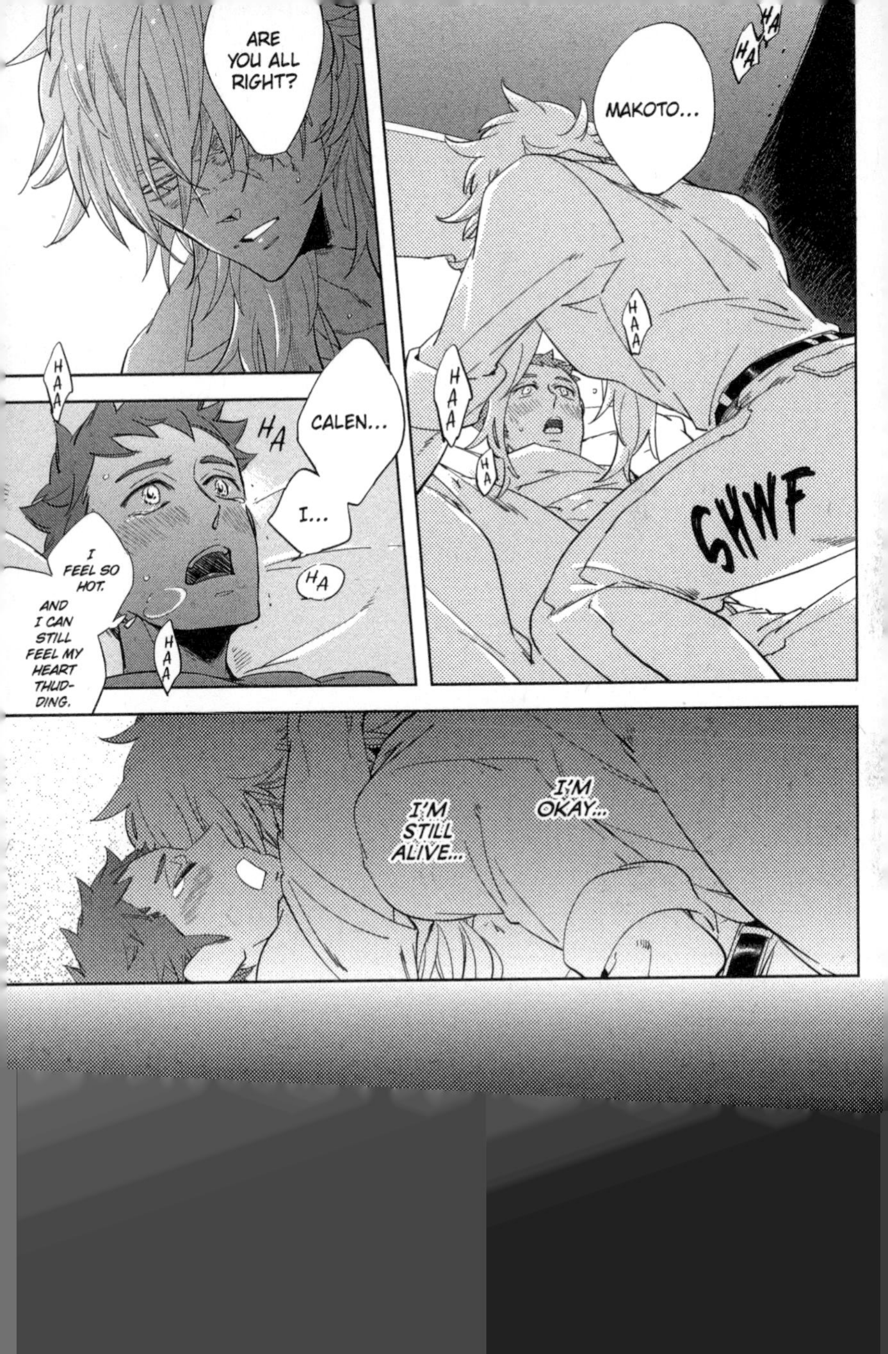
HA HA HA
MAKOTO...
HAA
HAA
HA
SHWF
ARE YOU ALL RIGHT?
HAA
HA
CALEN...
I...
HA
I FEEL SO HOT.
AND I CAN STILL FEEL MY HEART THUD-DING.
HAA
I'M OKAY...
I'M STILL ALIVE...

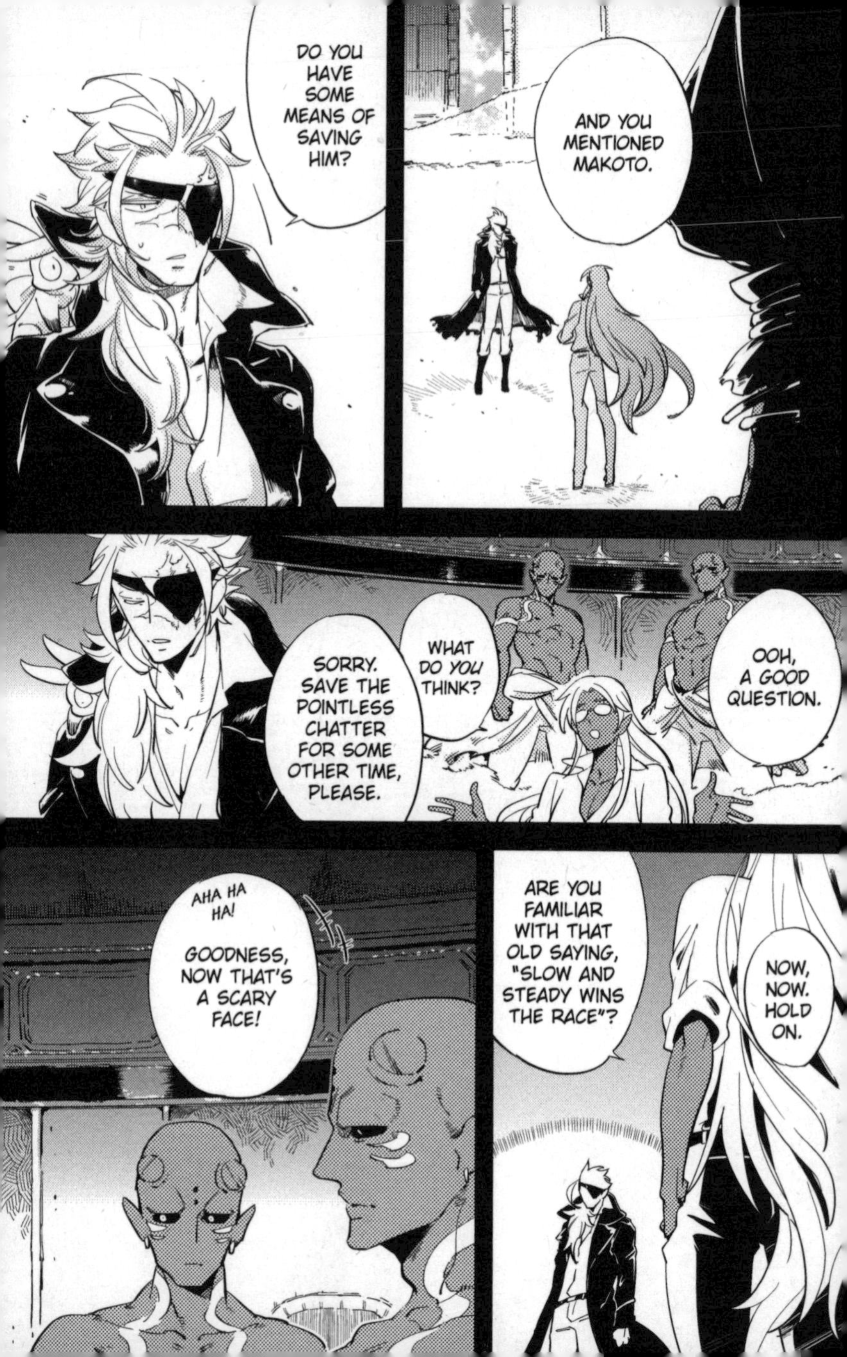
AND YOU MENTIONED MAKOTO.
DO YOU HAVE SOME MEANS OF SAVING HIM?
OOH, A GOOD QUESTION.
WHAT DO YOU THINK?
SORRY. SAVE THE POINTLESS CHATTER FOR SOME OTHER TIME, PLEASE.
NOW, NOW. HOLD ON.
ARE YOU FAMILIAR WITH THAT OLD SAYING, "SLOW AND STEADY WINS THE RACE"?
AHA HA HA!
GOODNESS, NOW THAT'S A SCARY FACE!

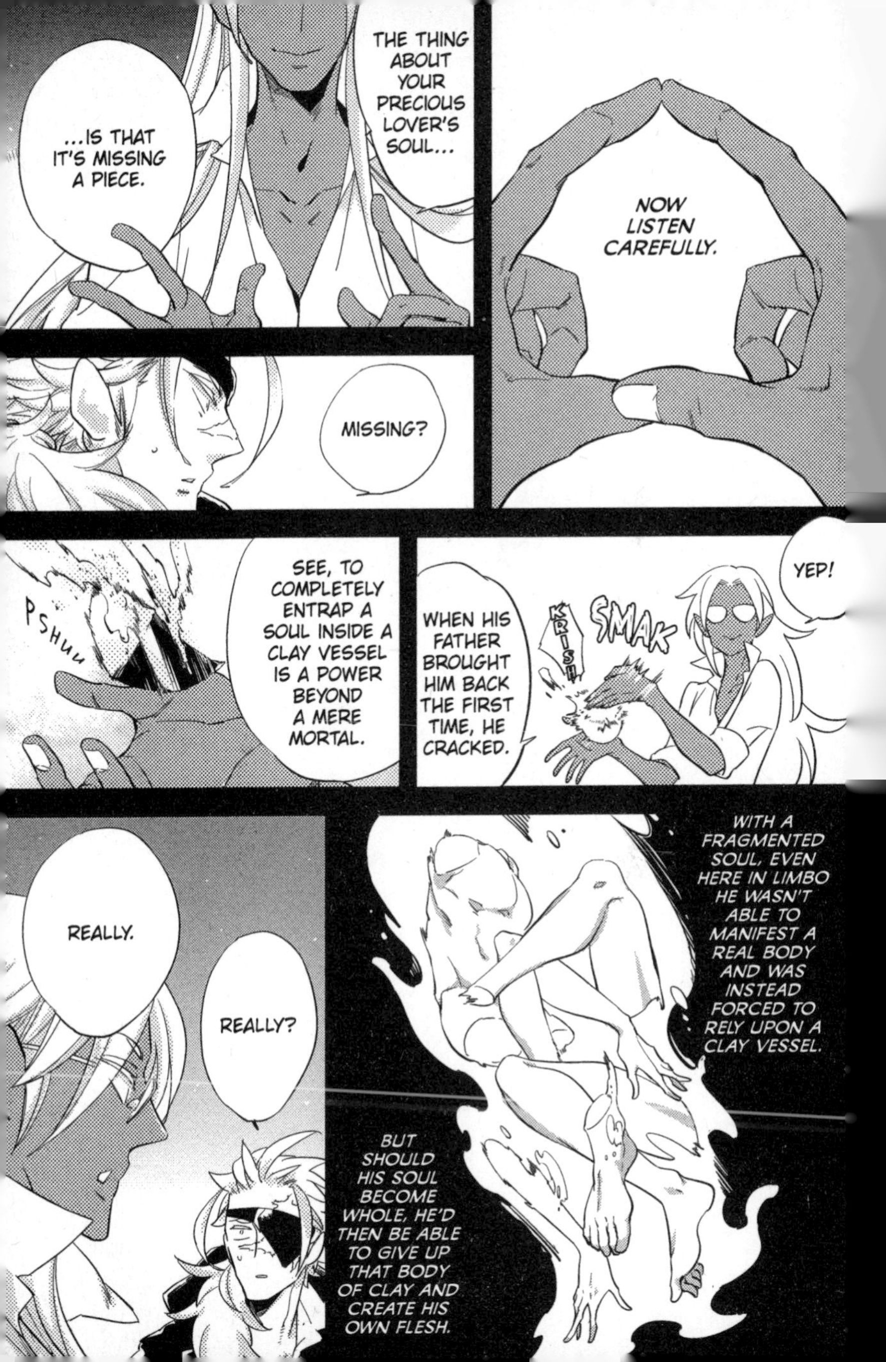
NOW LISTEN CAREFULLY.
THE THING ABOUT YOUR PRECIOUS LOVER'S SOUL...
...IS THAT IT'S MISSING A PIECE.
MISSING?
YEP!
SMAK
KRISH
WHEN HIS FATHER BROUGHT HIM BACK THE FIRST TIME, HE CRACKED.
SEE, TO COMPLETELY ENTRAP A SOUL INSIDE A CLAY VESSEL IS A POWER BEYOND A MERE MORTAL.
PSHUU
WITH A FRAGMENTED SOUL, EVEN HERE IN LIMBO HE WASN'T ABLE TO MANIFEST A REAL BODY AND WAS INSTEAD FORCED TO RELY UPON A CLAY VESSEL.
BUT SHOULD HIS SOUL BECOME WHOLE, HE'D THEN BE ABLE TO GIVE UP THAT BODY OF CLAY AND CREATE HIS OWN FLESH.
REALLY.
REALLY?

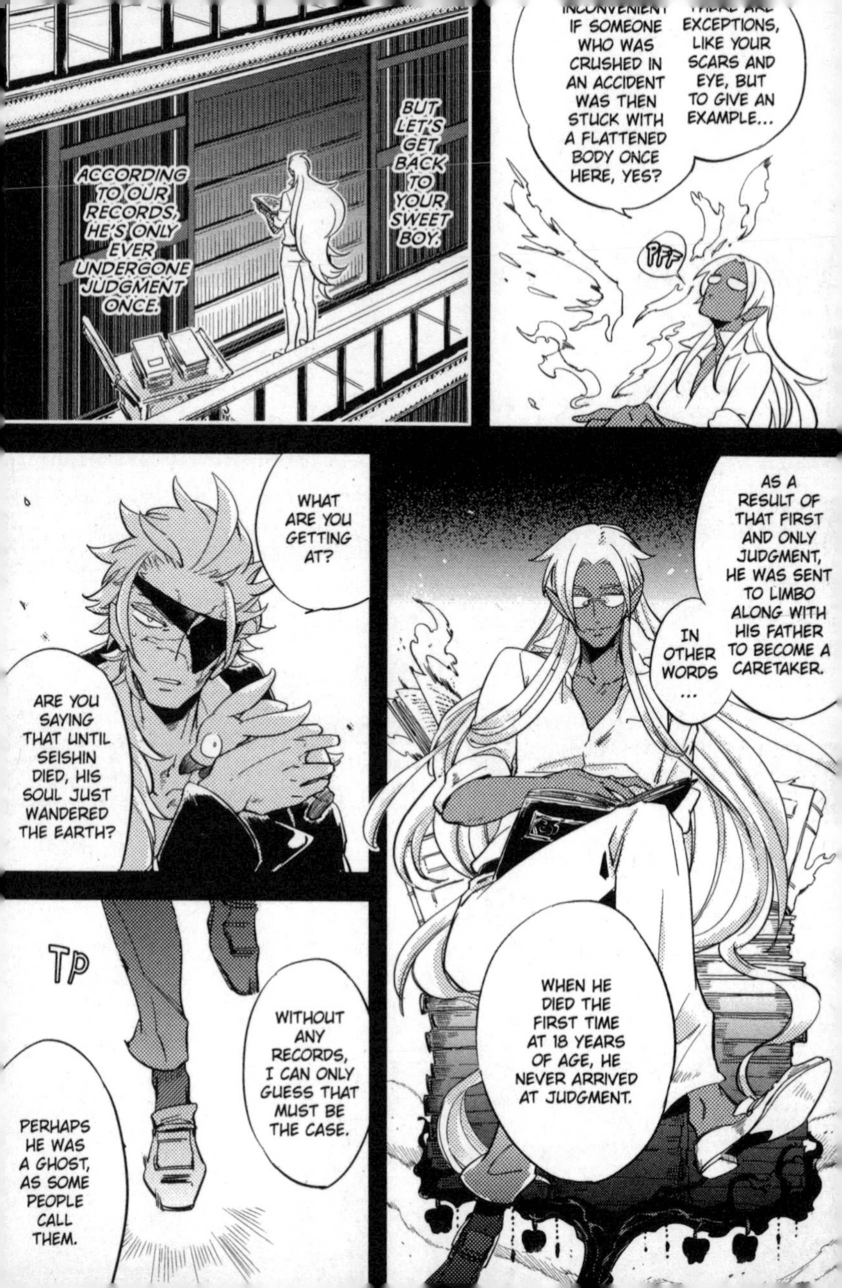
EXCEPTIONS, LIKE YOUR SCARS AND EYE, BUT TO GIVE AN EXAMPLE...
INCONVENIENT IF SOMEONE WHO WAS CRUSHED IN AN ACCIDENT WAS THEN STUCK WITH A FLATTENED BODY ONCE HERE, YES?
PFF
BUT LET'S GET BACK TO YOUR SWEET BOY.
ACCORDING TO OUR RECORDS, HE'S ONLY EVER UNDERGONE JUDGMENT ONCE.
AS A RESULT OF THAT FIRST AND ONLY JUDGMENT, HE WAS SENT TO LIMBO ALONG WITH HIS FATHER TO BECOME A CARETAKER.
IN OTHER WORDS...
WHEN HE DIED THE FIRST TIME AT 18 YEARS OF AGE, HE NEVER ARRIVED AT JUDGMENT.
WHAT ARE YOU GETTING AT?
ARE YOU SAYING THAT UNTIL SEISHIN DIED, HIS SOUL JUST WANDERED THE EARTH?
TP
WITHOUT ANY RECORDS, I CAN ONLY GUESS THAT MUST BE THE CASE.
PERHAPS HE WAS A GHOST, AS SOME PEOPLE CALL THEM.

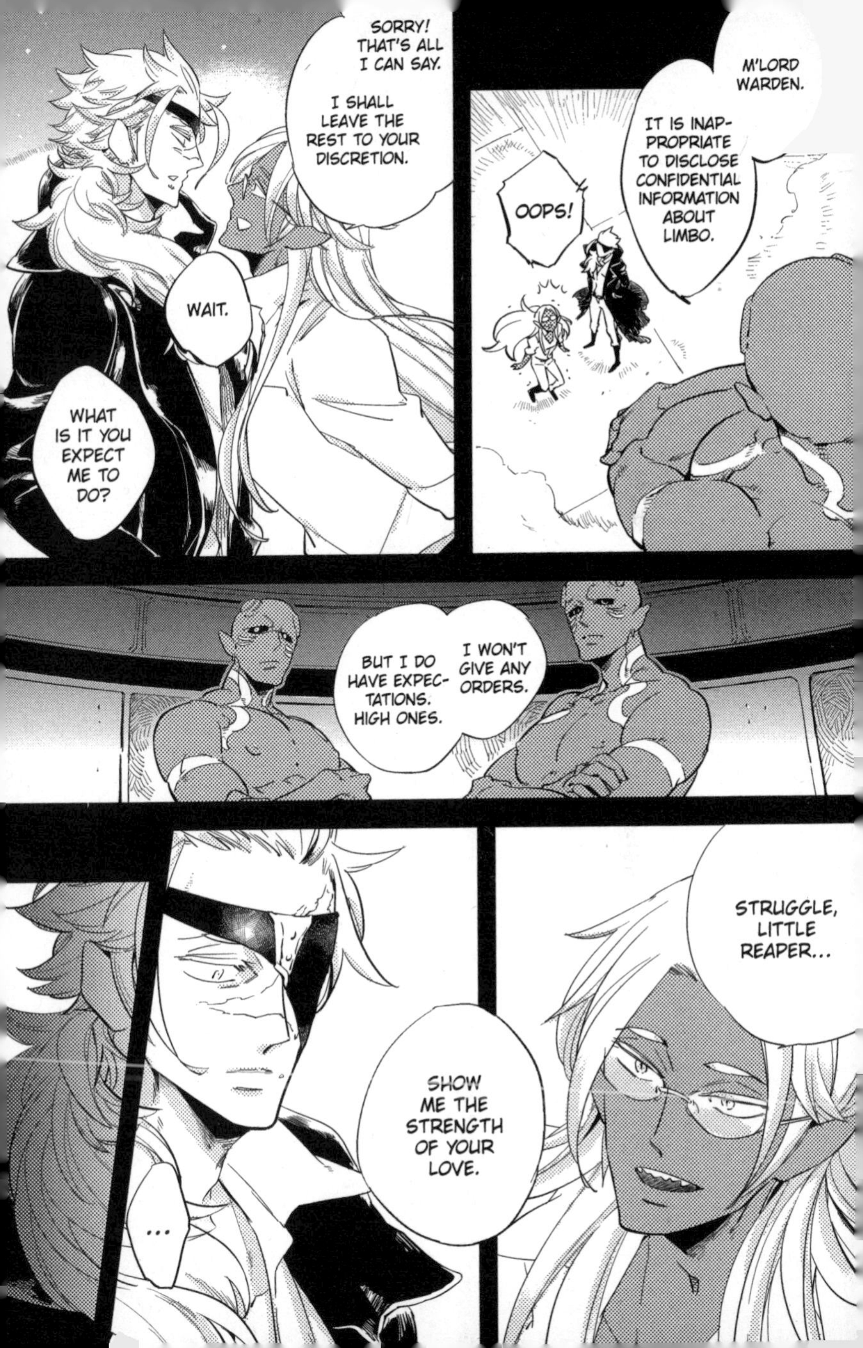
M'LORD WARDEN.
IT IS INAP-PROPRIATE TO DISCLOSE CONFIDENTIAL INFORMATION ABOUT LIMBO.
OOPS!
SORRY! THAT'S ALL I CAN SAY.
I SHALL LEAVE THE REST TO YOUR DISCRETION.
WAIT.
WHAT IS IT YOU EXPECT ME TO DO?
I WON'T GIVE ANY ORDERS.
BUT I DO HAVE EXPECTATIONS. HIGH ONES.
STRUGGLE, LITTLE REAPER...
SHOW ME THE STRENGTH OF YOUR LOVE.
...

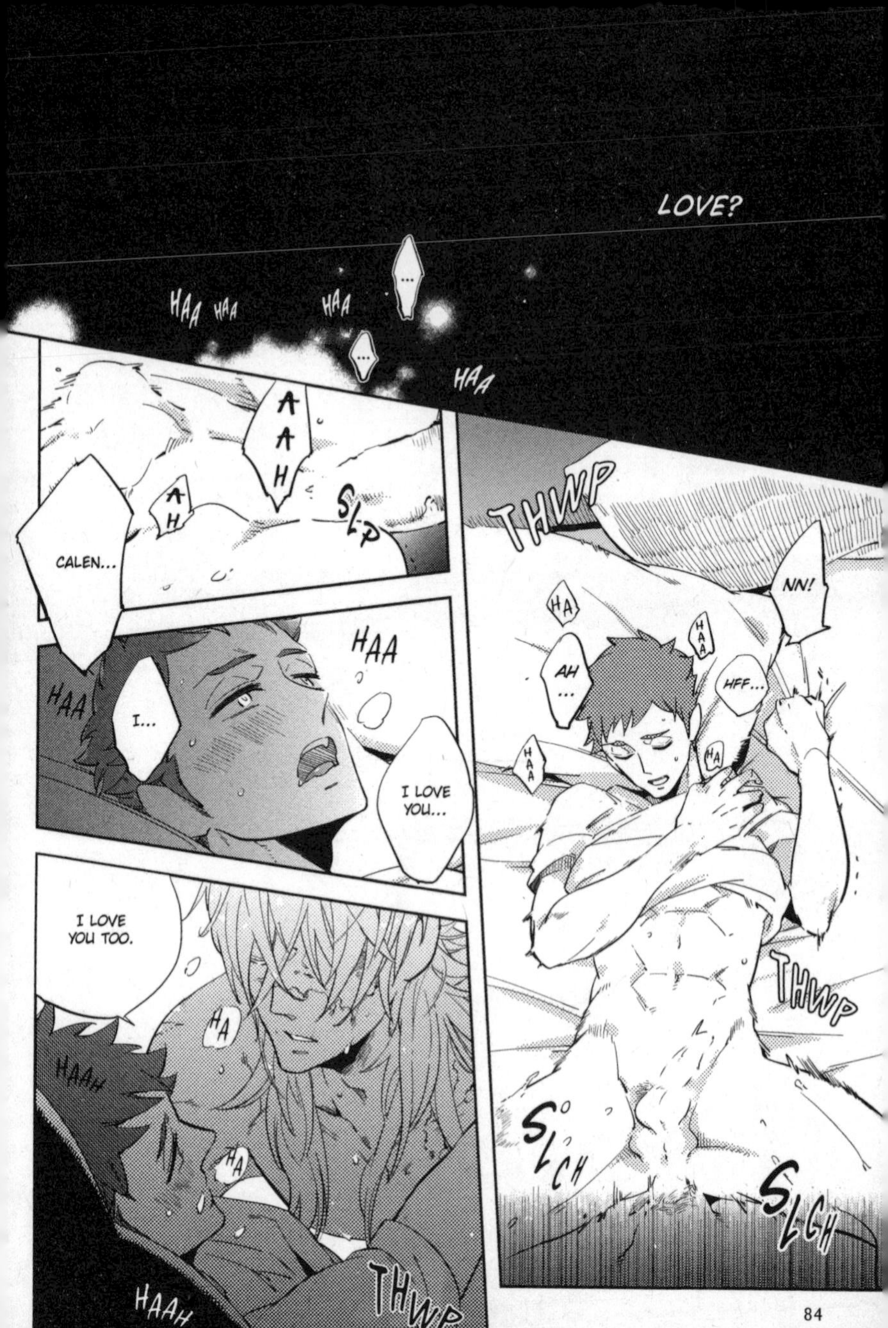
LOVE?
...
...
HAA HAA
HAA
HAA
THWP
NN!
HA
HAA
AH...
HFF...
HAA
HA
THWP
SLCH
SLCH
AAAH
AH
SLP
CALEN...
HAA
I...
HAA
I LOVE YOU...
I LOVE YOU TOO.
HA
HAAH
HA
HAAH
THWP

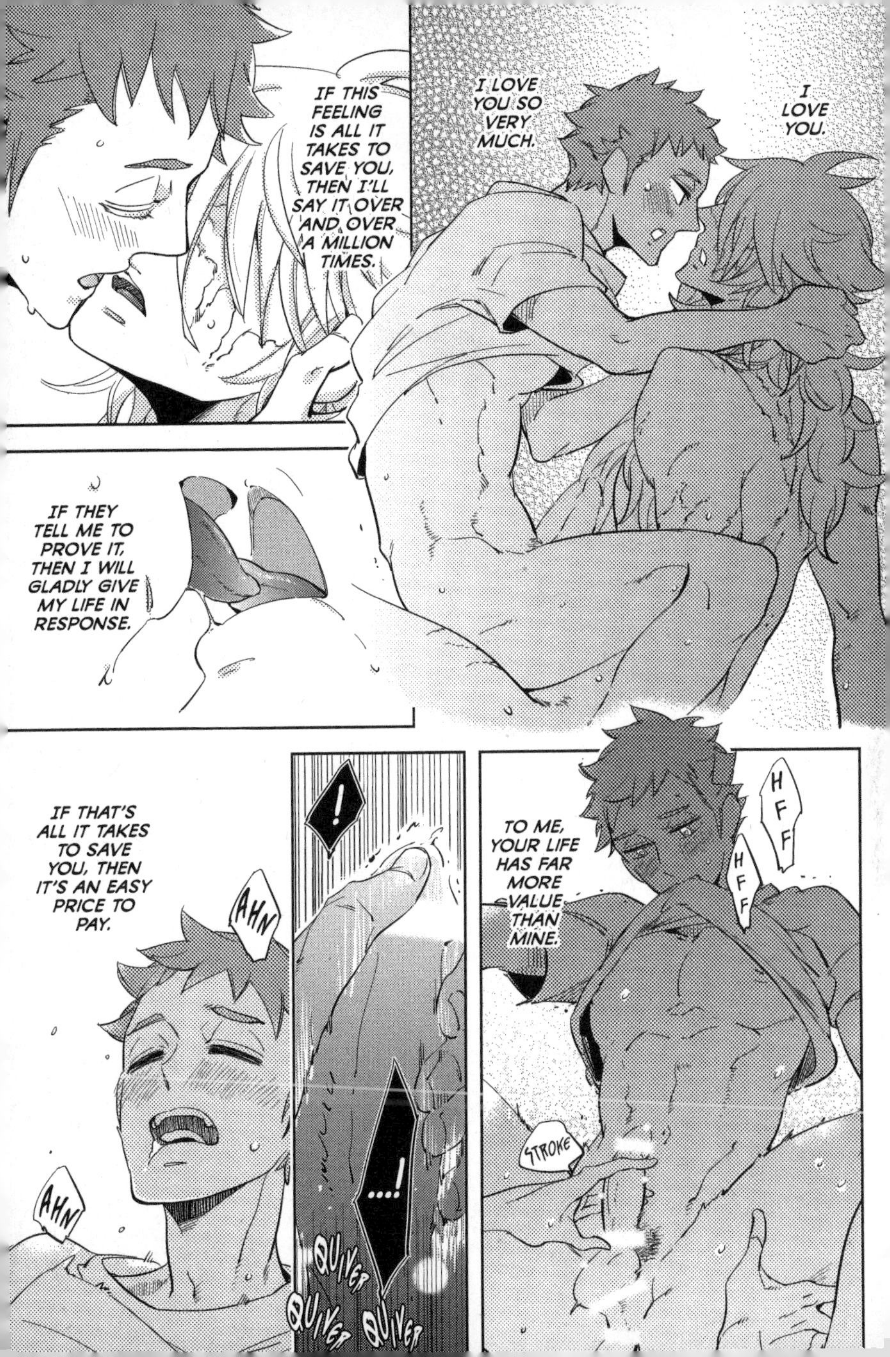

I LOVE YOU.
I LOVE YOU SO VERY MUCH.
IF THIS FEELING IS ALL IT TAKES TO SAVE YOU, THEN I'LL SAY IT OVER AND OVER A MILLION TIMES.
IF THEY TELL ME TO PROVE IT, THEN I WILL GLADLY GIVE MY LIFE IN RESPONSE.
HFF
HFF
TO ME, YOUR LIFE HAS FAR MORE VALUE THAN MINE.
STROKE
!
...!
QUIVER
QUIVER
QUIVER
IF THAT'S ALL IT TAKES TO SAVE YOU, THEN IT'S AN EASY PRICE TO PAY.
AHN
AHN

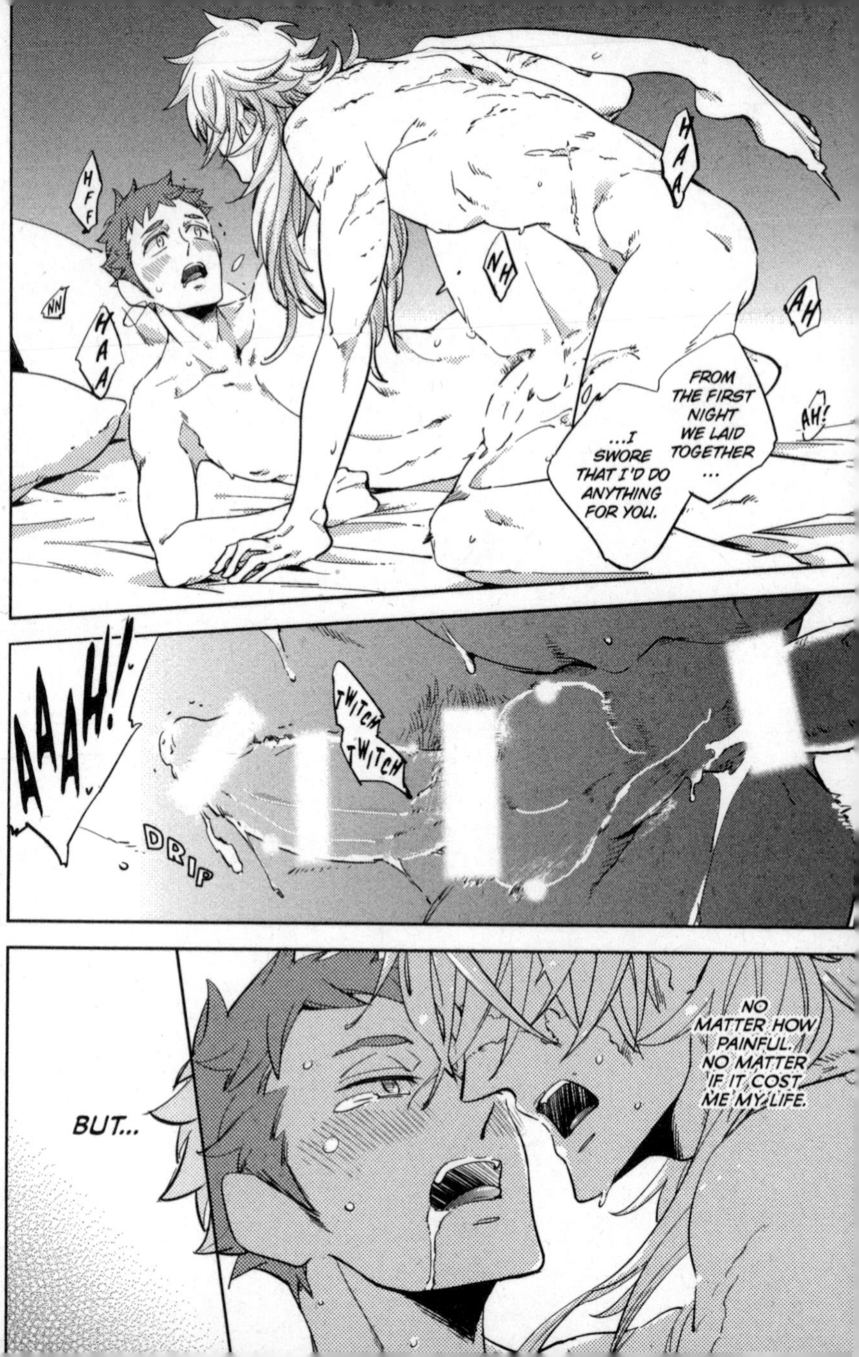
HAA
AH
FROM THE FIRST NIGHT WE LAID TOGETHER ...
AH!
NH
...I SWORE THAT I'D DO ANYTHING FOR YOU.
HFF
NN
HAA
TWITCH TWITCH
AAAH!
DRIP
NO MATTER HOW PAINFUL. NO MATTER IF IT COST ME MY LIFE.
BUT...

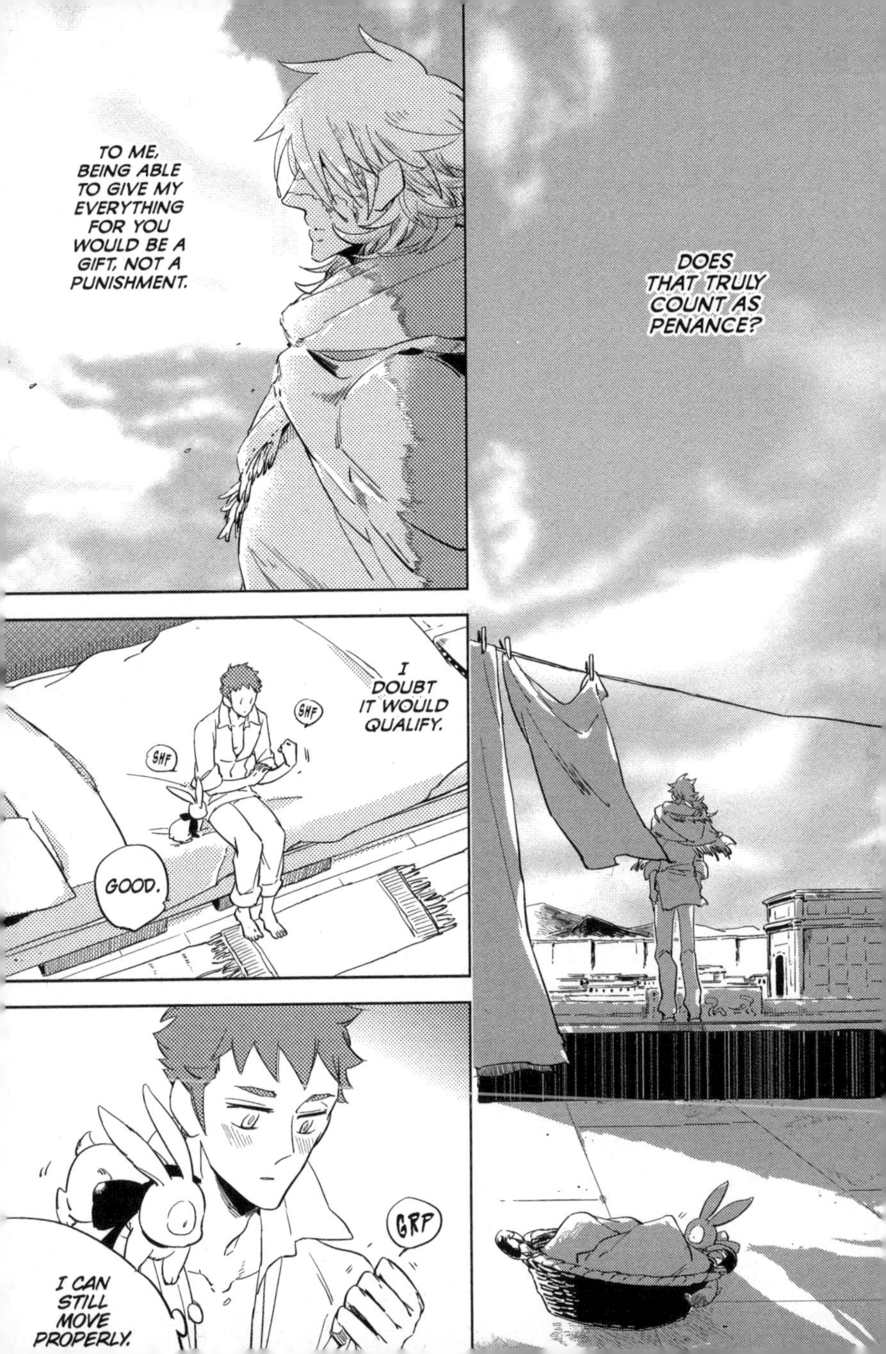
DOES THAT TRULY COUNT AS PENANCE?
TO ME, BEING ABLE TO GIVE MY EVERYTHING FOR YOU WOULD BE A GIFT, NOT A PUNISHMENT.
I DOUBT IT WOULD QUALIFY.
SHF
SHF
GOOD.
GRP
I CAN STILL MOVE PROPERLY.

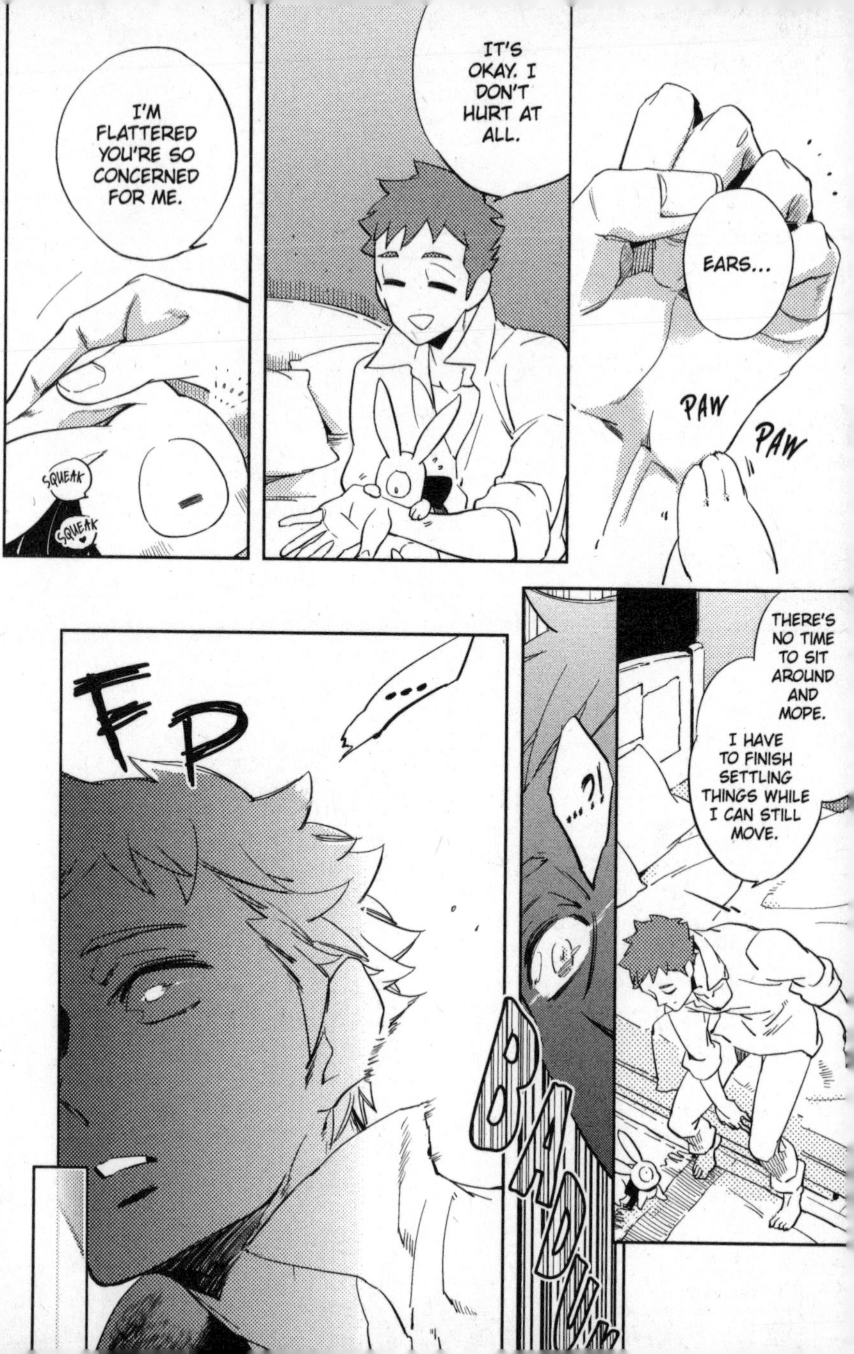
EARS...
PAW
PAW
IT'S OKAY. I DON'T HURT AT ALL.
I'M FLATTERED YOU'RE SO CONCERNED FOR ME.
SQUEAK
SQUEAK
THERE'S NO TIME TO SIT AROUND AND MOPE.
I HAVE TO FINISH SETTLING THINGS WHILE I CAN STILL MOVE.
...?!
FP
...

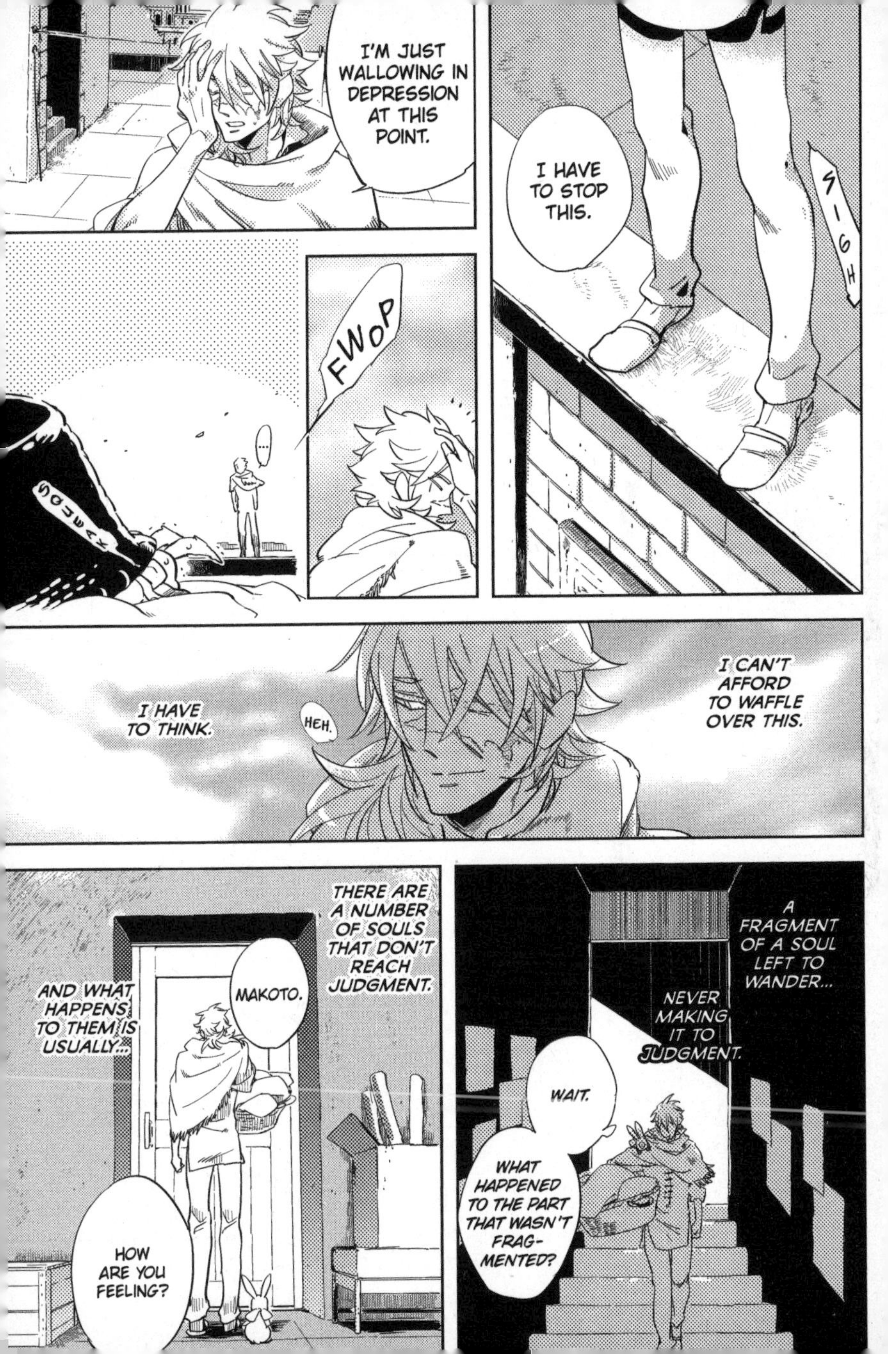
I HAVE TO STOP THIS.
SIGH
I'M JUST WALLOWING IN DEPRESSION AT THIS POINT.
FWOP
...
I CAN'T AFFORD TO WAFFLE OVER THIS.
HEH.
I HAVE TO THINK.
A FRAGMENT OF A SOUL LEFT TO WANDER...
NEVER MAKING IT TO JUDGMENT.
WAIT.
WHAT HAPPENED TO THE PART THAT WASN'T FRAG-MENTED?
THERE ARE A NUMBER OF SOULS THAT DON'T REACH JUDGMENT.
MAKOTO.
AND WHAT HAPPENS TO THEM IS USUALLY...
HOW ARE YOU FEELING?

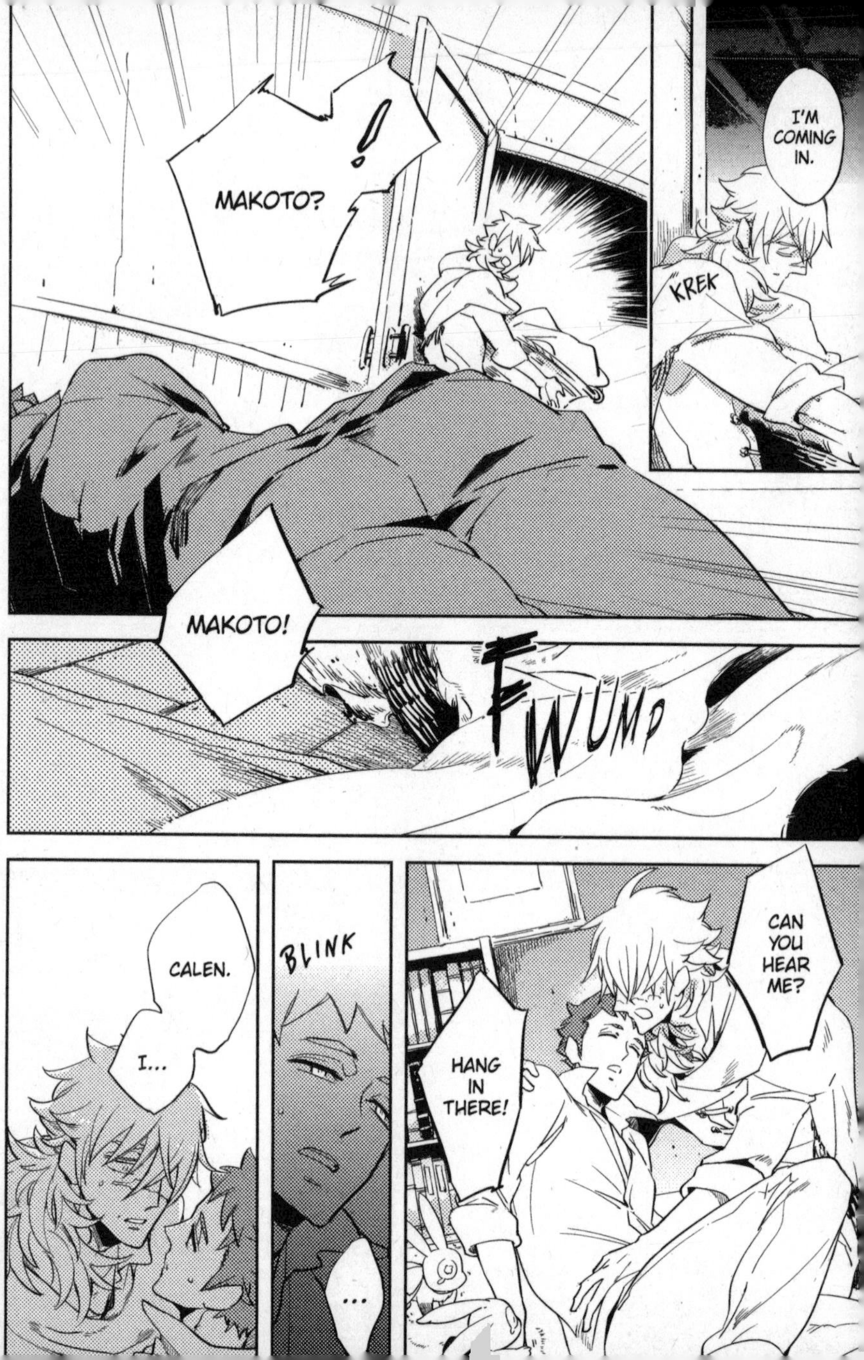
I'M COMING IN.
KREK
!
MAKOTO?
MAKOTO!
FWUMP
CAN YOU HEAR ME?
HANG IN THERE!
BLINK
...
CALEN.
I...

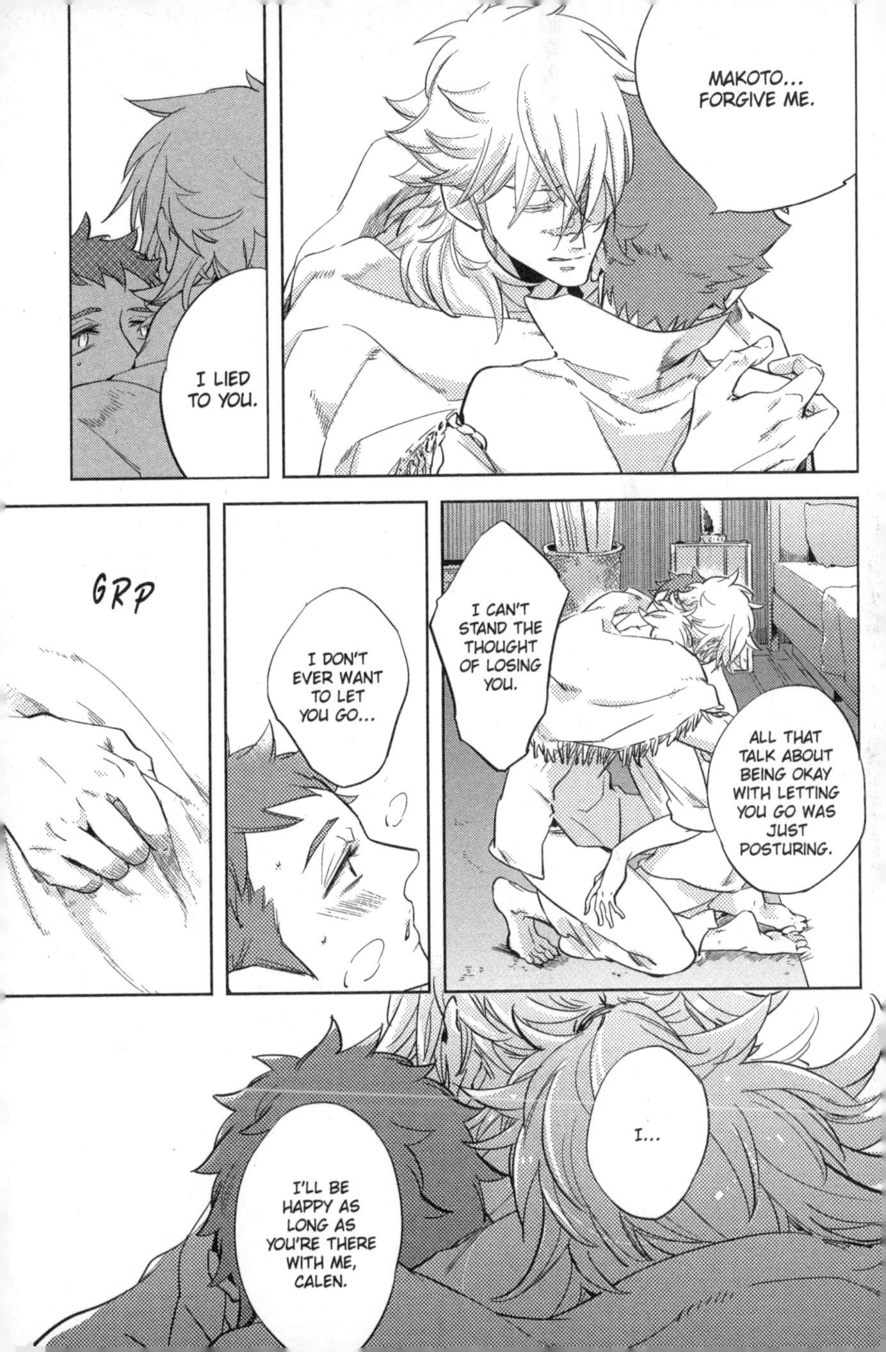
MAKOTO... FORGIVE ME.
I LIED TO YOU.
ALL THAT TALK ABOUT BEING OKAY WITH LETTING YOU GO WAS JUST POSTURING.
I CAN'T STAND THE THOUGHT OF LOSING YOU.
I DON'T EVER WANT TO LET YOU GO...
GRP
I...
I'LL BE HAPPY AS LONG AS YOU'RE THERE WITH ME, CALEN.

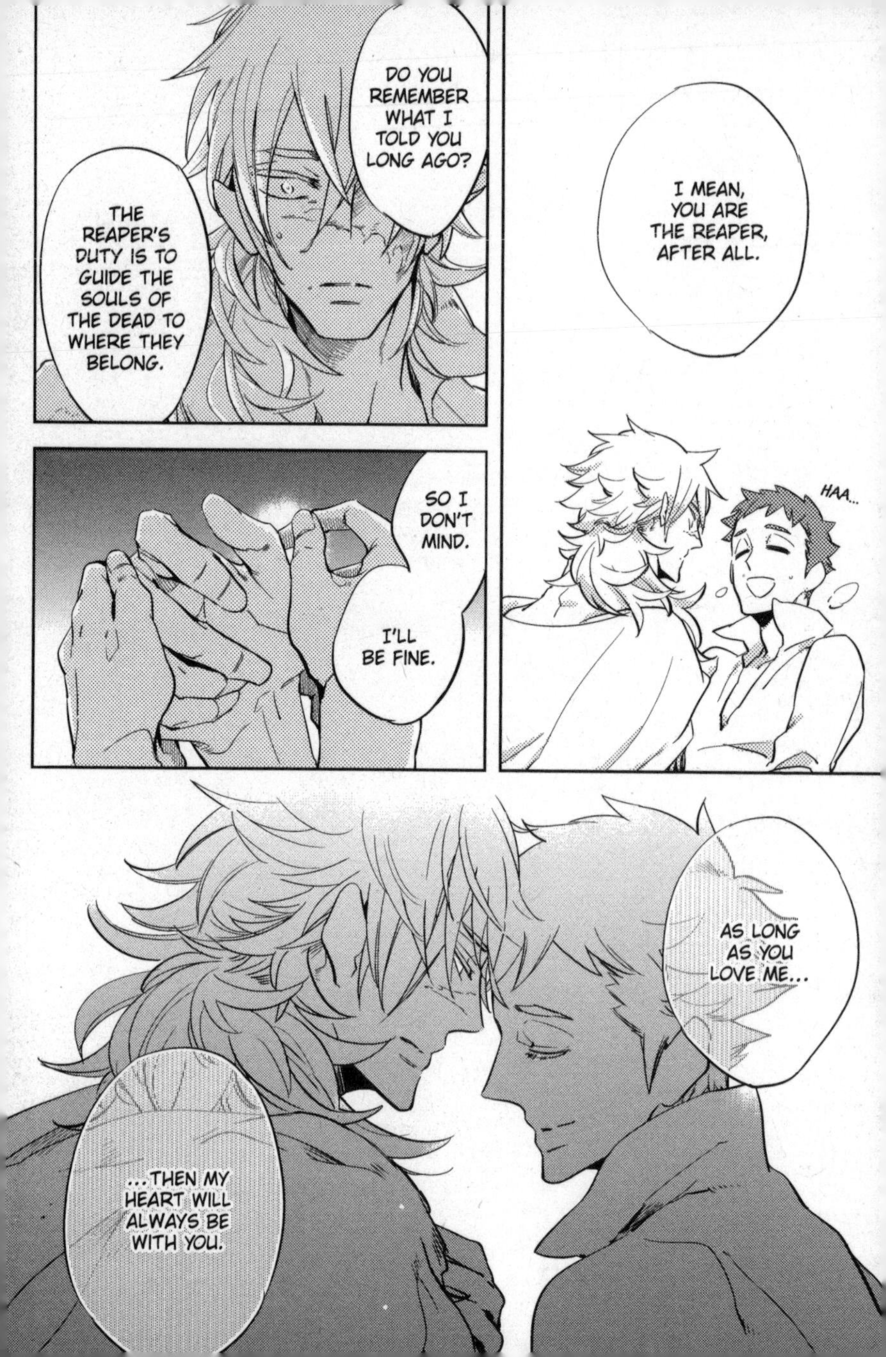
I MEAN, YOU ARE THE REAPER, AFTER ALL.
DO YOU REMEMBER WHAT I TOLD YOU LONG AGO?
THE REAPER'S DUTY IS TO GUIDE THE SOULS OF THE DEAD TO WHERE THEY BELONG.
HAA...
SO I DON'T MIND.
I'LL BE FINE.
AS LONG AS YOU LOVE ME...
...THEN MY HEART WILL ALWAYS BE WITH YOU.

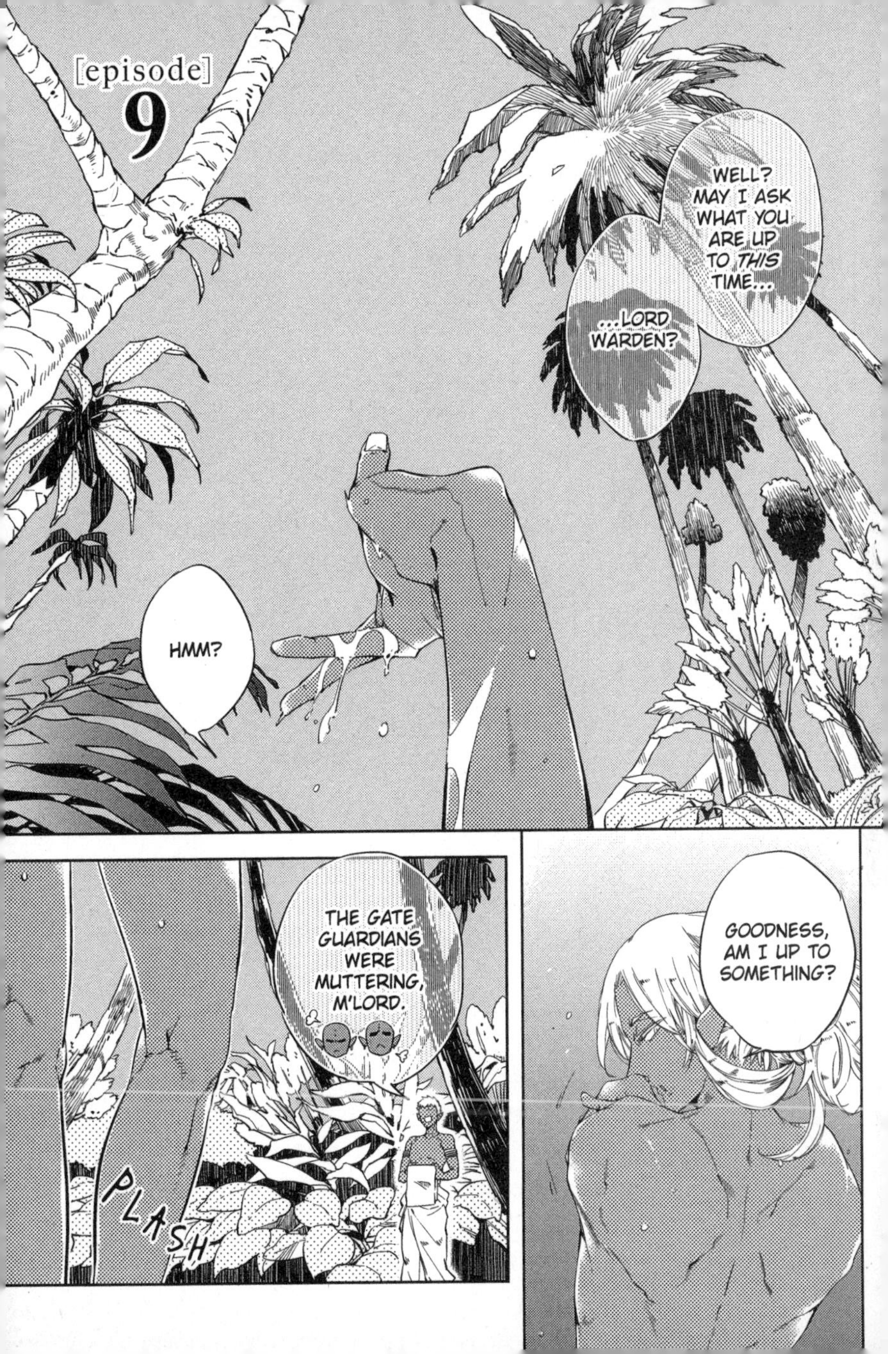
[episode] 9
WELL? MAY I ASK WHAT YOU ARE UP TO THIS TIME...
...LORD WARDEN?
HMM?
GOODNESS, AM I UP TO SOMETHING?
THE GATE GUARDIANS WERE MUTTERING, M'LORD.
PLASH

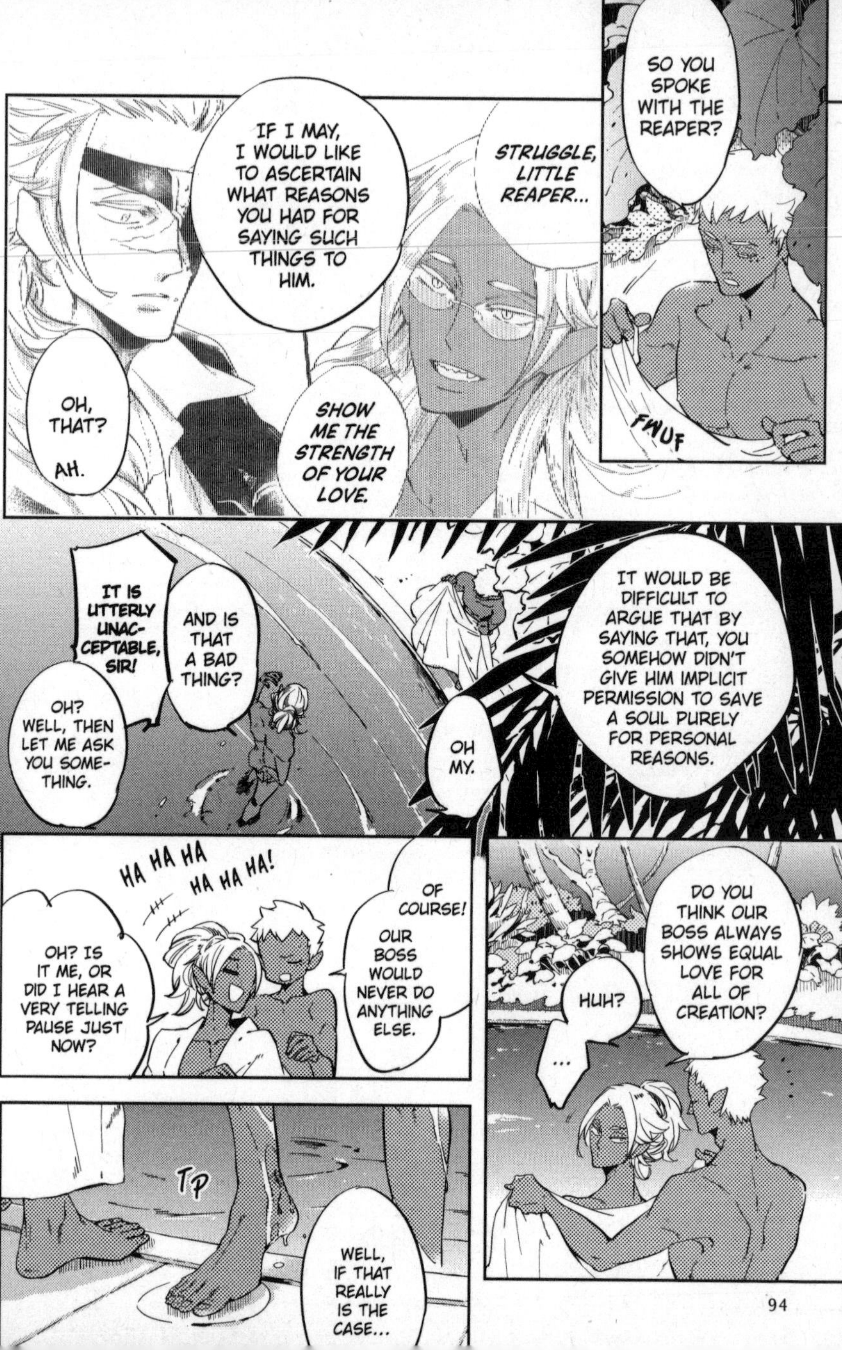
SO YOU SPOKE WITH THE REAPER?
FWUF
STRUGGLE, LITTLE REAPER...
IF I MAY, I WOULD LIKE TO ASCERTAIN WHAT REASONS YOU HAD FOR SAYING SUCH THINGS TO HIM.
SHOW ME THE STRENGTH OF YOUR LOVE.
OH, THAT?
AH.
IT WOULD BE DIFFICULT TO ARGUE THAT BY SAYING THAT, YOU SOMEHOW DIDN'T GIVE HIM IMPLICIT PERMISSION TO SAVE A SOUL PURELY FOR PERSONAL REASONS.
OH MY.
...
AND IS THAT A BAD THING?
IT IS UTTERLY UNACCEPTABLE, SIR!
OH? WELL, THEN LET ME ASK YOU SOMETHING.
DO YOU THINK OUR BOSS ALWAYS SHOWS EQUAL LOVE FOR ALL OF CREATION?
HUH?
...
OF COURSE!
OUR BOSS WOULD NEVER DO ANYTHING ELSE.
HA HA HA
HA HA HA!
OH? IS IT ME, OR DID I HEAR A VERY TELLING PAUSE JUST NOW?
TP
WELL, IF THAT REALLY IS THE CASE...

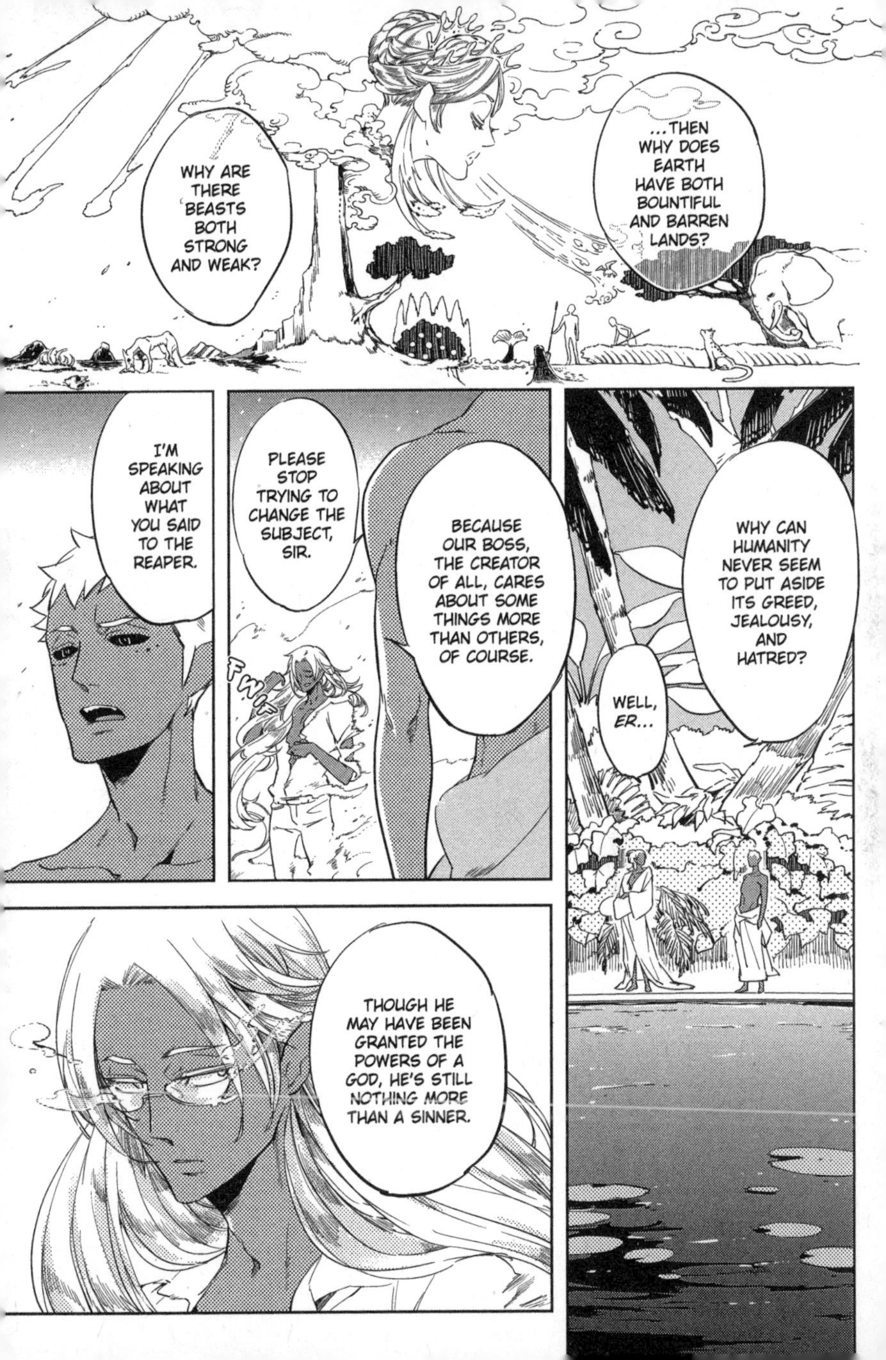
...THEN WHY DOES EARTH HAVE BOTH BOUNTIFUL AND BARREN LANDS?
WHY ARE THERE BEASTS BOTH STRONG AND WEAK?
WHY CAN HUMANITY NEVER SEEM TO PUT ASIDE ITS GREED, JEALOUSY, AND HATRED?
WELL, ER...
BECAUSE OUR BOSS, THE CREATOR OF ALL, CARES ABOUT SOME THINGS MORE THAN OTHERS, OF COURSE.
PLEASE STOP TRYING TO CHANGE THE SUBJECT, SIR.
FWIF
I'M SPEAKING ABOUT WHAT YOU SAID TO THE REAPER.
THOUGH HE MAY HAVE BEEN GRANTED THE POWERS OF A GOD, HE'S STILL NOTHING MORE THAN A SINNER.

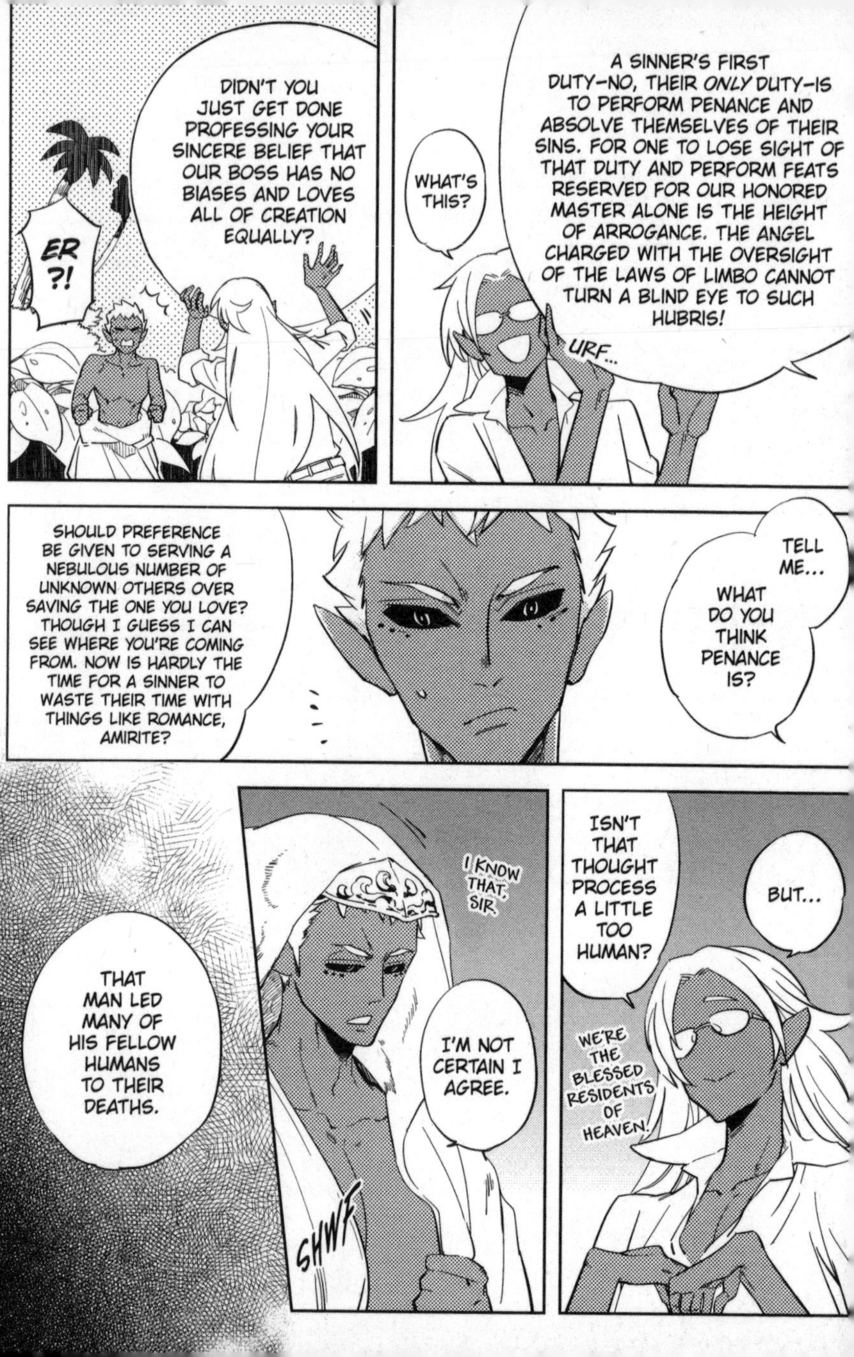
A SINNER'S FIRST DUTY—NO, THEIR *ONLY* DUTY—IS TO PERFORM PENANCE AND ABSOLVE THEMSELVES OF THEIR SINS. FOR ONE TO LOSE SIGHT OF THAT DUTY AND PERFORM FEATS RESERVED FOR OUR HONORED MASTER ALONE IS THE HEIGHT OF ARROGANCE. THE ANGEL CHARGED WITH THE OVERSIGHT OF THE LAWS OF LIMBO CANNOT TURN A BLIND EYE TO SUCH HUBRIS!
WHAT'S THIS?
URF...
DIDN'T YOU JUST GET DONE PROFESSING YOUR SINCERE BELIEF THAT OUR BOSS HAS NO BIASES AND LOVES ALL OF CREATION EQUALLY?
ER ?!
TELL ME...
WHAT DO YOU THINK PENANCE IS?
SHOULD PREFERENCE BE GIVEN TO SERVING A NEBULOUS NUMBER OF UNKNOWN OTHERS OVER SAVING THE ONE YOU LOVE? THOUGH I GUESS I CAN SEE WHERE YOU'RE COMING FROM. NOW IS HARDLY THE TIME FOR A SINNER TO WASTE THEIR TIME WITH THINGS LIKE ROMANCE, AMIRITE?
BUT...
ISN'T THAT THOUGHT PROCESS A LITTLE TOO HUMAN?
WE'RE THE BLESSED RESIDENTS OF HEAVEN.
I KNOW THAT, SIR.
THAT MAN LED MANY OF HIS FELLOW HUMANS TO THEIR DEATHS.
I'M NOT CERTAIN I AGREE.
SHWF

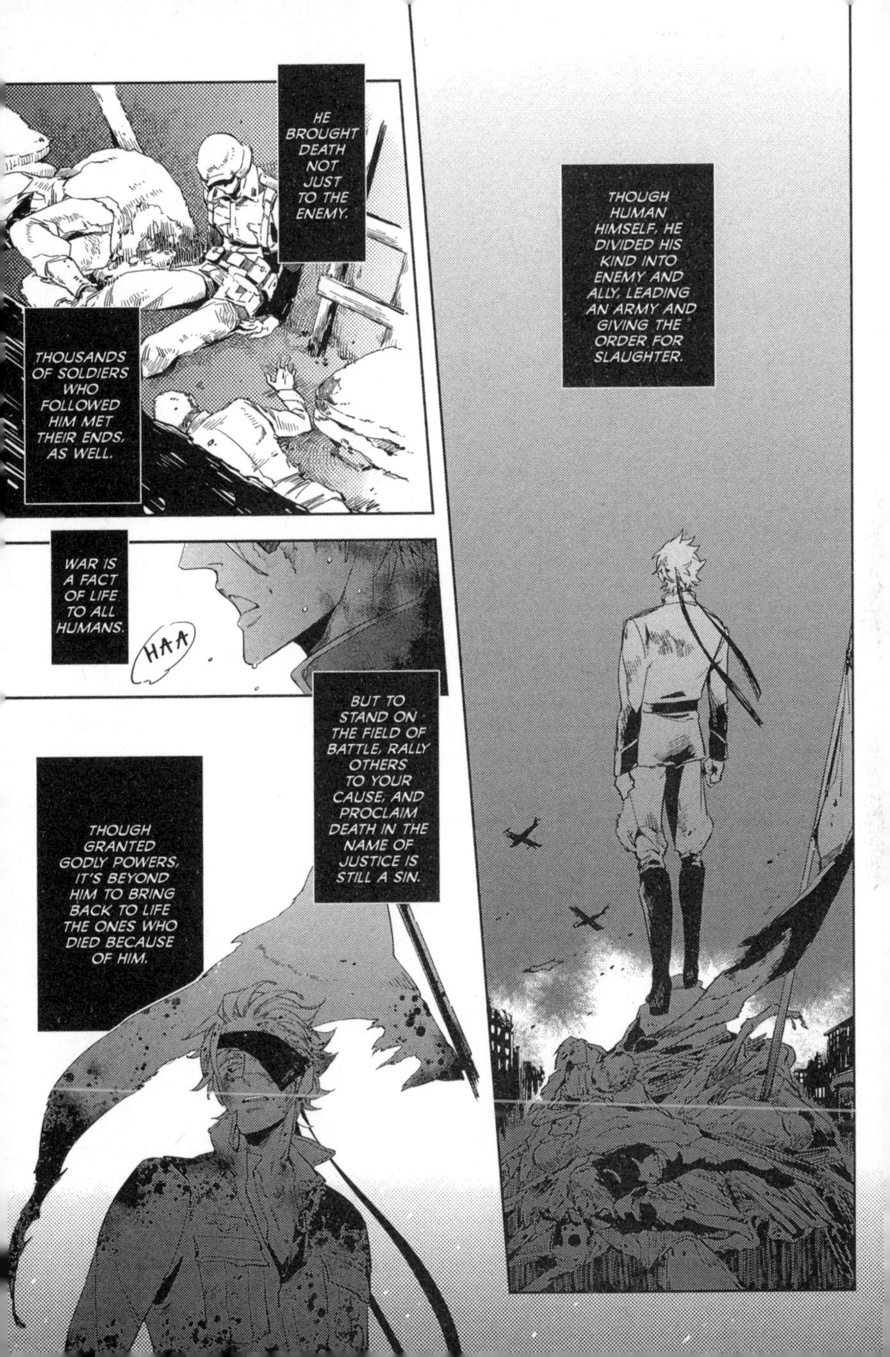
THOUGH HUMAN HIMSELF, HE DIVIDED HIS KIND INTO ENEMY AND ALLY, LEADING AN ARMY AND GIVING THE ORDER FOR SLAUGHTER.
HE BROUGHT DEATH NOT JUST TO THE ENEMY.
THOUSANDS OF SOLDIERS WHO FOLLOWED HIM MET THEIR ENDS, AS WELL.
WAR IS A FACT OF LIFE TO ALL HUMANS.
HAA
BUT TO STAND ON THE FIELD OF BATTLE, RALLY OTHERS TO YOUR CAUSE, AND PROCLAIM DEATH IN THE NAME OF JUSTICE IS STILL A SIN.
THOUGH GRANTED GODLY POWERS, IT'S BEYOND HIM TO BRING BACK TO LIFE THE ONES WHO DIED BECAUSE OF HIM.

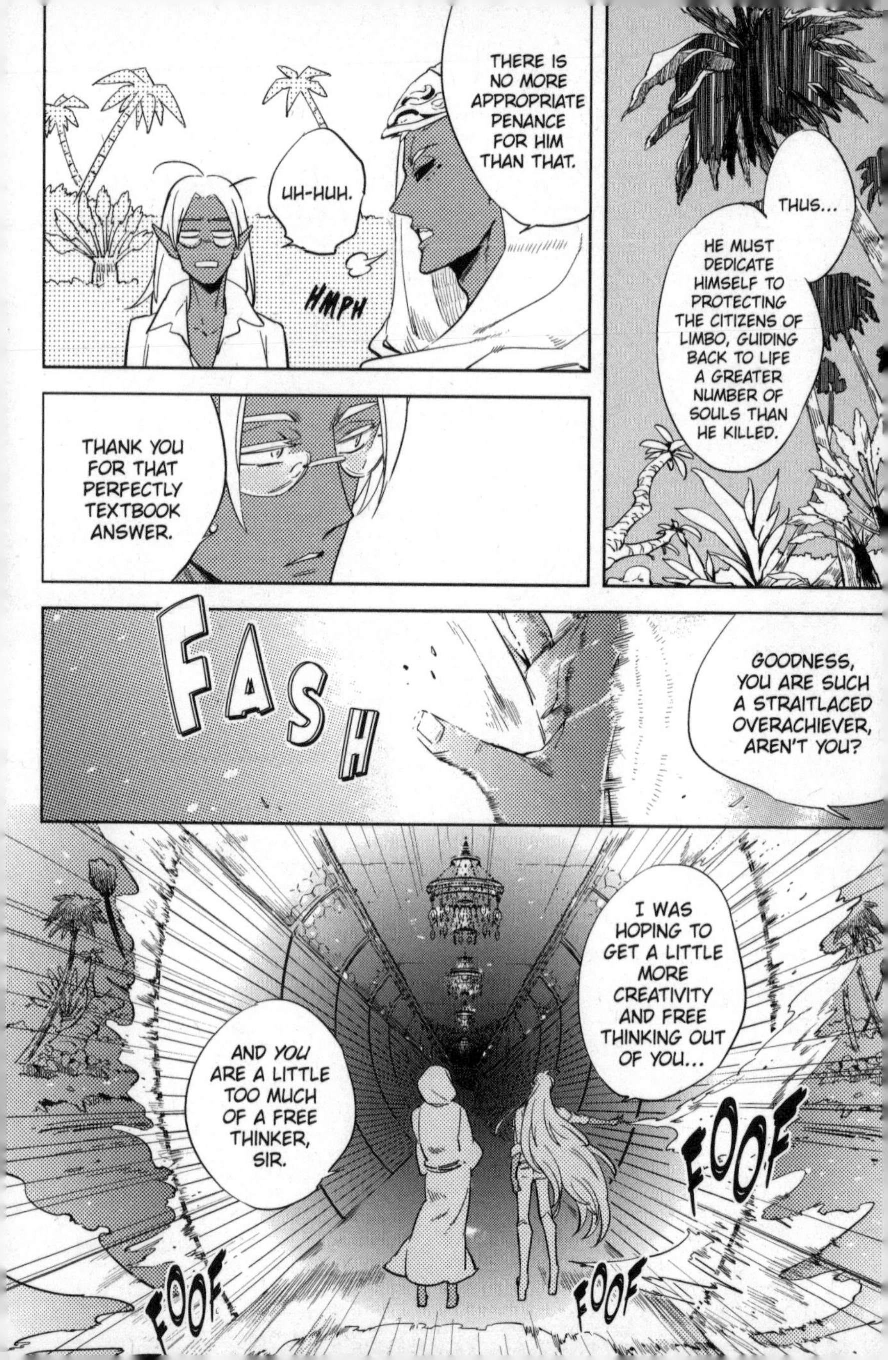
THUS...
HE MUST DEDICATE HIMSELF TO PROTECTING THE CITIZENS OF LIMBO, GUIDING BACK TO LIFE A GREATER NUMBER OF SOULS THAN HE KILLED.
THERE IS NO MORE APPROPRIATE PENANCE FOR HIM THAN THAT.
UH-HUH.
HMPH
THANK YOU FOR THAT PERFECTLY TEXTBOOK ANSWER.
GOODNESS, YOU ARE SUCH A STRAITLACED OVERACHIEVER, AREN'T YOU?
FASH
I WAS HOPING TO GET A LITTLE MORE CREATIVITY AND FREE THINKING OUT OF YOU...
FOOF
AND *YOU* ARE A LITTLE TOO MUCH OF A FREE THINKER, SIR.
FOOF
FOOF

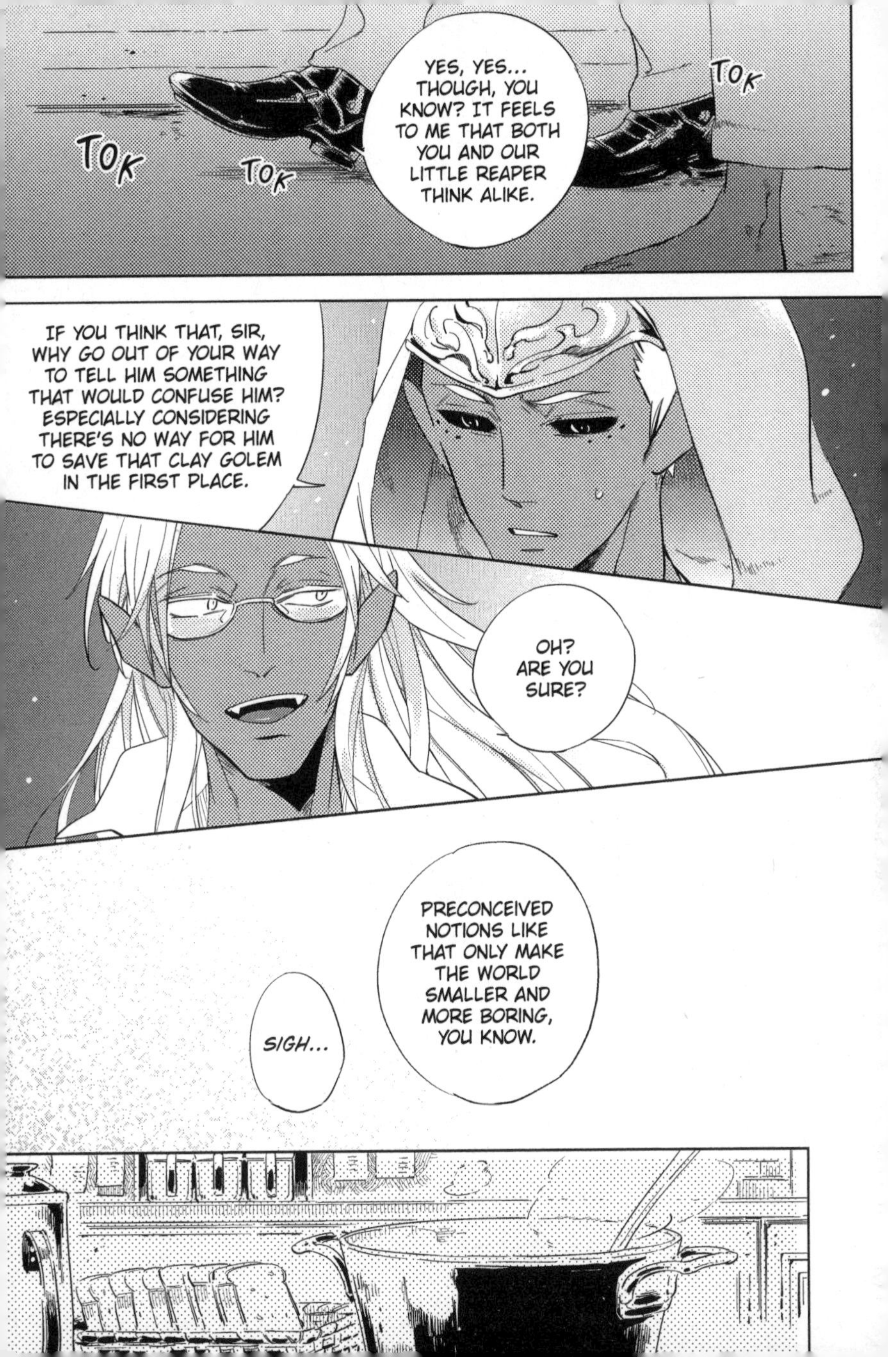
TOK
YES, YES... THOUGH, YOU KNOW? IT FEELS TO ME THAT BOTH YOU AND OUR LITTLE REAPER THINK ALIKE.
TOK
TOK
IF YOU THINK THAT, SIR, WHY GO OUT OF YOUR WAY TO TELL HIM SOMETHING THAT WOULD CONFUSE HIM? ESPECIALLY CONSIDERING THERE'S NO WAY FOR HIM TO SAVE THAT CLAY GOLEM IN THE FIRST PLACE.
OH? ARE YOU SURE?
PRECONCEIVED NOTIONS LIKE THAT ONLY MAKE THE WORLD SMALLER AND MORE BORING, YOU KNOW.
SIGH...

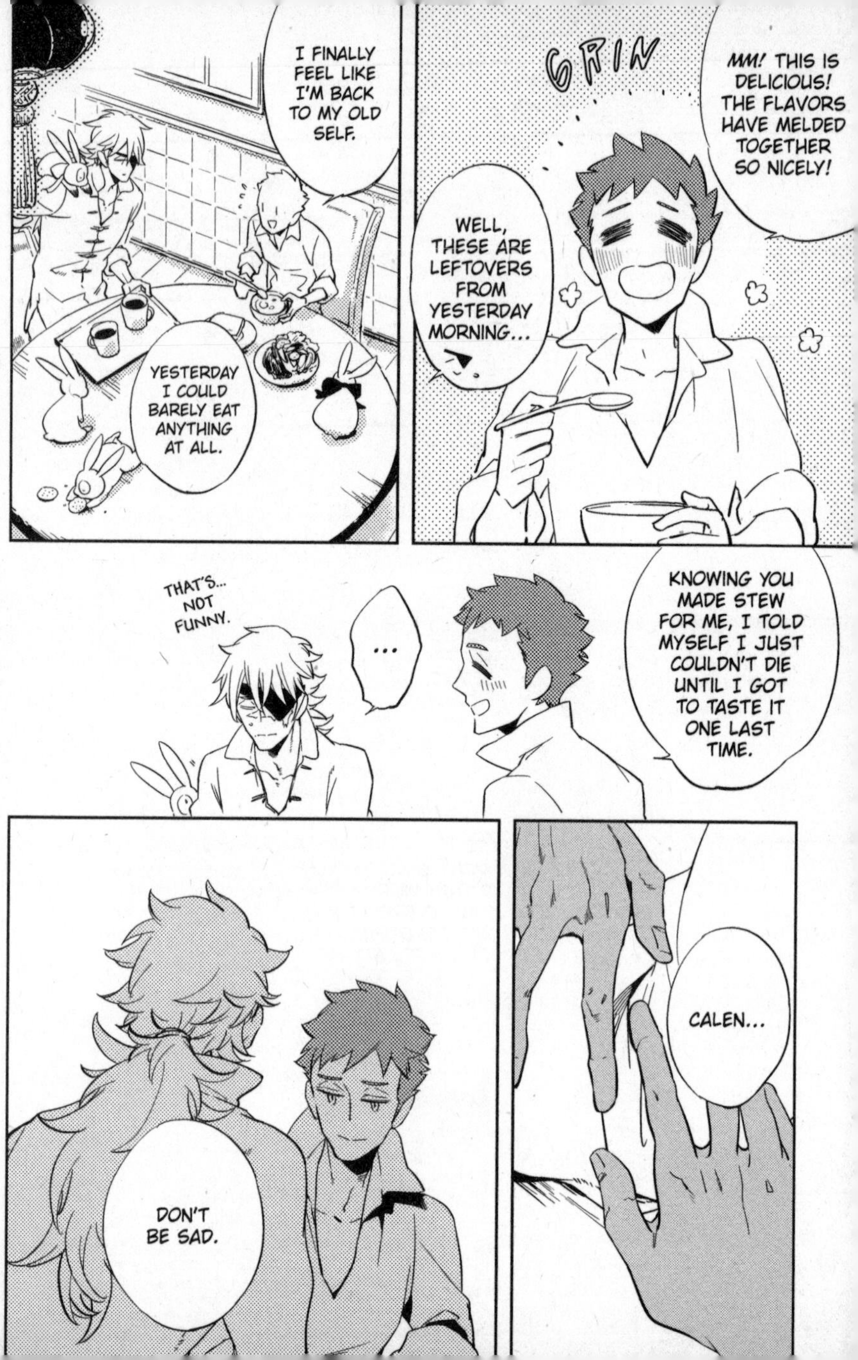
MM! THIS IS DELICIOUS! THE FLAVORS HAVE MELDED TOGETHER SO NICELY!
GRIN
WELL, THESE ARE LEFTOVERS FROM YESTERDAY MORNING...
I FINALLY FEEL LIKE I'M BACK TO MY OLD SELF.
YESTERDAY I COULD BARELY EAT ANYTHING AT ALL.
KNOWING YOU MADE STEW FOR ME, I TOLD MYSELF I JUST COULDN'T DIE UNTIL I GOT TO TASTE IT ONE LAST TIME.
...
THAT'S... NOT FUNNY.
CALEN...
DON'T BE SAD.

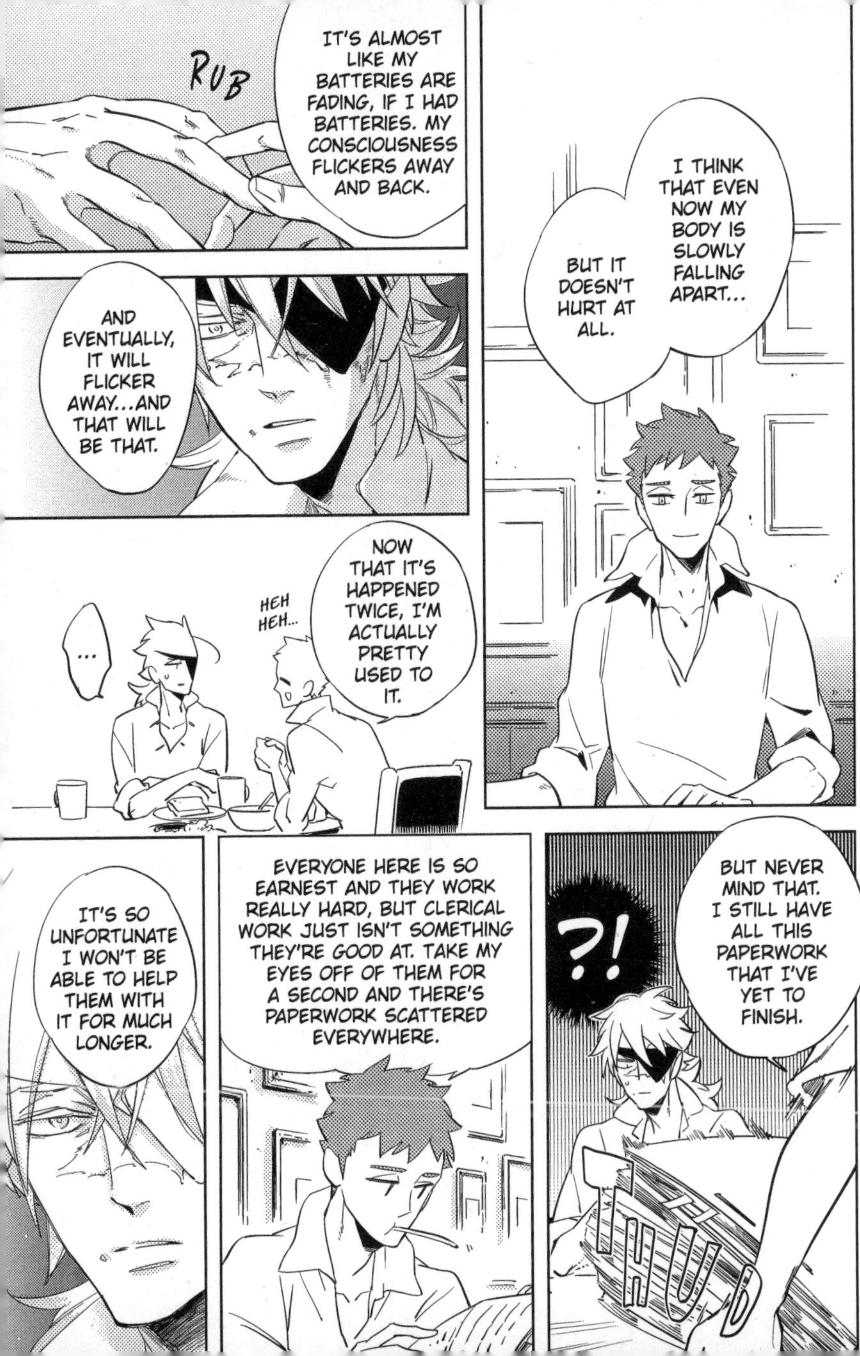
I THINK THAT EVEN NOW MY BODY IS SLOWLY FALLING APART...
BUT IT DOESN'T HURT AT ALL.
IT'S ALMOST LIKE MY BATTERIES ARE FADING, IF I HAD BATTERIES. MY CONSCIOUSNESS FLICKERS AWAY AND BACK.
RUB
AND EVENTUALLY, IT WILL FLICKER AWAY...AND THAT WILL BE THAT.
NOW THAT IT'S HAPPENED TWICE, I'M ACTUALLY PRETTY USED TO IT.
HEH HEH...
...
BUT NEVER MIND THAT. I STILL HAVE ALL THIS PAPERWORK THAT I'VE YET TO FINISH.
?!
THUD
EVERYONE HERE IS SO EARNEST AND THEY WORK REALLY HARD, BUT CLERICAL WORK JUST ISN'T SOMETHING THEY'RE GOOD AT. TAKE MY EYES OFF OF THEM FOR A SECOND AND THERE'S PAPERWORK SCATTERED EVERYWHERE.
IT'S SO UNFORTUNATE I WON'T BE ABLE TO HELP THEM WITH IT FOR MUCH LONGER.

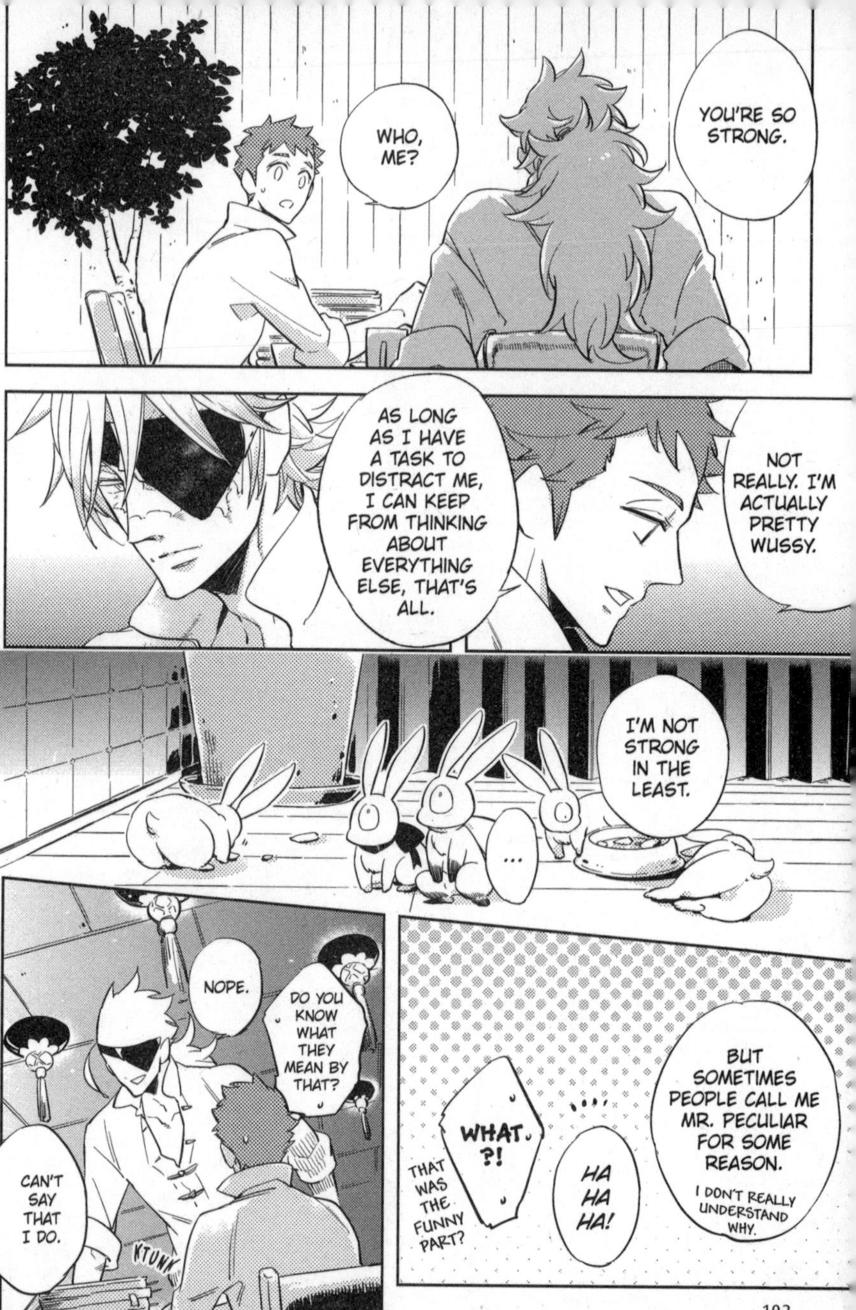
YOU'RE SO STRONG.
WHO, ME?
NOT REALLY. I'M ACTUALLY PRETTY WUSSY.
AS LONG AS I HAVE A TASK TO DISTRACT ME, I CAN KEEP FROM THINKING ABOUT EVERYTHING ELSE, THAT'S ALL.
I'M NOT STRONG IN THE LEAST.
...
BUT SOMETIMES PEOPLE CALL ME MR. PECULIAR FOR SOME REASON.
I DON'T REALLY UNDERSTAND WHY.
...!
HA HA HA!
WHAT?!
THAT WAS THE FUNNY PART?
DO YOU KNOW WHAT THEY MEAN BY THAT?
NOPE.
CAN'T SAY THAT I DO.
KTUNK

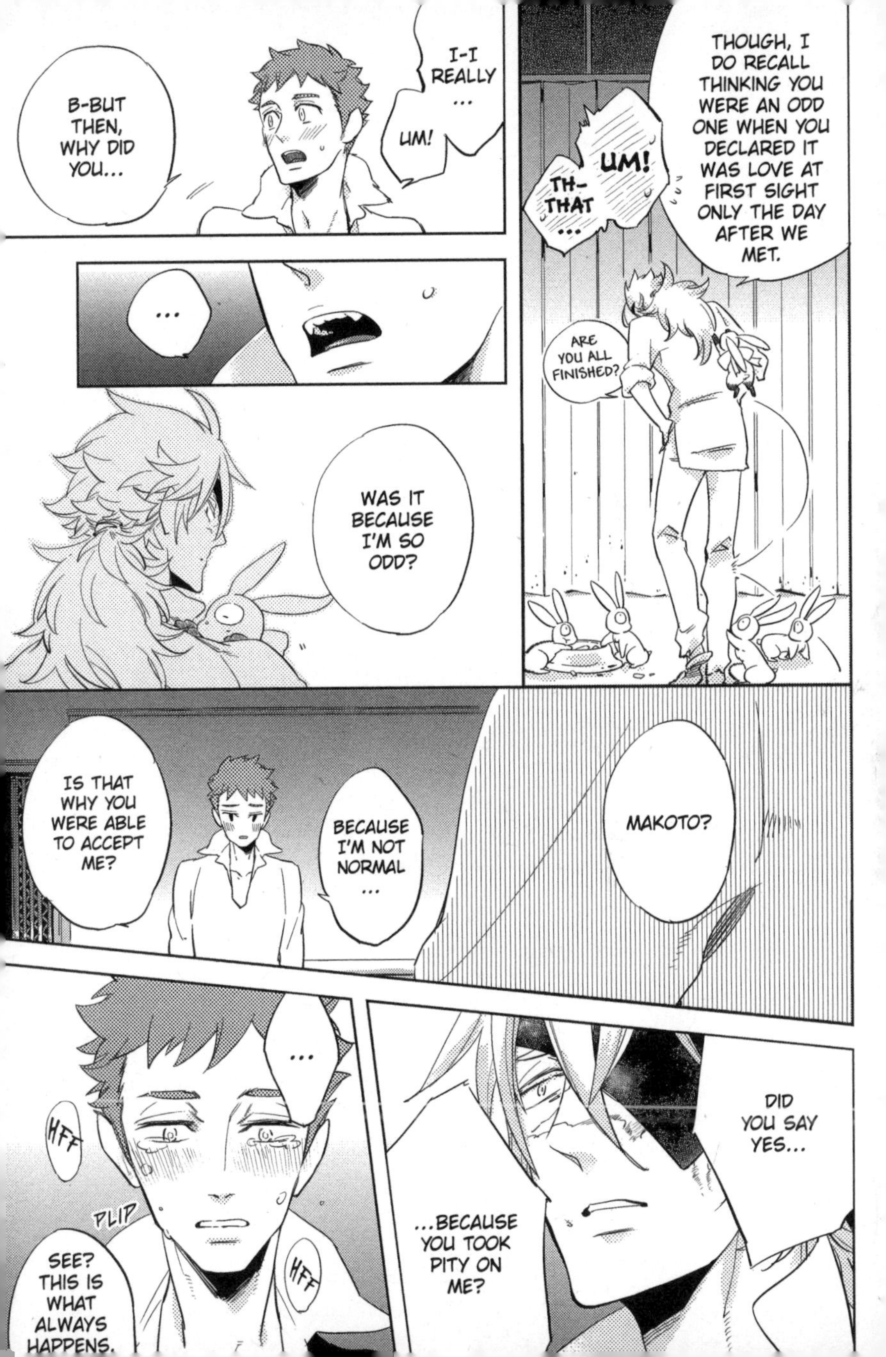
THOUGH, I DO RECALL THINKING YOU WERE AN ODD ONE WHEN YOU DECLARED IT WAS LOVE AT FIRST SIGHT ONLY THE DAY AFTER WE MET.
UM!
TH-THAT...
ARE YOU ALL FINISHED?
I-I REALLY... UM!
B-BUT THEN, WHY DID YOU...
...
WAS IT BECAUSE I'M SO ODD?
MAKOTO?
BECAUSE I'M NOT NORMAL...
IS THAT WHY YOU WERE ABLE TO ACCEPT ME?
DID YOU SAY YES...
...BECAUSE YOU TOOK PITY ON ME?
...
HFF
PLIP
HFF
SEE? THIS IS WHAT ALWAYS HAPPENS.

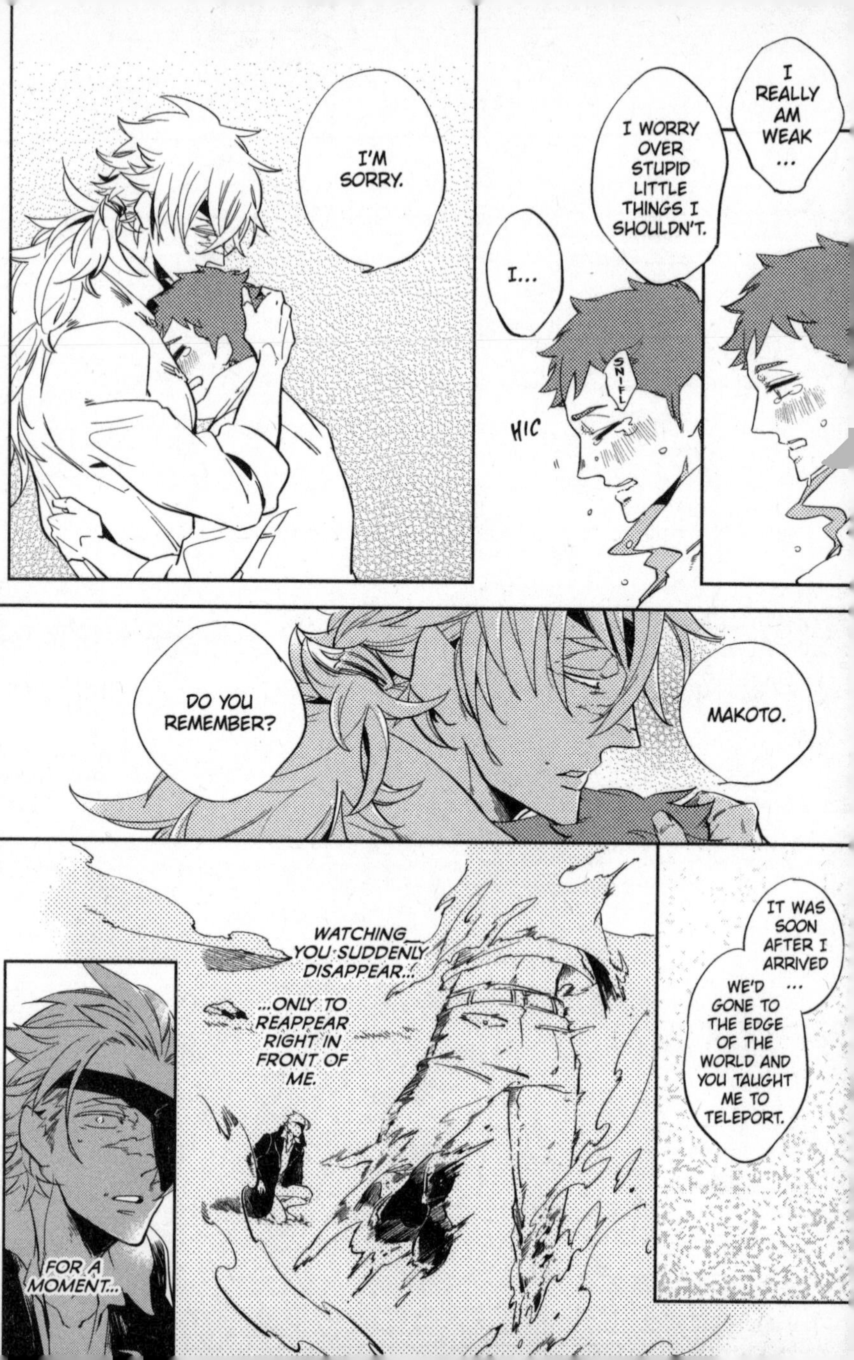
I REALLY AM WEAK ...
I WORRY OVER STUPID LITTLE THINGS I SHOULDN'T.
I...
SNIFL
HIC
I'M SORRY.
MAKOTO.
DO YOU REMEMBER?
IT WAS SOON AFTER I ARRIVED ...
WE'D GONE TO THE EDGE OF THE WORLD AND YOU TAUGHT ME TO TELEPORT.
WATCHING YOU SUDDENLY DISAPPEAR...
...ONLY TO REAPPEAR RIGHT IN FRONT OF ME.
FOR A MOMENT...

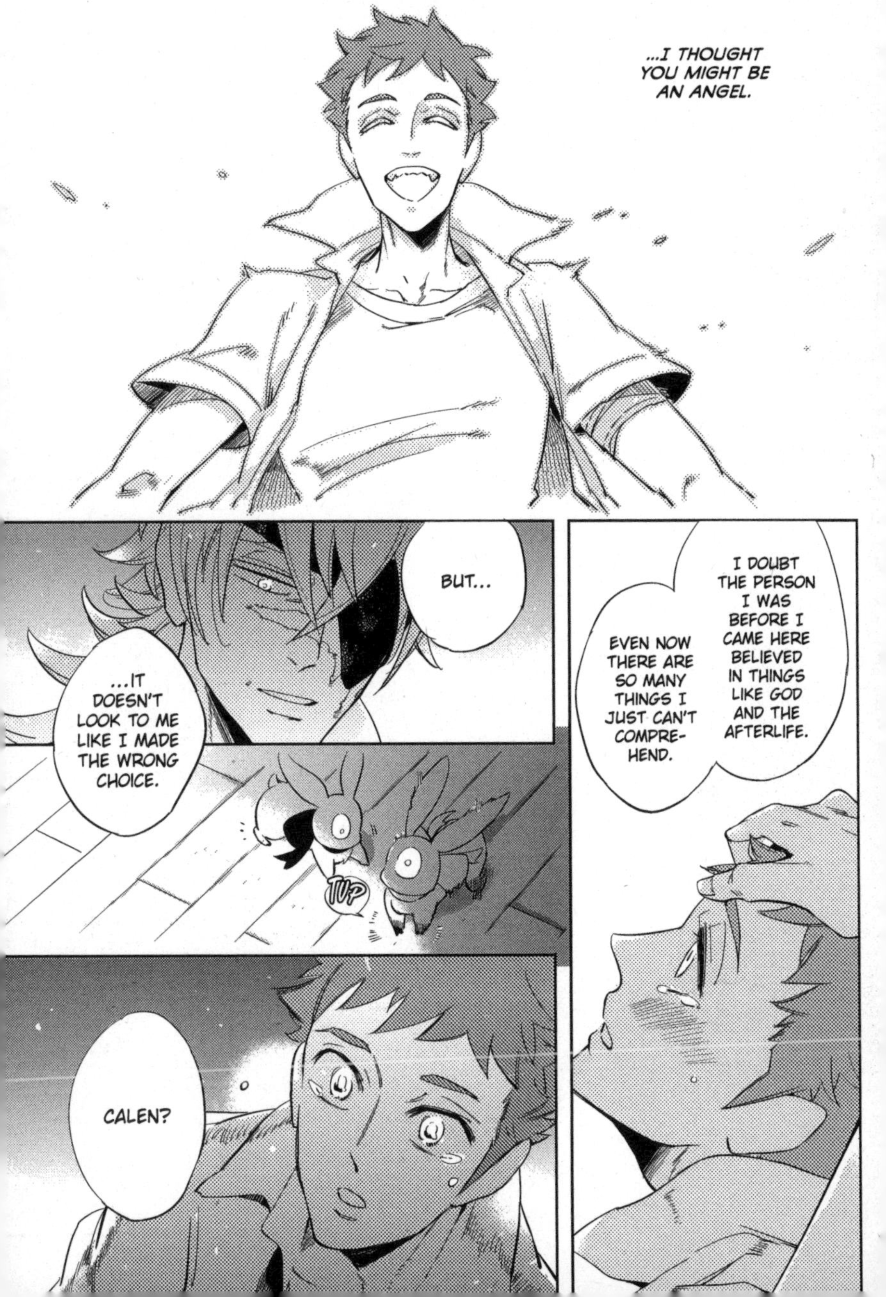
...I THOUGHT YOU MIGHT BE AN ANGEL.
I DOUBT THE PERSON I WAS BEFORE I CAME HERE BELIEVED IN THINGS LIKE GOD AND THE AFTERLIFE.
EVEN NOW THERE ARE SO MANY THINGS I JUST CAN'T COMPRE-HEND.
BUT...
...IT DOESN'T LOOK TO ME LIKE I MADE THE WRONG CHOICE.
TUP
CALEN?

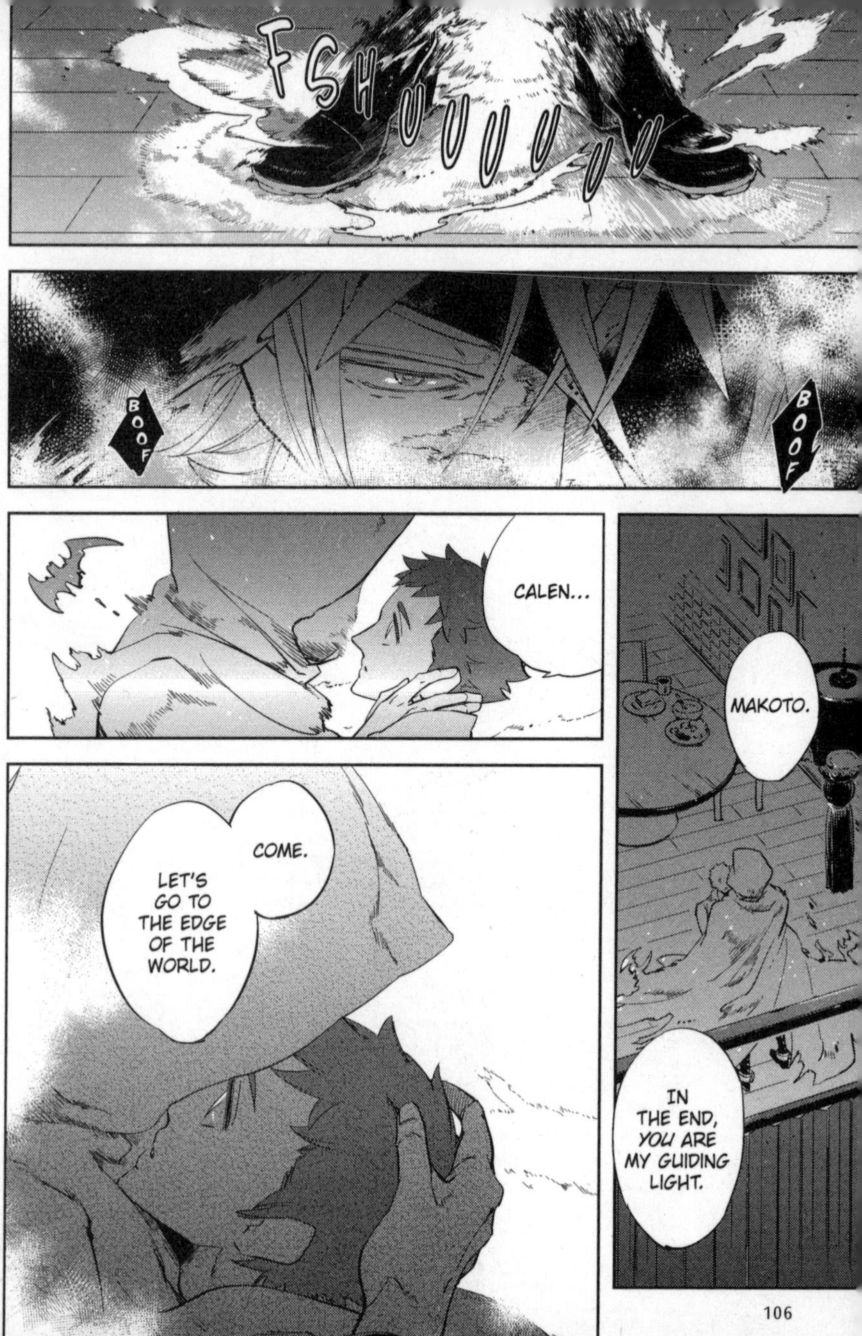
FSHUUUUUU
BOOF
BOOF
MAKOTO.
IN THE END, YOU ARE MY GUIDING LIGHT.
CALEN...
COME.
LET'S GO TO THE EDGE OF THE WORLD.

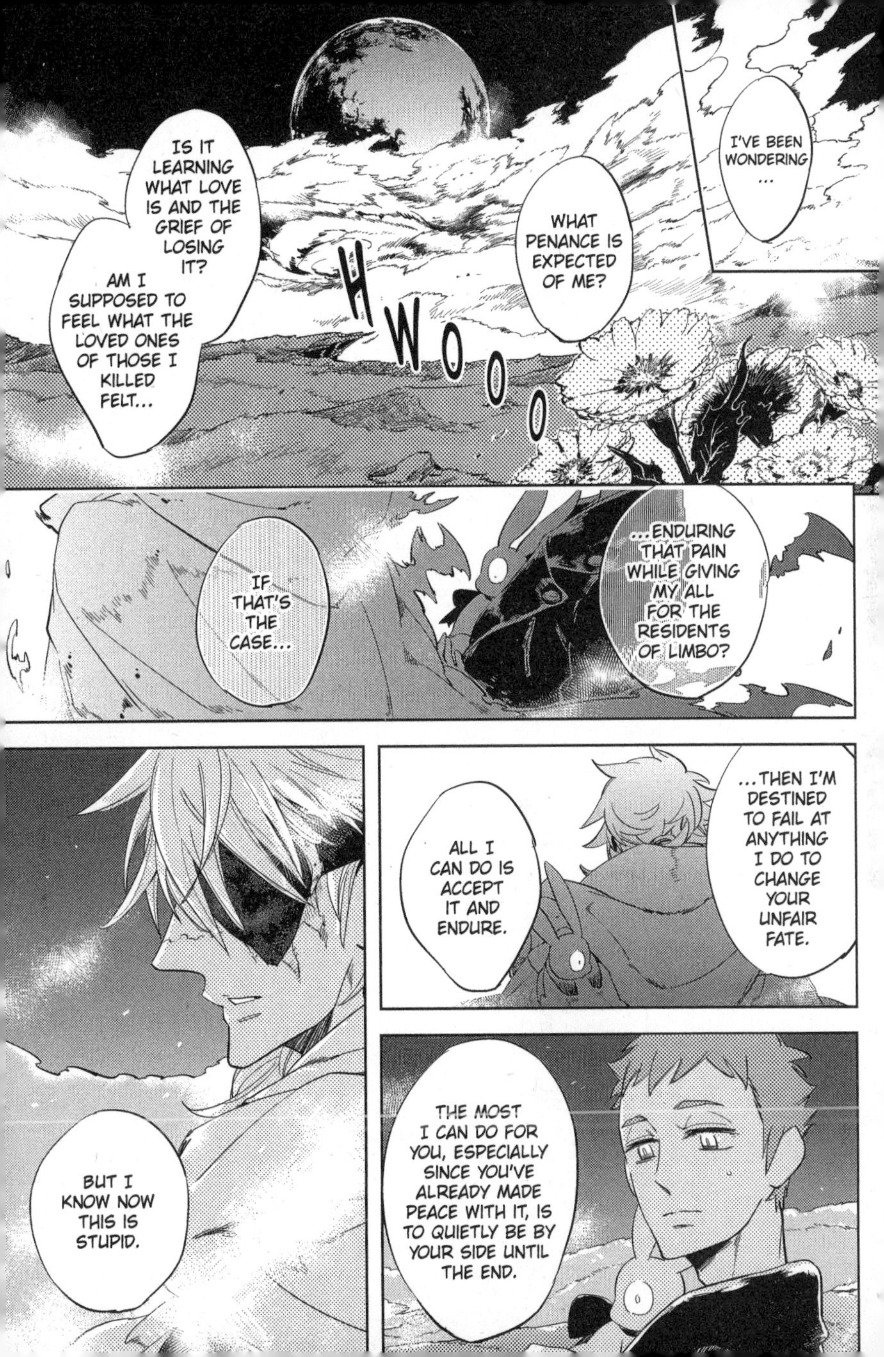
I'VE BEEN WONDERING ...
WHAT PENANCE IS EXPECTED OF ME?
HWOOO
IS IT LEARNING WHAT LOVE IS AND THE GRIEF OF LOSING IT?
AM I SUPPOSED TO FEEL WHAT THE LOVED ONES OF THOSE I KILLED FELT...
...ENDURING THAT PAIN WHILE GIVING MY ALL FOR THE RESIDENTS OF LIMBO?
IF THAT'S THE CASE...
...THEN I'M DESTINED TO FAIL AT ANYTHING I DO TO CHANGE YOUR UNFAIR FATE.
ALL I CAN DO IS ACCEPT IT AND ENDURE.
THE MOST I CAN DO FOR YOU, ESPECIALLY SINCE YOU'VE ALREADY MADE PEACE WITH IT, IS TO QUIETLY BE BY YOUR SIDE UNTIL THE END.
BUT I KNOW NOW THIS IS STUPID.

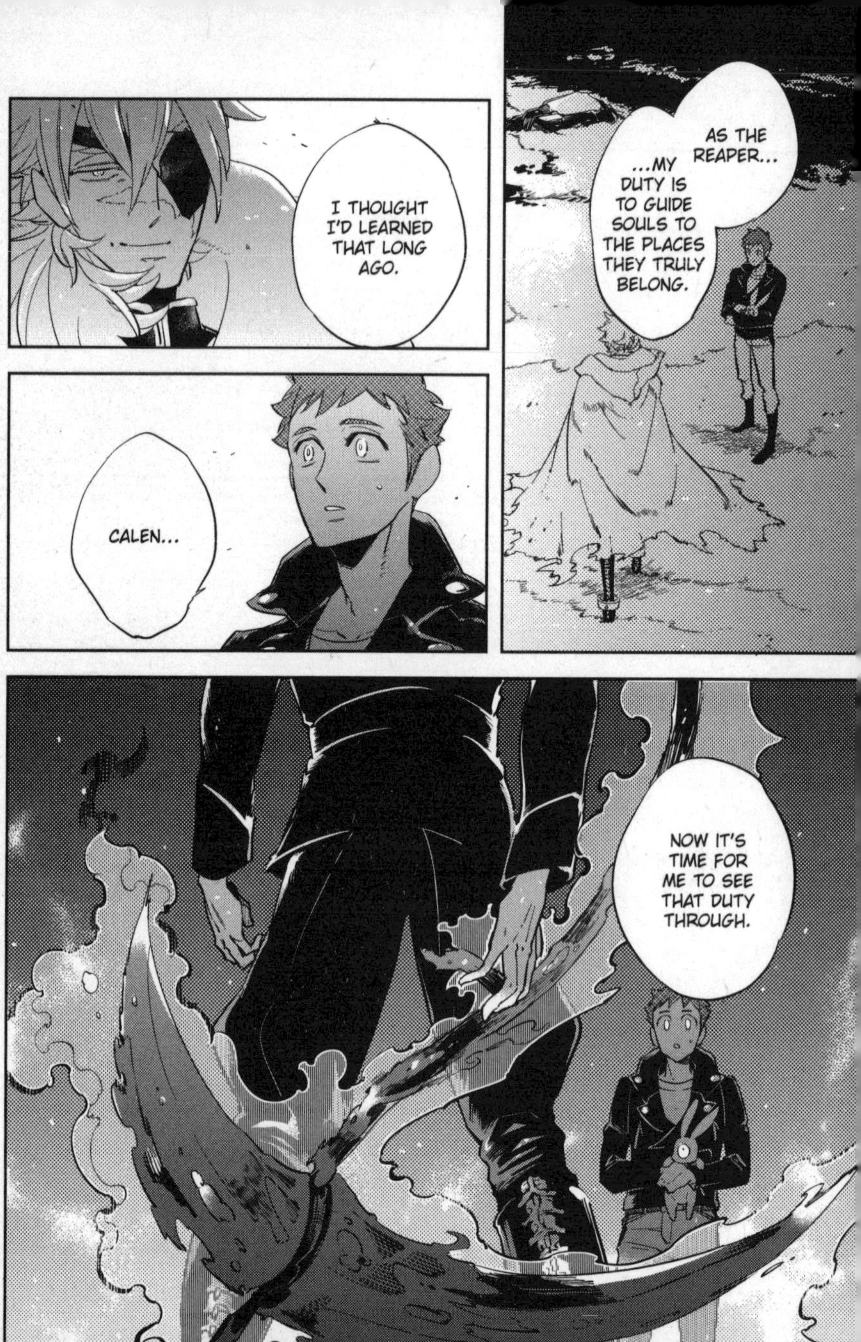
AS THE REAPER...
...MY DUTY IS TO GUIDE SOULS TO THE PLACES THEY TRULY BELONG.
I THOUGHT I'D LEARNED THAT LONG AGO.
CALEN...
NOW IT'S TIME FOR ME TO SEE THAT DUTY THROUGH.

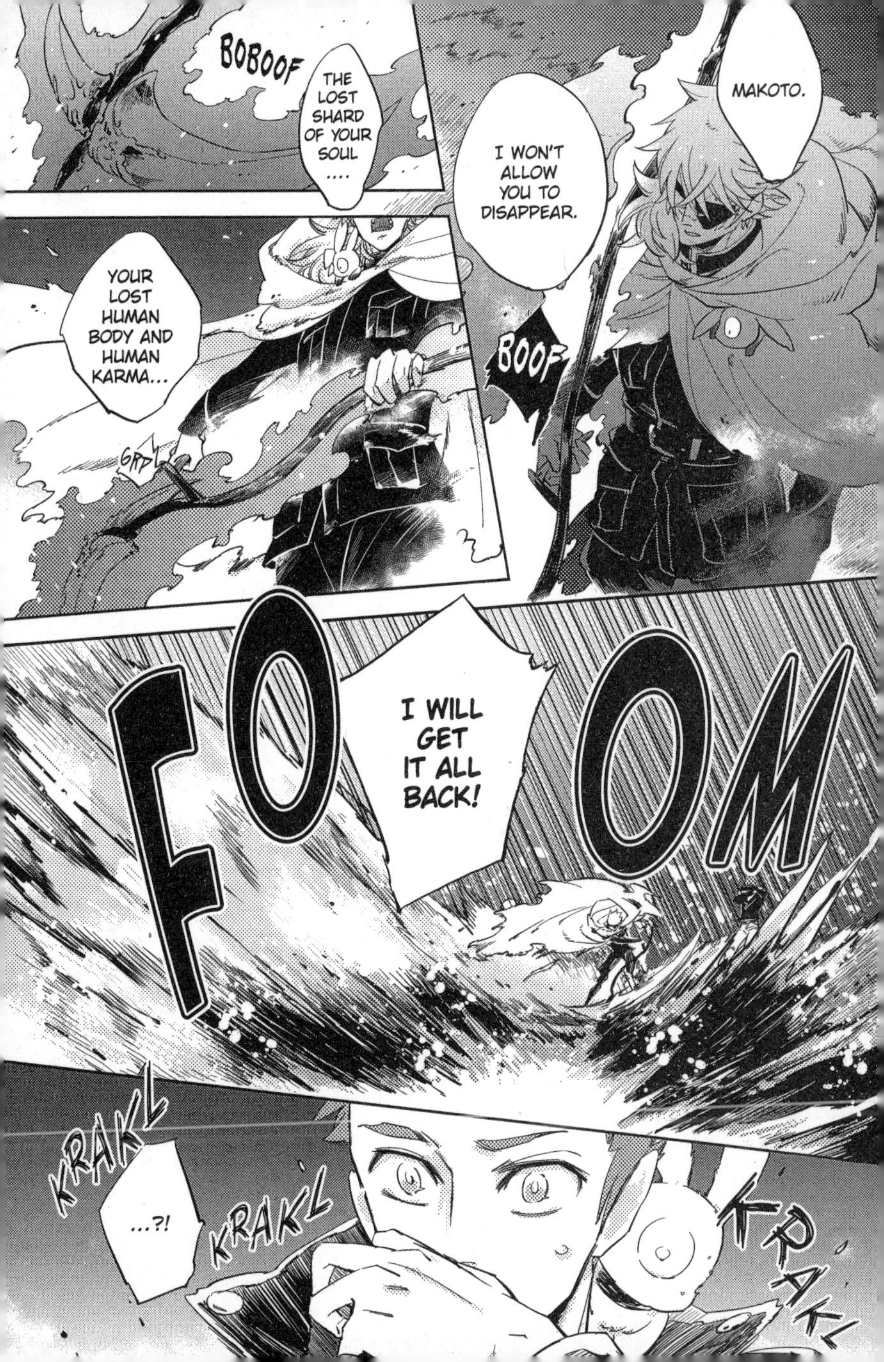
MAKOTO.
I WON'T ALLOW YOU TO DISAPPEAR.
BOOF
BOBOOF
THE LOST SHARD OF YOUR SOUL ....
YOUR LOST HUMAN BODY AND HUMAN KARMA...
GRP
FOOM
I WILL GET IT ALL BACK!
KRAKL
...?!
KRAKL
KRAKL

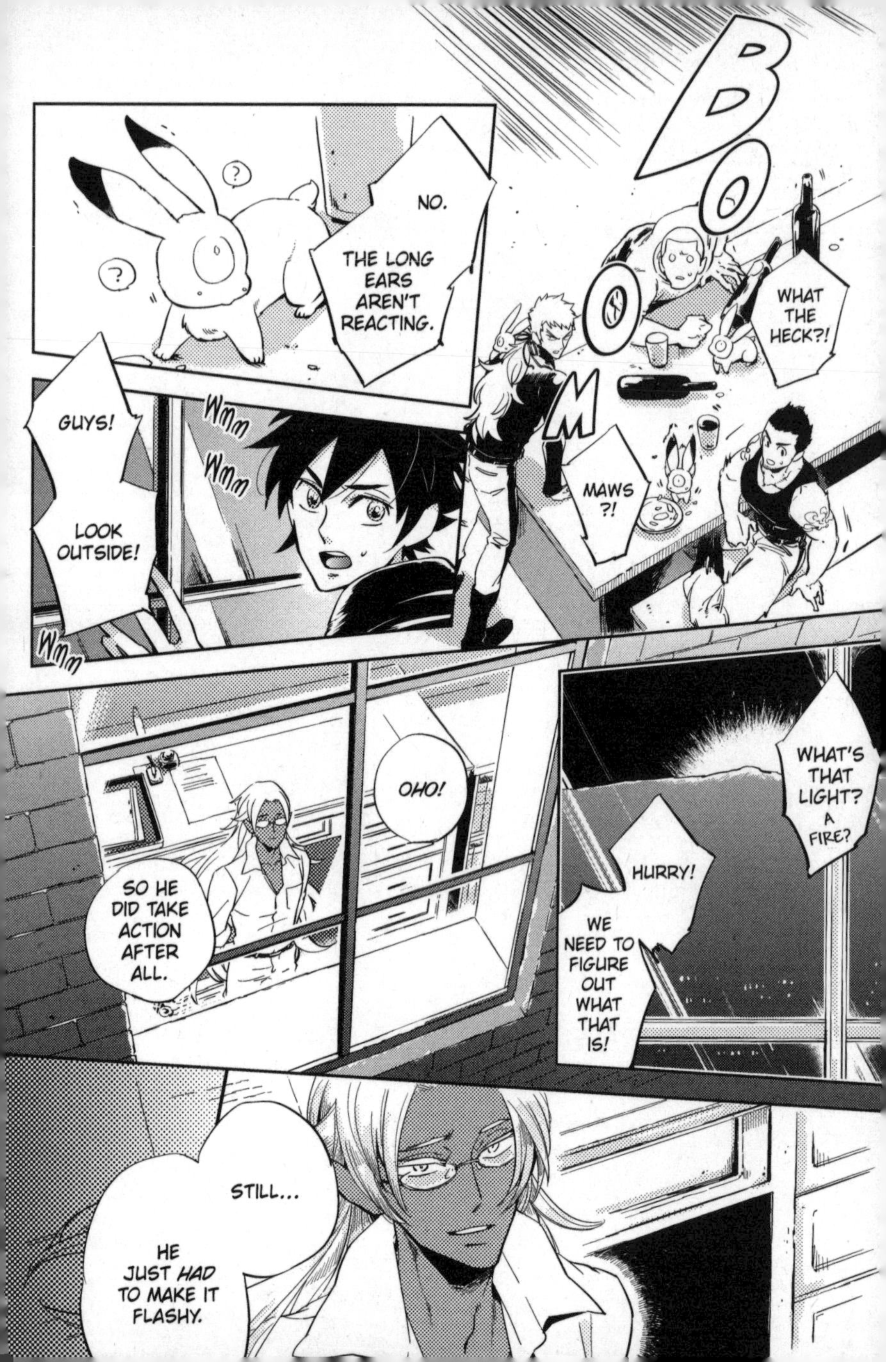
BOOM
WHAT THE HECK?!
MAWS ?!
?
?
NO.
THE LONG EARS AREN'T REACTING.
GUYS!
LOOK OUTSIDE!
Wmm
Wmm
Wmm
WHAT'S THAT LIGHT? A FIRE?
HURRY!
WE NEED TO FIGURE OUT WHAT THAT IS!
OHO!
SO HE DID TAKE ACTION AFTER ALL.
STILL...
HE JUST *HAD* TO MAKE IT FLASHY.

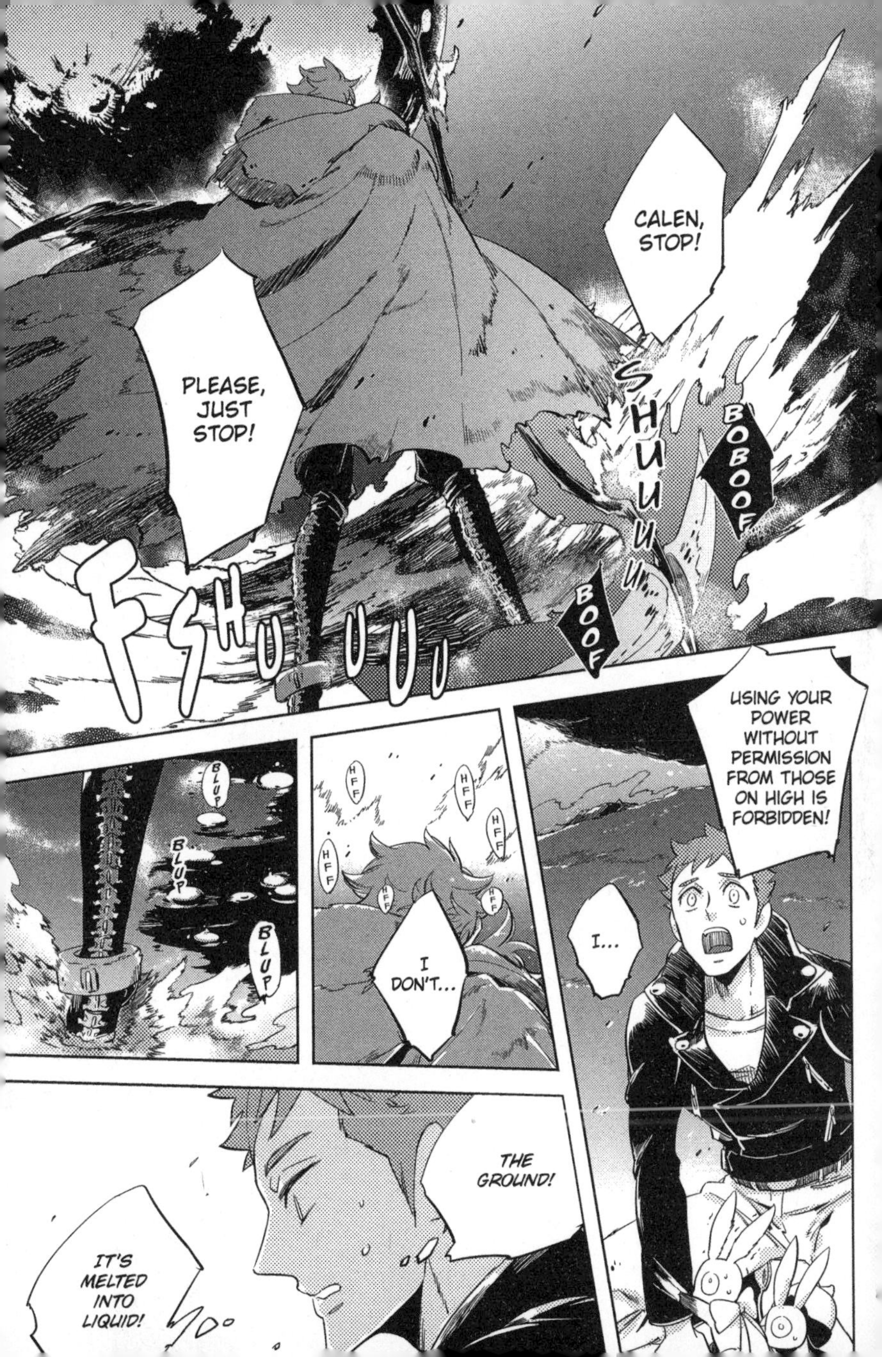
CALEN, STOP!
PLEASE, JUST STOP!
BOBOOF
SHUUUUU
BOOF
FSHUUUU
USING YOUR POWER WITHOUT PERMISSION FROM THOSE ON HIGH IS FORBIDDEN!
I...
HFF
HFF
HFF
HFF
HFF
HFF
I DON'T...
BLUP
BLUP
BLUP
THE GROUND!
IT'S MELTED INTO LIQUID!

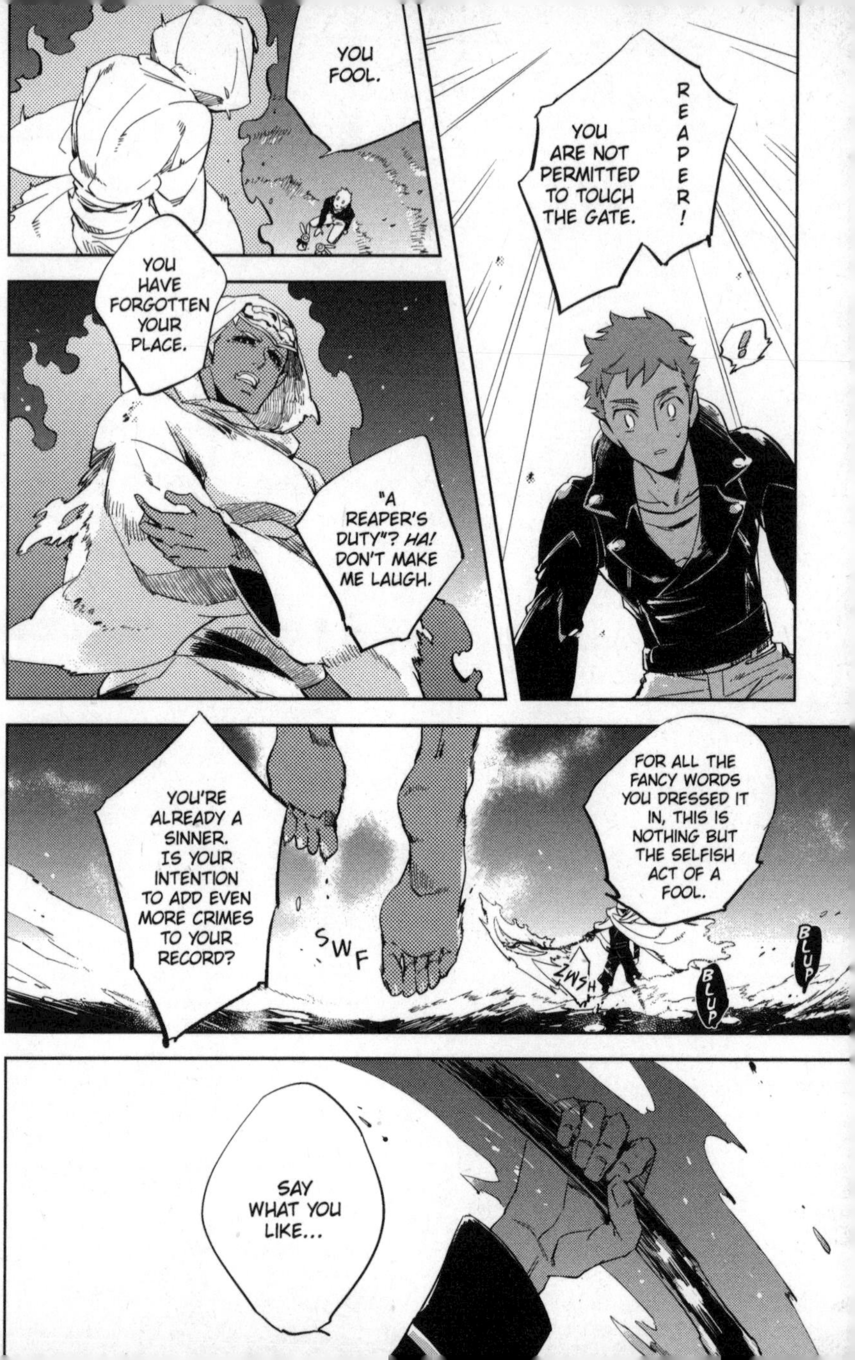
REAPER!
YOU ARE NOT PERMITTED TO TOUCH THE GATE.
!
YOU FOOL.
YOU HAVE FORGOTTEN YOUR PLACE.
"A REAPER'S DUTY"? *HA!* DON'T MAKE ME LAUGH.
FOR ALL THE FANCY WORDS YOU DRESSED IT IN, THIS IS NOTHING BUT THE SELFISH ACT OF A FOOL.
BLUP
BLUP
ZWSH
SWF
YOU'RE ALREADY A SINNER. IS YOUR INTENTION TO ADD EVEN MORE CRIMES TO YOUR RECORD?
SAY WHAT YOU LIKE...

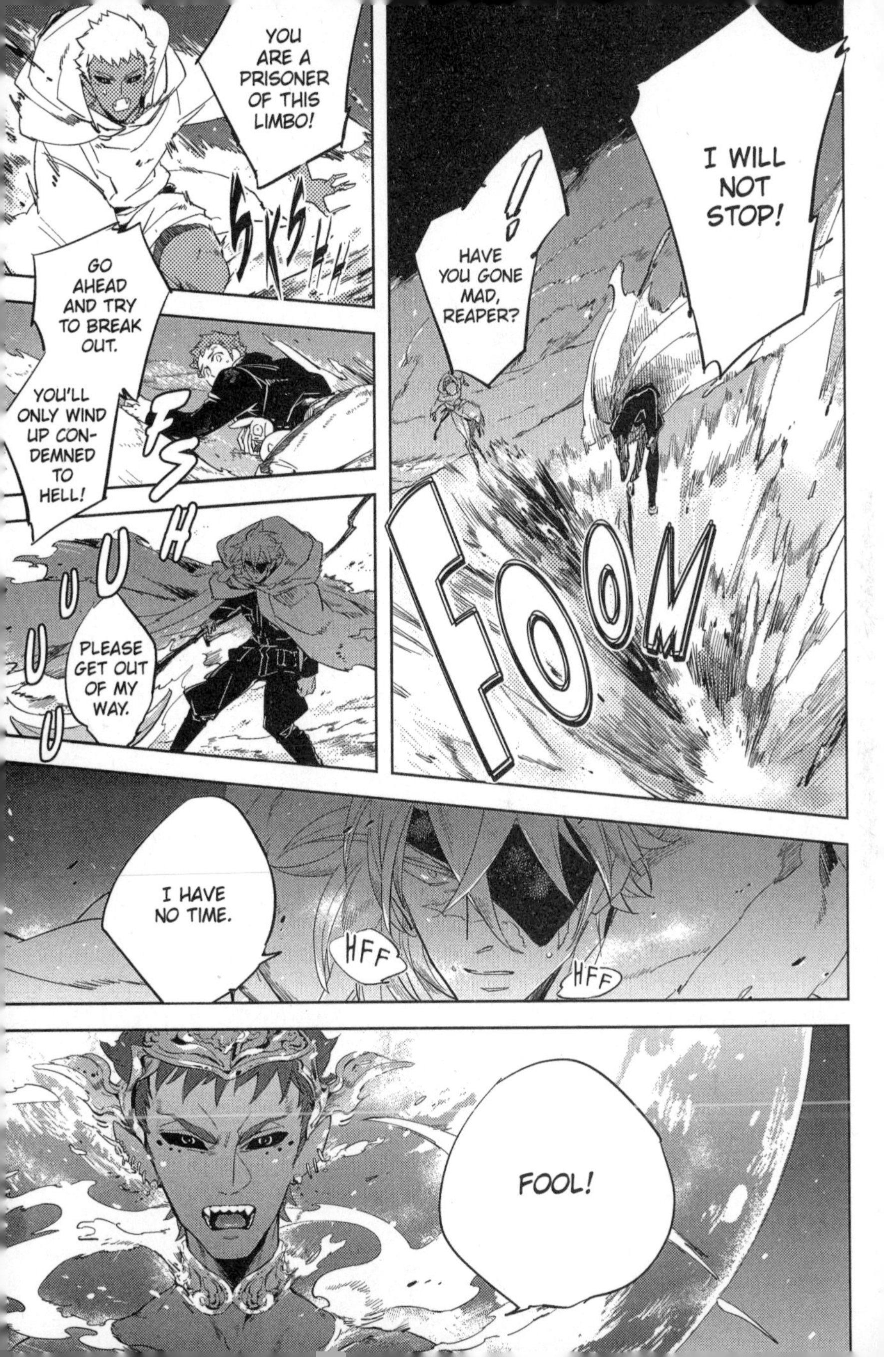
I WILL NOT STOP!
!
HAVE YOU GONE MAD, REAPER?
FOOM
YOU ARE A PRISONER OF THIS LIMBO!
SHSHH
GO AHEAD AND TRY TO BREAK OUT.
YOU'LL ONLY WIND UP CON-DEMNED TO HELL!
FS
UUUUH
PLEASE GET OUT OF MY WAY.
I HAVE NO TIME.
HFF
HFF
FOOL!

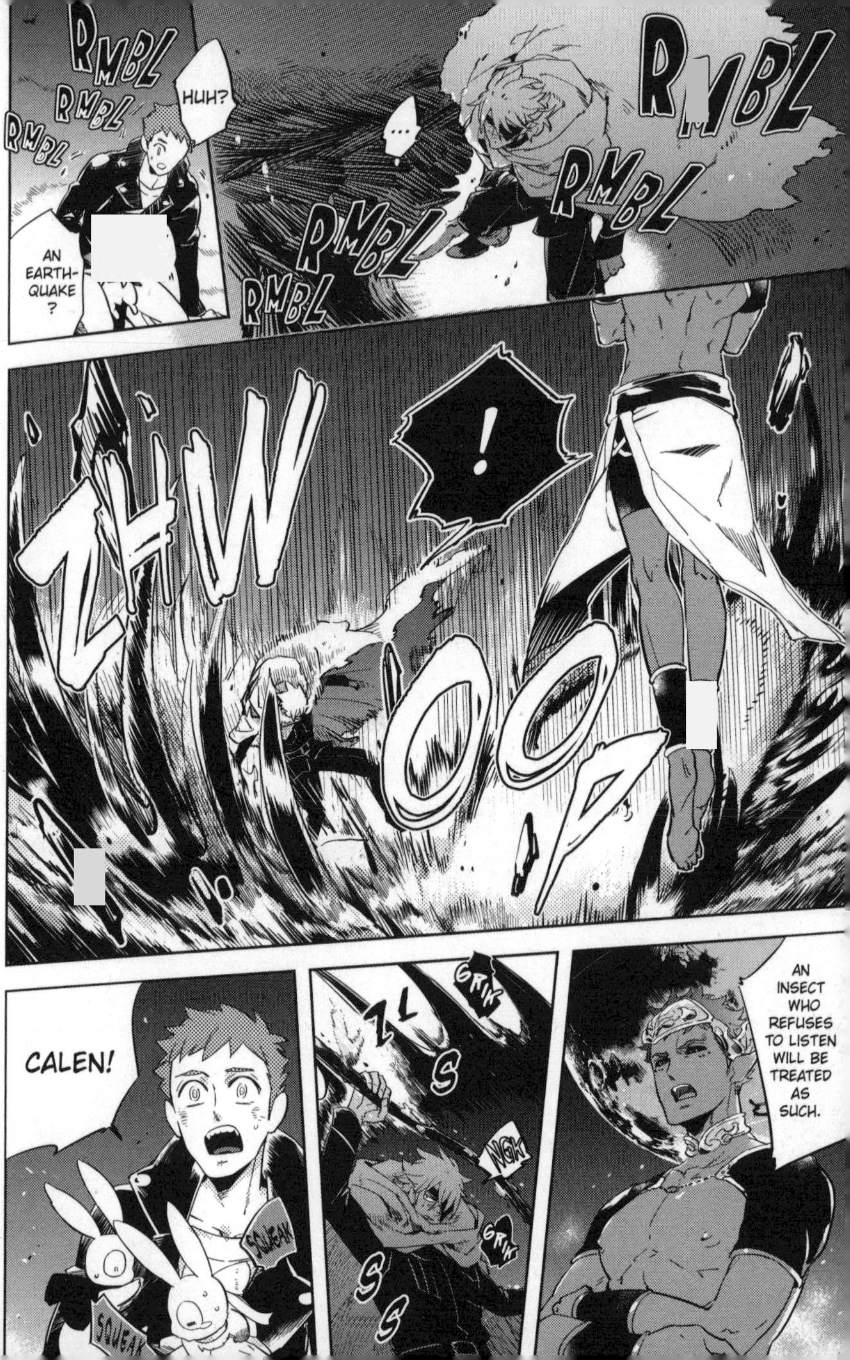
RMBL
...
RMBL
RMBL
RMBL
RMBL
RMBL
RMBL
HUH?
AN EARTH-QUAKE?
!
ZHWOOP
AN INSECT WHO REFUSES TO LISTEN WILL BE TREATED AS SUCH.
GRIK
ZZL
SS
NGK
GRIK
SS
CALEN!
SQUEAK
SQUEAK

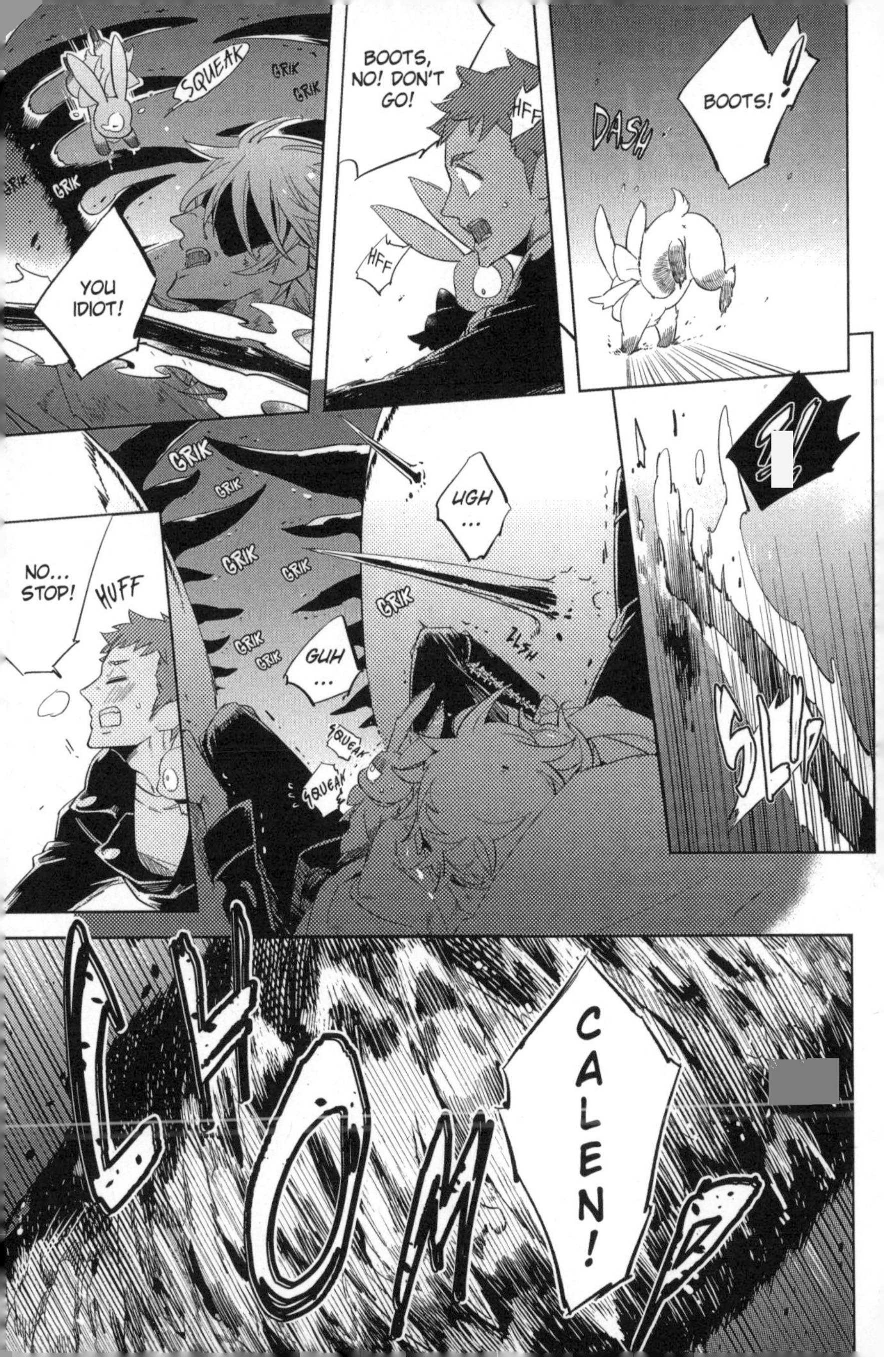
BOOTS!
!
DASH
BOOTS, NO! DON'T GO!
HFF
HFF
SQUEAK
GRIK
GRIK
GRIK
YOU IDIOT!
SLIP
UGH ...
GRIK
GRIK
GRIK
GRIK
GRIK
ZLSH
GRIK
GRIK
GUH ...
SQUEAK
SQUEAK
NO... STOP!
HUFF
CALEN!
CHOMP

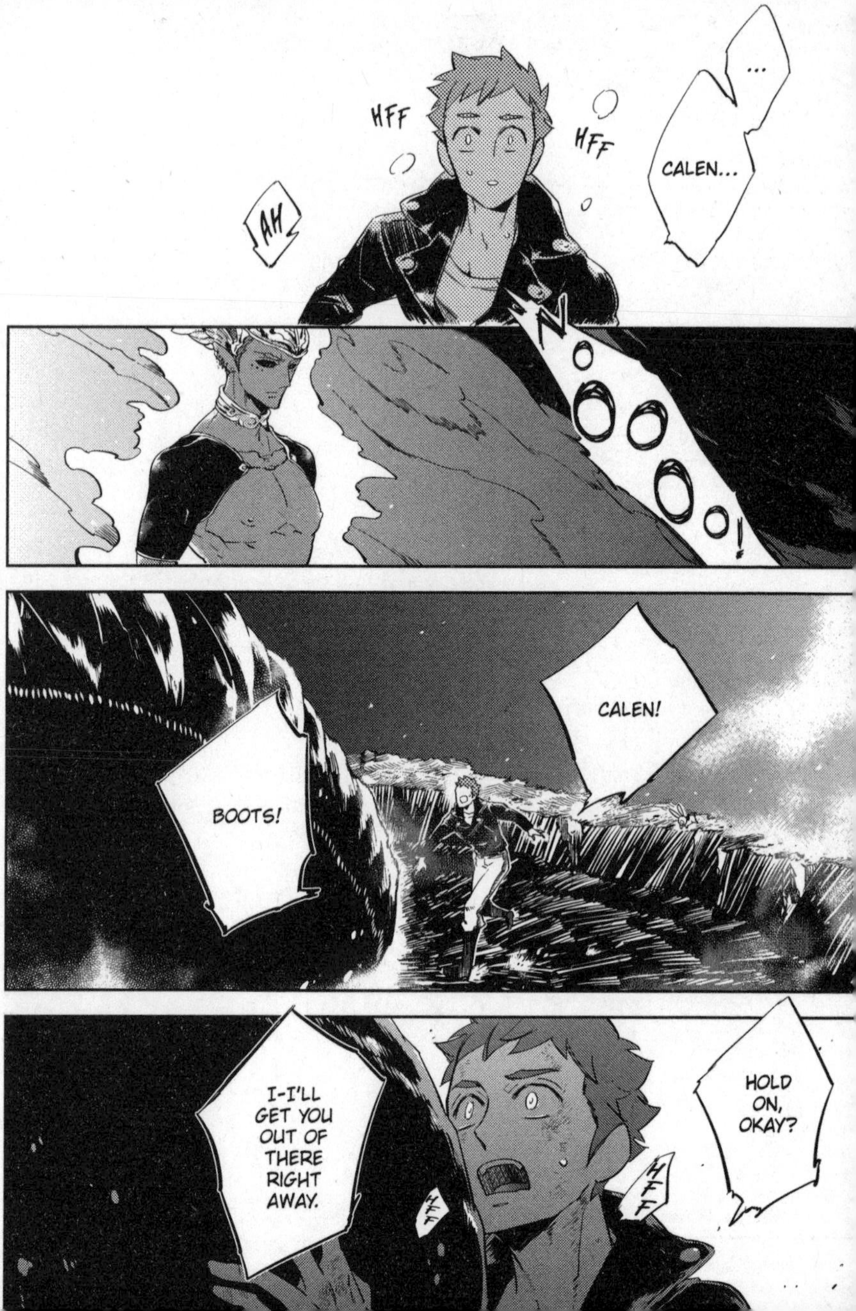
...
CALEN...
HFF
HFF
AH
NOOOOO!
CALEN!
BOOTS!
HOLD ON, OKAY?
HFF
HFF
I-I'LL GET YOU OUT OF THERE RIGHT AWAY.

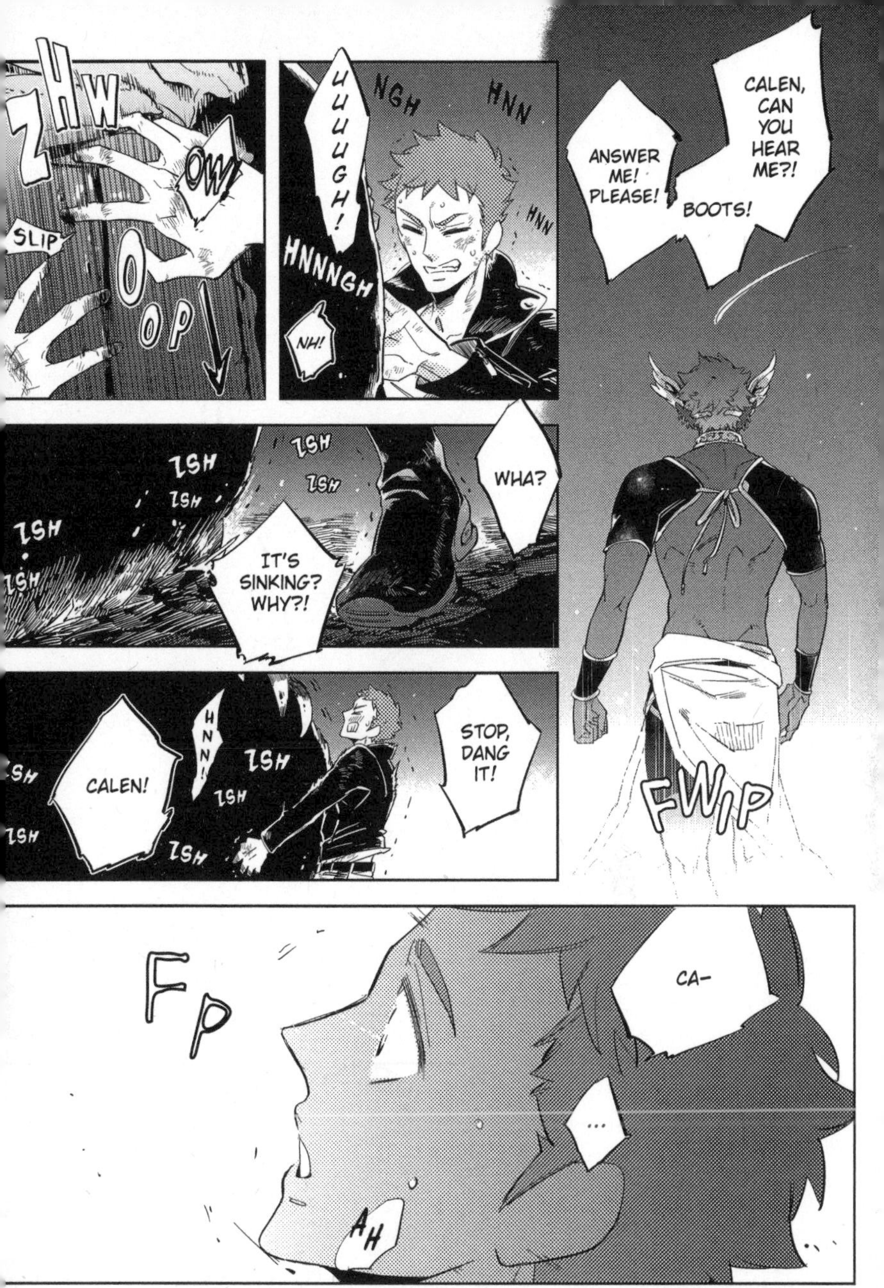
CALEN, CAN YOU HEAR ME?!
BOOTS!
ANSWER ME! PLEASE!
FWIP
NGH
HNN
UUUUGH!
HNN
HNNNGH
NH!
ZHW
OW
SLIP
OOP
WHA?
ZSH
ZSH
IT'S SINKING? WHY?!
ZSH
ZSH
ZSH
ZSH
STOP, DANG IT!
HNN!
ZSH
ZSH
ZSH
CALEN!
ZSH
ZSH
CA-
...
AH
Fp

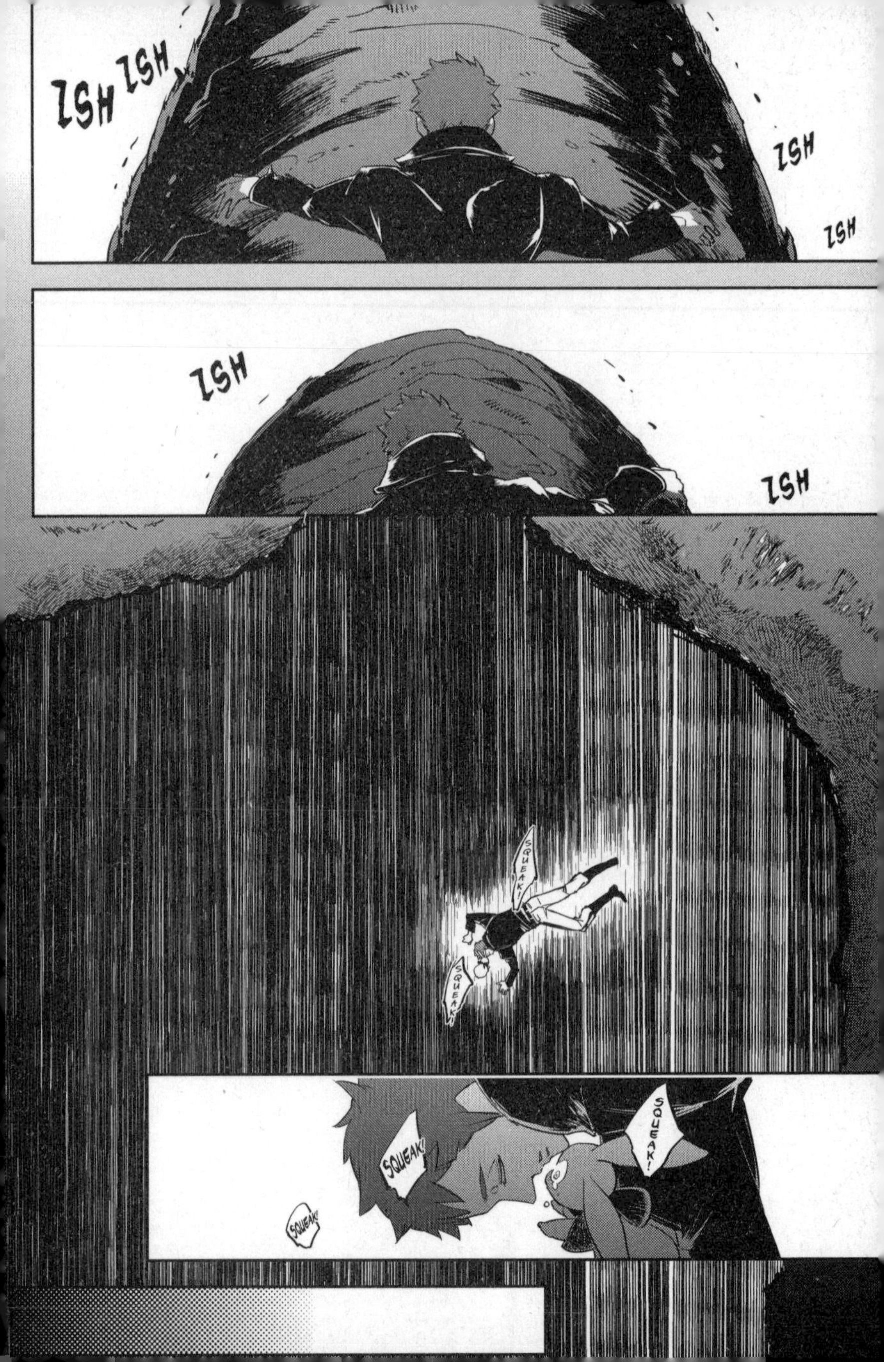
ZSH ZSH
ZSH
ZSH
ZSH
ZSH
SQUEAK!
SQUEAK!
SQUEAK!
SQUEAK!
SQUEAK!

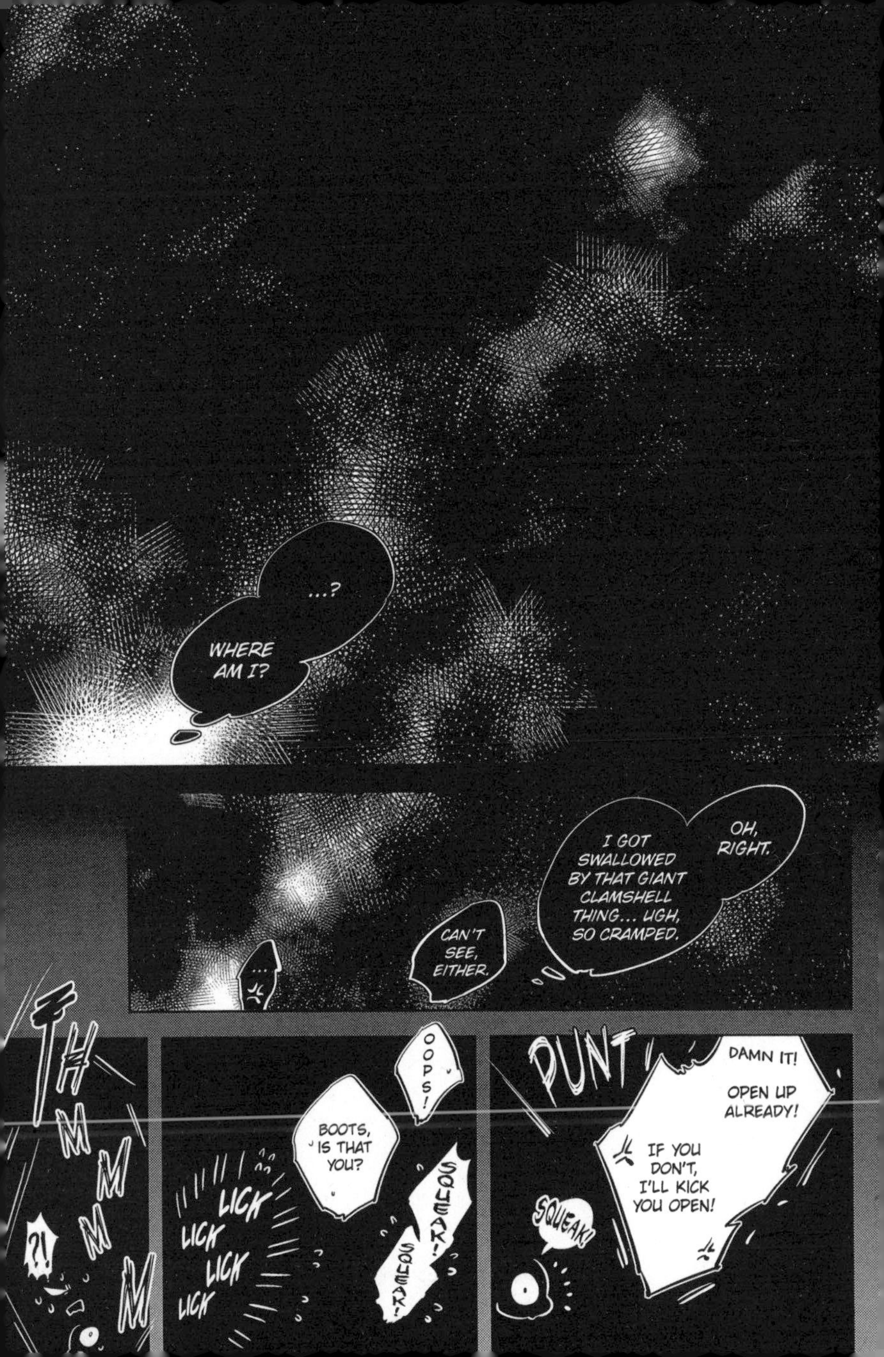
...?
WHERE AM I?
OH, RIGHT.
I GOT SWALLOWED BY THAT GIANT CLAMSHELL THING... UGH, SO CRAMPED.
CAN'T SEE, EITHER.
...
DAMN IT! OPEN UP ALREADY!
IF YOU DON'T, I'LL KICK YOU OPEN!
PUNT
SQUEAK!
OOPS!
BOOTS, IS THAT YOU?
SQUEAK!
SQUEAK!
LICK LICK LICK LICK
THMMMM
?!

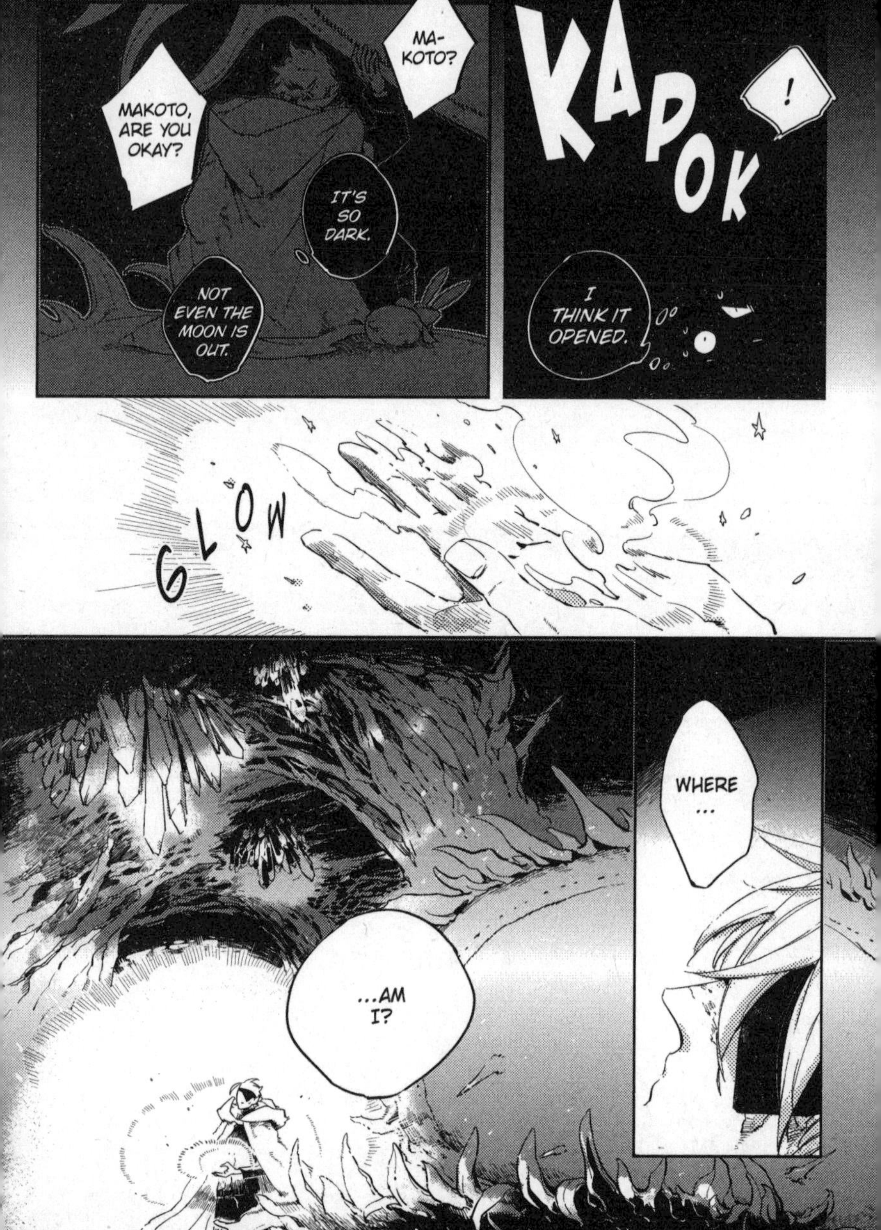
KAPOK
!
I THINK IT OPENED.
MA-KOTO?
MAKOTO, ARE YOU OKAY?
IT'S SO DARK.
NOT EVEN THE MOON IS OUT.
GLOW
WHERE...
...AM I?

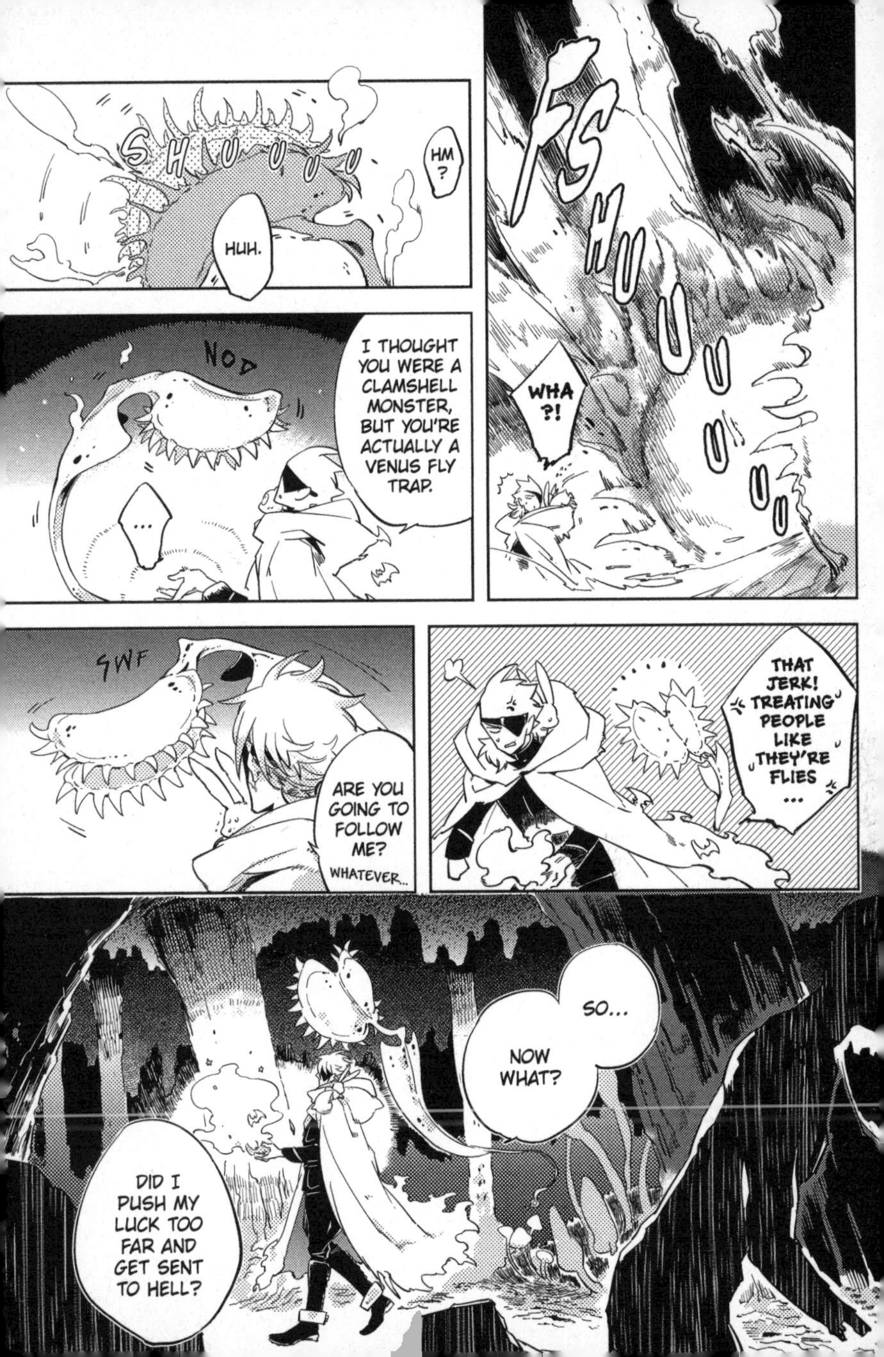

FSHUUUUUU
WHA?!
SHUUUU
HM?
HUH.
NOD
I THOUGHT YOU WERE A CLAMSHELL MONSTER, BUT YOU'RE ACTUALLY A VENUS FLY TRAP.
...
THAT JERK! TREATING PEOPLE LIKE THEY'RE FLIES...
SWF
ARE YOU GOING TO FOLLOW ME?
WHATEVER...
SO...
NOW WHAT?
DID I PUSH MY LUCK TOO FAR AND GET SENT TO HELL?

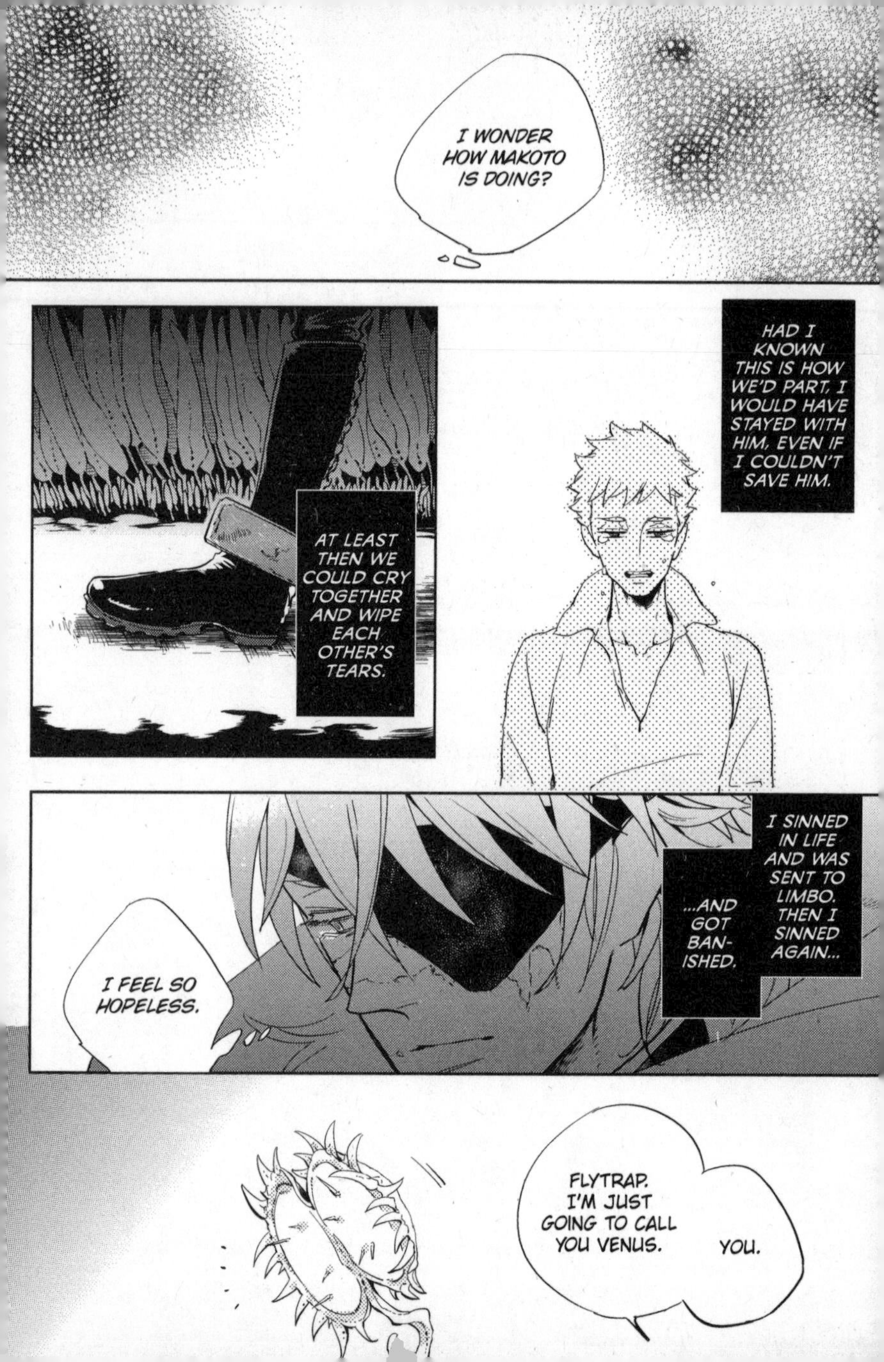

I WONDER HOW MAKOTO IS DOING?
HAD I KNOWN THIS IS HOW WE'D PART, I WOULD HAVE STAYED WITH HIM, EVEN IF I COULDN'T SAVE HIM.
AT LEAST THEN WE COULD CRY TOGETHER AND WIPE EACH OTHER'S TEARS.
I SINNED IN LIFE AND WAS SENT TO LIMBO. THEN I SINNED AGAIN...
...AND GOT BAN-ISHED.
I FEEL SO HOPELESS.
YOU.
FLYTRAP. I'M JUST GOING TO CALL YOU VENUS.

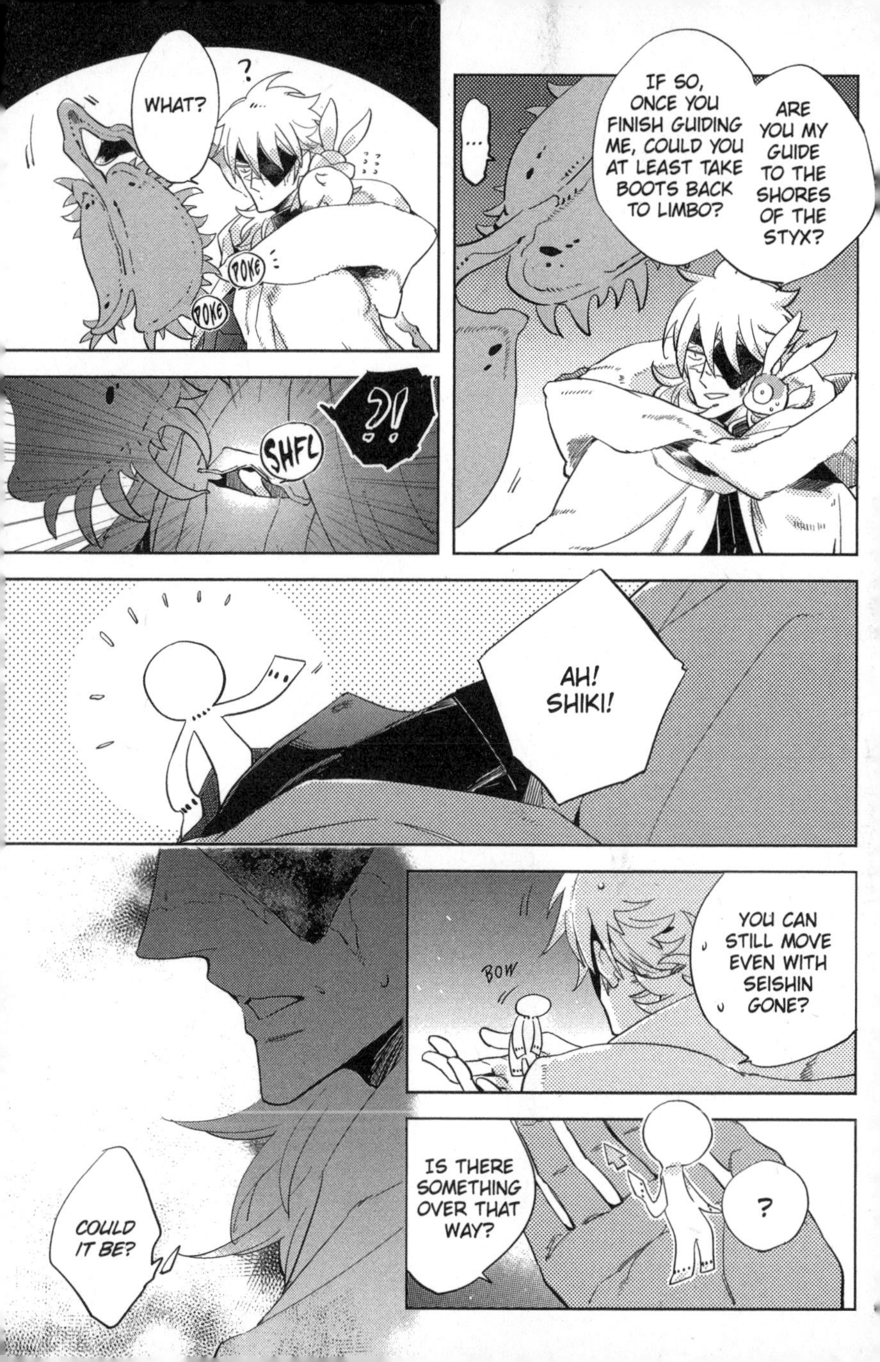
ARE YOU MY GUIDE TO THE SHORES OF THE STYX?
IF SO, ONCE YOU FINISH GUIDING ME, COULD YOU AT LEAST TAKE BOOTS BACK TO LIMBO?
...
WHAT?
?
POKE
POKE
?!
SHFL
AH! SHIKI!
YOU CAN STILL MOVE EVEN WITH SEISHIN GONE?
BOW
?
IS THERE SOMETHING OVER THAT WAY?
COULD IT BE?

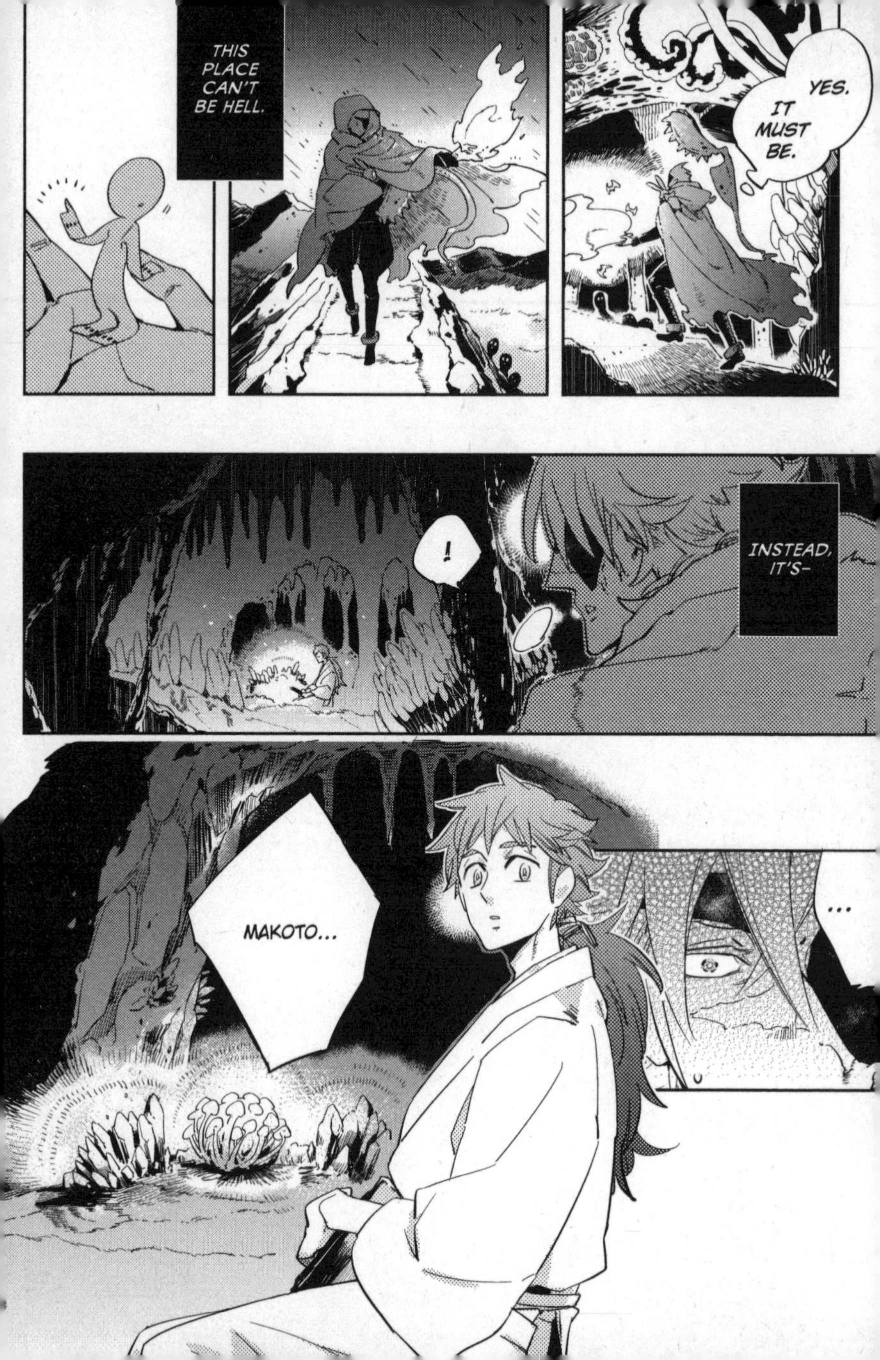
YES. IT MUST BE.
THIS PLACE CAN'T BE HELL.
INSTEAD, IT'S-
!
...
MAKOTO...

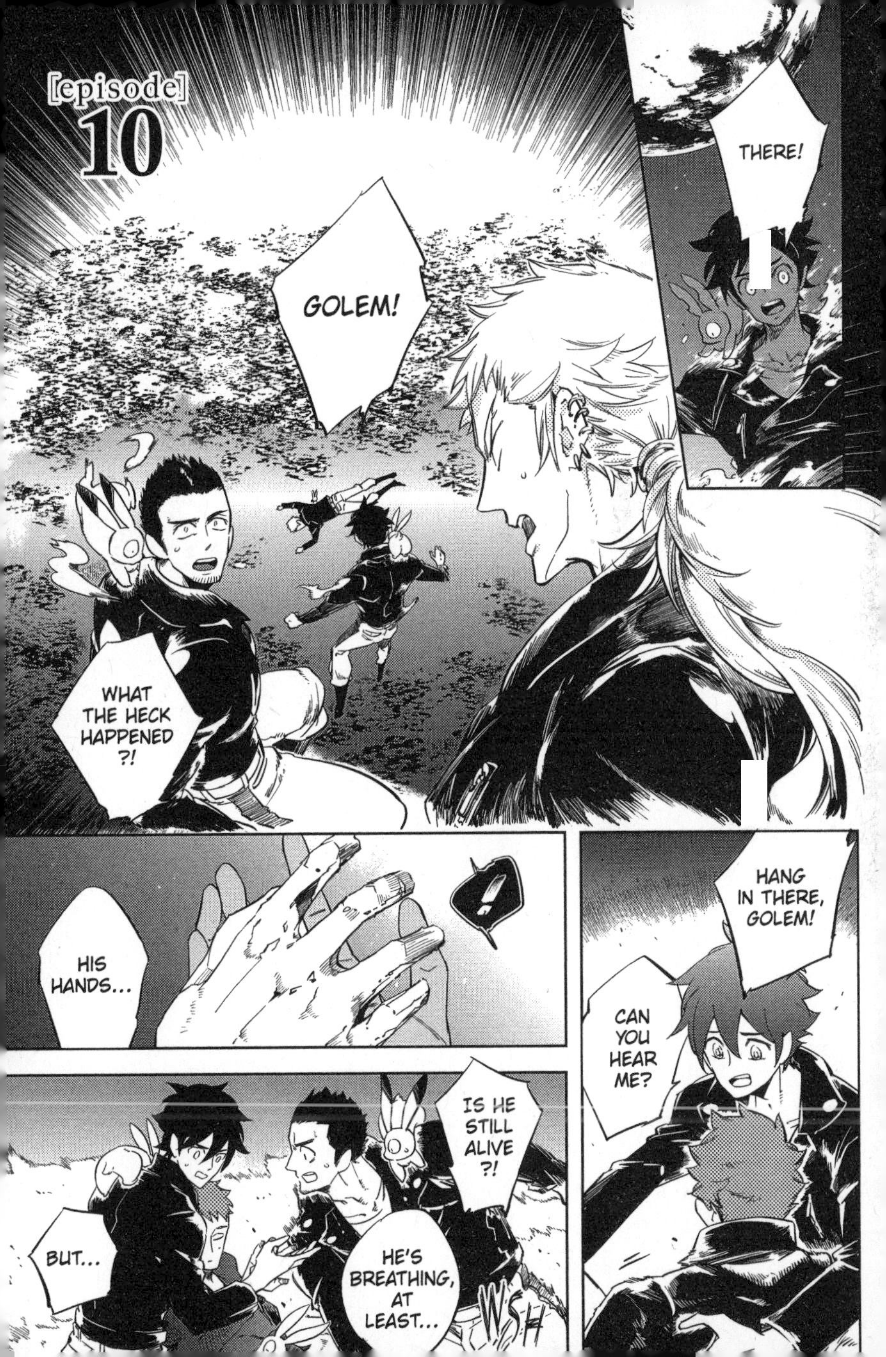
[episode] 10
THERE!
GOLEM!
WHAT THE HECK HAPPENED ?!
HANG IN THERE, GOLEM!
CAN YOU HEAR ME?
HIS HANDS...
IS HE STILL ALIVE ?!
HE'S BREATHING, AT LEAST...
BUT...
WSH

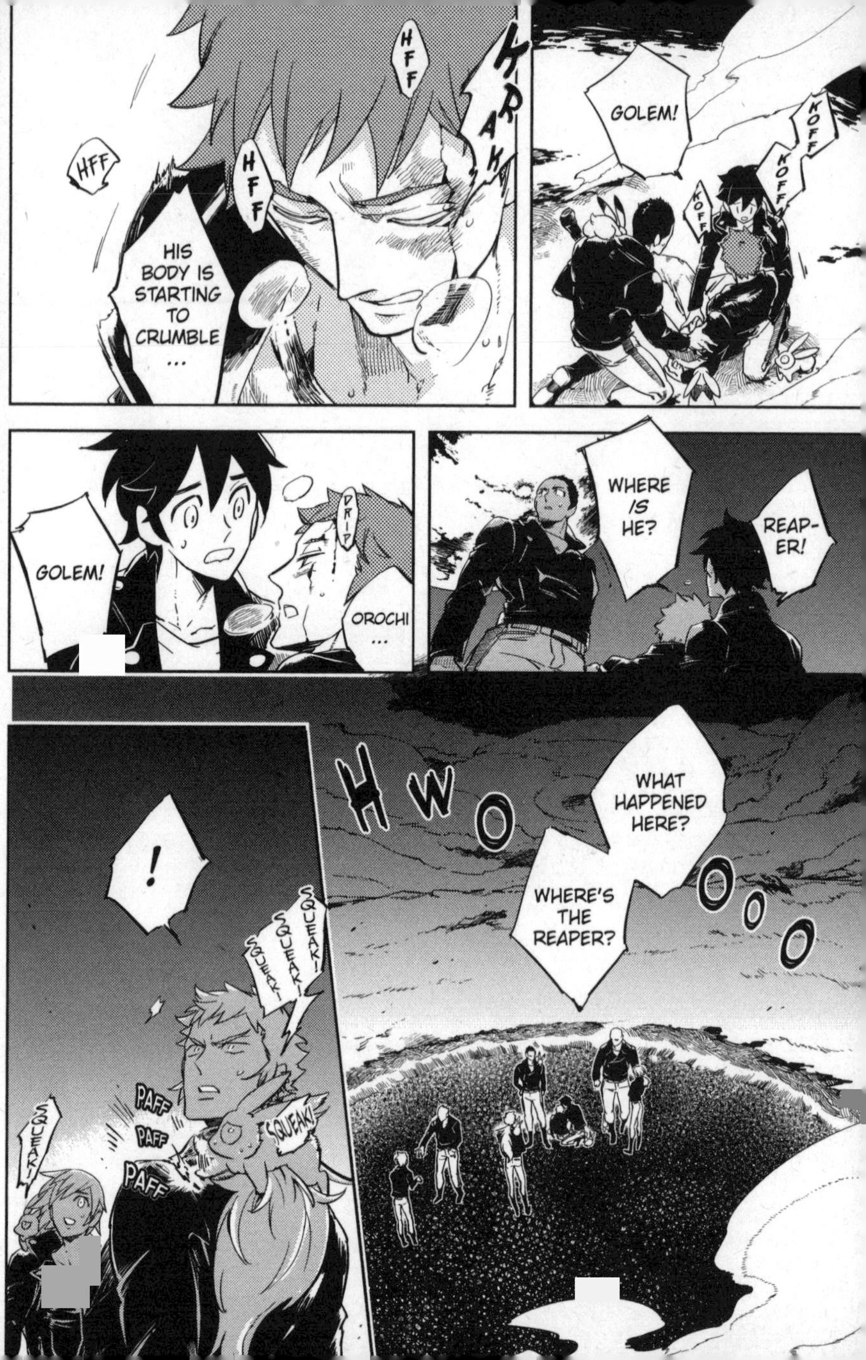
KOFF KOFF
GOLEM!
KOFF
KRAK
HFF
HFF
HFF
HIS BODY IS STARTING TO CRUMBLE ...
REAPER!
WHERE IS HE?
OROCHI ...
DRIP
GOLEM!
WHAT HAPPENED HERE?
HWOOOOO
WHERE'S THE REAPER?
!
SQUEAK! SQUEAK! SQUEAK!
SQUEAK!
PAFF PAFF PAFF
SQUEAK!

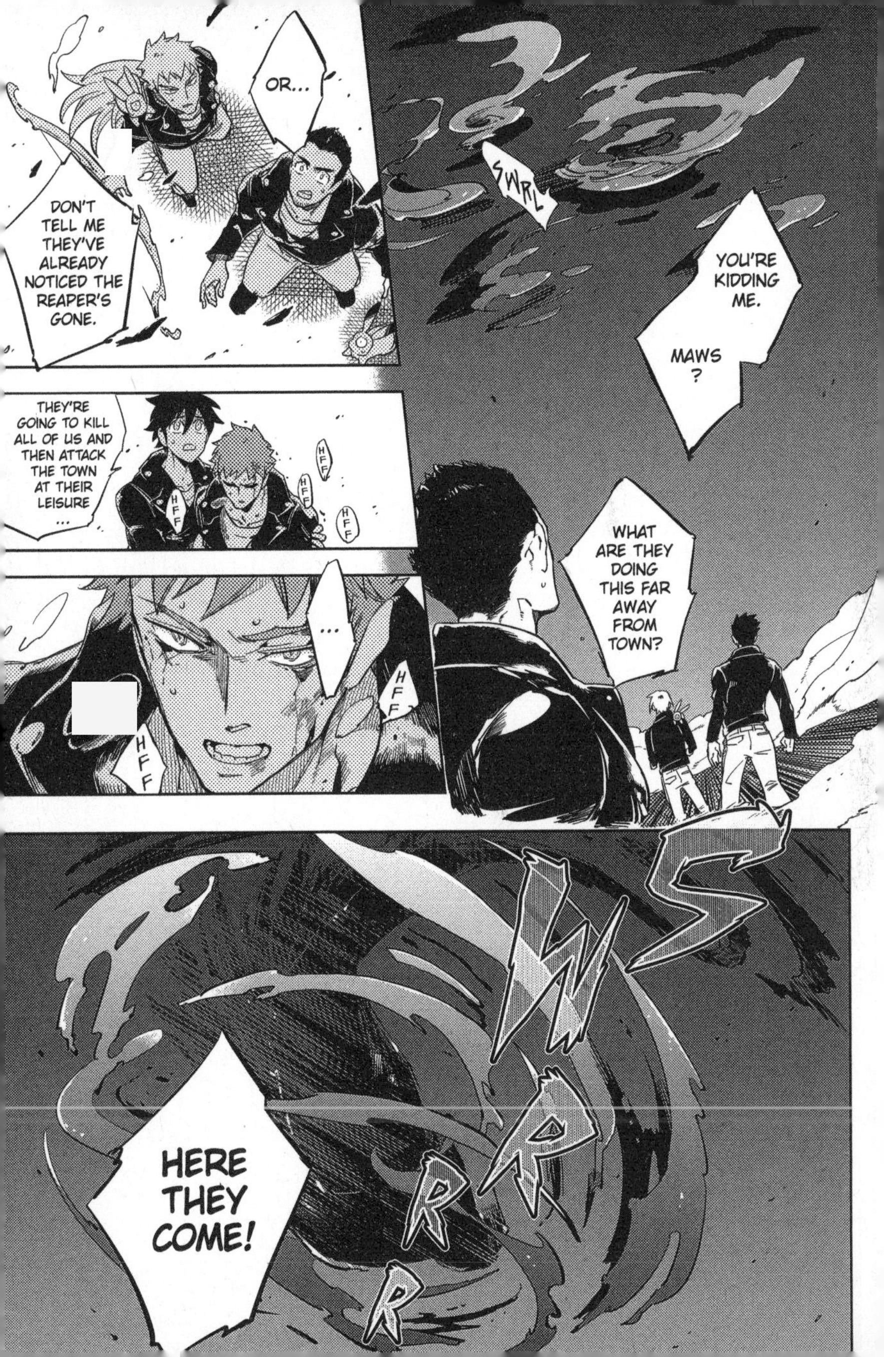
SWRL
YOU'RE KIDDING ME.
MAWS?
WHAT ARE THEY DOING THIS FAR AWAY FROM TOWN?
OR...
DON'T TELL ME THEY'VE ALREADY NOTICED THE REAPER'S GONE.
THEY'RE GOING TO KILL ALL OF US AND THEN ATTACK THE TOWN AT THEIR LEISURE...
HFF HFF HFF
...
HFF HFF
WSRRR
HERE THEY COME!

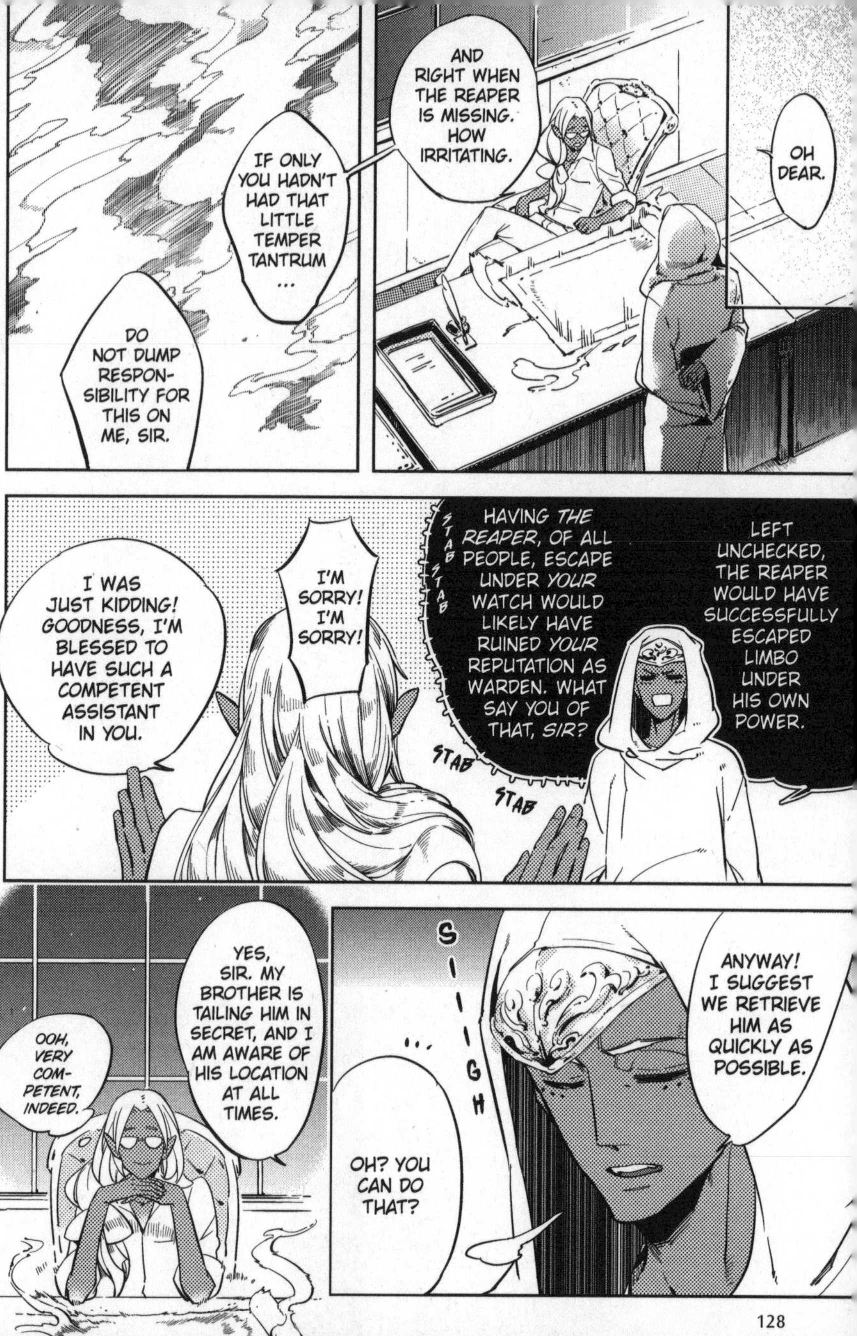
OH DEAR.
AND RIGHT WHEN THE REAPER IS MISSING. HOW IRRITATING.
IF ONLY YOU HADN'T HAD THAT LITTLE TEMPER TANTRUM ...
DO NOT DUMP RESPON-SIBILITY FOR THIS ON ME, SIR.
LEFT UNCHECKED, THE REAPER WOULD HAVE SUCCESSFULLY ESCAPED LIMBO UNDER HIS OWN POWER.
HAVING *THE REAPER*, OF ALL PEOPLE, ESCAPE UNDER *YOUR* WATCH WOULD LIKELY HAVE RUINED *YOUR* REPUTATION AS WARDEN. WHAT SAY YOU OF THAT, *SIR*?
STAB STAB
STAB
STAB
I'M SORRY! I'M SORRY!
I WAS JUST KIDDING! GOODNESS, I'M BLESSED TO HAVE SUCH A COMPETENT ASSISTANT IN YOU.
ANYWAY! I SUGGEST WE RETRIEVE HIM AS QUICKLY AS POSSIBLE.
SIGH
...
OH? YOU CAN DO THAT?
YES, SIR. MY BROTHER IS TAILING HIM IN SECRET, AND I AM AWARE OF HIS LOCATION AT ALL TIMES.
OOH, VERY COM-PETENT, INDEED.

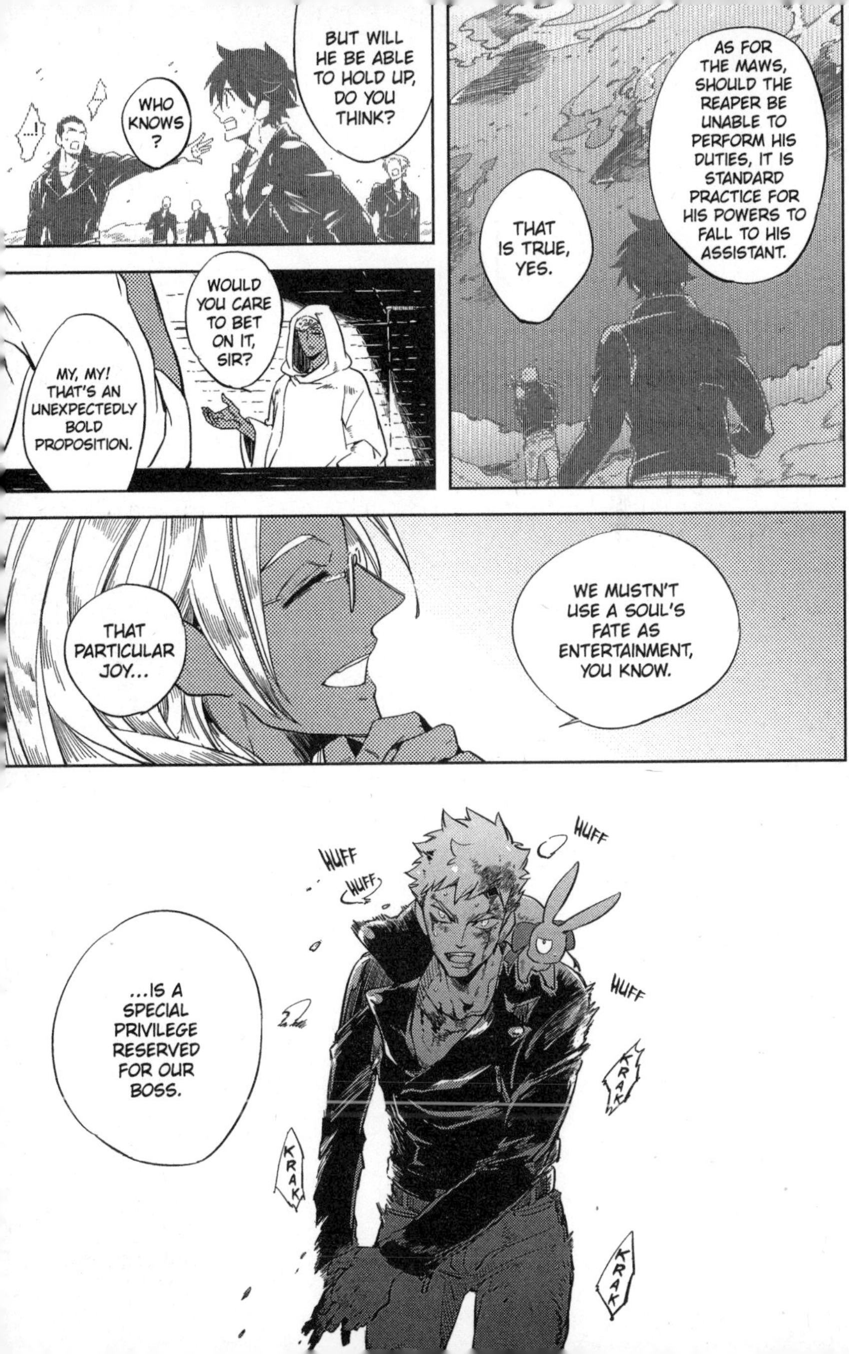
AS FOR THE MAWS, SHOULD THE REAPER BE UNABLE TO PERFORM HIS DUTIES, IT IS STANDARD PRACTICE FOR HIS POWERS TO FALL TO HIS ASSISTANT.
THAT IS TRUE, YES.
BUT WILL HE BE ABLE TO HOLD UP, DO YOU THINK?
WHO KNOWS?
...!
WOULD YOU CARE TO BET ON IT, SIR?
MY, MY! THAT'S AN UNEXPECTEDLY BOLD PROPOSITION.
WE MUSTN'T USE A SOUL'S FATE AS ENTERTAINMENT, YOU KNOW.
THAT PARTICULAR JOY...
HUFF
HUFF
HUFF
HUFF
...IS A SPECIAL PRIVILEGE RESERVED FOR OUR BOSS.
KRAK
KRAK
KRAK

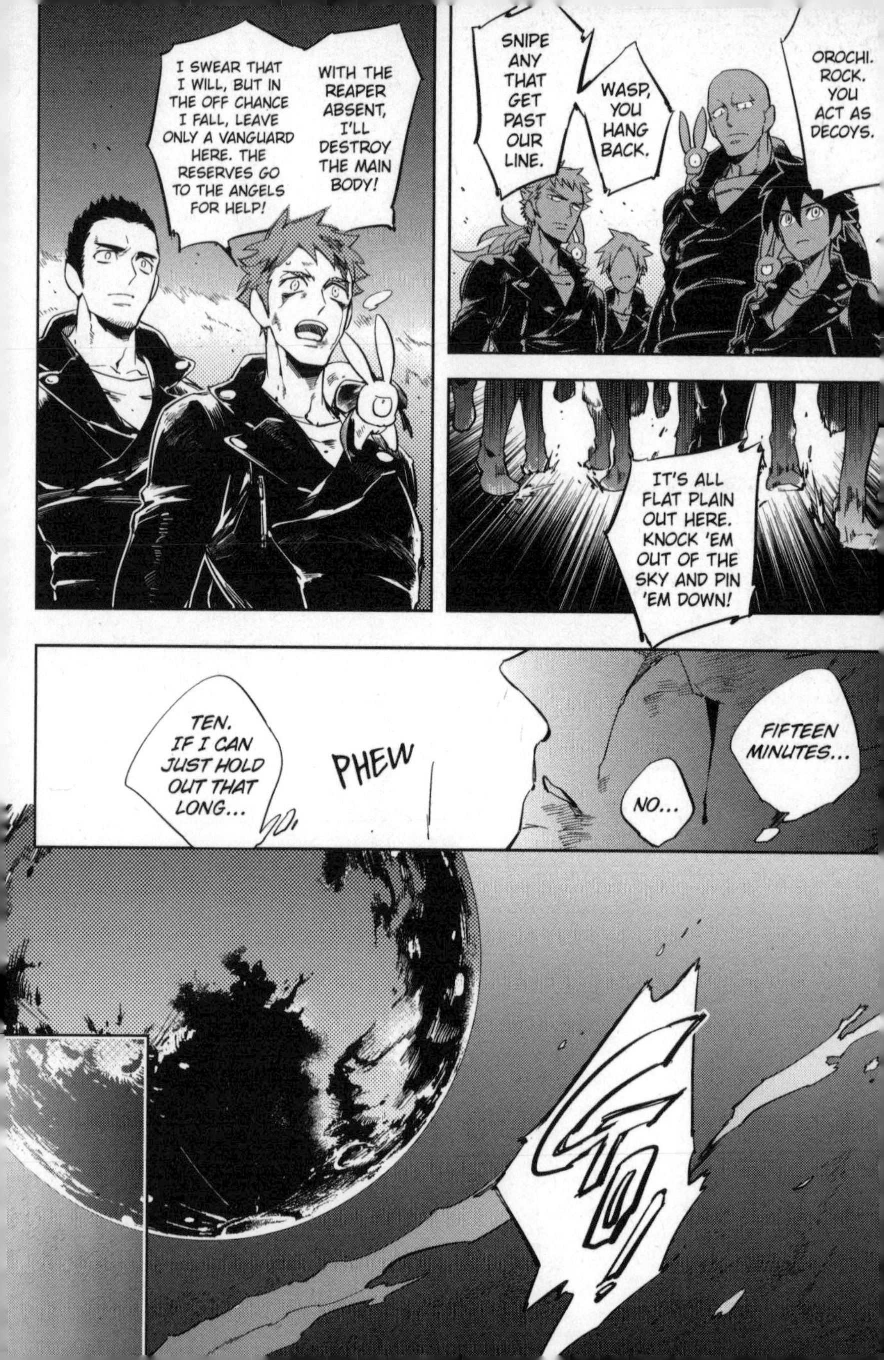
OROCHI. ROCK. YOU ACT AS DECOYS.
WASP, YOU HANG BACK.
SNIPE ANY THAT GET PAST OUR LINE.
IT'S ALL FLAT PLAIN OUT HERE. KNOCK 'EM OUT OF THE SKY AND PIN 'EM DOWN!
WITH THE REAPER ABSENT, I'LL DESTROY THE MAIN BODY!
I SWEAR THAT I WILL, BUT IN THE OFF CHANCE I FALL, LEAVE ONLY A VANGUARD HERE. THE RESERVES GO TO THE ANGELS FOR HELP!
FIFTEEN MINUTES...
NO...
PHEW
TEN. IF I CAN JUST HOLD OUT THAT LONG...
GO!

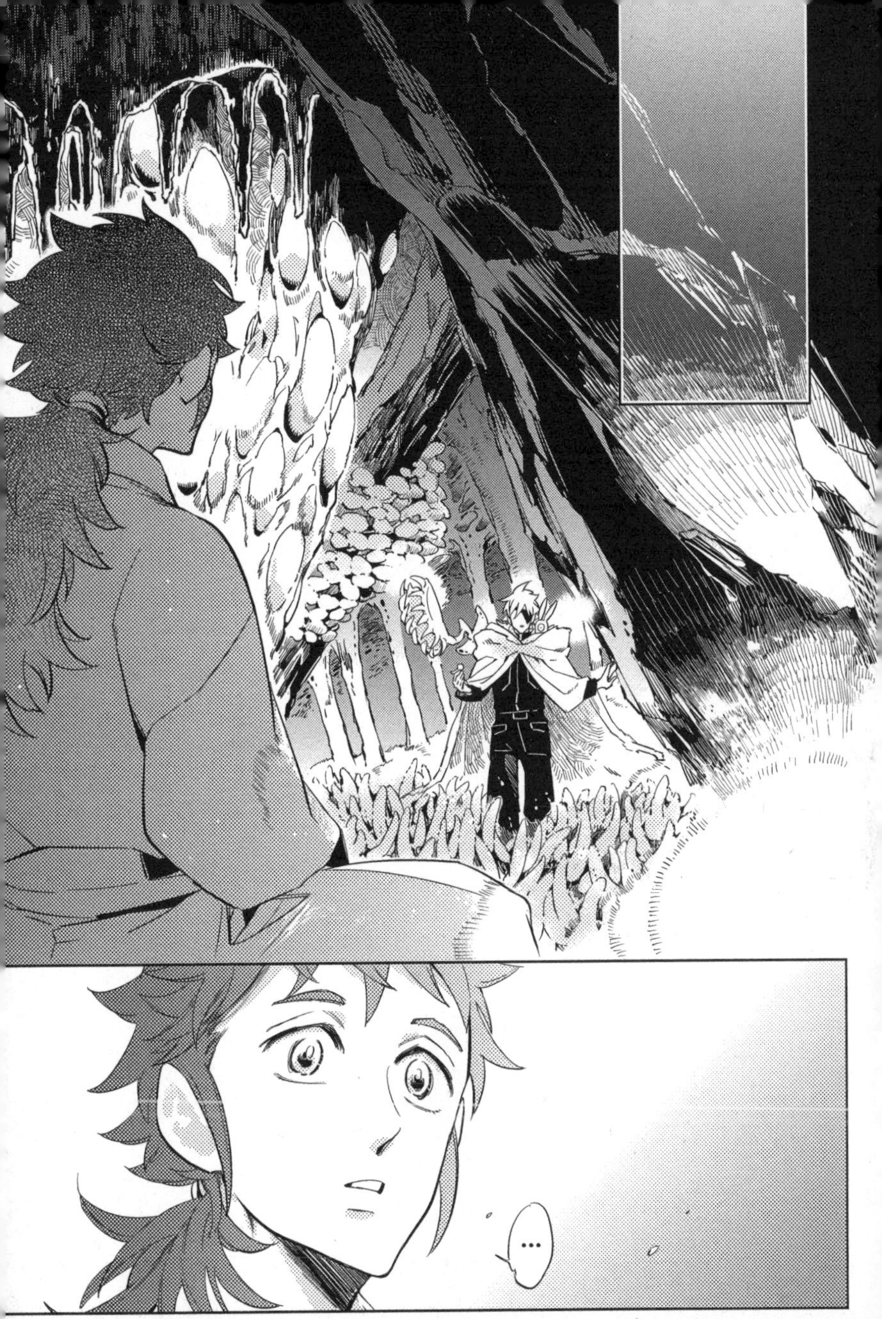
...

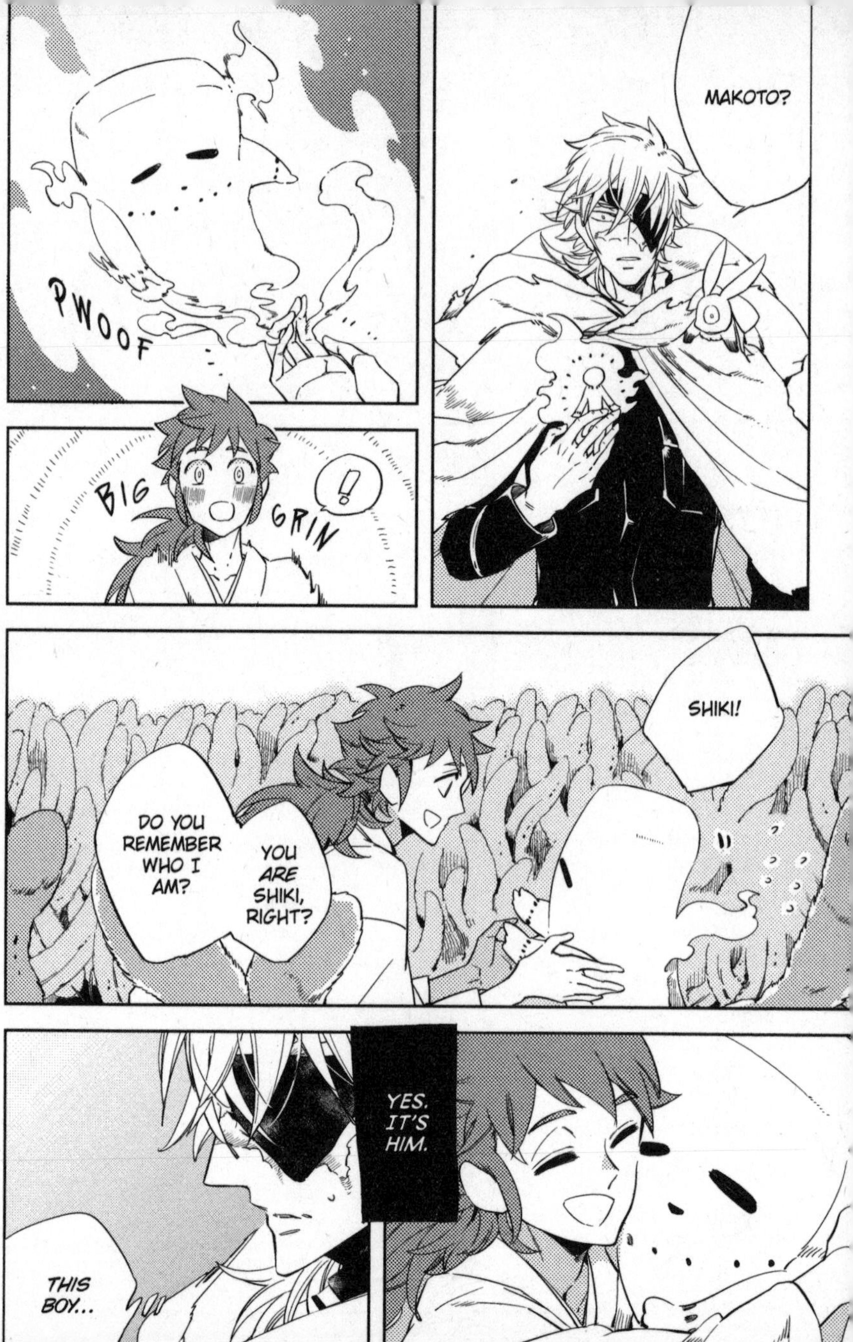
MAKOTO?
PWOOF
BIG GRIN
!
SHIKI!
YOU ARE SHIKI, RIGHT?
DO YOU REMEMBER WHO I AM?
YES. IT'S HIM.
THIS BOY...

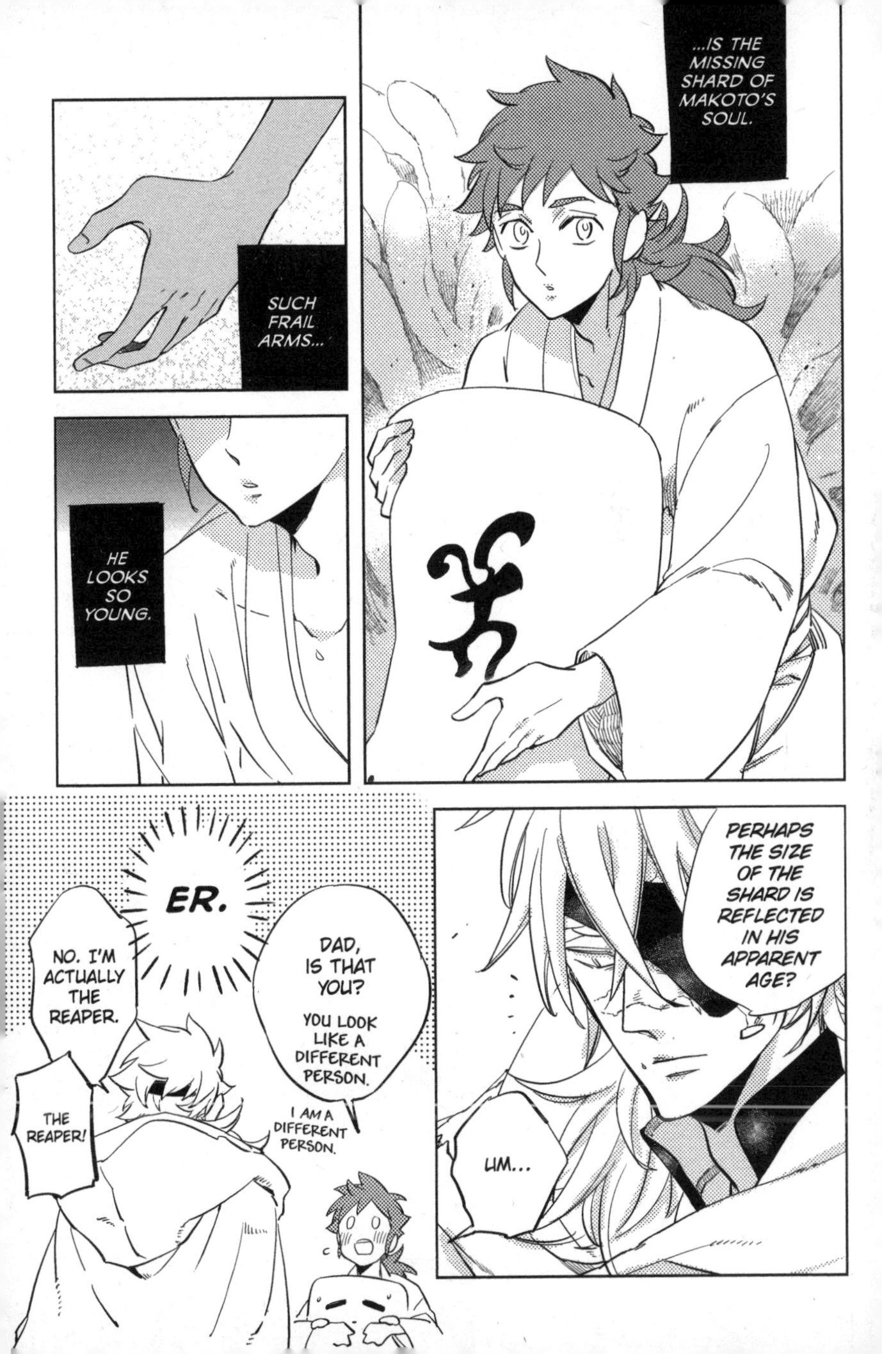
...IS THE MISSING SHARD OF MAKOTO'S SOUL.
SUCH FRAIL ARMS...
HE LOOKS SO YOUNG.
PERHAPS THE SIZE OF THE SHARD IS REFLECTED IN HIS APPARENT AGE?
UM...
DAD, IS THAT YOU?
YOU LOOK LIKE A DIFFERENT PERSON.
ER.
NO. I'M ACTUALLY THE REAPER.
I AM A DIFFERENT PERSON.
THE REAPER!

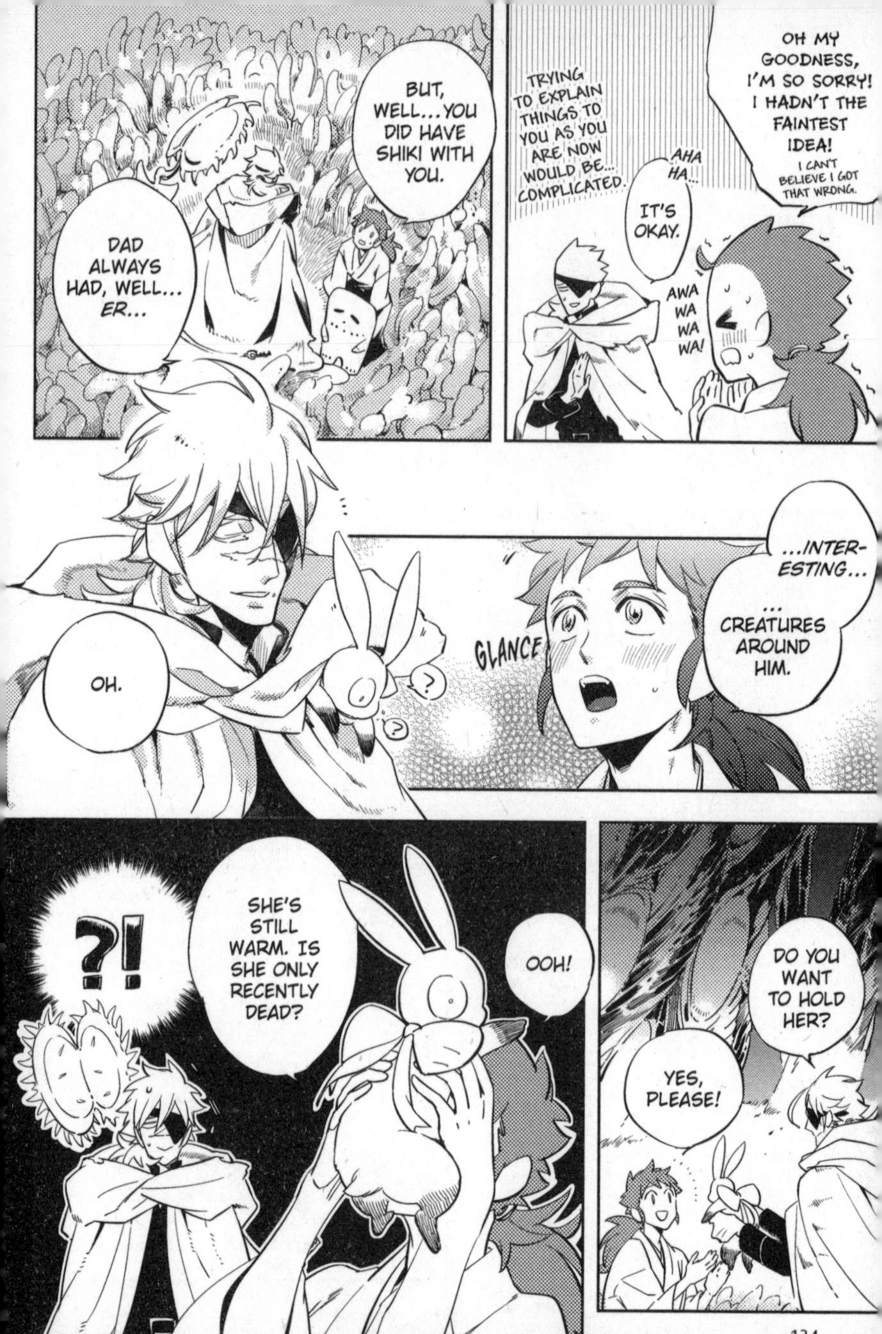
DAD ALWAYS HAD, WELL... ER...
BUT, WELL... YOU DID HAVE SHIKI WITH YOU.
OH MY GOODNESS, I'M SO SORRY! I HADN'T THE FAINTEST IDEA!
I CAN'T BELIEVE I GOT THAT WRONG.
AWA WA WA WA!
AHA HA...
IT'S OKAY.
TRYING TO EXPLAIN THINGS TO YOU AS YOU ARE NOW WOULD BE... COMPLICATED.
OH.
GLANCE
...INTER-ESTING...
... CREATURES AROUND HIM.
?!
SHE'S STILL WARM. IS SHE ONLY RECENTLY DEAD?
OOH!
DO YOU WANT TO HOLD HER?
YES, PLEASE!

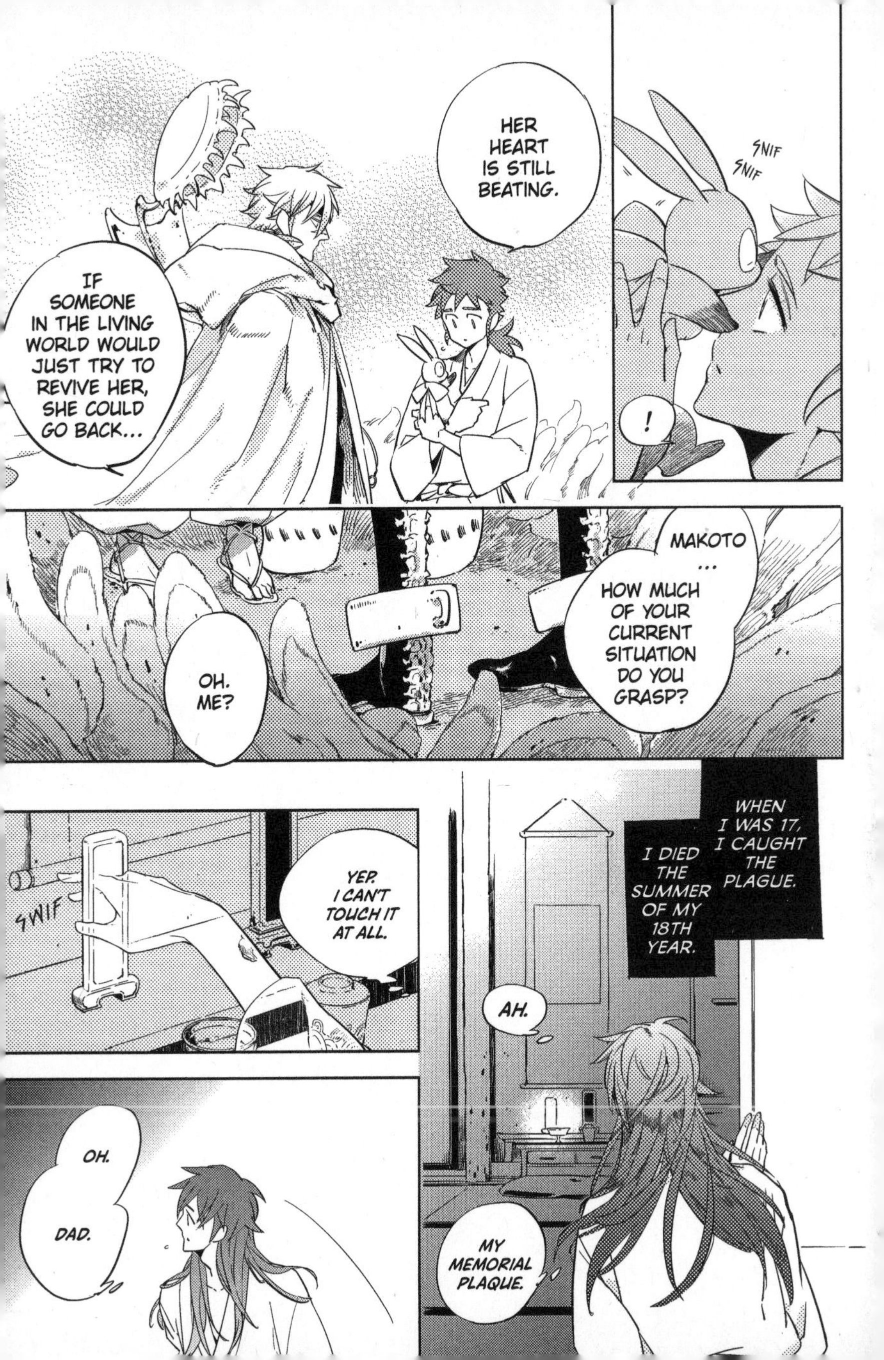
SNIF
SNIF
!
HER HEART IS STILL BEATING.
IF SOMEONE IN THE LIVING WORLD WOULD JUST TRY TO REVIVE HER, SHE COULD GO BACK...
MAKOTO... HOW MUCH OF YOUR CURRENT SITUATION DO YOU GRASP?
OH. ME?
WHEN I WAS 17, I CAUGHT THE PLAGUE.
I DIED THE SUMMER OF MY 18TH YEAR.
AH.
MY MEMORIAL PLAQUE.
SWIF
YEP. I CAN'T TOUCH IT AT ALL.
OH.
DAD.

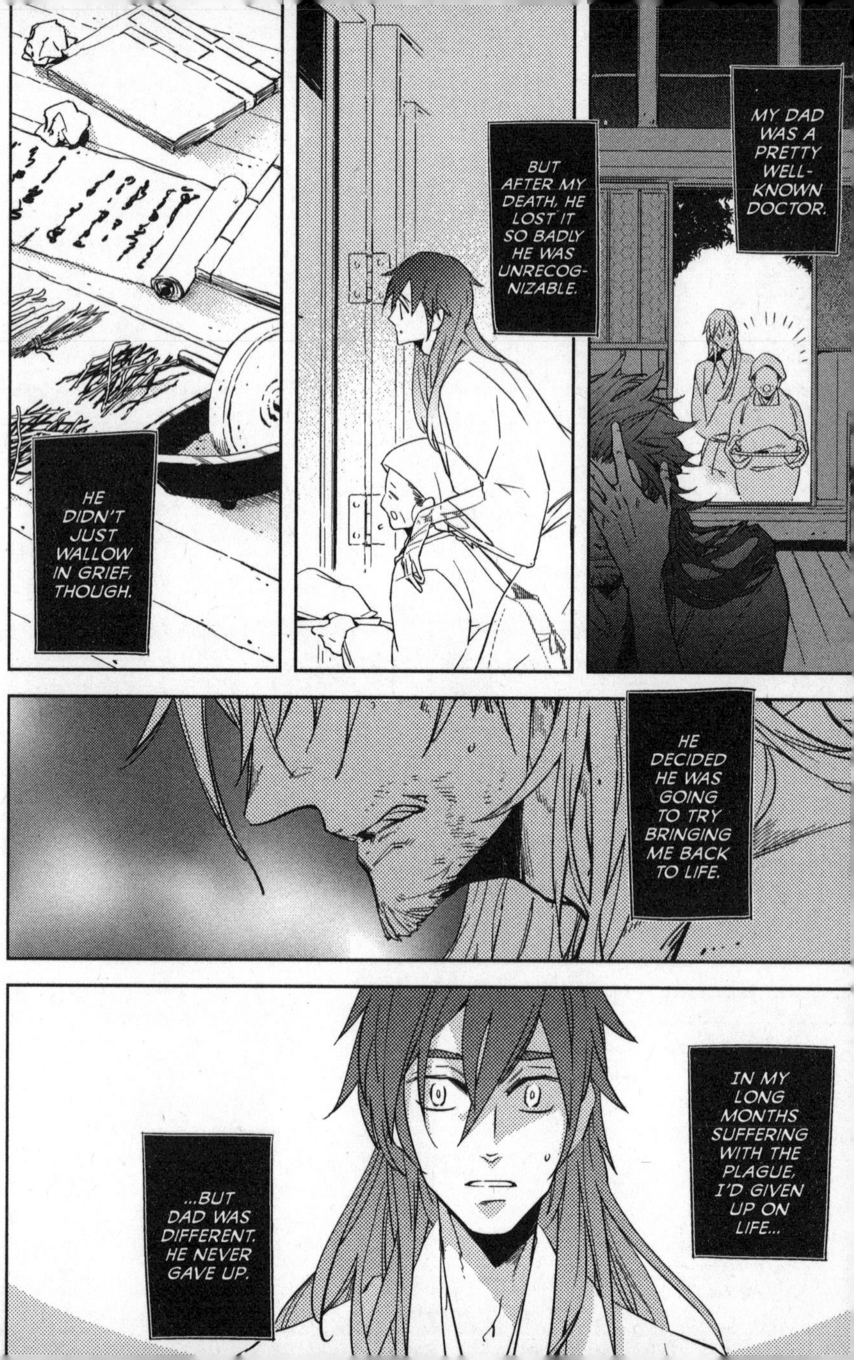
MY DAD WAS A PRETTY WELL-KNOWN DOCTOR.
BUT AFTER MY DEATH, HE LOST IT SO BADLY HE WAS UNRECOG-NIZABLE.
HE DIDN'T JUST WALLOW IN GRIEF, THOUGH.
HE DECIDED HE WAS GOING TO TRY BRINGING ME BACK TO LIFE.
IN MY LONG MONTHS SUFFERING WITH THE PLAGUE, I'D GIVEN UP ON LIFE...
...BUT DAD WAS DIFFERENT. HE NEVER GAVE UP.

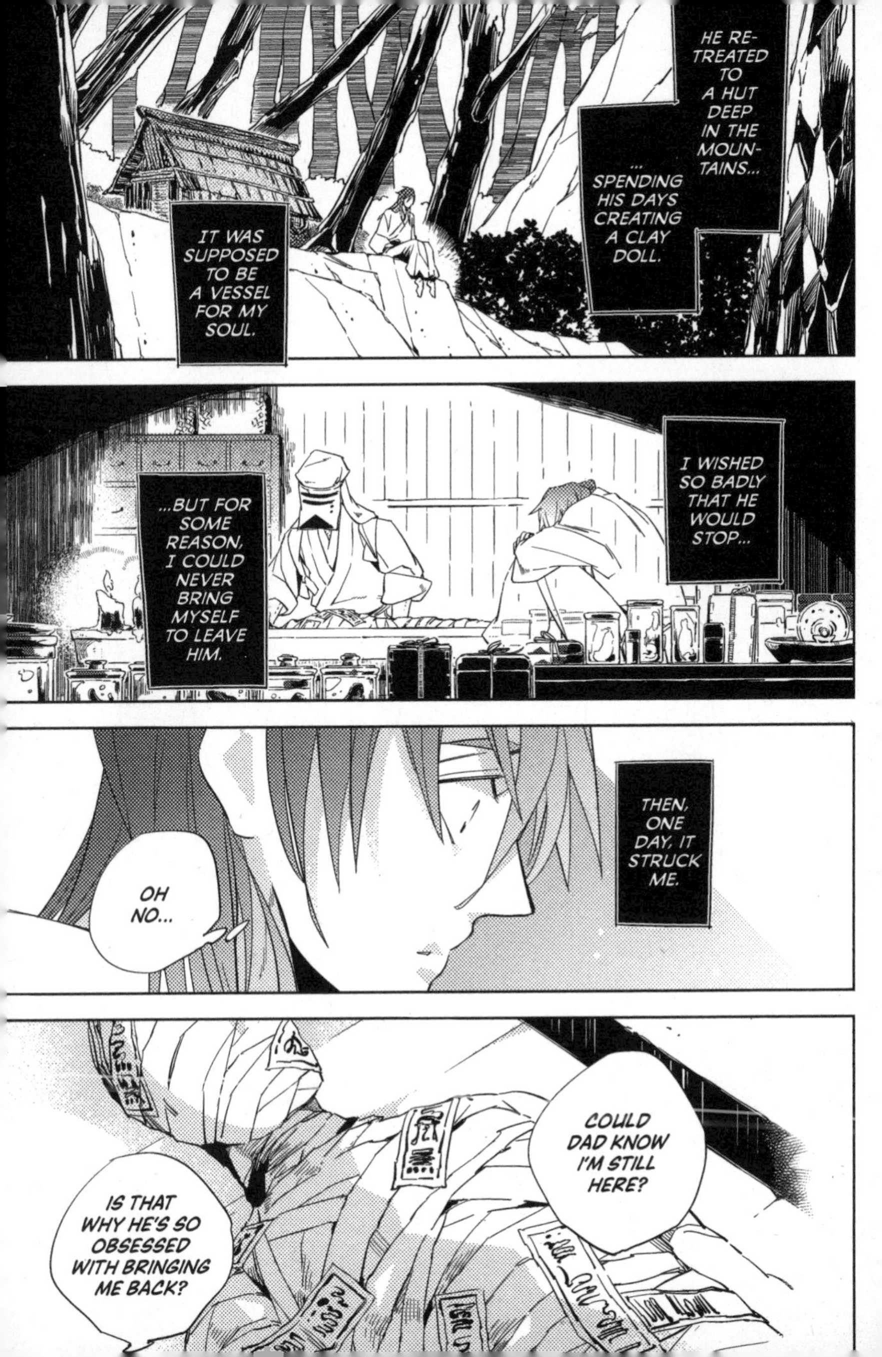
HE RE-TREATED TO A HUT DEEP IN THE MOUN-TAINS...
...SPENDING HIS DAYS CREATING A CLAY DOLL.
IT WAS SUPPOSED TO BE A VESSEL FOR MY SOUL.
I WISHED SO BADLY THAT HE WOULD STOP...
...BUT FOR SOME REASON, I COULD NEVER BRING MYSELF TO LEAVE HIM.
THEN, ONE DAY, IT STRUCK ME.
OH NO...
COULD DAD KNOW I'M STILL HERE?
IS THAT WHY HE'S SO OBSESSED WITH BRINGING ME BACK?

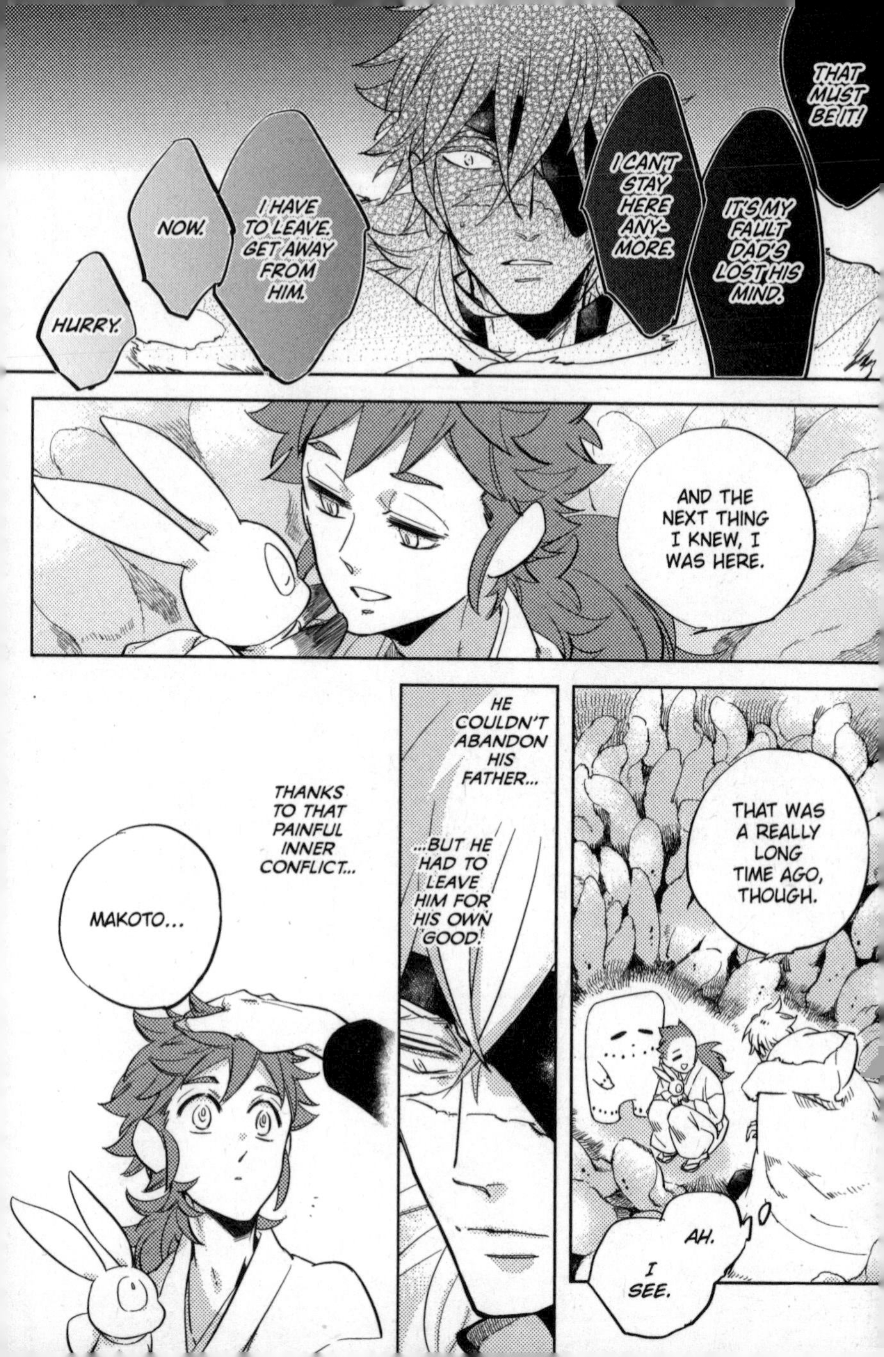
THAT MUST BE IT!
IT'S MY FAULT DAD'S LOST HIS MIND.
I CAN'T STAY HERE ANY-MORE.
I HAVE TO LEAVE. GET AWAY FROM HIM.
NOW.
HURRY.
AND THE NEXT THING I KNEW, I WAS HERE.
THAT WAS A REALLY LONG TIME AGO, THOUGH.
AH. I SEE.
HE COULDN'T ABANDON HIS FATHER...
...BUT HE HAD TO LEAVE HIM FOR HIS OWN GOOD.
THANKS TO THAT PAINFUL INNER CONFLICT...
MAKOTO...

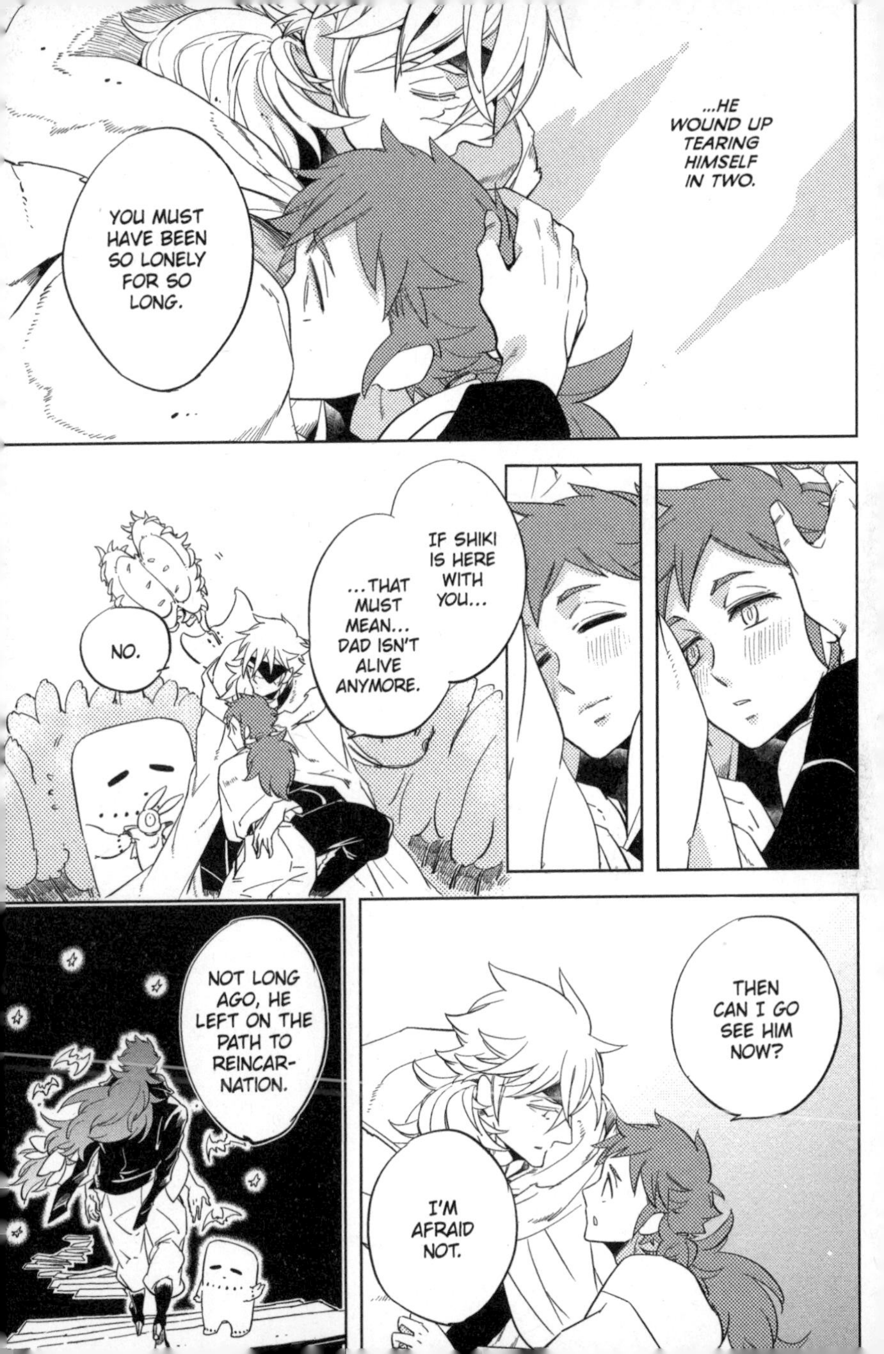
...HE WOUND UP TEARING HIMSELF IN TWO.
YOU MUST HAVE BEEN SO LONELY FOR SO LONG.
IF SHIKI IS HERE WITH YOU...
...THAT MUST MEAN... DAD ISN'T ALIVE ANYMORE.
NO.
THEN CAN I GO SEE HIM NOW?
I'M AFRAID NOT.
NOT LONG AGO, HE LEFT ON THE PATH TO REINCAR-NATION.

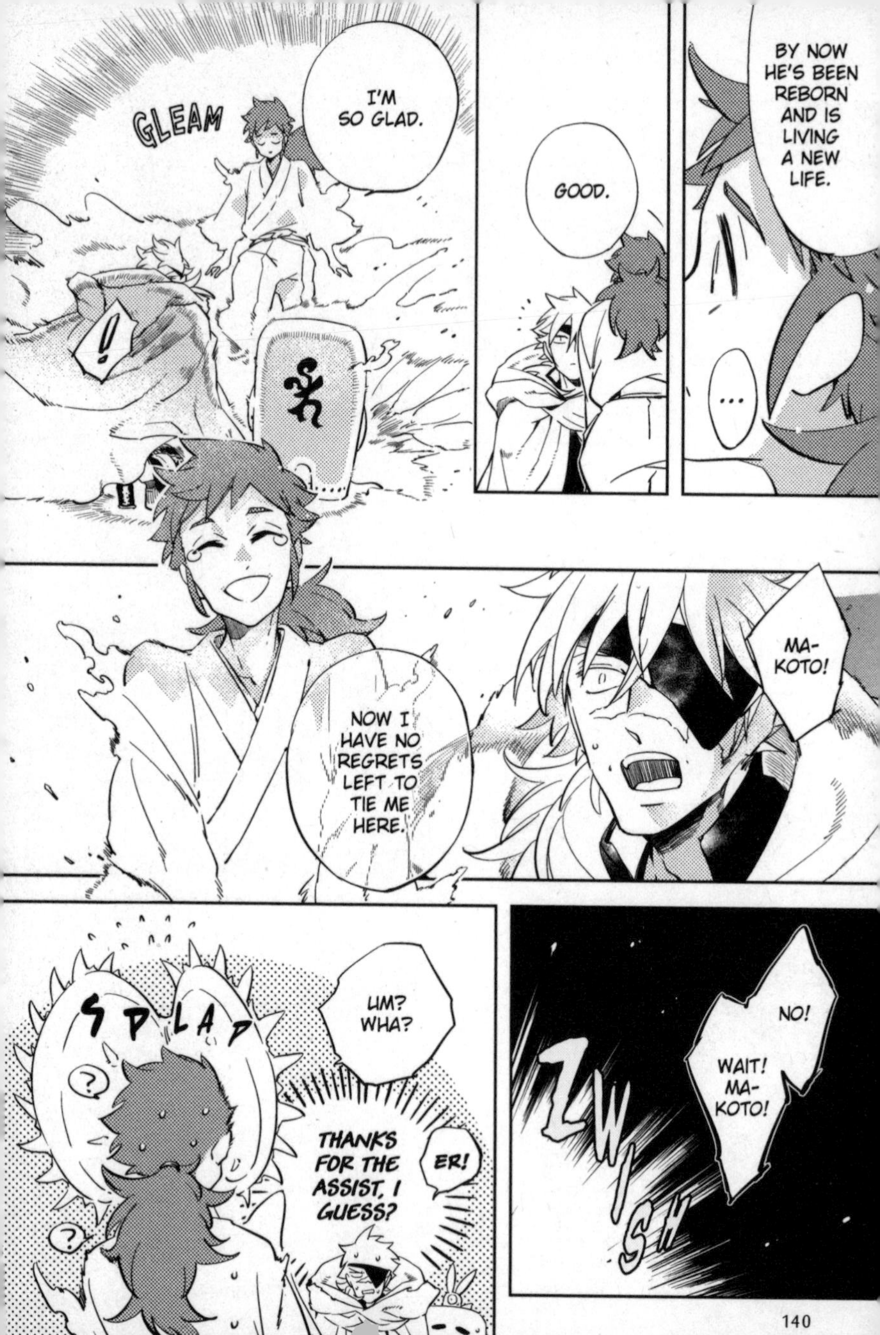

BY NOW HE'S BEEN REBORN AND IS LIVING A NEW LIFE.
...
GOOD.
GLEAM
I'M SO GLAD.
!
!!
MA-KOTO!
NOW I HAVE NO REGRETS LEFT TO TIE ME HERE.
ZWISH
NO!
WAIT! MA-KOTO!
UM? WHA?
SPLAP
?
THANKS FOR THE ASSIST, I GUESS?
ER!
?

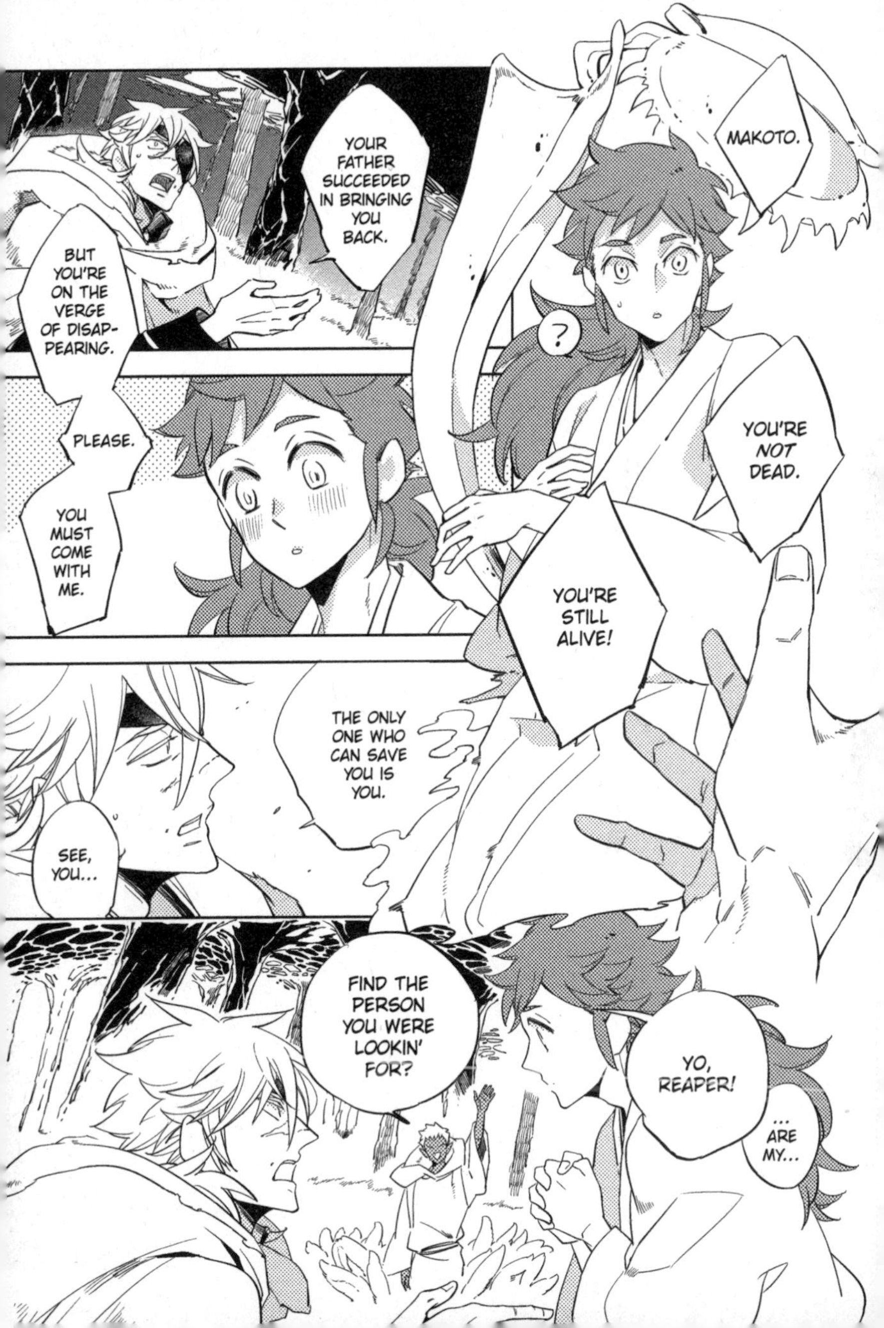
MAKOTO.
?
YOU'RE NOT DEAD.
YOU'RE STILL ALIVE!
YOUR FATHER SUCCEEDED IN BRINGING YOU BACK.
BUT YOU'RE ON THE VERGE OF DISAP-PEARING.
PLEASE.
YOU MUST COME WITH ME.
THE ONLY ONE WHO CAN SAVE YOU IS YOU.
SEE, YOU...
YO, REAPER!
... ARE MY...
FIND THE PERSON YOU WERE LOOKIN' FOR?

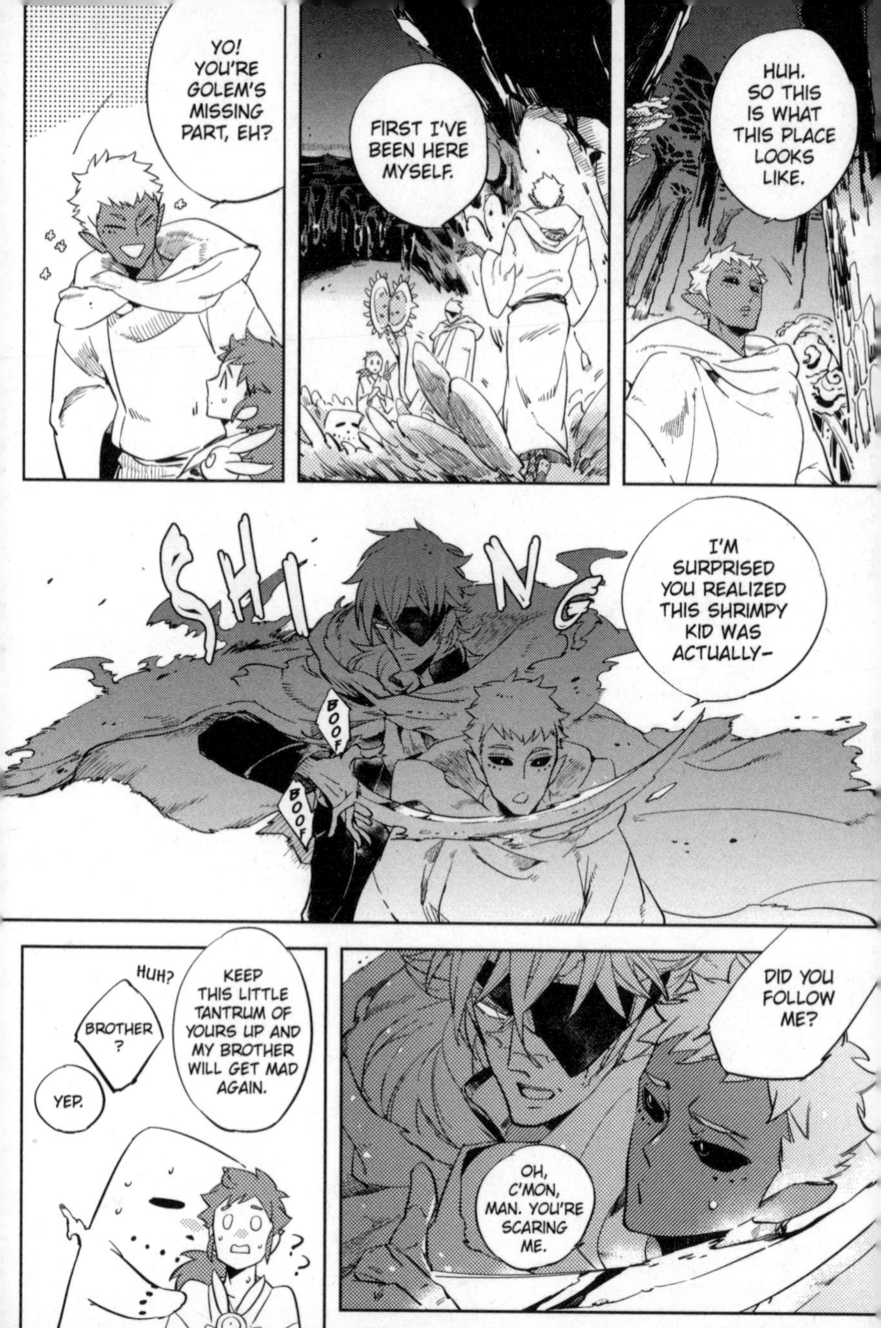
HUH. SO THIS IS WHAT THIS PLACE LOOKS LIKE.
FIRST I'VE BEEN HERE MYSELF.
YO! YOU'RE GOLEM'S MISSING PART, EH?
I'M SURPRISED YOU REALIZED THIS SHRIMPY KID WAS ACTUALLY-
SHING
BOOF
BOOF
DID YOU FOLLOW ME?
OH, C'MON, MAN. YOU'RE SCARING ME.
KEEP THIS LITTLE TANTRUM OF YOURS UP AND MY BROTHER WILL GET MAD AGAIN.
HUH?
BROTHER?
YEP.

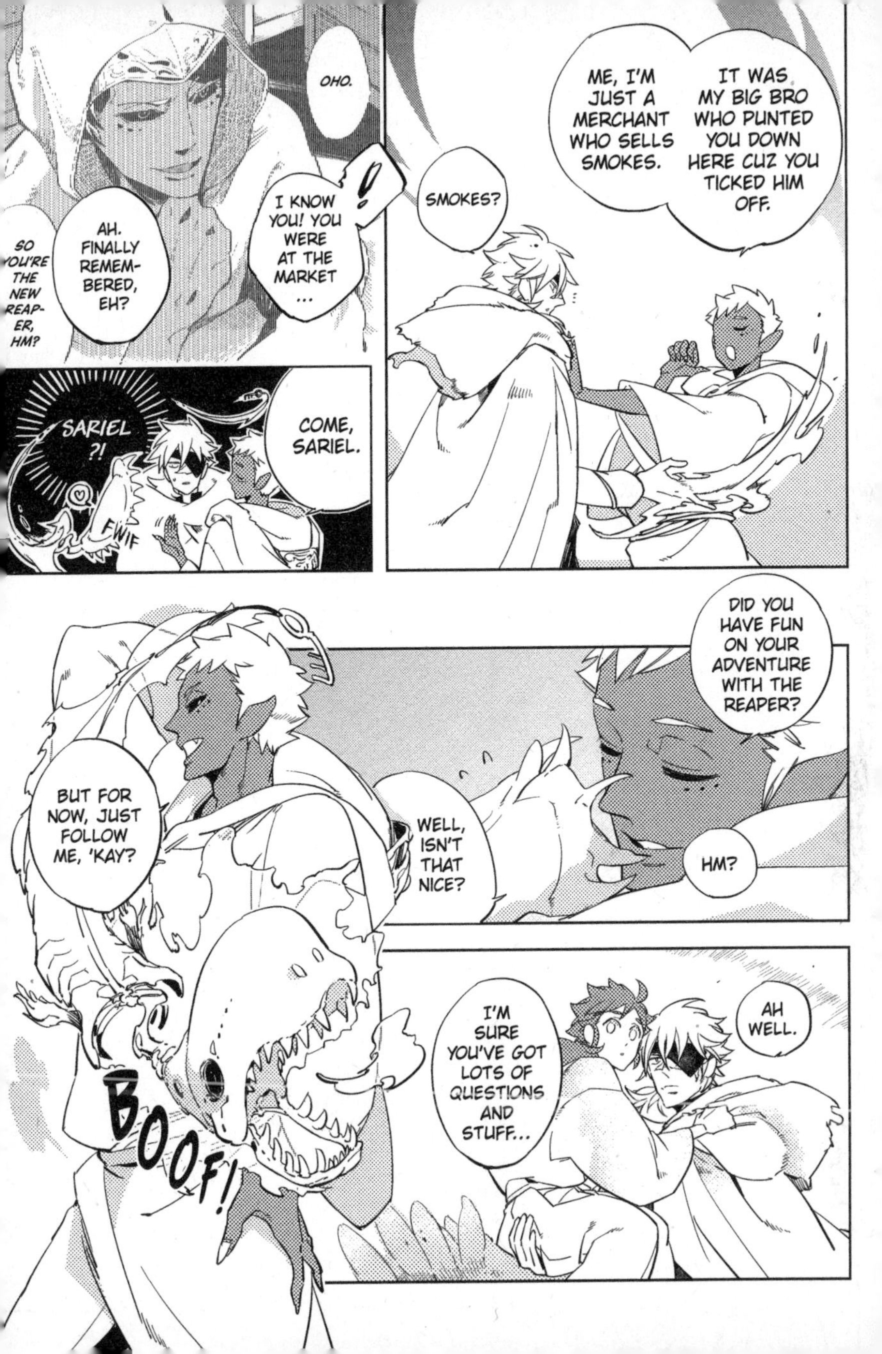
IT WAS MY BIG BRO WHO PUNTED YOU DOWN HERE CUZ YOU TICKED HIM OFF.
ME, I'M JUST A MERCHANT WHO SELLS SMOKES.
SMOKES?
OHO.
!
I KNOW YOU! YOU WERE AT THE MARKET ...
AH. FINALLY REMEMBERED, EH?
SO YOU'RE THE NEW REAPER, HM?
COME, SARIEL.
SARIEL ?!
FWIF
DID YOU HAVE FUN ON YOUR ADVENTURE WITH THE REAPER?
HM?
WELL, ISN'T THAT NICE?
AH WELL.
I'M SURE YOU'VE GOT LOTS OF QUESTIONS AND STUFF...
BUT FOR NOW, JUST FOLLOW ME, 'KAY?
BOOOF!

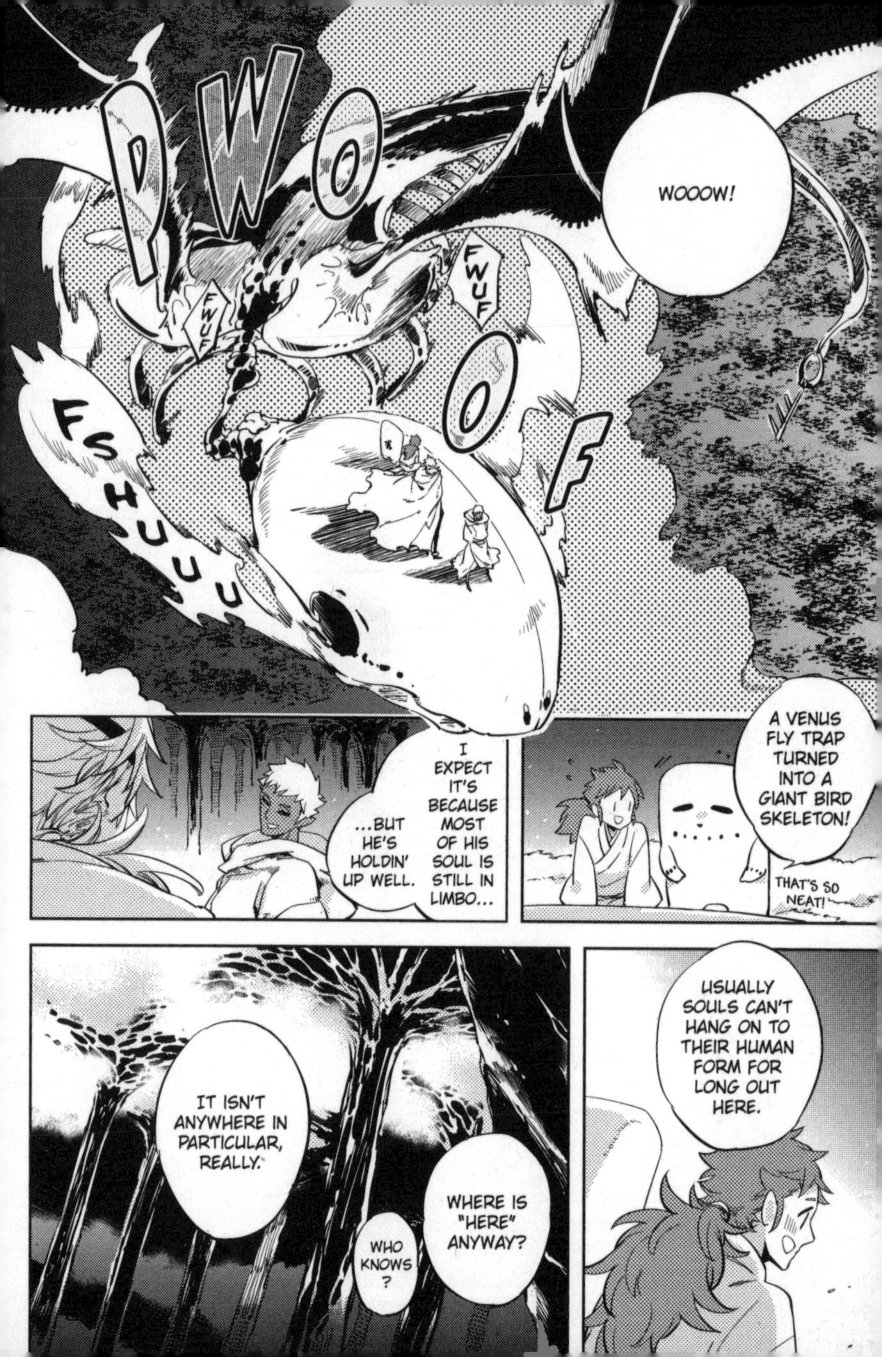
WOOOW!
PWOOF
FWUF
FWUF
FSHUUUU
A VENUS FLY TRAP TURNED INTO A GIANT BIRD SKELETON!
THAT'S SO NEAT!
I EXPECT IT'S BECAUSE MOST OF HIS SOUL IS STILL IN LIMBO...
...BUT HE'S HOLDIN' UP WELL.
USUALLY SOULS CAN'T HANG ON TO THEIR HUMAN FORM FOR LONG OUT HERE.
WHERE IS "HERE" ANYWAY?
WHO KNOWS?
IT ISN'T ANYWHERE IN PARTICULAR, REALLY.

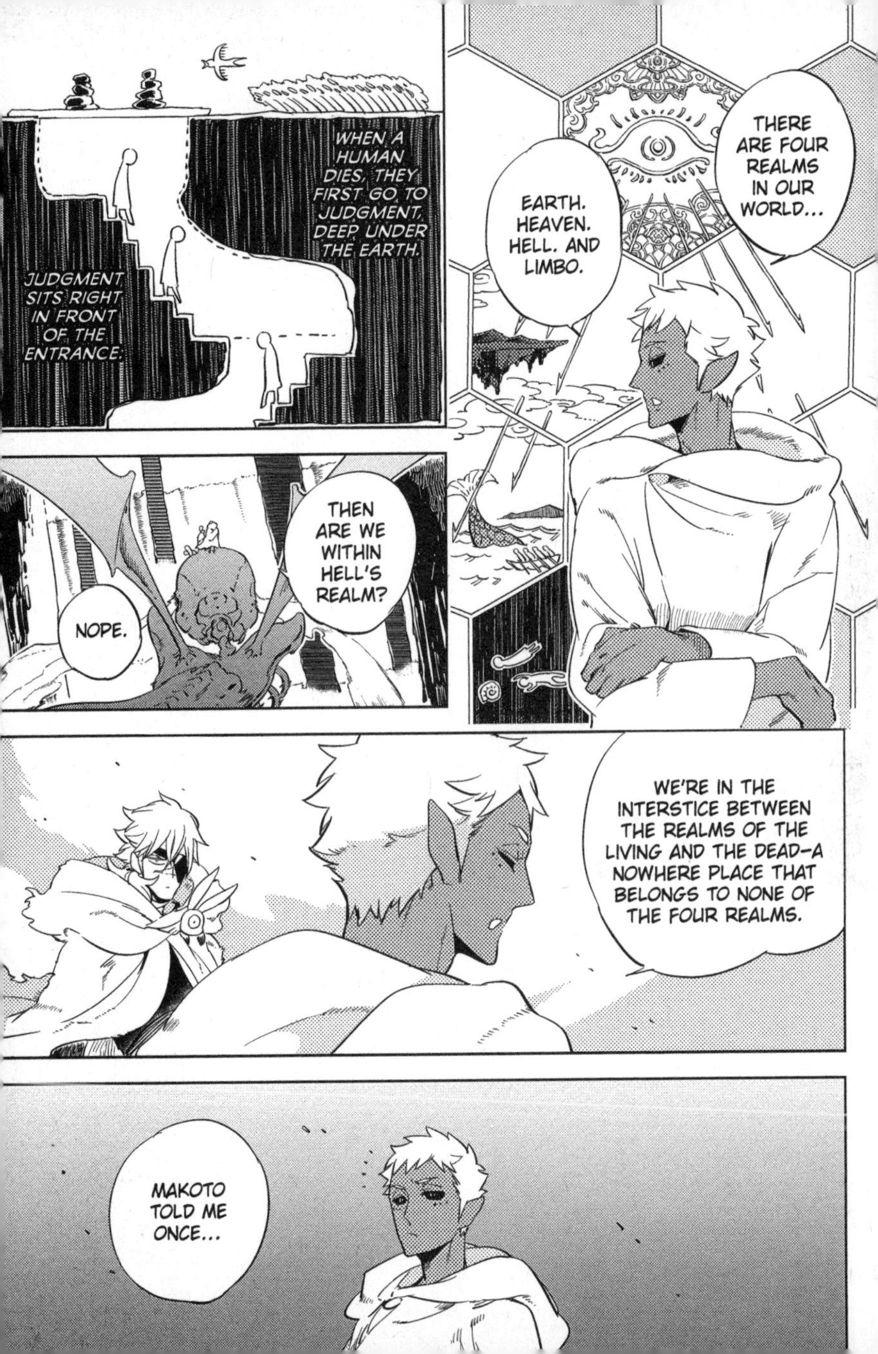
THERE ARE FOUR REALMS IN OUR WORLD...
EARTH. HEAVEN. HELL. AND LIMBO.
WHEN A HUMAN DIES, THEY FIRST GO TO JUDGMENT, DEEP UNDER THE EARTH.
JUDGMENT SITS RIGHT IN FRONT OF THE ENTRANCE.
THEN ARE WE WITHIN HELL'S REALM?
NOPE.
WE'RE IN THE INTERSTICE BETWEEN THE REALMS OF THE LIVING AND THE DEAD—A NOWHERE PLACE THAT BELONGS TO NONE OF THE FOUR REALMS.
MAKOTO TOLD ME ONCE...

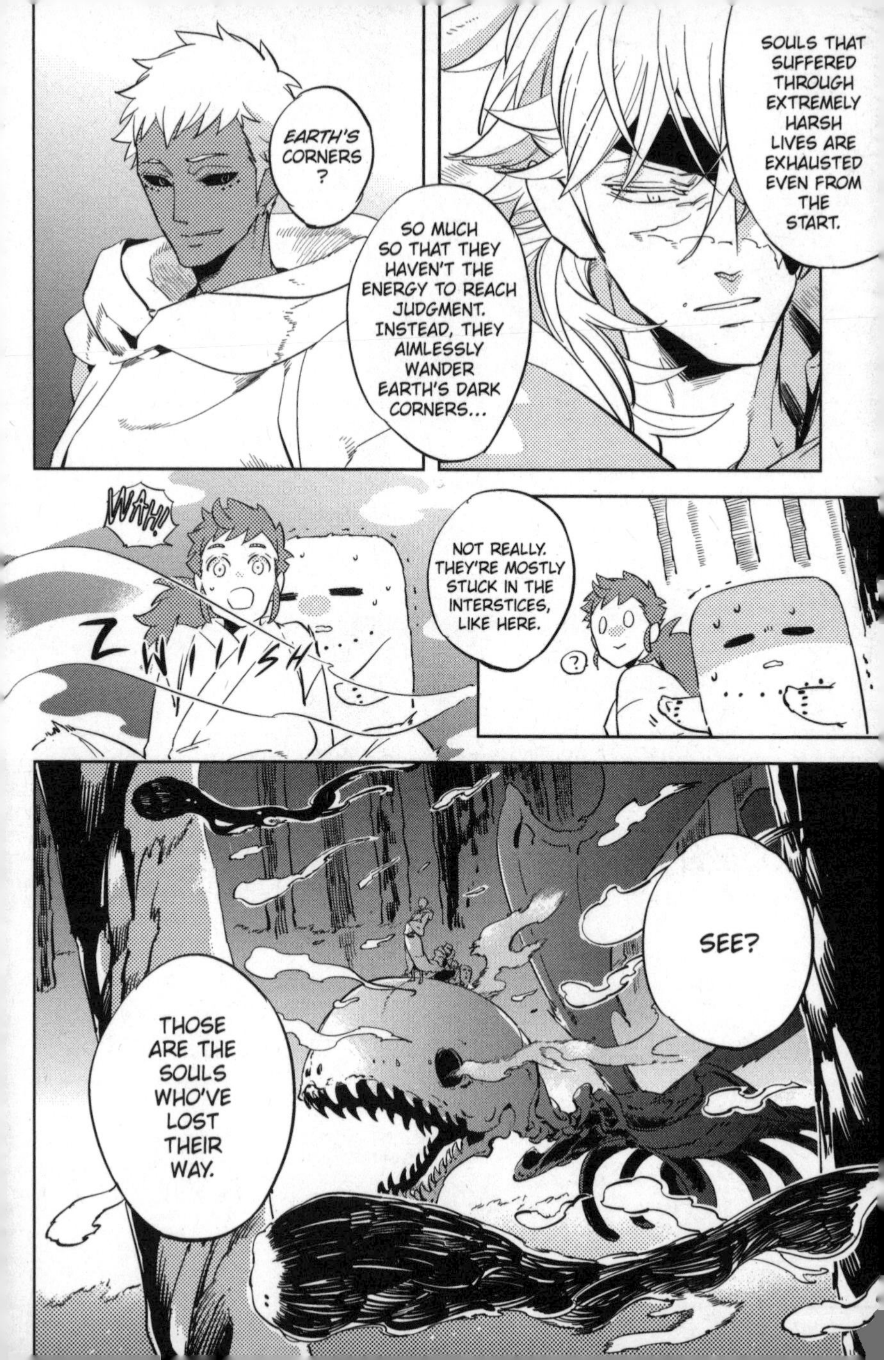
SOULS THAT SUFFERED THROUGH EXTREMELY HARSH LIVES ARE EXHAUSTED EVEN FROM THE START.
SO MUCH SO THAT THEY HAVEN'T THE ENERGY TO REACH JUDGMENT. INSTEAD, THEY AIMLESSLY WANDER EARTH'S DARK CORNERS...
EARTH'S CORNERS?
NOT REALLY. THEY'RE MOSTLY STUCK IN THE INTERSTICES, LIKE HERE.
?
WAH!
ZWIIISH
SEE?
THOSE ARE THE SOULS WHO'VE LOST THEIR WAY.

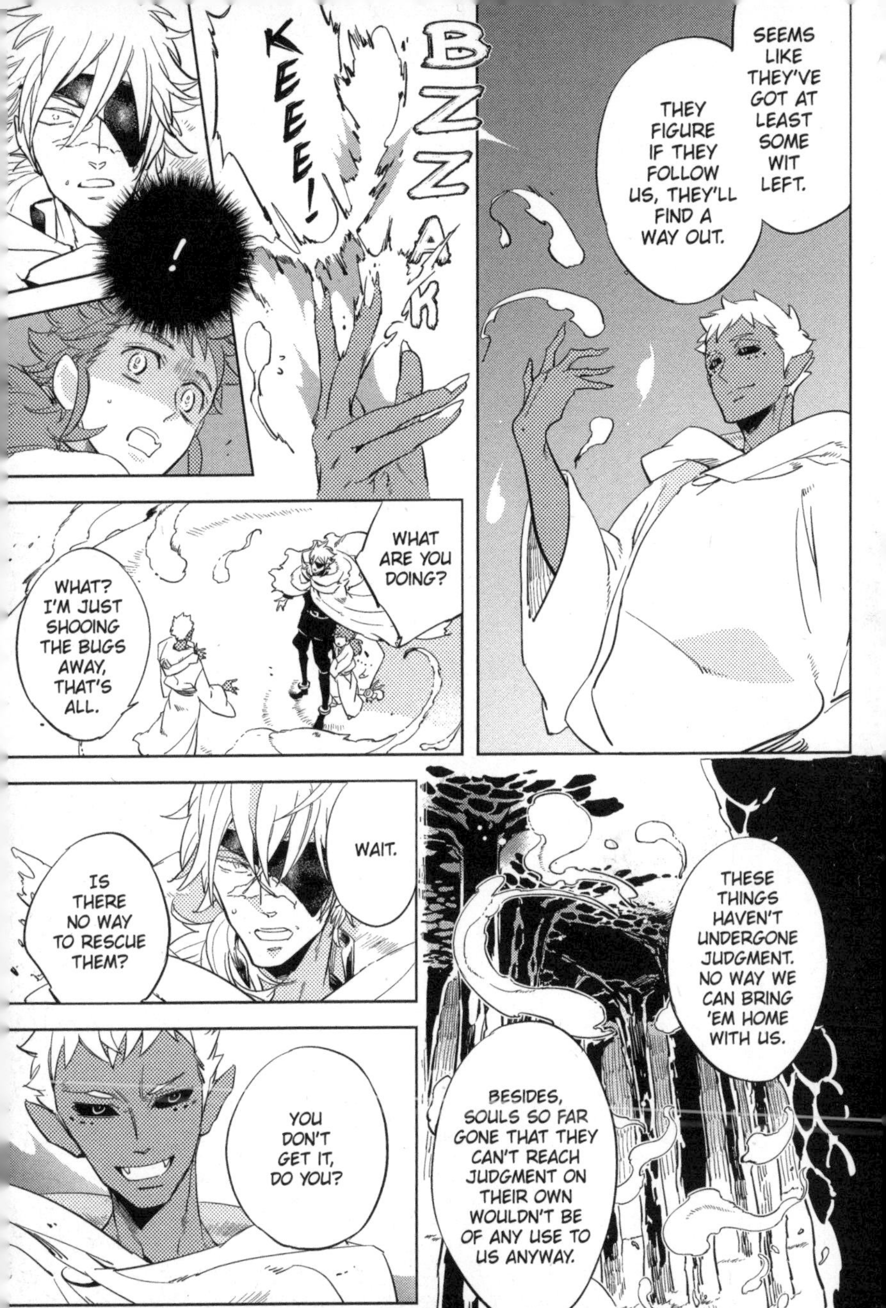
SEEMS LIKE THEY'VE GOT AT LEAST SOME WIT LEFT.
THEY FIGURE IF THEY FOLLOW US, THEY'LL FIND A WAY OUT.
BZZ
KEEEE!
AK
!
WHAT ARE YOU DOING?
WHAT? I'M JUST SHOOING THE BUGS AWAY, THAT'S ALL.
THESE THINGS HAVEN'T UNDERGONE JUDGMENT. NO WAY WE CAN BRING 'EM HOME WITH US.
BESIDES, SOULS SO FAR GONE THAT THEY CAN'T REACH JUDGMENT ON THEIR OWN WOULDN'T BE OF ANY USE TO US ANYWAY.
WAIT.
IS THERE NO WAY TO RESCUE THEM?
YOU DON'T GET IT, DO YOU?

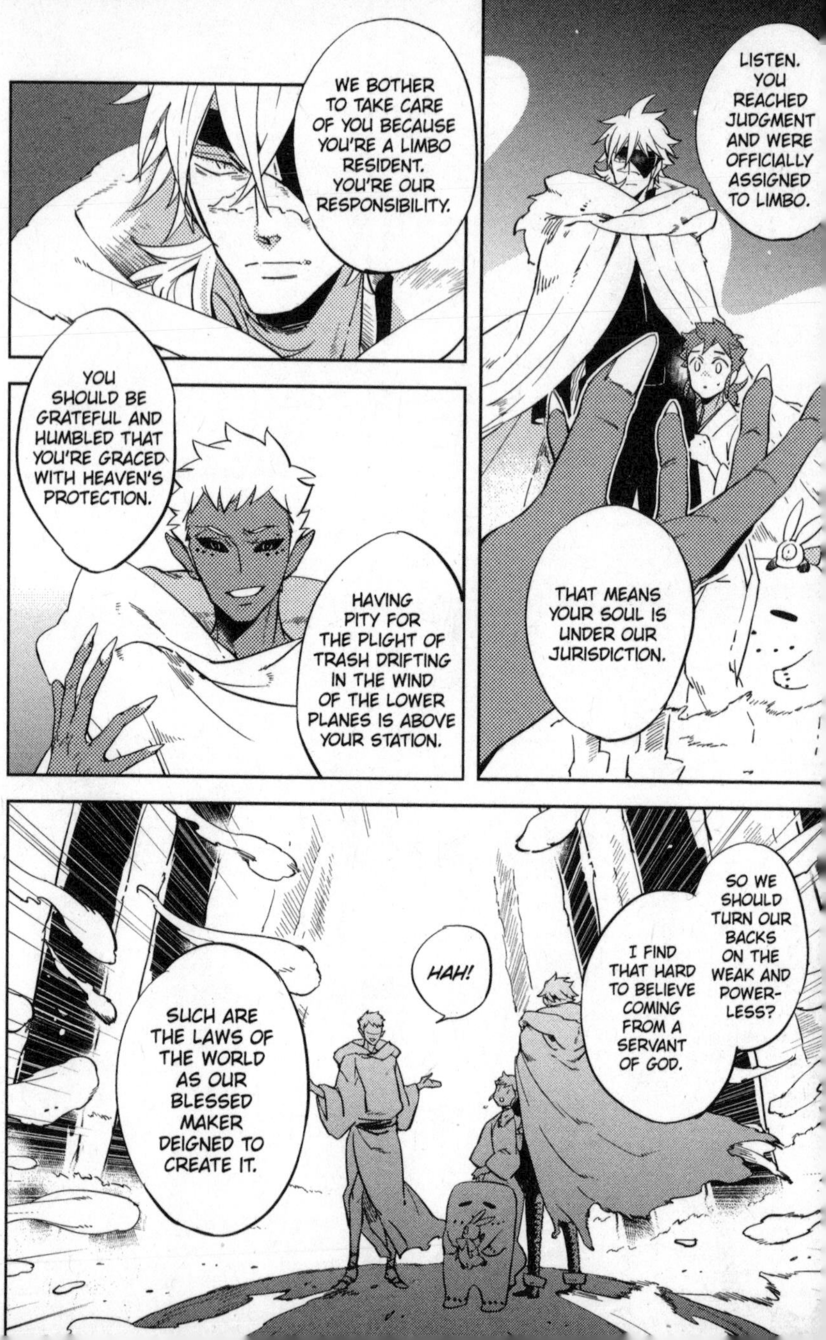
LISTEN. YOU REACHED JUDGMENT AND WERE OFFICIALLY ASSIGNED TO LIMBO.
THAT MEANS YOUR SOUL IS UNDER OUR JURISDICTION.
WE BOTHER TO TAKE CARE OF YOU BECAUSE YOU'RE A LIMBO RESIDENT. YOU'RE OUR RESPONSIBILITY.
YOU SHOULD BE GRATEFUL AND HUMBLED THAT YOU'RE GRACED WITH HEAVEN'S PROTECTION.
HAVING PITY FOR THE PLIGHT OF TRASH DRIFTING IN THE WIND OF THE LOWER PLANES IS ABOVE YOUR STATION.
SO WE SHOULD TURN OUR BACKS ON THE WEAK AND POWER-LESS?
I FIND THAT HARD TO BELIEVE COMING FROM A SERVANT OF GOD.
HAH!
SUCH ARE THE LAWS OF THE WORLD AS OUR BLESSED MAKER DEIGNED TO CREATE IT.

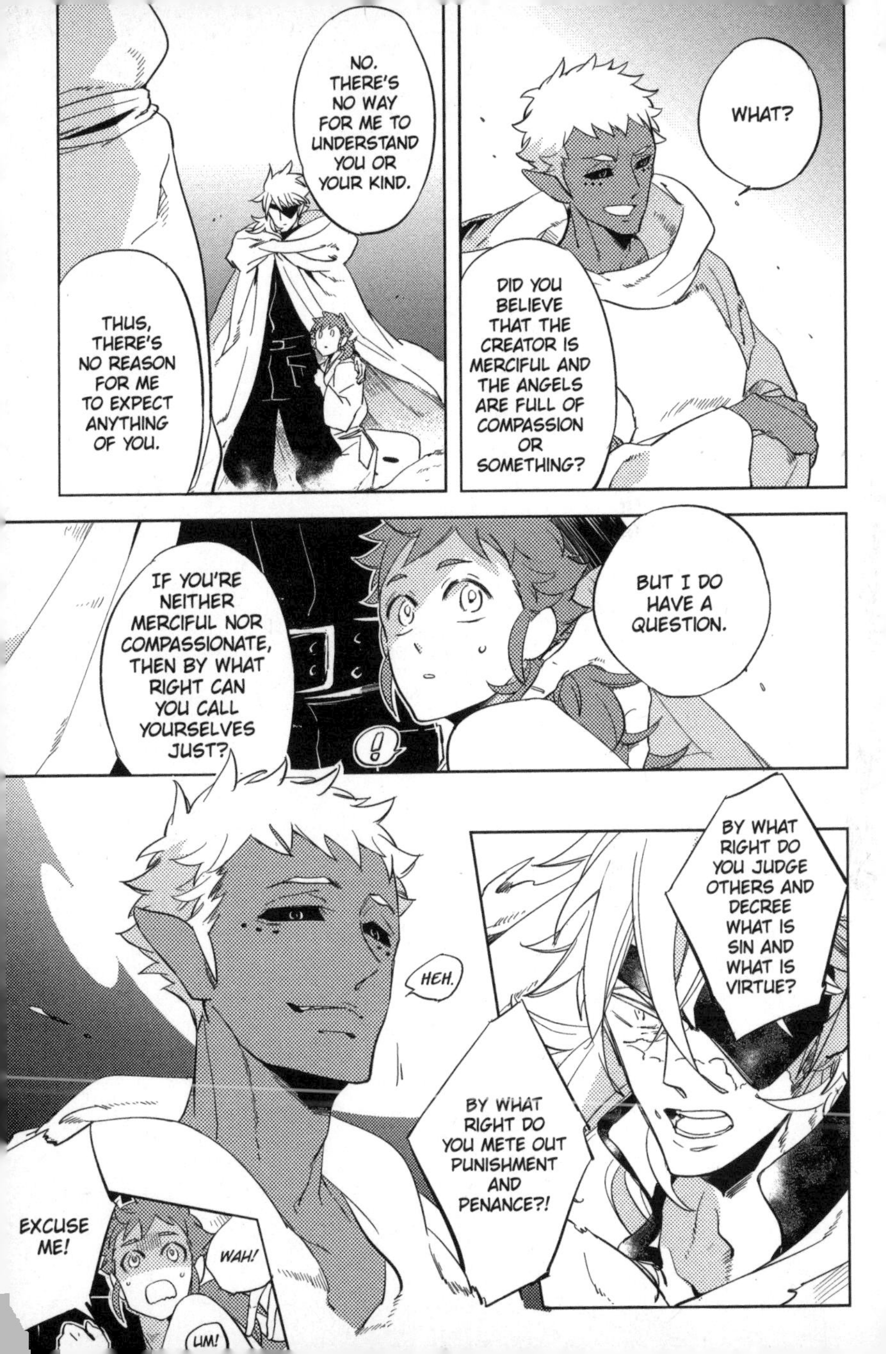
WHAT?
DID YOU BELIEVE THAT THE CREATOR IS MERCIFUL AND THE ANGELS ARE FULL OF COMPASSION OR SOMETHING?
NO. THERE'S NO WAY FOR ME TO UNDERSTAND YOU OR YOUR KIND.
THUS, THERE'S NO REASON FOR ME TO EXPECT ANYTHING OF YOU.
BUT I DO HAVE A QUESTION.
!
IF YOU'RE NEITHER MERCIFUL NOR COMPASSIONATE, THEN BY WHAT RIGHT CAN YOU CALL YOURSELVES JUST?
BY WHAT RIGHT DO YOU JUDGE OTHERS AND DECREE WHAT IS SIN AND WHAT IS VIRTUE?
BY WHAT RIGHT DO YOU METE OUT PUNISHMENT AND PENANCE?!
HEH.
WAH!
EXCUSE ME!
UM!

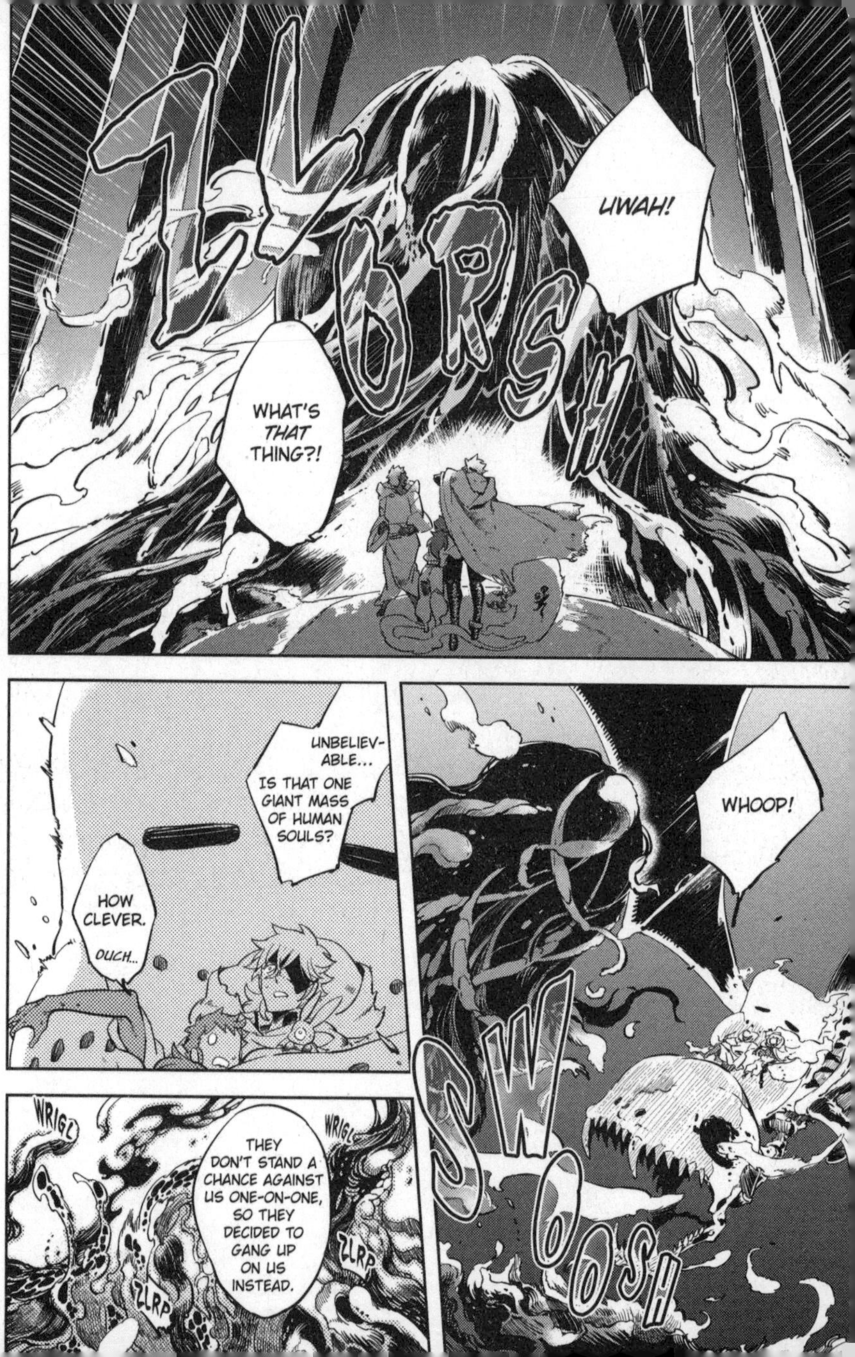
UWAH!
ZLORSH
WHAT'S THAT THING?!
WHOOP!
SWOOSH
UNBELIEVABLE... IS THAT ONE GIANT MASS OF HUMAN SOULS?
HOW CLEVER.
OUCH...
WRIGL
WRIGL
THEY DON'T STAND A CHANCE AGAINST US ONE-ON-ONE, SO THEY DECIDED TO GANG UP ON US INSTEAD.
ZLRP
ZLRP

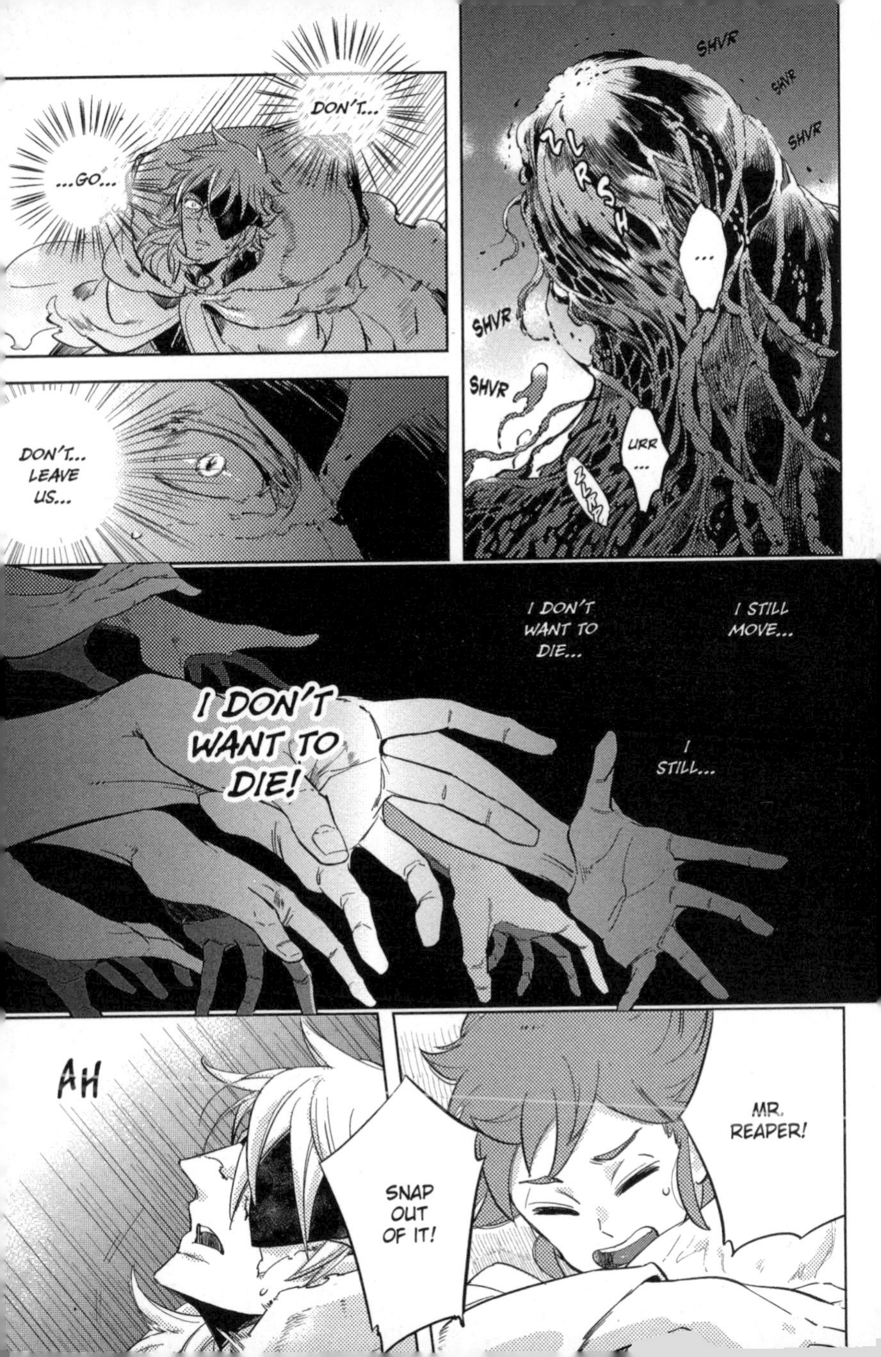
SHVR
SHVR
SHVR
ZLRSH
...
SHVR
SHVR
URR...
DON'T...
...GO...
DON'T... LEAVE US...
I STILL MOVE...
I DON'T WANT TO DIE...
I STILL...
I DON'T WANT TO DIE!
MR. REAPER!
SNAP OUT OF IT!
AH

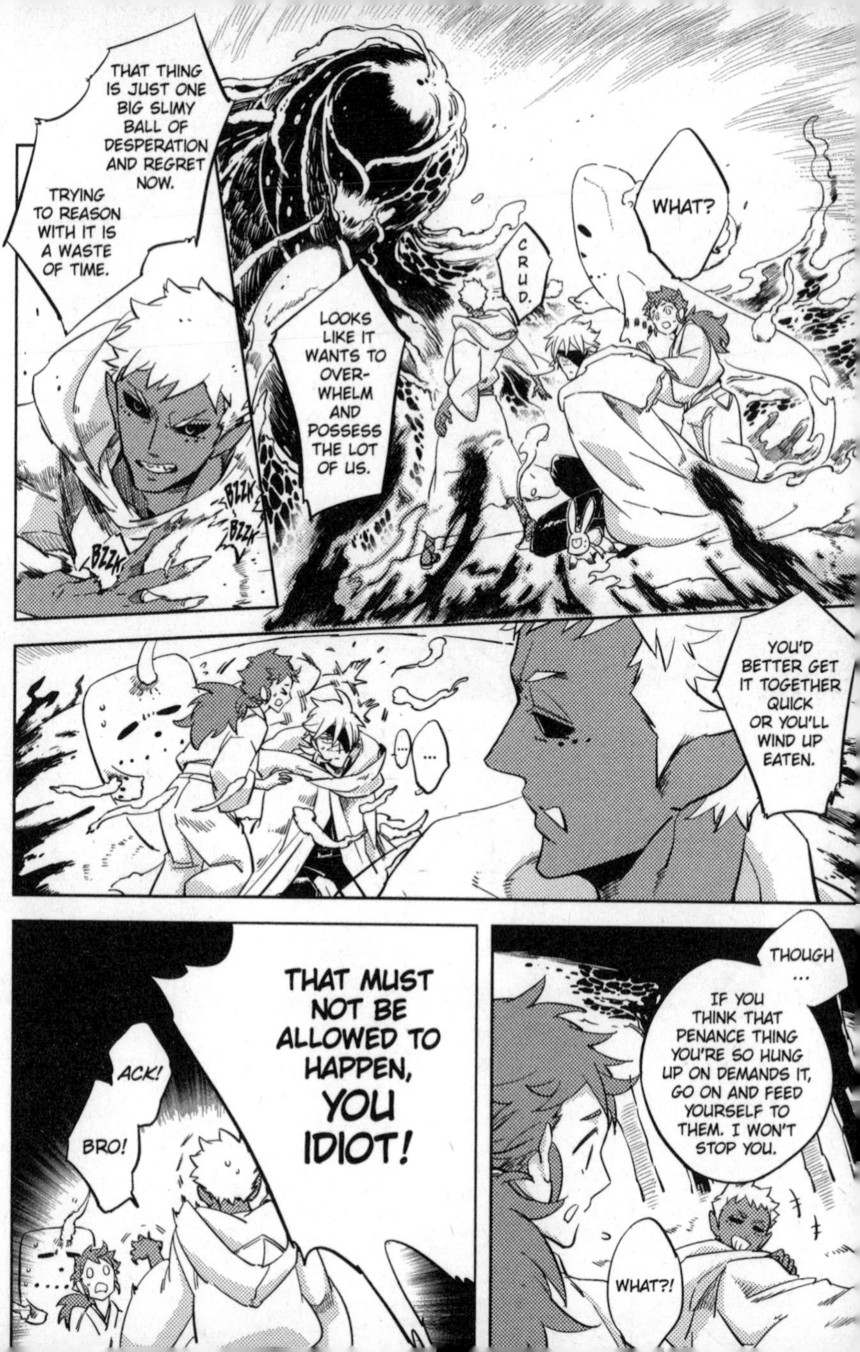
WHAT?
CRUD.
LOOKS LIKE IT WANTS TO OVER-WHELM AND POSSESS THE LOT OF US.
THAT THING IS JUST ONE BIG SLIMY BALL OF DESPERATION AND REGRET NOW.
TRYING TO REASON WITH IT IS A WASTE OF TIME.
BZZK
BZZK
BZZK
YOU'D BETTER GET IT TOGETHER QUICK OR YOU'LL WIND UP EATEN.
...
...
THOUGH ...
IF YOU THINK THAT PENANCE THING YOU'RE SO HUNG UP ON DEMANDS IT, GO ON AND FEED YOURSELF TO THEM. I WON'T STOP YOU.
WHAT?!
THAT MUST NOT BE ALLOWED TO HAPPEN, YOU IDIOT!
ACK!
BRO!
...

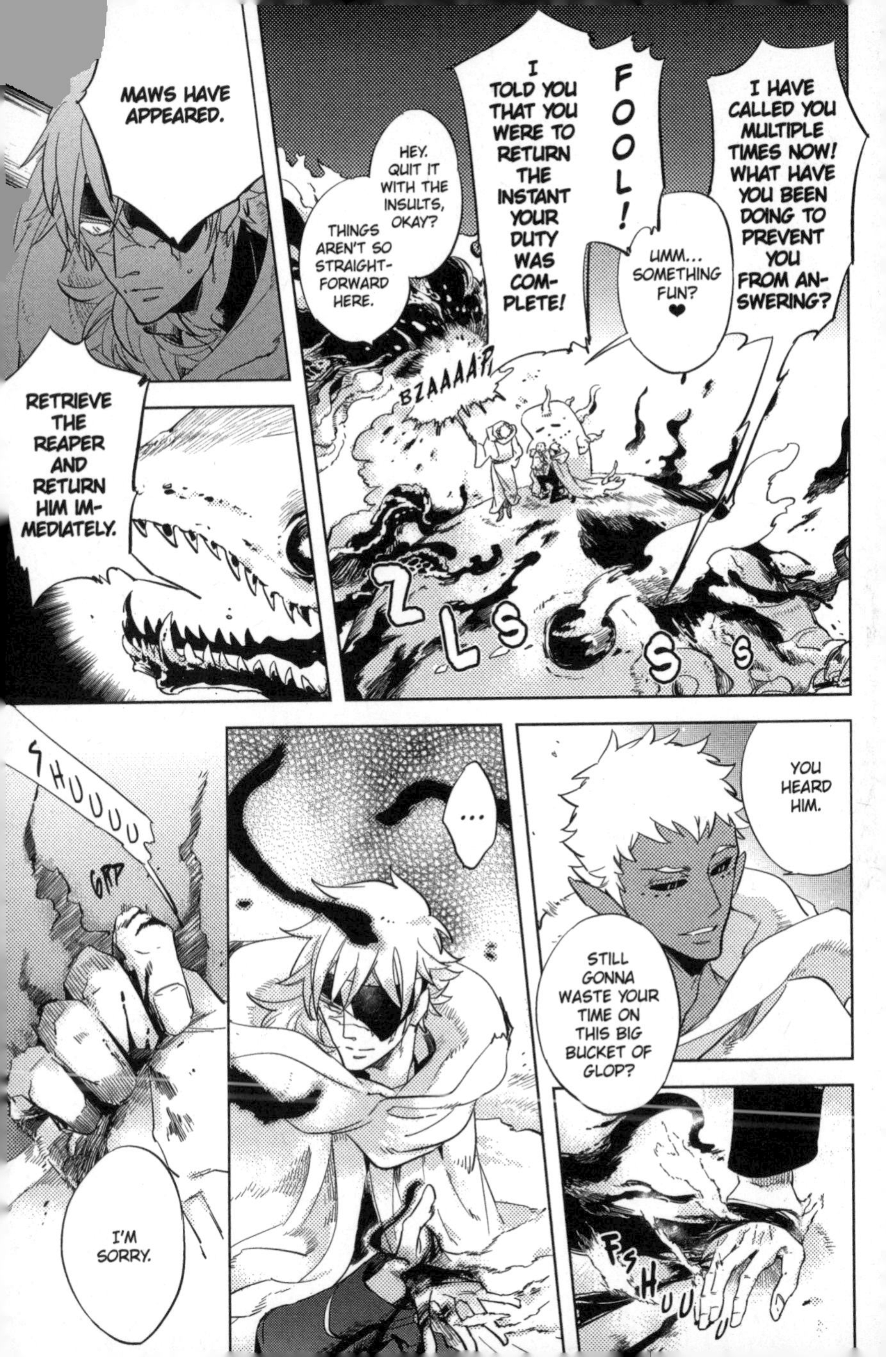
I HAVE CALLED YOU MULTIPLE TIMES NOW! WHAT HAVE YOU BEEN DOING TO PREVENT YOU FROM ANSWERING?
UMM... SOMETHING FUN? ❤
FOOL!
I TOLD YOU THAT YOU WERE TO RETURN THE INSTANT YOUR DUTY WAS COMPLETE!
HEY. QUIT IT WITH THE INSULTS, OKAY?
THINGS AREN'T SO STRAIGHTFORWARD HERE.
BZAAAAP
ZLSSSS
MAWS HAVE APPEARED.
RETRIEVE THE REAPER AND RETURN HIM IMMEDIATELY.
YOU HEARD HIM.
STILL GONNA WASTE YOUR TIME ON THIS BIG BUCKET OF GLOP?
FSHUUU
...
SHUUUUU
GRP
I'M SORRY.

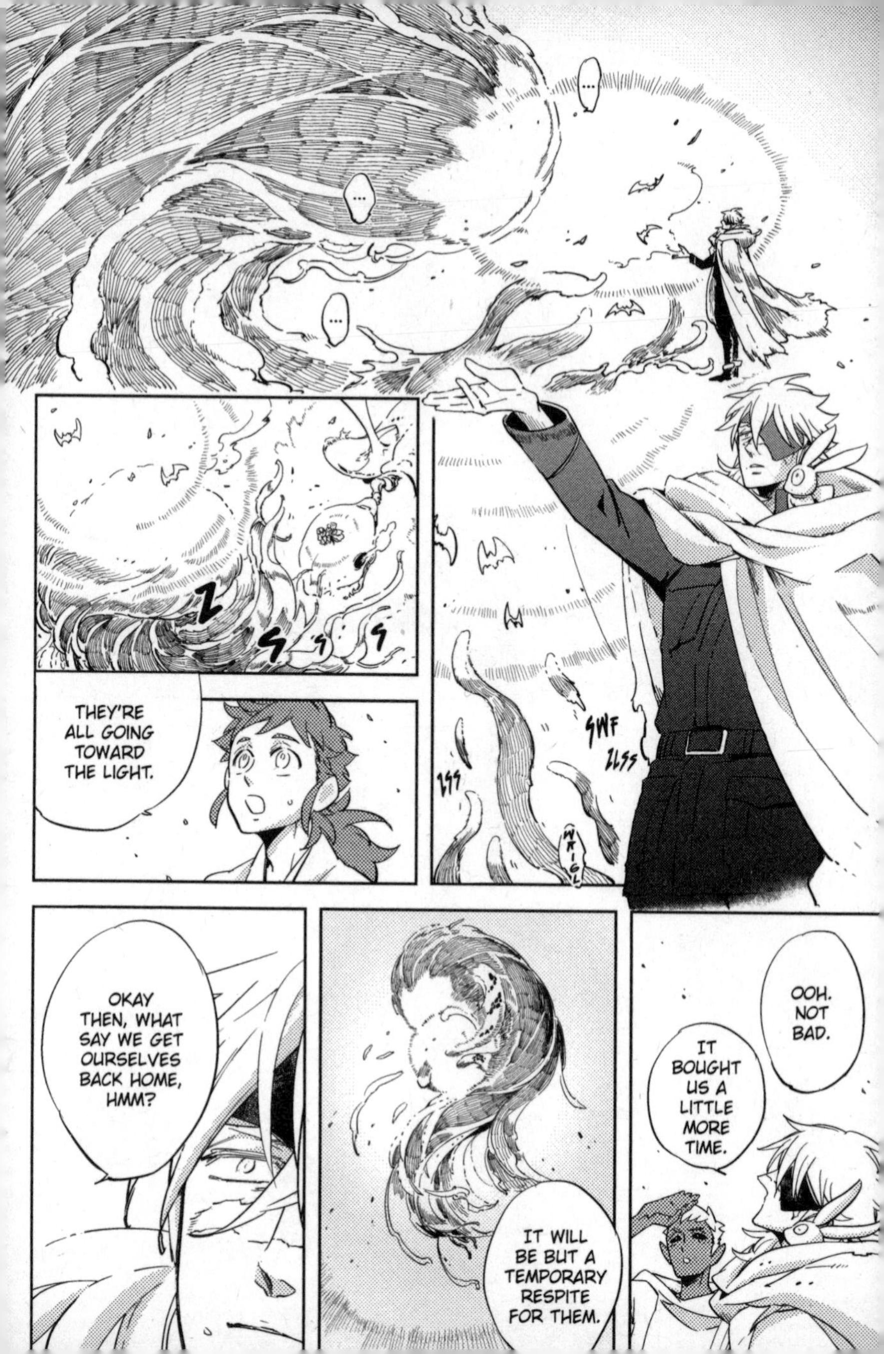
...
...
...
SWF
ZLSS
ZSS
WRIGL
THEY'RE ALL GOING TOWARD THE LIGHT.
OOH. NOT BAD.
IT BOUGHT US A LITTLE MORE TIME.
IT WILL BE BUT A TEMPORARY RESPITE FOR THEM.
OKAY THEN, WHAT SAY WE GET OURSELVES BACK HOME, HMM?

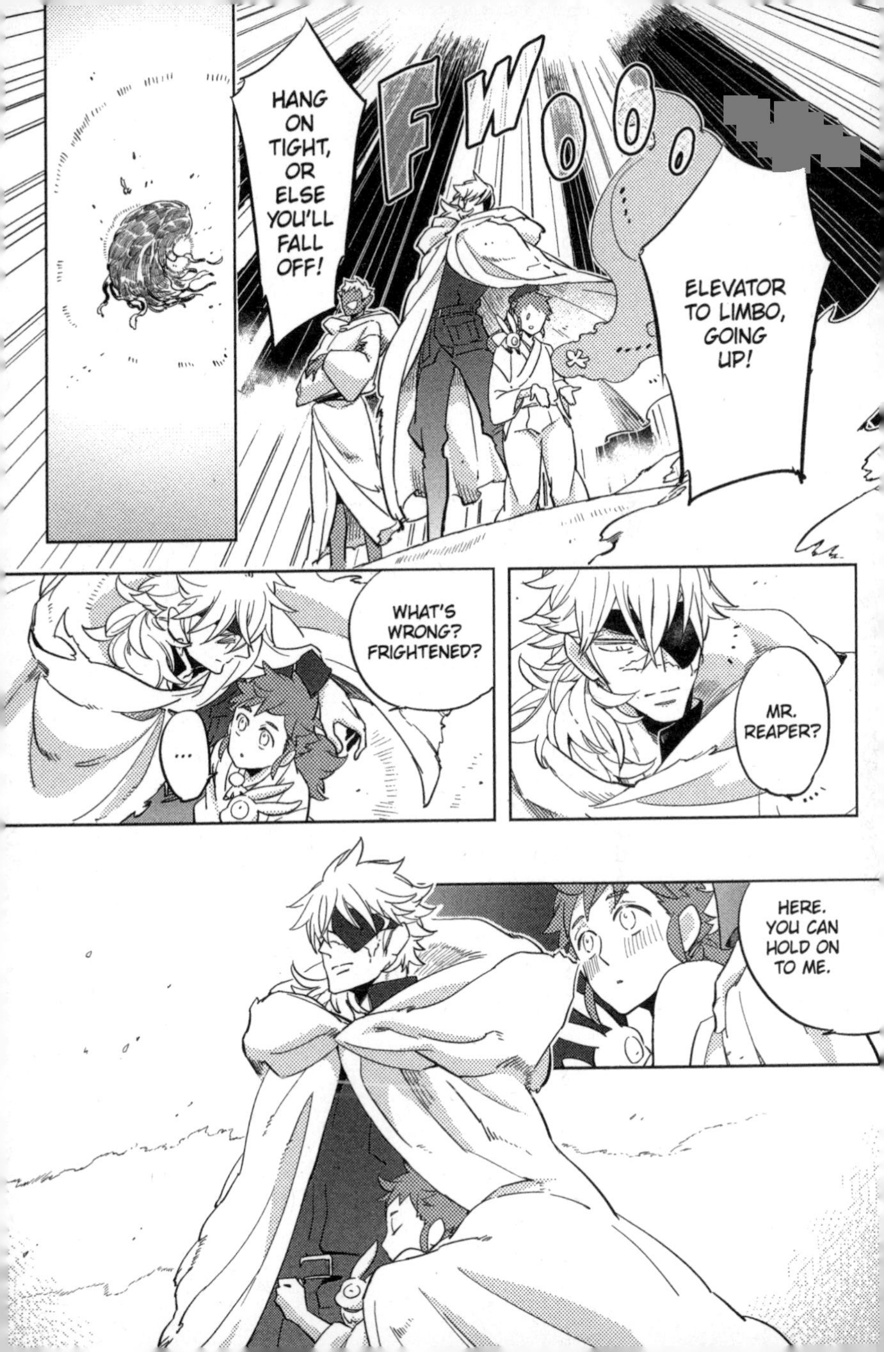
FWOOO
ELEVATOR TO LIMBO, GOING UP!
HANG ON TIGHT, OR ELSE YOU'LL FALL OFF!
MR. REAPER?
WHAT'S WRONG? FRIGHTENED?
...
HERE. YOU CAN HOLD ON TO ME.

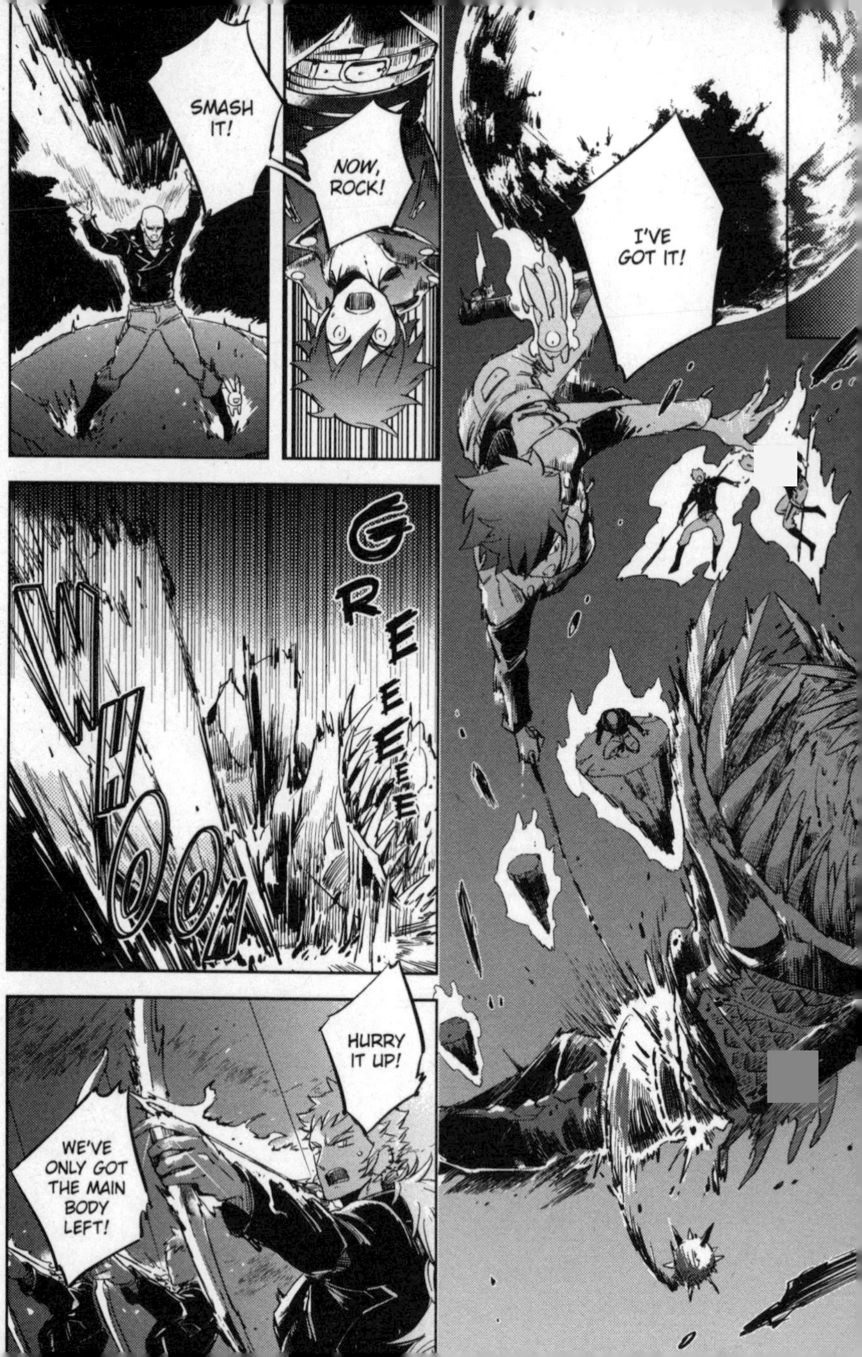
I'VE GOT IT!
NOW, ROCK!
SMASH IT!
GREEEEEE
WHOOOM
HURRY IT UP!
WE'VE ONLY GOT THE MAIN BODY LEFT!

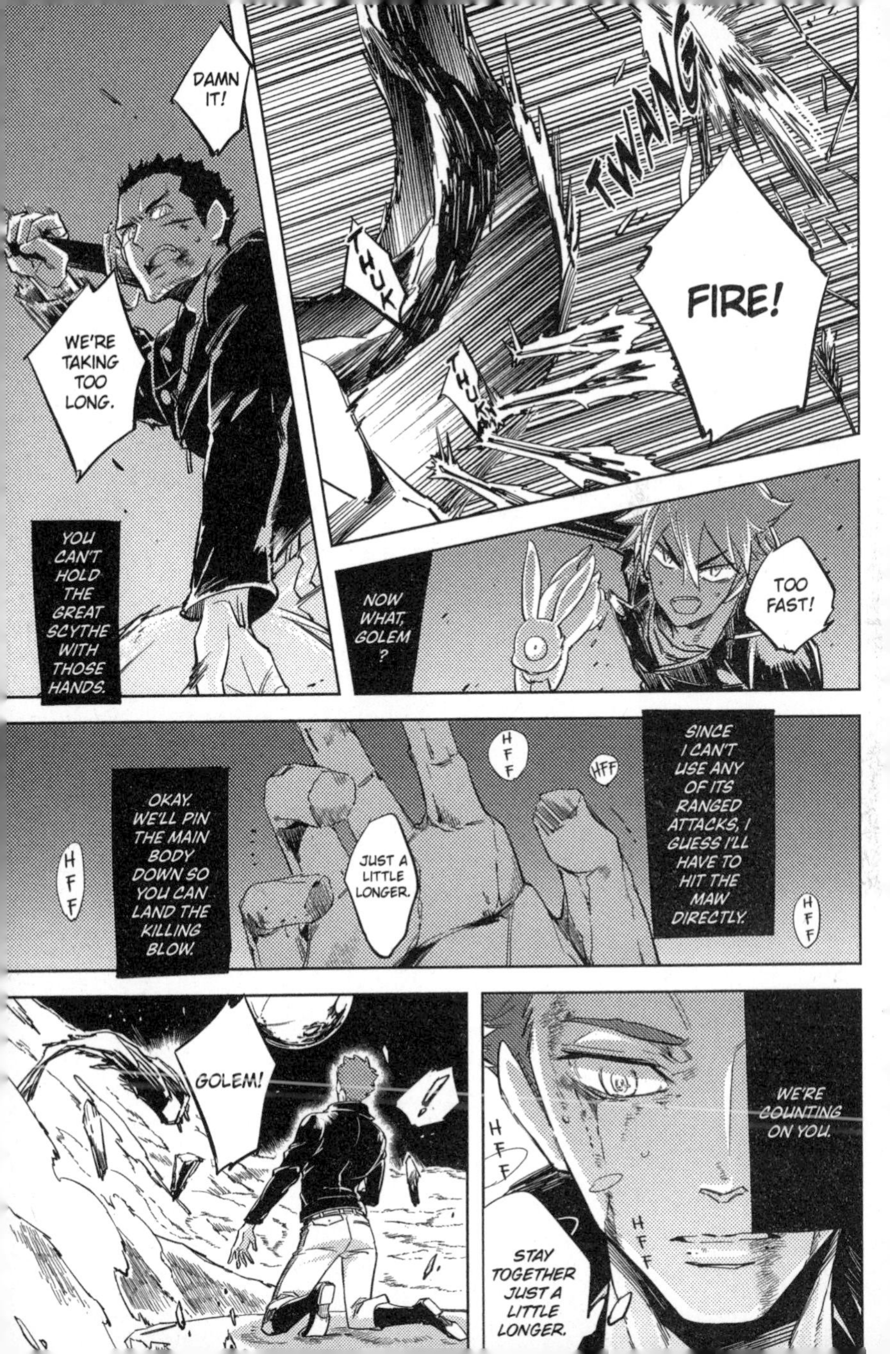
TWANG
FIRE!
THUK
THUK
TOO FAST!
NOW WHAT, GOLEM?
DAMN IT!
WE'RE TAKING TOO LONG.
YOU CAN'T HOLD THE GREAT SCYTHE WITH THOSE HANDS.
SINCE I CAN'T USE ANY OF ITS RANGED ATTACKS, I GUESS I'LL HAVE TO HIT THE MAW DIRECTLY.
HFF
HFF
HFF
JUST A LITTLE LONGER.
OKAY. WE'LL PIN THE MAIN BODY DOWN SO YOU CAN LAND THE KILLING BLOW.
HFF
WE'RE COUNTING ON YOU.
HFF
HFF
STAY TOGETHER JUST A LITTLE LONGER.
GOLEM!
!

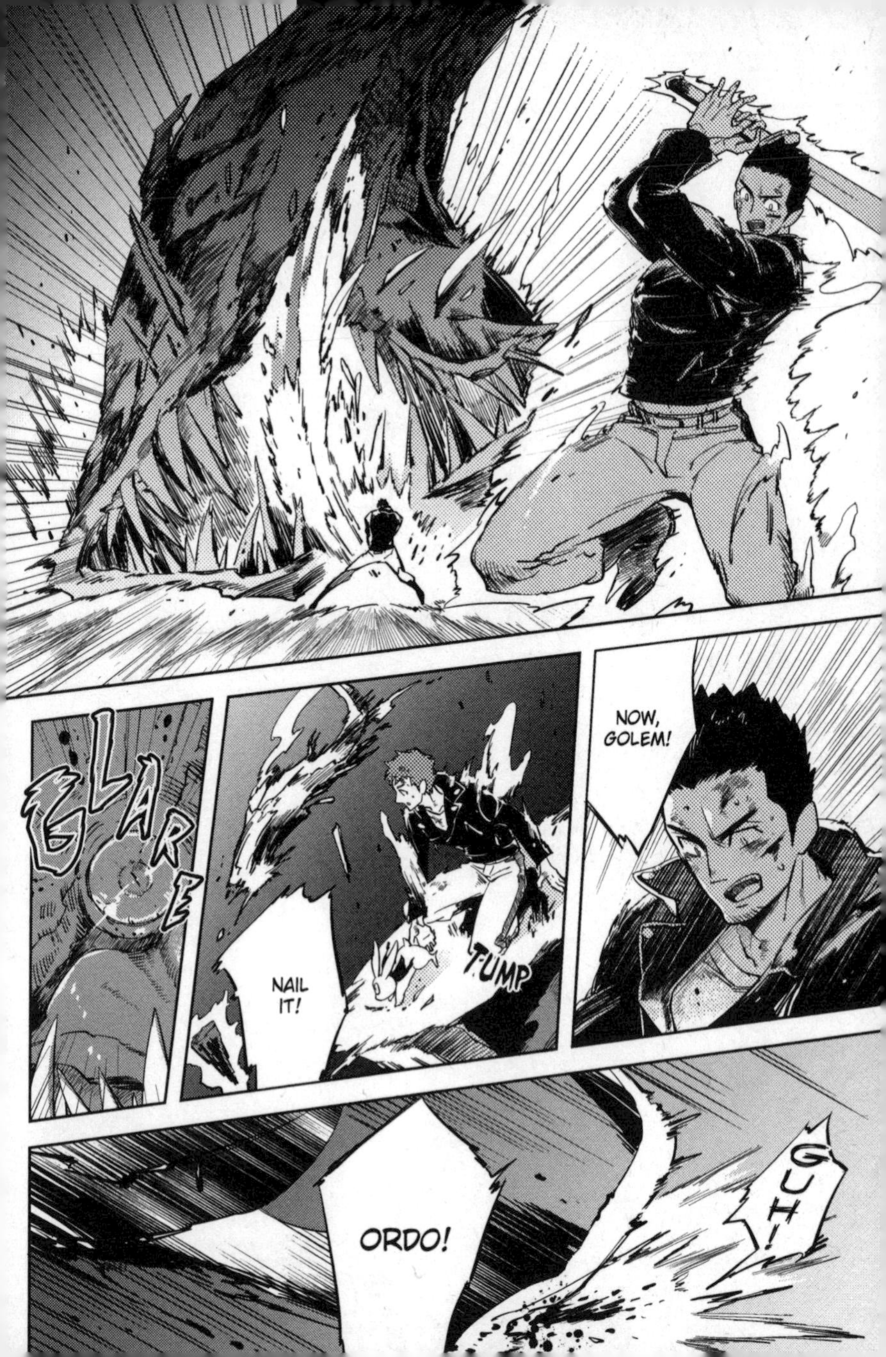
NOW, GOLEM!
NAIL IT!
TUMP
GLARE
GUH!
ORDO!

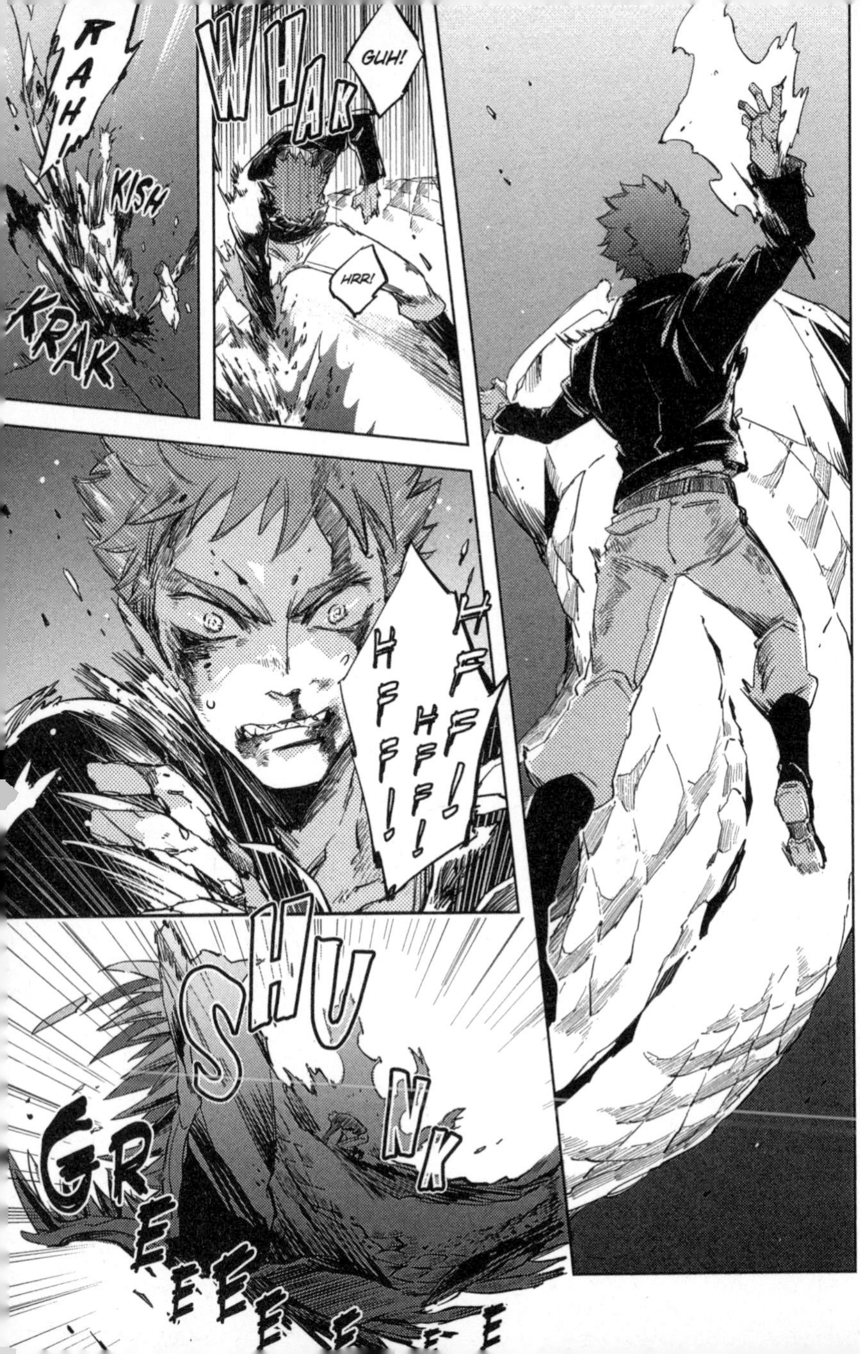
WHAK
GUH!
HRR!
RAH!
KISH
KRAK
HFF!
HFF!
HFF!
SHUNK
GREEEEEEEE

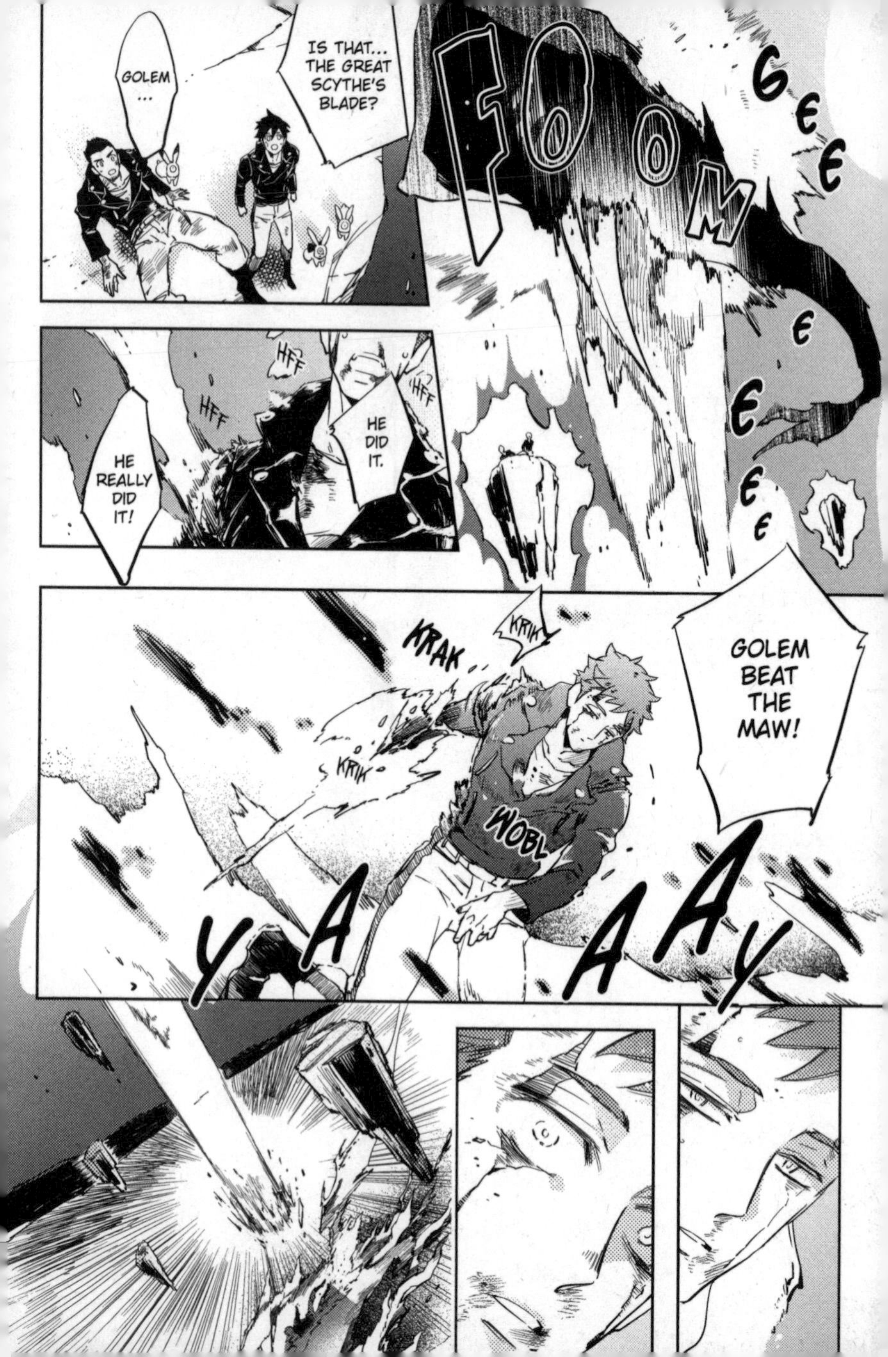
FOOOM
GEEEEEEE
IS THAT... THE GREAT SCYTHE'S BLADE?
GOLEM...
HFF
HFF
HE DID IT.
HFF
HE REALLY DID IT!
GOLEM BEAT THE MAW!
KRIK
KRAK
KRIK
WOBL
YAAAY

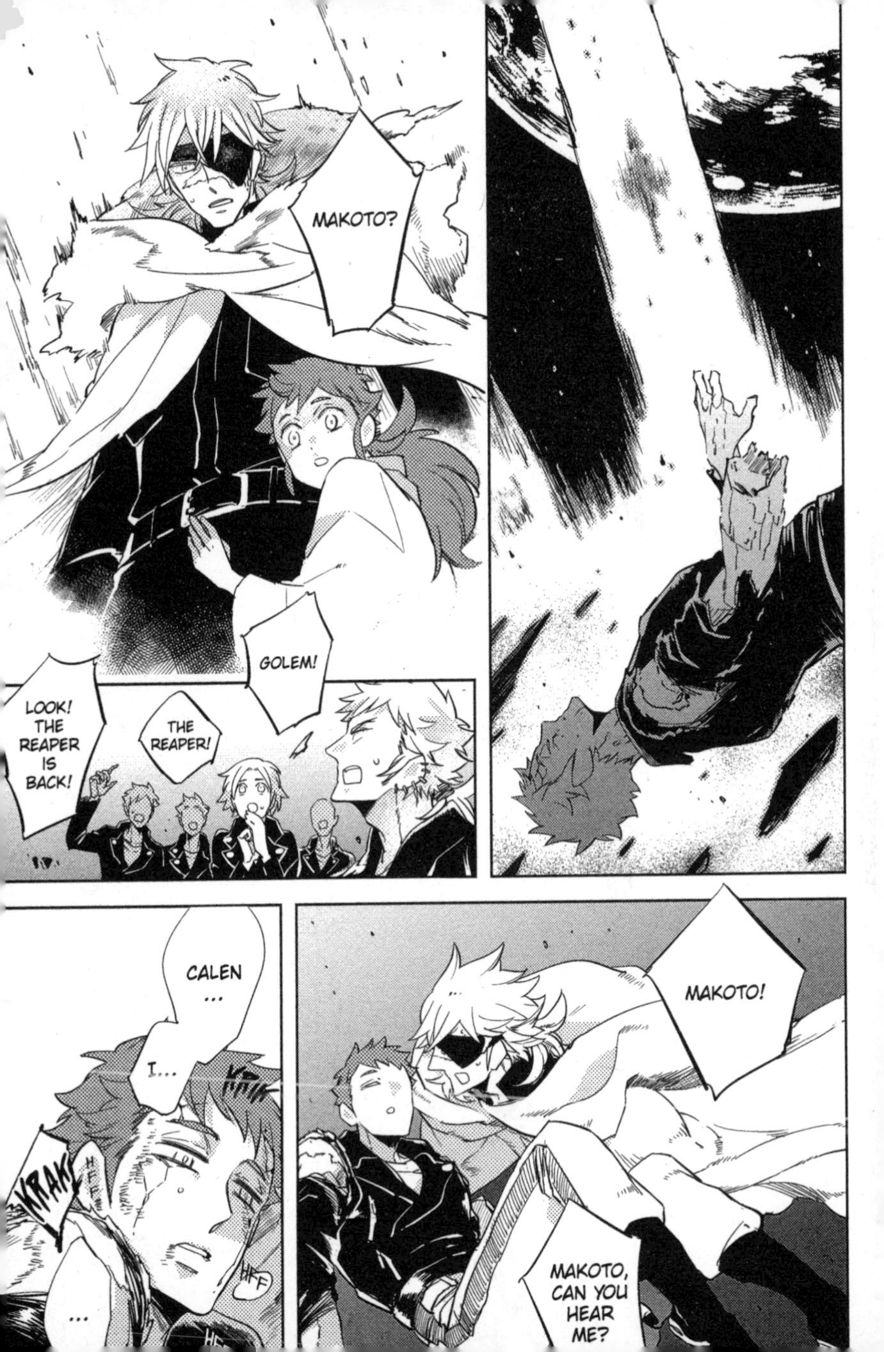
MAKOTO?
GOLEM!
LOOK! THE REAPER IS BACK!
THE REAPER!
MAKOTO!
MAKOTO, CAN YOU HEAR ME?
CALEN ...
I...
KRAK
HFF
HFF
...

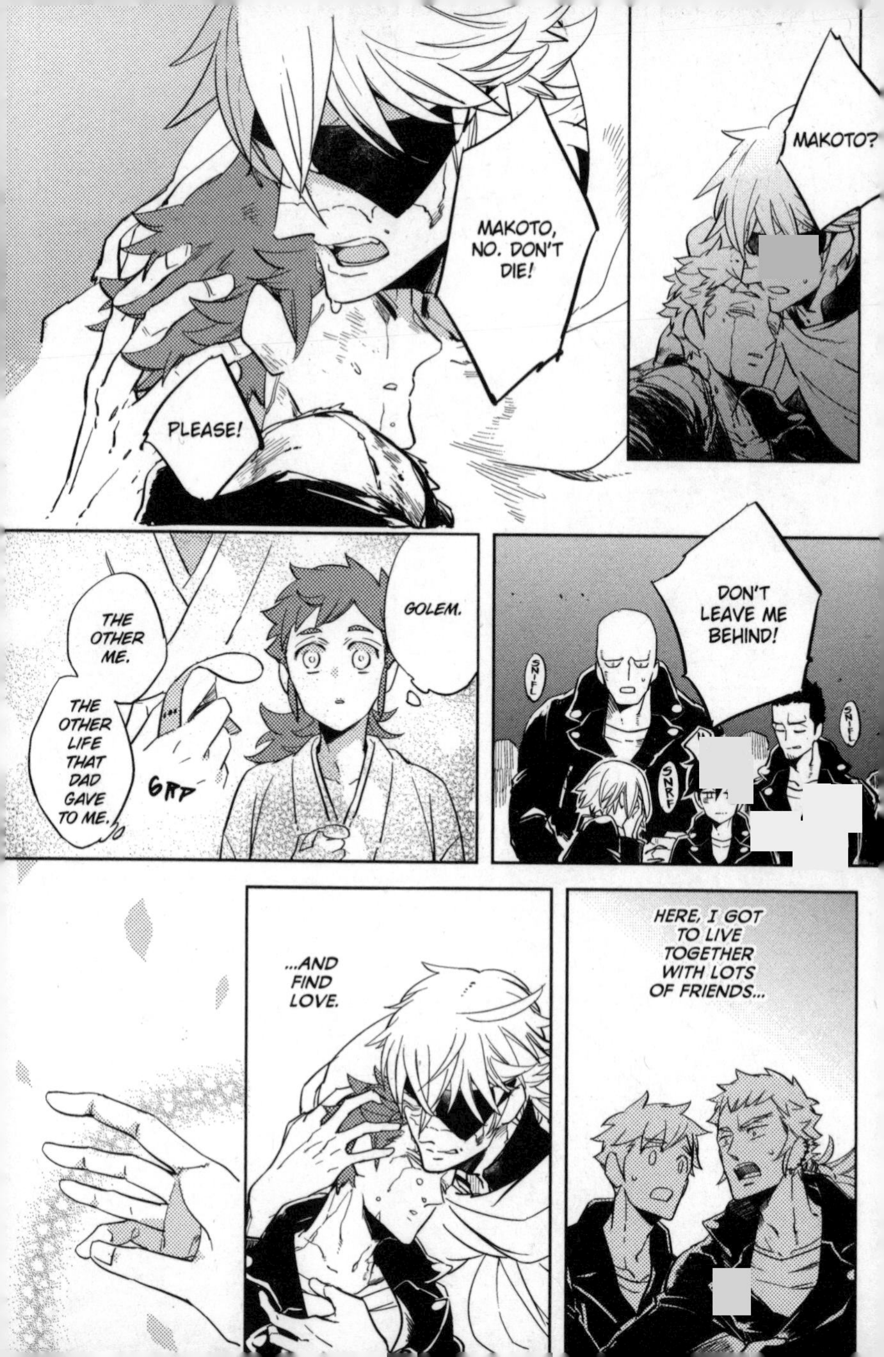
MAKOTO?
MAKOTO, NO. DON'T DIE!
PLEASE!
DON'T LEAVE ME BEHIND!
SNIFL
SNRF
SNIFL
GOLEM.
THE OTHER ME.
THE OTHER LIFE THAT DAD GAVE TO ME.
GRP
HERE, I GOT TO LIVE TOGETHER WITH LOTS OF FRIENDS...
...AND FIND LOVE.

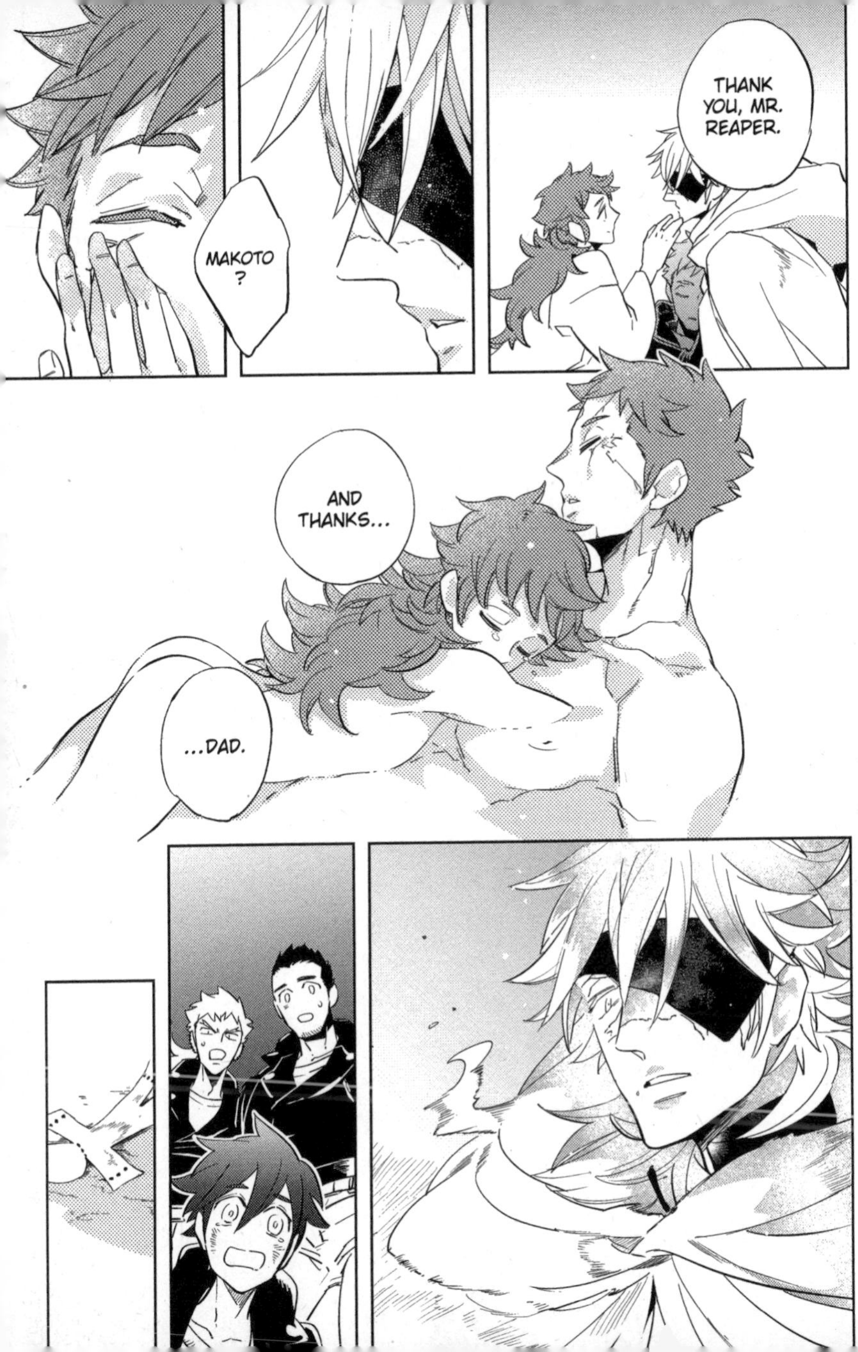
THANK YOU, MR. REAPER.
MAKOTO ?
AND THANKS...
...DAD.

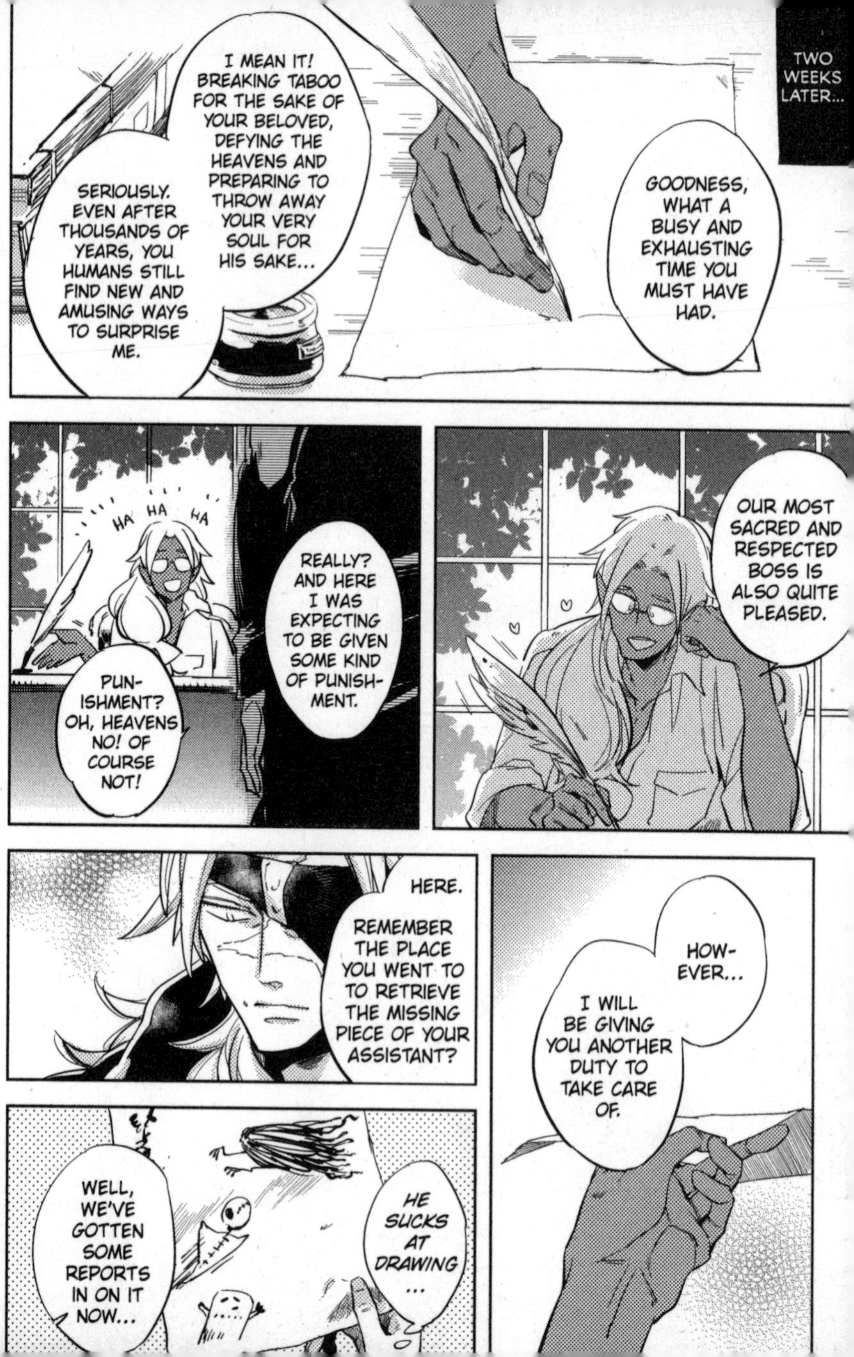
TWO WEEKS LATER...
GOODNESS, WHAT A BUSY AND EXHAUSTING TIME YOU MUST HAVE HAD.
SERIOUSLY. EVEN AFTER THOUSANDS OF YEARS, YOU HUMANS STILL FIND NEW AND AMUSING WAYS TO SURPRISE ME.
I MEAN IT! BREAKING TABOO FOR THE SAKE OF YOUR BELOVED, DEFYING THE HEAVENS AND PREPARING TO THROW AWAY YOUR VERY SOUL FOR HIS SAKE...
OUR MOST SACRED AND RESPECTED BOSS IS ALSO QUITE PLEASED.
REALLY? AND HERE I WAS EXPECTING TO BE GIVEN SOME KIND OF PUNISHMENT.
HA HA HA
PUN-ISHMENT? OH, HEAVENS NO! OF COURSE NOT!
HOW-EVER...
I WILL BE GIVING YOU ANOTHER DUTY TO TAKE CARE OF.
HERE.
REMEMBER THE PLACE YOU WENT TO TO RETRIEVE THE MISSING PIECE OF YOUR ASSISTANT?
HE SUCKS AT DRAWING...
WELL, WE'VE GOTTEN SOME REPORTS IN ON IT NOW...

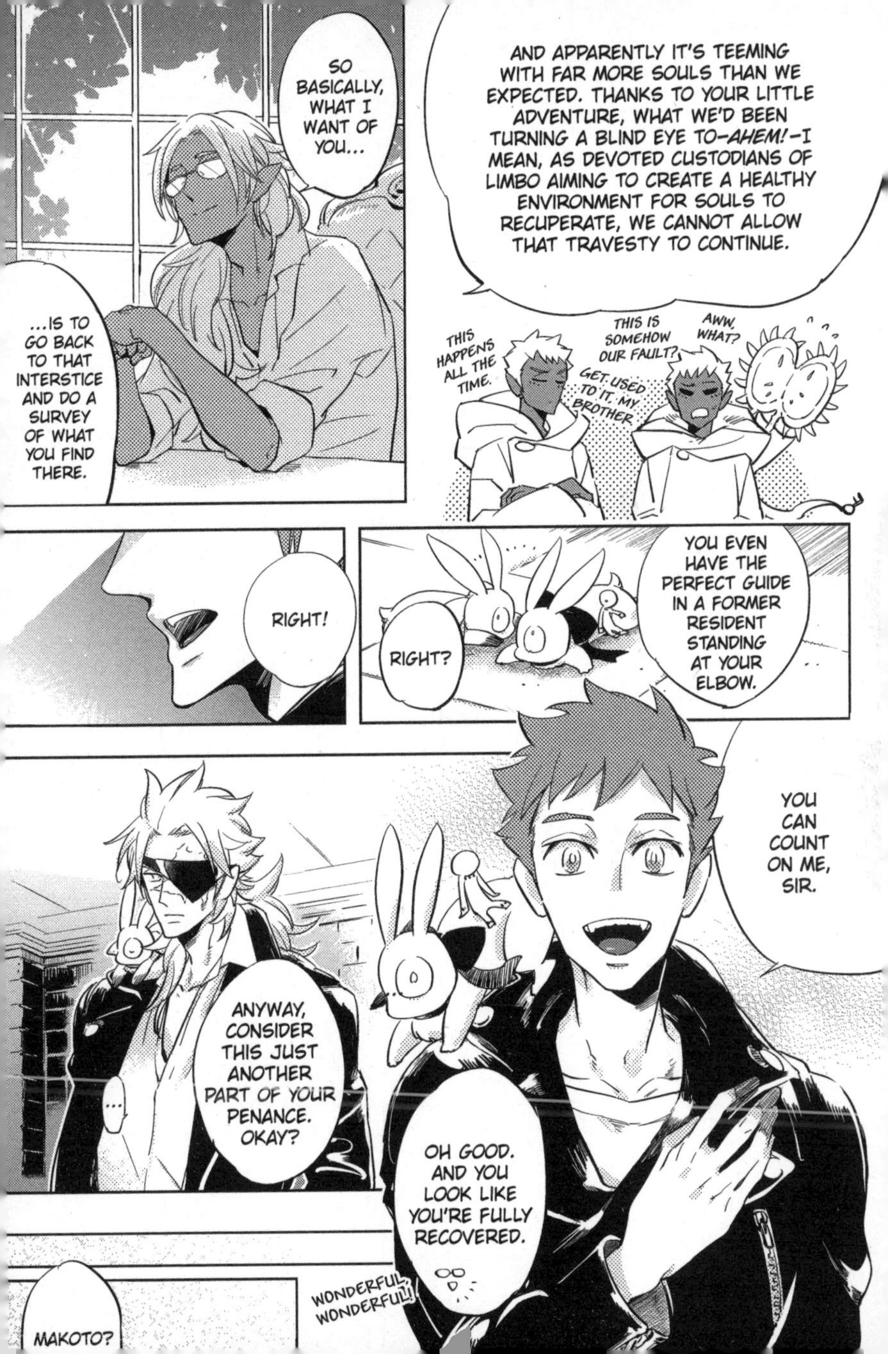
AND APPARENTLY IT'S TEEMING WITH FAR MORE SOULS THAN WE EXPECTED. THANKS TO YOUR LITTLE ADVENTURE, WHAT WE'D BEEN TURNING A BLIND EYE TO–*AHEM!*–I MEAN, AS DEVOTED CUSTODIANS OF LIMBO AIMING TO CREATE A HEALTHY ENVIRONMENT FOR SOULS TO RECUPERATE, WE CANNOT ALLOW THAT TRAVESTY TO CONTINUE.
AWW, WHAT?
THIS IS SOMEHOW OUR FAULT?
THIS HAPPENS ALL THE TIME.
GET USED TO IT, MY BROTHER.
SO BASICALLY, WHAT I WANT OF YOU...
...IS TO GO BACK TO THAT INTERSTICE AND DO A SURVEY OF WHAT YOU FIND THERE.
YOU EVEN HAVE THE PERFECT GUIDE IN A FORMER RESIDENT STANDING AT YOUR ELBOW.
RIGHT?
RIGHT!
YOU CAN COUNT ON ME, SIR.
ANYWAY, CONSIDER THIS JUST ANOTHER PART OF YOUR PENANCE. OKAY?
...
OH GOOD. AND YOU LOOK LIKE YOU'RE FULLY RECOVERED.
WONDERFUL, WONDERFUL!
MAKOTO?

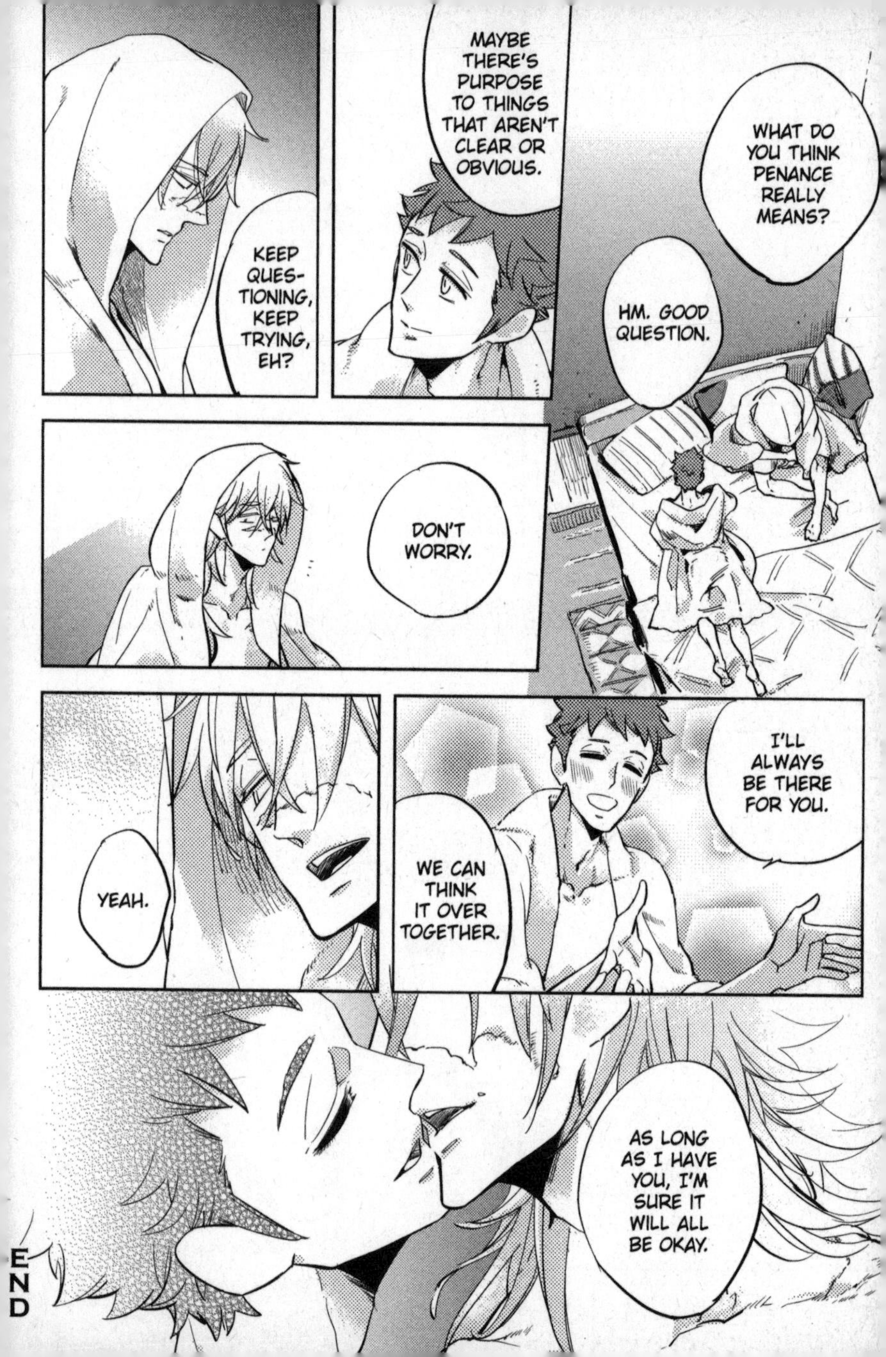
WHAT DO YOU THINK PENANCE REALLY MEANS?
HM. GOOD QUESTION.
MAYBE THERE'S PURPOSE TO THINGS THAT AREN'T CLEAR OR OBVIOUS.
KEEP QUES-TIONING, KEEP TRYING, EH?
DON'T WORRY.
I'LL ALWAYS BE THERE FOR YOU.
WE CAN THINK IT OVER TOGETHER.
YEAH.
AS LONG AS I HAVE YOU, I'M SURE IT WILL ALL BE OKAY.
END

[Final episode]

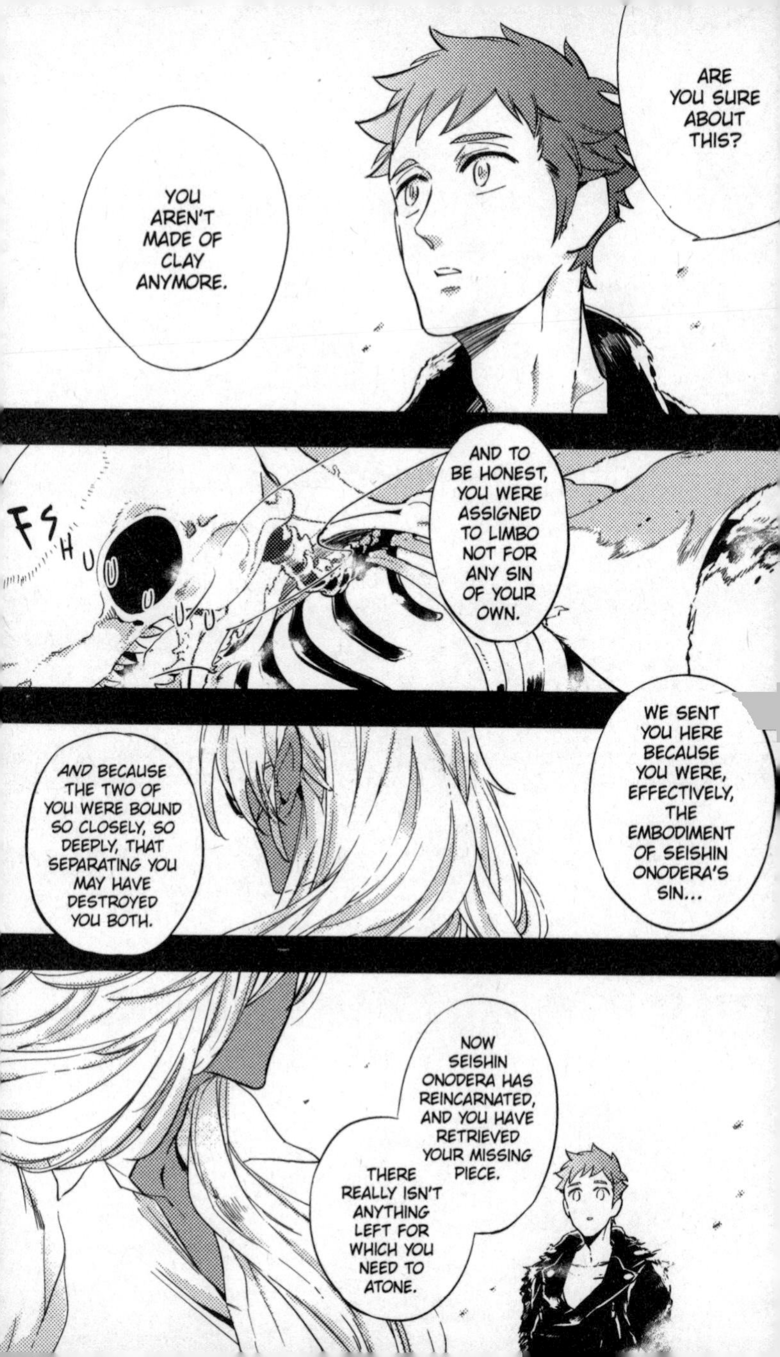
ARE YOU SURE ABOUT THIS?
YOU AREN'T MADE OF CLAY ANYMORE.
AND TO BE HONEST, YOU WERE ASSIGNED TO LIMBO NOT FOR ANY SIN OF YOUR OWN.
FSHU
WE SENT YOU HERE BECAUSE YOU WERE, EFFECTIVELY, THE EMBODIMENT OF SEISHIN ONODERA'S SIN...
AND BECAUSE THE TWO OF YOU WERE BOUND SO CLOSELY, SO DEEPLY, THAT SEPARATING YOU MAY HAVE DESTROYED YOU BOTH.
NOW SEISHIN ONODERA HAS REINCARNATED, AND YOU HAVE RETRIEVED YOUR MISSING PIECE.
THERE REALLY ISN'T ANYTHING LEFT FOR WHICH YOU NEED TO ATONE.

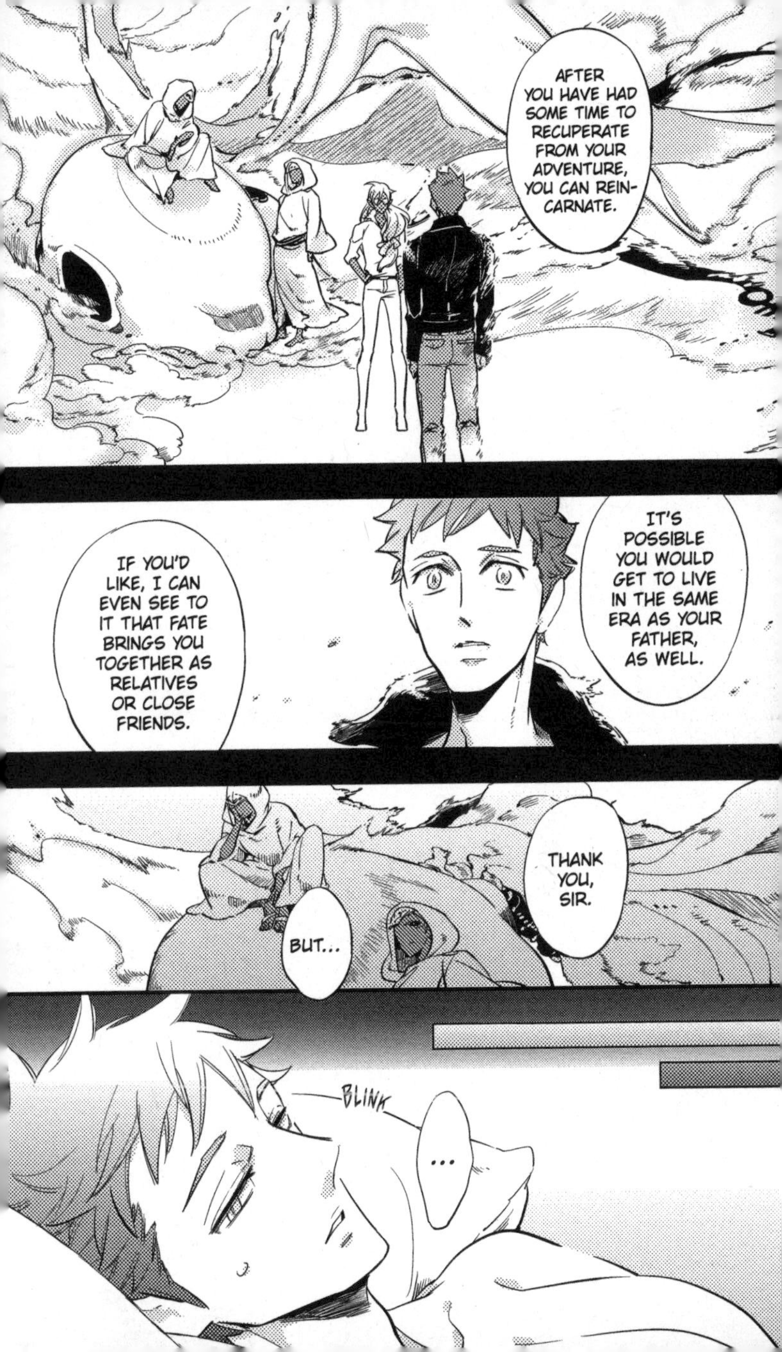
AFTER YOU HAVE HAD SOME TIME TO RECUPERATE FROM YOUR ADVENTURE, YOU CAN REIN-CARNATE.
IT'S POSSIBLE YOU WOULD GET TO LIVE IN THE SAME ERA AS YOUR FATHER, AS WELL.
IF YOU'D LIKE, I CAN EVEN SEE TO IT THAT FATE BRINGS YOU TOGETHER AS RELATIVES OR CLOSE FRIENDS.
THANK YOU, SIR.
BUT...
BLINK
...

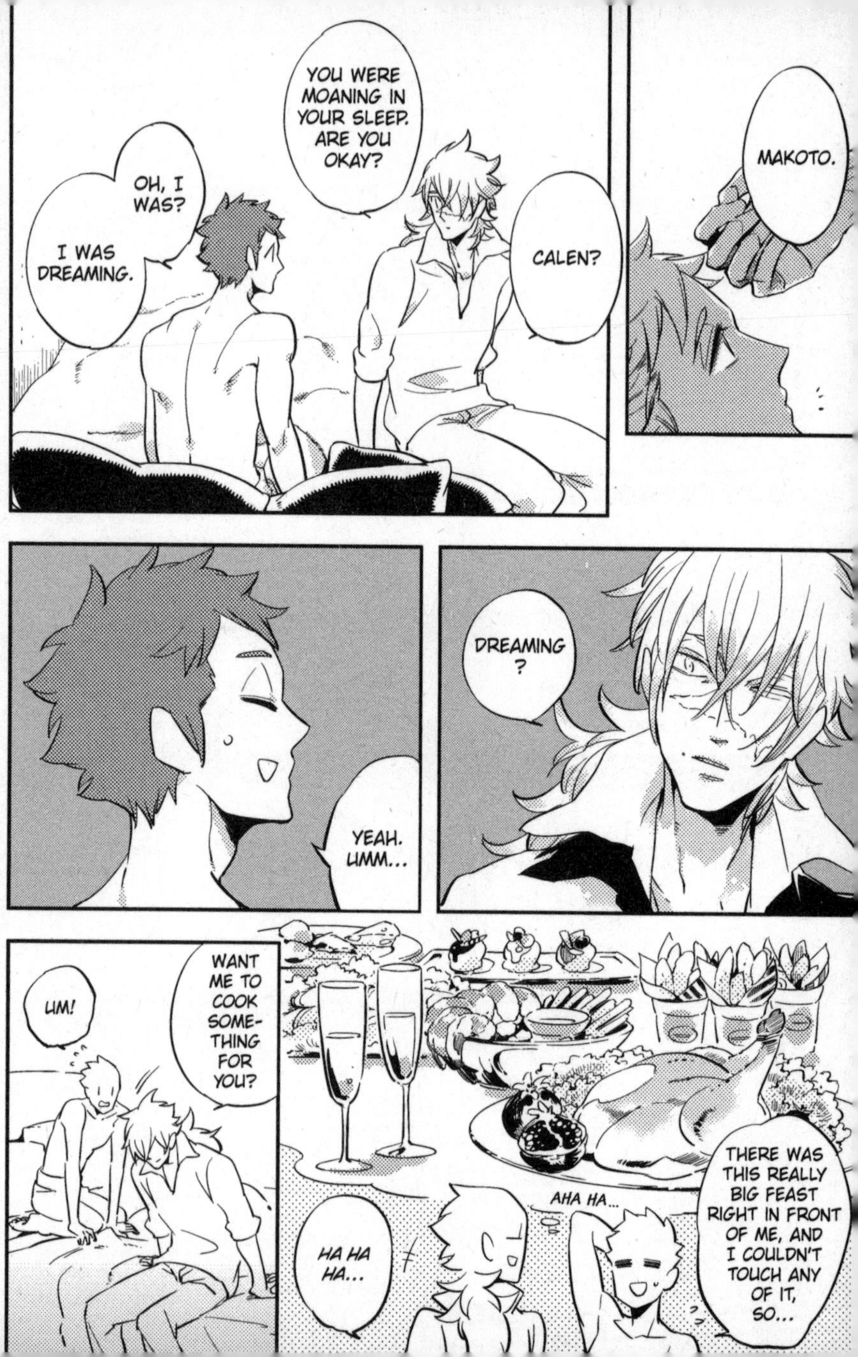
MAKOTO.
CALEN?
YOU WERE MOANING IN YOUR SLEEP. ARE YOU OKAY?
OH, I WAS?
I WAS DREAMING.
DREAMING?
YEAH. UMM...
THERE WAS THIS REALLY BIG FEAST RIGHT IN FRONT OF ME, AND I COULDN'T TOUCH ANY OF IT, SO...
AHA HA...
HA HA HA...
WANT ME TO COOK SOMETHING FOR YOU?
UM!

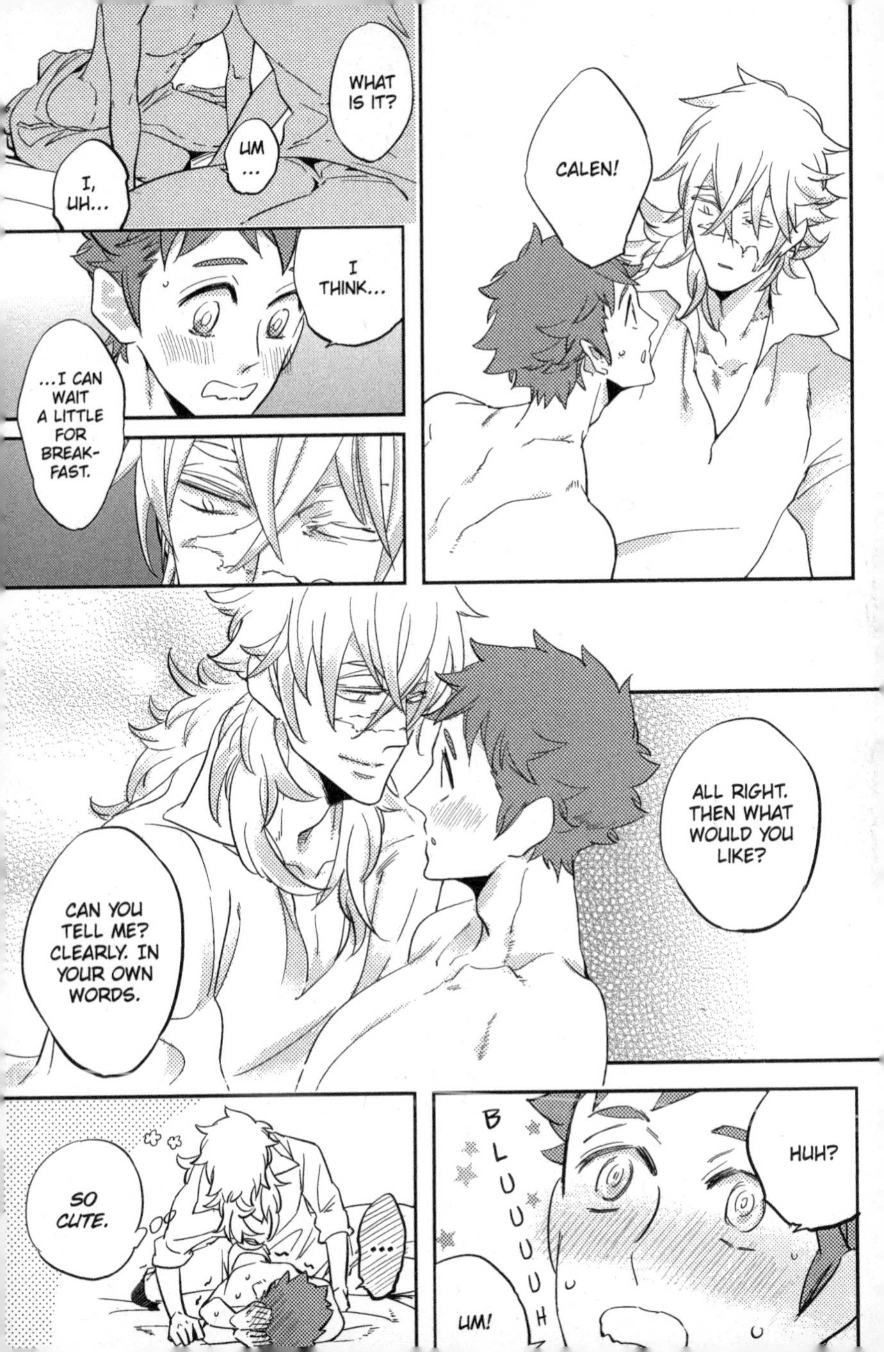
CALEN!
WHAT IS IT?
UM ...
I, UH...
I THINK...
...I CAN WAIT A LITTLE FOR BREAK-FAST.
ALL RIGHT. THEN WHAT WOULD YOU LIKE?
CAN YOU TELL ME? CLEARLY. IN YOUR OWN WORDS.
HUH?
BLUUUUUH
UM!
SO CUTE.
...

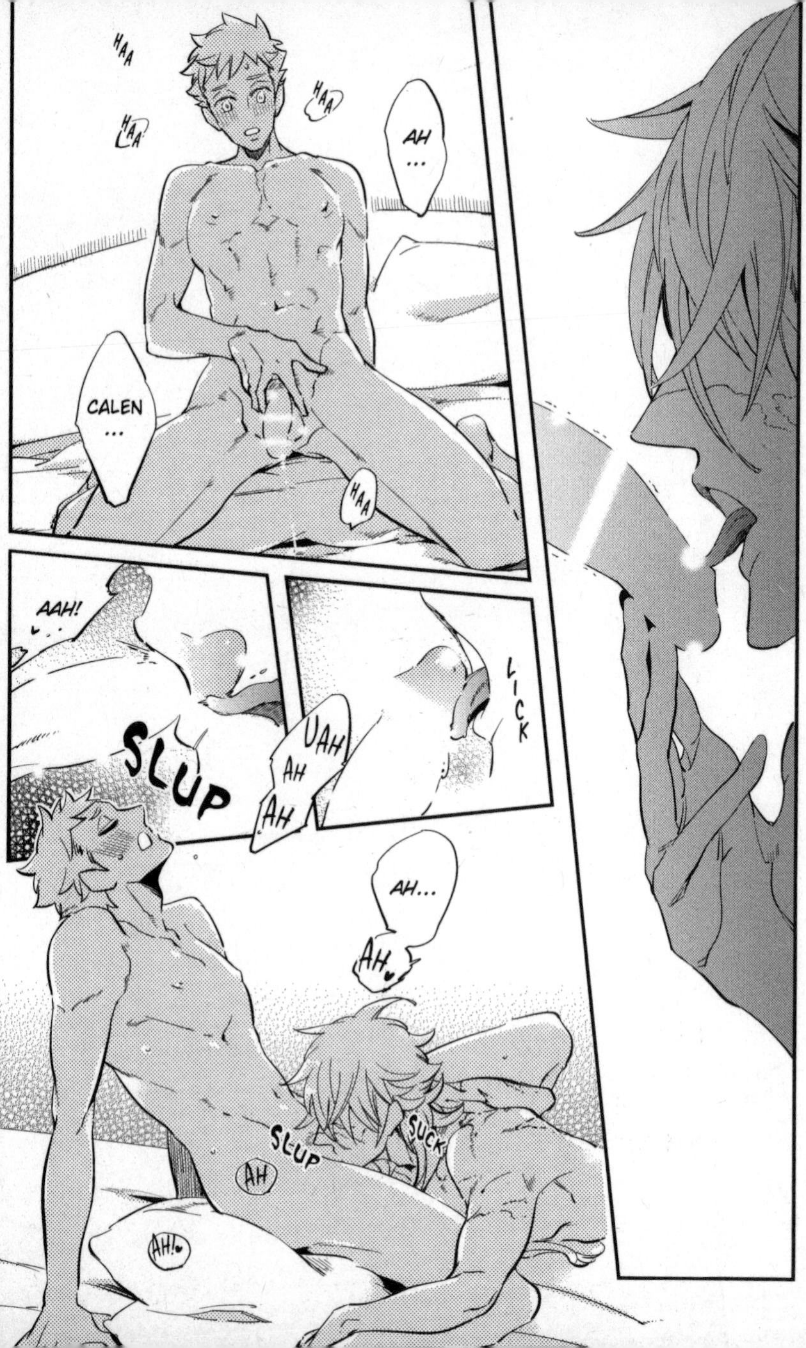
AH ...
HAA
HAA
HAA
CALEN ...
HAA
LICK
UAH AH AH
AAH! ...
SLUP
AH... AH♥
SUCK
SLUP
AH
AH!♥

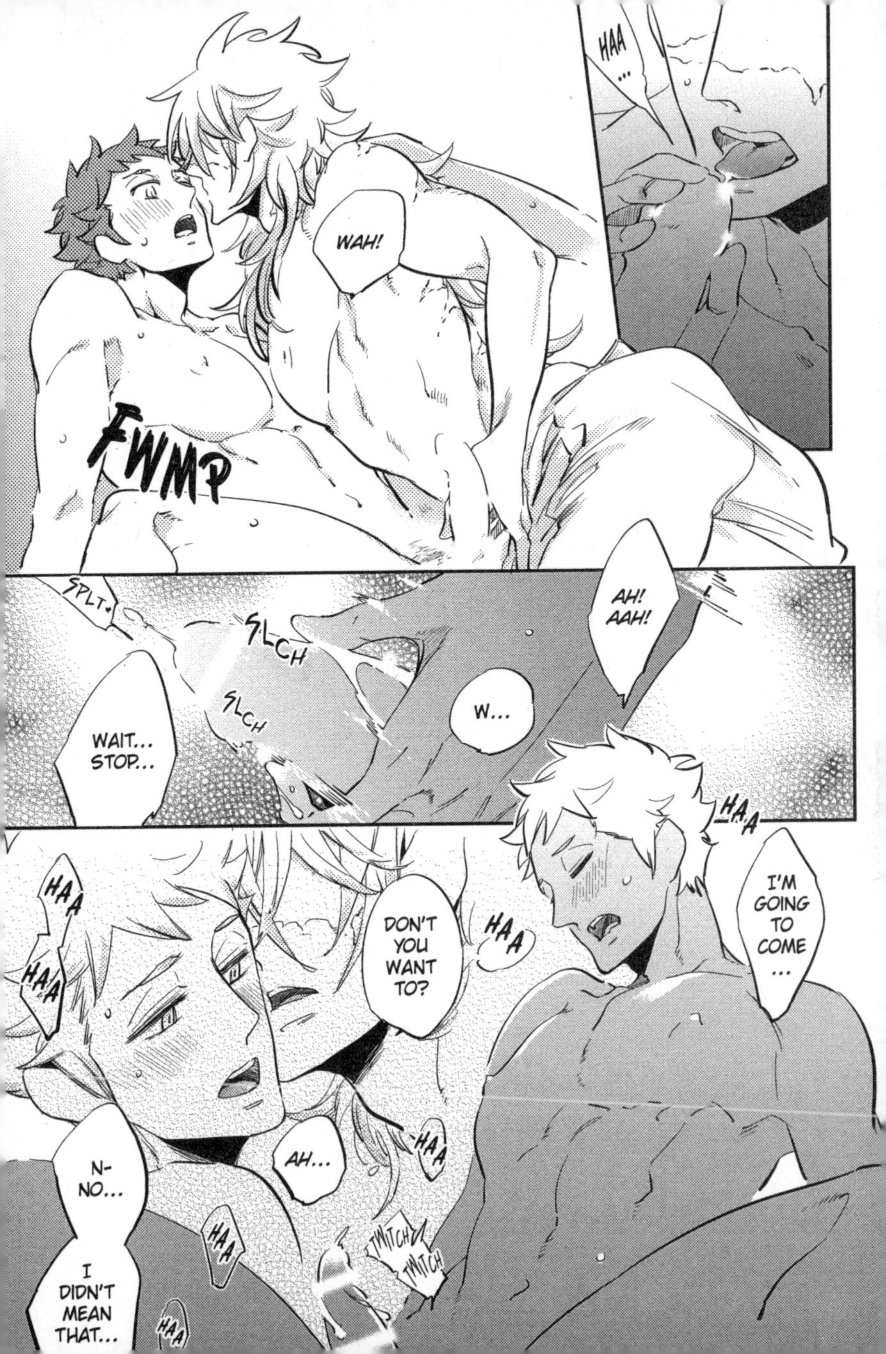
HAA...
WAH!
FWMP
AH! AAH!
W...
SLCH
SLCH
SPLT
WAIT... STOP...
HAA
I'M GOING TO COME...
HAA
DON'T YOU WANT TO?
HAA
HAA
HAA
AH...
TWITCH TWITCH
HAA
N- NO...
I DIDN'T MEAN THAT...
HAA

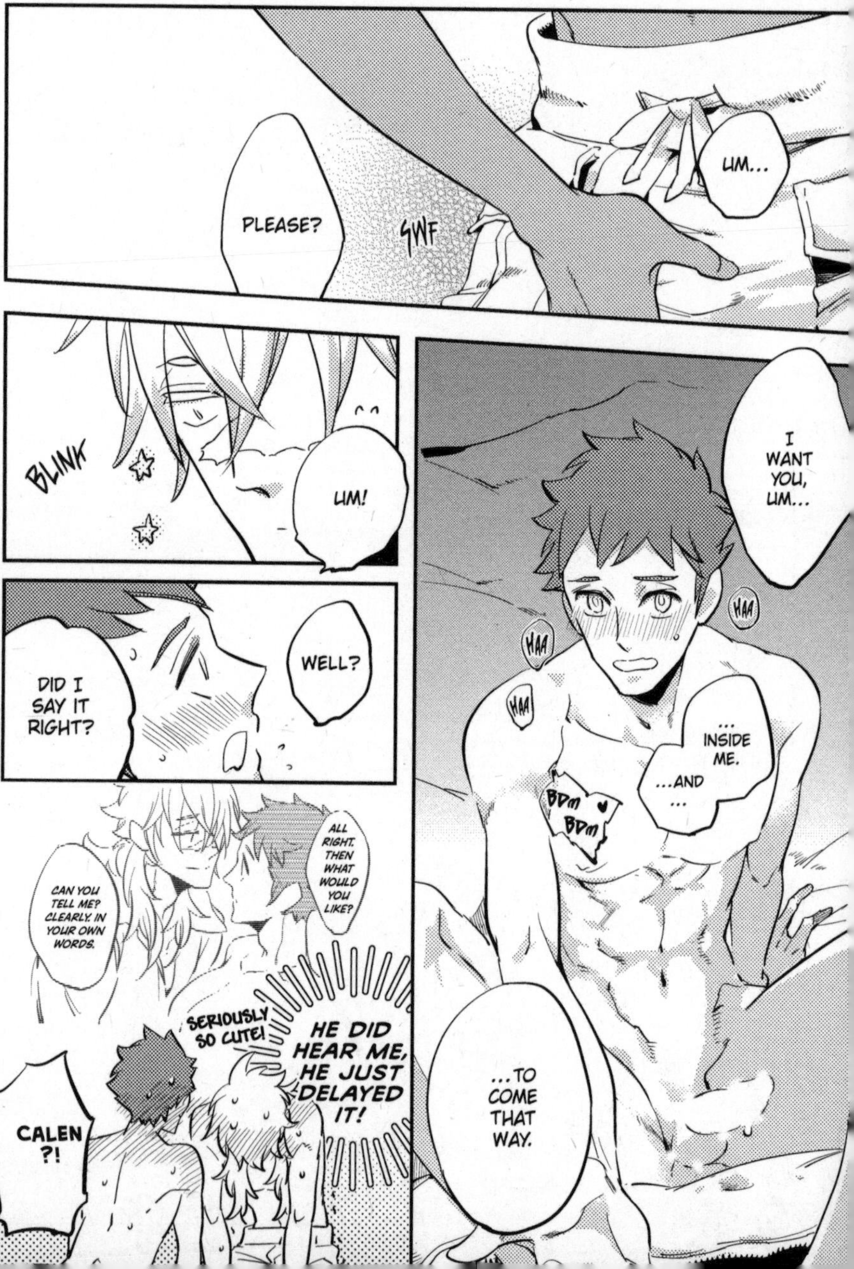

UM...
SWF
PLEASE?
I WANT YOU, UM...
HAA
HAA
HAA
... INSIDE ME.
...AND ...
BDM BDM
...TO COME THAT WAY.
UM!
BLINK
WELL?
DID I SAY IT RIGHT?
ALL RIGHT. THEN WHAT WOULD YOU LIKE?
CAN YOU TELL ME? CLEARLY. IN YOUR OWN WORDS.
HE DID HEAR ME, HE JUST DELAYED IT!
SERIOUSLY SO CUTE!
CALEN ?!

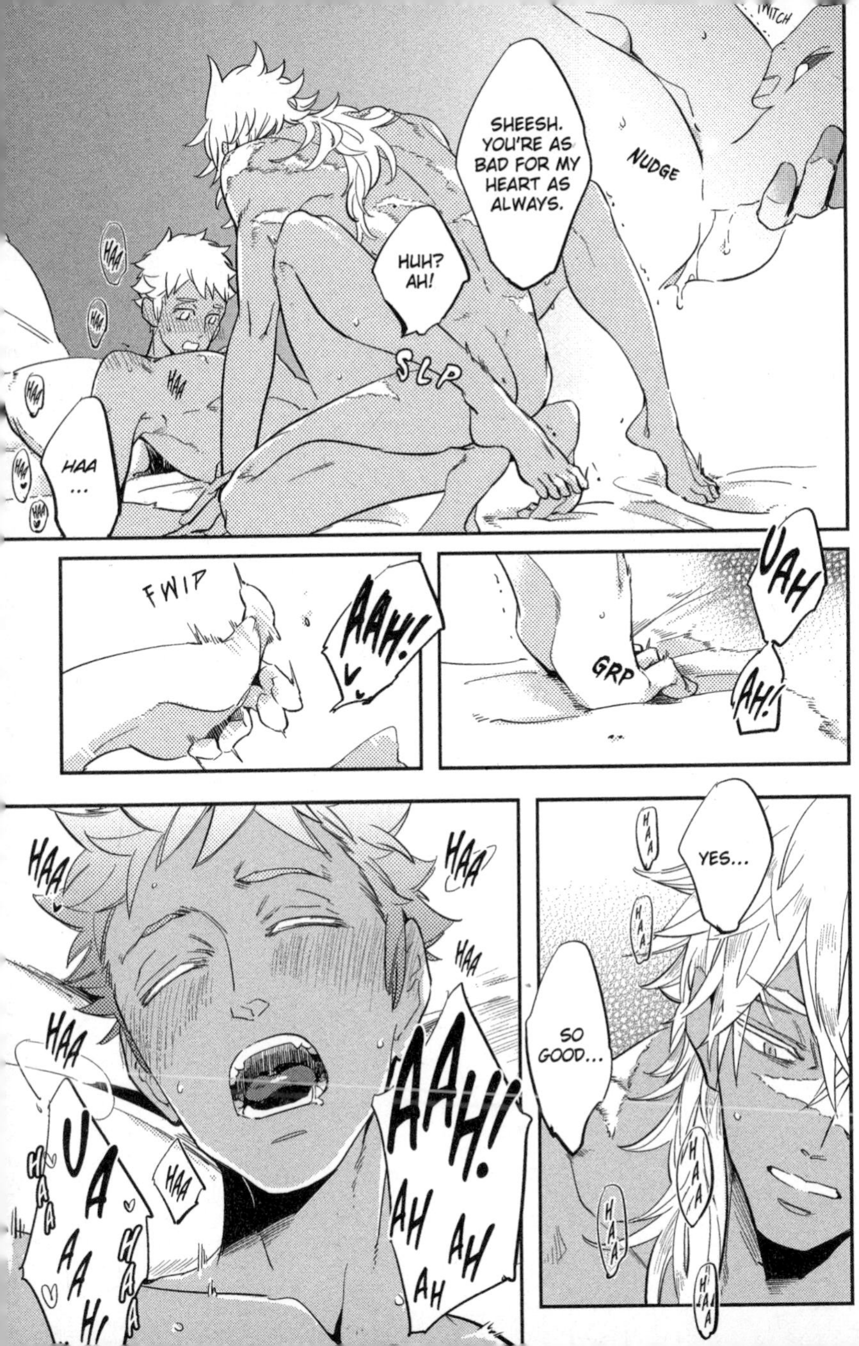
TWITCH
NUDGE
SHEESH. YOU'RE AS BAD FOR MY HEART AS ALWAYS.
HUH? AH!
SLP
HAA
HAA
HAA
HAA
HAA ...
UAH
AH!
GRP
AAH!
FWIP
HAA
YES...
HAA
SO GOOD...
HAA
HAA
HAA
HAA
HAA
HAA
AAH!
AH
AH
AH
HAA
HAA
UA
AAH!

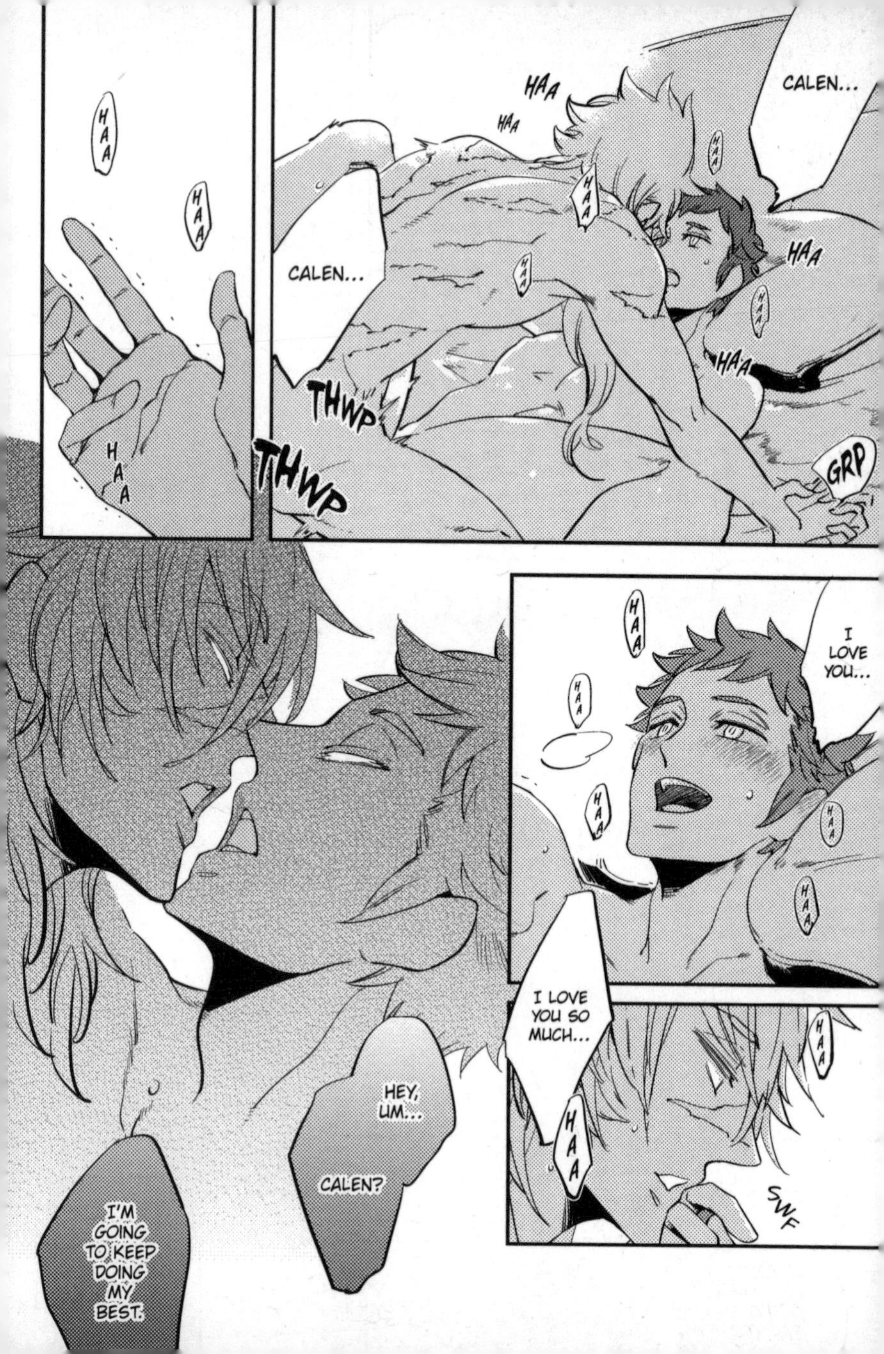
CALEN...
HAA
HAA
HAA
HAA
HAA
CALEN...
HAA
HAA
HAA
GRP
THWP
THWP
HAA
HAA
HAA
I LOVE YOU...
HAA
HAA
HAA
HAA
HAA
HAA
I LOVE YOU SO MUCH...
HAA
SWF
HEY, UM...
CALEN?
I'M GOING TO KEEP DOING MY BEST.

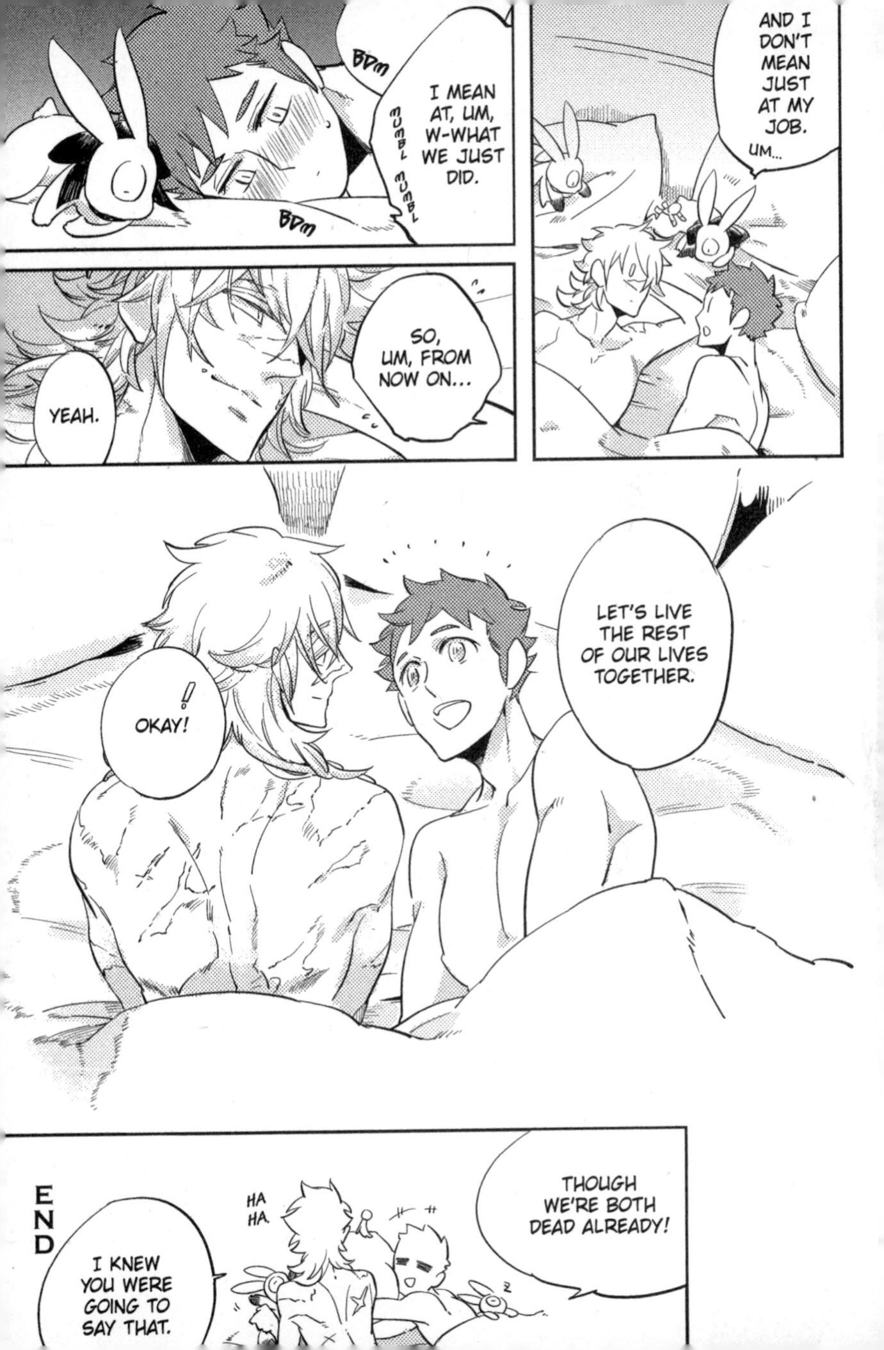
AND I DON'T MEAN JUST AT MY JOB.
UM...
BDm
I MEAN AT, UM, W-WHAT WE JUST DID.
MUMBL MUMBL
BDm
SO, UM, FROM NOW ON...
YEAH.
LET'S LIVE THE REST OF OUR LIVES TOGETHER.
OKAY!
THOUGH WE'RE BOTH DEAD ALREADY!
HA HA.
I KNEW YOU WERE GOING TO SAY THAT.
END

AFTERWORD

THANK YOU VERY MUCH FOR READING THIS FAR.

THERE WAS A TIME WHEN I THOUGHT I MIGHT TOUCH ON CALEN'S MEMORIES AND PAST IN THE BONUS CHAPTER AT THE END, BUT THEN I SAID TO HECK WITH IT AND GAVE IN TO THE DESIRE TO WRITE SOME OOH-LA-LA TIME FOR OUR TWO MAIN CHARACTERS.

PART OF ME WANTS TO TALK ABOUT ALL KINDS OF THINGS THAT I WASN'T ABLE TO PUT IN THE MAIN STORY, WHILE ANOTHER PART IS LIKE WHATEVER WASN'T ADDED DOESN'T COUNT AS REAL, SO WHY BOTHER PONTIFICATING ABOUT IT, LEAVING ME SITTING HERE WRITING THIS AFTERWORD AND THEN ERASING IT AND THEN WRITING AND ERASING IT AGAIN. YOU KNOW WHAT? IF IT ISN'T COMING EASILY, IT WILL ONLY BE AN UGLY MESS, SO LET'S STOP THINKING ABOUT IT!

ANYWAY, THOUGH THIS STORY IS OVER, CALEN AND MAKOTO'S AFTERLIFE IN LIMBO WILL CONTINUE ON. I'M SURE THEY'LL HAVE MANY SAD, DIFFICULT TIMES, AS WELL AS TIMES BRIMMING WITH HAPPINESS AND LAUGHTER. ON THE ONE HAND, I HAVE FUN THINKING ABOUT HOW THE TWO OF THEM WILL GO ON LIVING TOGETHER, ENJOYING GOOD FOOD AND GOOD COMPANY IN BOTH THE HAPPY TIMES AND THE ROUGH TIMES, WHILE ON THE OTHER HAND, I GET SAD THINKING ABOUT HOW THEIR STORY IS NOW OVER—AND ON THE THIRD HAND, I HAVE TO WONDER WHERE I'M GOING TO END THIS SUPERLONG SENTENCE (HOW ABOUT HERE?).

FINALLY, TO MY EDITOR, EVERYONE INVOLVED IN THE MAKING OF THIS SERIES, MY FRIENDS AND FAMILY WHO SUPPORTED ME, AND LAST BUT NOT LEAST, EVERYONE WHO PICKED UP AND READ THESE BOOKS, THANK YOU!

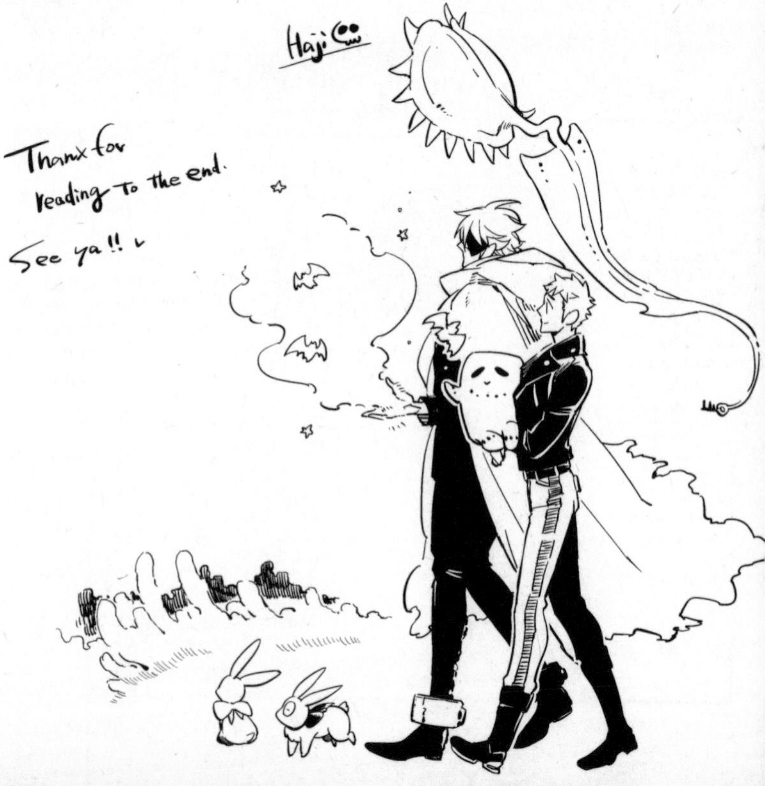
Haji
Thanx for reading to the end.
See ya!!

BONUS SHORT

LUNCH SOAPS IN LIMBO

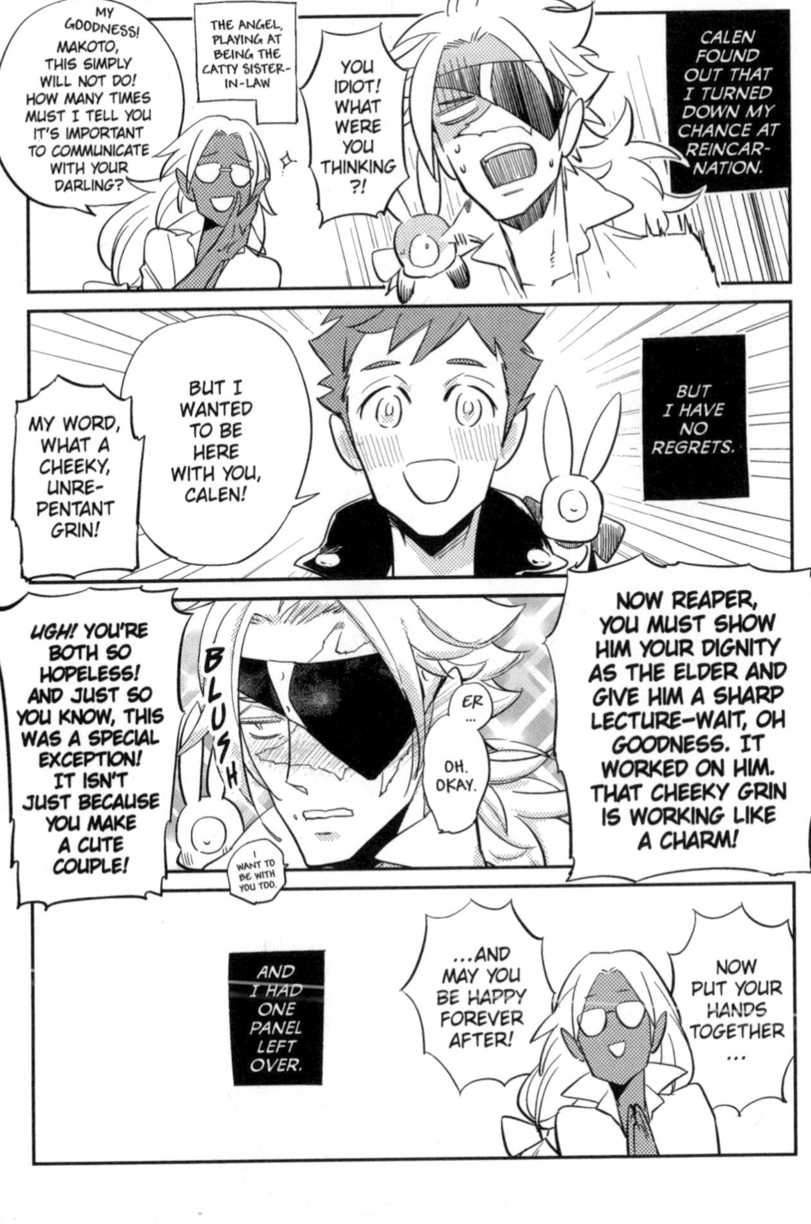
CALEN FOUND OUT THAT I TURNED DOWN MY CHANCE AT REINCARNATION.
YOU IDIOT! WHAT WERE YOU THINKING?!
THE ANGEL, PLAYING AT BEING THE CATTY SISTER-IN-LAW
MY GOODNESS! MAKOTO, THIS SIMPLY WILL NOT DO! HOW MANY TIMES MUST I TELL YOU IT'S IMPORTANT TO COMMUNICATE WITH YOUR DARLING?
BUT I HAVE NO REGRETS.
BUT I WANTED TO BE HERE WITH YOU, CALEN!
MY WORD, WHAT A CHEEKY, UNREPENTANT GRIN!
NOW REAPER, YOU MUST SHOW HIM YOUR DIGNITY AS THE ELDER AND GIVE HIM A SHARP LECTURE—WAIT, OH GOODNESS. IT WORKED ON HIM. THAT CHEEKY GRIN IS WORKING LIKE A CHARM!
ER...
OH. OKAY.
BLUSH
UGH! YOU'RE BOTH SO HOPELESS! AND JUST SO YOU KNOW, THIS WAS A SPECIAL EXCEPTION! IT ISN'T JUST BECAUSE YOU MAKE A CUTE COUPLE!
I WANT TO BE WITH YOU TOO.
NOW PUT YOUR HANDS TOGETHER...
...AND MAY YOU BE HAPPY FOREVER AFTER!
AND I HAD ONE PANEL LEFT OVER.

They're all dead already, but that isn't stopping them from living as hard as they can. I hope you enjoy this fantasy set in not just another world, but the otherworld!

About the Author

This is **HAJI**'s first English-language release. She also publishes *doujinshi* (independent comics) under the circle name "69de74." Born June 18, she's a Gemini with a B blood type. You can find out more about Haji on her Twitter page, **@69de74haji**.

Love in Limbo

Volume 2

SuBLime Manga Edition

Story and Art by **HAJI**

Translation—**Adrienne Beck**
Touch-Up Art and Lettering—**Mara Coman**
Cover and Graphic Design—**Julian [JR] Robinson**
Editor—**Jennifer LeBlanc**

Printed in the U.S.A.

Published by SuBLime Manga
P.O. Box 77010
San Francisco, CA 94107

10 9 8 7 6 5 4 3 2 1
First printing, August 2019

M
MATURE

PARENTAL ADVISORY
LOVE IN LIMBO is rated M for Mature and is recommended for mature readers. This volume contains graphic imagery and mature themes.

SUBLIME
www.SuBLimeManga.com

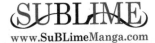

For more information

on all our products, along with the most up-to-date news on releases, series announcements, and contests, please visit us at:

 SuBLimeManga.com

 twitter.com/**SuBLimeManga**

 facebook.com/**SuBLimeManga**

 instagram.com/**SuBLimeManga**

 SuBLimeManga.tumblr.com

Downloading is as easy as:

1

Login/Email
Password

LOGIN
REGISTER NOW
Forgot Password

2

PAY with PayPal

— OR —

Pay Now with amazon
The Simple, Trusted Way to Pay

Digital Edition includes **BOTH**
Download-to-own PDF and
online viewing option.

3

View your purchase as:

DOWNLOAD-TO-OWN PDF